A·N·N·U·A·L E·D·I·T·I·O·N·S

S0-BYZ-249

World History
Volume I

Seventh Edition

Prehistory to 1500

EDITOR

David McComb
Colorado State University

David McComb received his Ph.D. from the University of Texas at Austin and is currently a professor of history at Colorado State University. Dr. McComb has written 8 books and over 100 articles and book reviews, and he teaches courses in the history of the United States, sports, and the world. He has traveled twice around the world as a Semester at Sea faculty member of the University of Pittsburgh, and he has spent additional time in India and Mexico. Currently, he is a member of the executive council of the World History Association.

McGraw-Hill/Dushkin
530 Old Whitfield Street, Guilford, Connecticut 06437

Visit us on the Internet
http://www.dushkin.com

Credits

1. Natural History and the Spread of Humankind
Unit photo—© 2001 PhotoDisc, Inc.
2. The Beginnings of Culture, Agriculture, and Cities
Unit photo—WHO photo.
3. The Early Civilizations to 500 B.C.E.
Unit photo—© 2001 PhotoDisc, Inc.
4. The Later Civilizations to 500 C.E.
Unit photo—United Nations photo.
5. The Great Religions
Unit photo—Courtesy of Brian Spykerman.
6. The World of the Middle Ages, 500-1500
Unit photo—Photo by Rheinisches Bildarchiv, Germany.
7. 1500: The Era of Global Explorations
Unit photo—Library of Congress Collection photo.

Cataloging in Publication Data
Main entry under title: Annual Editions: World history, Vol. I: Prehistory to 1500. 7/E.
    1. World history—Periodicals. 2. Civilization, Modern—Periodicals. 3. Social problems—Periodicals. I. McComb, David,
comp. II. Title: World history, vol. I: Prehistory to 1500.
905   ISBN 0-07-250311-4   90-656260   ISSN 1054-2779

© 2002 by McGraw-Hill/Dushkin, Guilford, CT 06437, A Division of The McGraw-Hill Companies.

Seventh Edition

Cover image © 2002 PhotoDisc, Inc.

Printed in the United States of America   1234567890BAHBAH54322   Printed on Recycled Paper

Copyright

Editors/Advisory Board

Staff

In publishing ANNUAL EDITIONS we recognize the enormous role played by the magazines, newspapers, and journals of the public press in providing current, first-rate educational information in a broad spectrum of interest areas. Many of these articles are appropriate for students, researchers, and professionals seeking accurate, current material to help bridge the gap between principles and theories and the real world. These articles, however, become more useful for study when those of lasting value are carefully collected, organized, indexed, and reproduced in a low-cost format, which provides easy and permanent access when the material is needed. That is the role played by ANNUAL EDITIONS.

It has become almost a cliché to state that well-informed citizens need to know world history in order to understand the modern world. Although trite, the thought is nonetheless true. Increasingly, the United States government and its people are swept up in a daily vortex of international concerns—terrorism in the Middle East, ethnic wars in the Balkans, viral diseases in Africa, air pollution from industries that threaten global warming, endangered species, mad cow disease from Europe, financial disruptions from Southeast Asia, to name but a few. There are also cultural imports of art, music, literature, fashion, and religion that demand an explanation for their appreciation and tolerance. It is impossible to comprehend even a local newspaper without knowledge of the world, and responsible citizenship requires a broad education in order to act and vote intelligently for the welfare of the individual, the nation, and the planet. Although history is not infallible as a guide to the future, the study of the past helps to explain how the world came to its present condition. That knowledge is important for understanding current situations and to serve as a foundation for action and response.

Educators have reacted by making world history courses, along with United States history courses, a central curriculum feature in the secondary schools. In addition, since the early 1980s world history courses have spread through higher education and the first generation of world history scholars has emerged. These academics have a particular interest in global themes and comparing historical developments in time and place. The *Journal of World History,* a marking point of interest in the field, is 12 years old, and the World History Association with 1,300 members is 20 years old.

The organizational problems of teaching world history include the traditional difficulties of scope and relevance. What should be included and what may be left out? How can diverse material be arranged to make sense of the past? In all history courses choices must be made, particularly in the surveys. No one learns about each country of Europe in a survey of Western civilization, or about each state in a survey of the United States with the hope that the details add up to a comprehensible story. Instead, there is an emphasis upon ideas, technology, turning points, significant people, movements, and chronology. Efforts are made by historians and teachers to place events in context in order to demonstrate cause and effect, and to focus upon what brings change to the human condition.

World history is no exception, but the range of choices is greater. There are simply more people, places, and events in the history of the world. There is more material, and thus world history courses require the broadest level of abstraction from teachers and students. A few global historians have even enlarged their scope to teach "big history," a one-semester course that covers the beginning of the universe from the "big bang" to the present time on Earth. World historians, however, generally focus upon civilizations, cultures, global economic systems, and international relationships. Often they attempt cross-cultural comparisons and struggle with special historiographical problems.

Probably the most difficult theoretical question involves periodization—how to subdivide history into meaningful time units. In Western civilization courses the division of ancient, medieval, and modern serves nicely. In world history, however, this time division does not fit so neatly because civilizations have evolved at different rates. The development of medieval Europe makes little sense for Asia, the Middle East, Africa, or the Americas. World historians, however, have reached a grumbling consensus about the following: the two most important technological events in human history are the invention of agriculture and the industrial revolution; the development of the great religions are significant for understanding human motivation; the thousand years before Columbus are important because of the rise of Islam, the development of Eurasian trading routes, the evolution of civilizations in the Western Hemisphere, and the power of China; and 1500 C.E. is a practical dividing point for a two-semester sequence because of the European explorations and their global consequences.

In this volume I use a periodization structure starting with early civilization to 500 B.C.E., later civilizations to 500 C.E., and the world to 1500 C.E. This is fairly traditional, but there are additional units on natural history and the spread of human beings, the great religions, and exploration. Within the broad units one can find information about women, technology, the family, historiography, urbanization, sports, and other subjects. Since the development of Western civilization is a part of world history, Western topics are also included. The topic guide is a useful index for this varied information. This edition of *Annual Editions: World History, Volume I* also contains *Web sites* that are cross-referenced by topics and that can be hot-linked through the *Annual Editions* home page at *www.dushkin.com/annualeditions.*

The articles were selected for readability, accuracy, relevance, interest, and freshness. They are meant to supplement a course in order to provide depth, and to add spice and spark. The articles do not cover everything; that is impossible, of course. Sometimes older selections have been included to provide balance when nothing new is available. You may know of other articles that would do a better job. If so, please return the prepaid *article rating form* at the back of this book with your suggestions. Thank you.

David McComb
Editor

Contents

UNIT 1

Natural History and the Spread of Humankind

Five articles discuss how humans
may have evolved and what impact
the environment had on the shaping
of early human society.

Contents

The concepts in bold italics are developed in the article. For further expansion please refer to the Topic Guide and the Index.   **v**

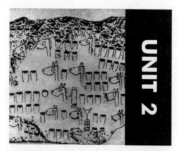

UNIT 2

The Beginnings of Culture, Agriculture, and Cities

Five selections examine early milestones in the history of humankind: the origin of writing, the beginnings of agriculture, and urbanization.

UNIT 3

The Early Civilizations to 500 B.C.E.

Six articles consider the growing diversity of human life as civilization evolved in the ancient world.

The concepts in bold italics are developed in the article. For further expansion please refer to the Topic Guide and the Index.

UNIT 4

The Later
Civilizations
to 500 c.e.

Six articles discuss some of the
dynamics of culture in the New
World, Egypt, and Greece.

UNIT 5

The Great Religions

Six articles discuss the beginnings of the world's great religions, including Judaism, Christianity, Islam, Hinduism, and Buddhism.

The concepts in bold italics are developed in the article. For further expansion please refer to the Topic Guide and the Index.

UNIT 6

The World of the Middle Ages, 500–1500

Seven selections examine
the development of world
cultures during this period:
in the Western Hemisphere,
flourishing Mesoamerican cities; in
the West, feudalism and the growth
of the nation-state; in the East, the
golden age of peak development.

The concepts in bold italics are developed in the article. For further expansion please refer to the Topic Guide and the Index.

UNIT 7

1500: The Era of Global Explorations

Five articles examine the enormous global impact of the voyages of discovery, essentially by the Europeans.

The concepts in bold italics are developed in the article. For further expansion please refer to the Topic Guide and the Index.

The concepts in bold italics are developed in the article. For further expansion please refer to the Topic Guide and the Index.

Topic Guide

This topic guide suggests how the selections in this book relate to the subjects covered in your course.

The Web icon (⊙) under the topic articles easily identifies the relevant Web sites, which are numbered and annotated on the next two pages. By linking the articles and the Web sites by topic, this ANNUAL EDITIONS reader becomes a powerful learning and research tool.

TOPIC AREA	TREATED IN	TOPIC AREA	TREATED IN
Africa	1. Once We Were Not Alone 15. Out of Africa 20. Cleopatra 36. 1492: The Prequel ⊙ **3, 4, 5, 16, 21, 22, 24**		21. Year One 32. Arab Roots of European Medicine 33. Iberian Chemistry 34. Age of the Vikings 35. Clocks 37. Columbus and the Labyrinth of History 39. Taste of Adventure 40. After Dire Straits, an Agonizing Haul Across the Pacific ⊙ **1, 2, 3, 8, 14, 20, 21, 25, 31, 34, 35, 36, 37**
Agriculture	6. New Clues Show Where People Made the Great Leap to Agriculture 7. In Dawn of Society 30. Americas ⊙ **1, 4, 18**		
Americas	5. Diffusionists Have Landed 9. Tale of Two Cultures 17. Tiny Sacrifices at 22,000 Feet 30. Americas 31. Chaco Death Squads 37. Columbus and the Labyrinth of History 38. How Many People Were Here Before Columbus? ⊙ **15, 18, 32, 33, 35, 36**	**Geography**	3. Mapping the Past 4. Japanese Roots 5. Diffusionists Have Landed 9. Tale of Two Cultures 12. In China, Ancient History Kindles Modern Doubts 20. Cleopatra 24. What Is the Koran? 37. Columbus and the Labyrinth of History ⊙ **1, 4, 8, 21, 32, 35, 36, 37**
Asian Civilization	2. Scavenging of "Peking Man" 4. Japanese Roots 9. Tale of Two Cultures 12. In China, Ancient History Kindles Modern Doubts 23. Ancient Jewel 28. Confucius 36. 1492: The Prequel ⊙ **4, 5, 15, 16, 19, 21, 26, 27, 30**	**Greek Civilization**	16. Scythian Gold 18. In Classical Athens 19. Old Sports 32. Arab Roots of European Medicine
		Hinduism	23. Ancient Jewel 27. Other Jesus 29. If You Had Lived Back Then ⊙ **30**
Buddhism	23. Ancient Jewel 27. Other Jesus 29. If You Had Lived Back Then ⊙ **28, 30**	**Historiography**	5. Diffusionists Have Landed 27. Other Jesus 33. Iberian Chemistry
Christianity	21. Year One 25. Dome of the Rock 26. 2000 Years of Jesus 27. Other Jesus 33. Iberian Chemistry ⊙ **28, 29**	**Indian Civilization**	11. Indus Valley, Inc. 23. Ancient Jewel 39. Taste of Adventure ⊙ **5, 21, 30**
Economics	10. Cradle of Cash 14. Nabada 16. Scythian Gold 22. Secrets of a Desert Metropolis 39. Taste of Adventure ⊙ **21, 34, 35, 36**	**Islamic Civilization**	23. What Is the Koran? 25. Dome of the Rock 27. Other Jesus 32. Arab Roots of European Medicine 33. Iberian Chemistry ⊙ **21, 27, 28, 30**
Egyptian Civilization	15. Out of Africa 19. Old Sports ⊙ **22, 24**	**Judaism**	25. Dome of the Rock 36. 1492: The Prequel 38. How Many People Were Here Before Columbus? 39. Taste of Adventure 40. After Dire Straits, an Agonizing Haul Across the Pacific ⊙ **29**
Environment	22. Secrets of a Desert Metropolis 31. Chaco Death Squads ⊙ **11, 35, 37**		
Europe	16. Scythian Gold 18. In Classical Athens		

● AE: World History, Volume I

The following World Wide Web sites have been carefully researched and selected to support the articles found in this reader. The sites are cross-referenced by number and the Web icon (●) in the topic guide. In addition, it is possible to link directly to these Web sites through our DUSHKIN ONLINE support site at *http://www.dushkin.com/online/*.

The following sites were available at the time of publication. Visit our Web site—we update DUSHKIN ONLINE regularly to reflect any changes.

General Sites

1. The Historical Text Archive
http://www.geocities.com/Athens/Forum/9061/index.html
This award-winning site contains links to world history, regional or national, and topical history and resources. For speed, use the text version.

2. The History Index
http://www.ukans.edu/history/VL/
Here you'll find an immense collection of links (4,000) to sites devoted to different aspects and periods of history, for example, Prehistory, Ancient Egypt, Ancient Greece, Archaeology, Byzantine Empire, Maritime History, Military History, Women's, Medieval, Renaissance, and many more.

3. History of Science, Technology, and Medicine
http://www.asap.unimelb.edu.au/hstm/
A database of information on science, technology, and medicine with alphabetical listing of resources, this site has search features and multiple links.

4. Hyperhistory Online
http://www.hyperhistory.com
At this Web site, click on "hyperhistory" and navigate through 3,000 years of world history. Links to important historical persons, events, and maps are also here.

5. International Network Information Systems at University of Texas
http://inic.utexas.edu
This gateway has pointers to international study sites for Africa, India, China, Japan, and many other countries.

6. National Humanities Institute Home Page
http://www.nhumanities.org
This Web site includes philosophical, cultural, and historical worldwide links, including archives, history sites, and an electronic library of full texts and documents, which is useful for research in history and the humanities.

7. WWW Virtual Library—Humanities
http://www.hum.gu.se/w3vl/VL.html
This main subject index leads to many humanities-related research subjects, many of which relate to historical studies.

Natural History and the Spread of Humankind

8. The Ancient World
http://www.omnibusol.com/ancient.html
The first part of this online book, *The Amazing Ancient World of Western Civilization*, begins with the dinosaurs and moves to Stonehenge.

9. Discussion of Evolutionism, Diffusionism, Functionalism and History
http://www.arts.ubc.ca/anso/menzies/anth470h.htm
Visit this site to explore information regarding evolutionism, diffusionism, and functionalism, and how they relate to history.

10. Fossil Hominids
http://www.talkorigins.org/faqs/homs/
Information and links concerning hominid fossils and paleoanthropology can be found on this page created by The Talk Origins Archive. Visit here to investigate the diversity of hominids referenced in the first article.

11. The Origin and Evolution of Life
http://cmex-www.arc.nasa.gov/VikingCD/Puzzle/EvoLife.htm
This site contains NASA's Planetary Biology Program, which is chartered to investigate the origin and evolution of life.

12. Peking Man
http://www.talkorigins.org/faqs/homs/peking.html
Here you can compare Peking Man with *Homo erectus* and view creationist arguments about Peking Man.

13. Talk-Origins
http://www.talkorigins.org
This is the site of a newsgroup devoted to debate on the biological and physical origins of the world. Many articles are archived here and there are links to other Web sites. Be sure to click on "The Origin of Humankind," a comprehensive source for students of human evolution, which has the latest news about new discoveries, a link to an exhibition of human prehistory, and links to many other related sites, including Yahoo's creation/evolution material.

14. WWW-VL Prehistoric Web Index
http://easyweb.easynet.co.uk/~aburnham/database/index.htm
This site is an index to prehistoric, megalithic, and ancient sites in Europe.

The Beginnings of Culture, Agriculture, and Cities

15. Ancient World Web
http://www.julen.net/ancient/Language_and_Literature/
Early language is explored at this fascinating Web site, which includes Akkadian, Ogham (Celtic/Irish), Mesoamerican writing systems, ancient Berber script, and even 5500-year-old pottery shards found at Harappa in Pakistan.

16. Assyria-on-Line
http://www.aina.org/aol/
All there is to know about ancient Assyria, including the epic of Gilgamesh and Hammurabi's Code, can be found at this Web site.

17. Diotima: Women and Gender in the Ancient World
http://www.stoa.org/diotima/
Historical information about women in the ancient world is available at this site, which also includes search possibilities.

18. Civilization of the Olmec
http://loki.stockton.edu/~gilmorew/consorti/1bcenso.htm
Robert Knaak is the curator of this complete Olmec site, which includes history and origins, achievements, and archaeological sites of this "hearth culture" of Central America, whose traditions have carried over through the centuries.

19. Oriental Institute

http://www-oi.uchicago.edu/OI/DEPT/RA/ABZU/
Click on *ABZU.htm* in the index of the University of Chicago's Oriental Institute for information about ancient Near East archaeology and a bibliographic reference on women in the areas covered.

The Early Civilizations to 500 B.C.E.

20. Ancient City of Athens

http://www.indiana.edu/~kglowack/athens/
Look in the Index for images of ancient Athens as well as insights into Greek history and links to other Greek historical sites.

21. Exploring Ancient World Cultures

http://eawc.evansville.edu
Eight ancient world cultures can be explored from this starting point. They include Ancient China, Egypt, India, Greece, Rome, Near East, Early Islam, and Medieval Europe.

22. Reeder's Egypt Page

http://www.sirius.com/~reeder/
Click on the tomb opening to reveal a wealth of historical and archaeological information about Egypt, including a tour of the tombs of Niankhkhnum and Khnumhotep.

The Later Civilizations to 500 C.E.

23. Britannica.com: Scythian Art

http://www.britannica.com/eb/article?eu=68148
The Encyclopedia Britannica provides this description and information about Scythian art and culture.

24. The Institute of Egyptian Art and Archaeology

http://www.memphis.edu/egypt/main.html
This site offers an exhibit of artifacts, a color tour of Egypt, and links to other Web sites about Egypt.

25. World of Late Antiquity

http://ccat.sas.upenn.edu/jod/
Click on "World of Late Antiquity" in the left side panel for interesting documents, many concerning military history, about late Roman and early medieval times.

The Great Religions

26. Confucius

http://www.crystalinks.com/confucious.html
Here is a Web site on Confucius, which includes a biography, an overview of Confucius's teachings, and quotations.

27. Islam Page

http://www.geocities.com/Athens/Aegean/8264/
Features of this page include an introduction for non-Muslims, the Holy Quran, the prophet Mohammad, the fundamental beliefs of Islam, prayer, and other information about Muslim character and culture.

28. Major World Religions

http://www.omsakthi.org/religions.html
Information at this site provides short introductions to the major world religions. There are also links to great books on religion and spirituality.

29. Religion Search Engines: Christianity and Judaism

http://www.suite101.com/article.cfm/search_engines/13501/
Paula Dragutsky's collection of search engines will lead to a wide-ranging directory of Christian Web sites. Shamash is a comprehensive search engine for Jewish information.

30. Religion Search Engines: Islam, Hinduism, Buddhism and Baha'i

http://www.suite101.com/article.cfm/search_engines/14603/
Specialized search engines reviewed on this page can be very helpful in leading to original and interpretive documents that explain the philosophy and practices of Islam, Hinduism, Buddhism, and Baha'i.

The World of the Middle Ages, 500–1500

31. Labyrinth Home Page to Medieval Studies

http://www.georgetown.edu/labyrinth/
Complete information about medieval studies on the Web can be found here. Site also has a search capability.

32. Lords of the Earth: Maya/Aztec/Inca Exchange

http://www.mayalords.org
History, geography, and art about the indigenous inhabitants of the Americas before the arrival of Columbus is available here.

33. The Maya Astronomy Page

http://www.astro.uva.nl/~michielb/maya/astro.html
The focus here is on Mayan civilization, especially astronomy, mathematics, and the Mayan calendar. There are also links to other Maya-related sites. Click on "Maya Astronomy Page."

34. WWW Medieval Resources

http://ebbs.english.vt.edu/medieval/medieval.ebbs.html
This site has links to different resources concerning medieval times.

1500: The Era of Global Explorations

35. The Age of Exploration

http://www.teleport.com/~dleahy/themes/explore.htm
A complete index to the age of exploration is available at this page, which includes a tutorial about the Spanish and Portuguese in the fifteenth and sixteenth centuries. Individual explorers of important sites are available here.

36. Gander Academy's European Explorers Resources on the World Wide Web

http://www.stemnet.nf.ca/CITE/explorer.htm
Access to resources for each of the European explorers of the "New World" is available here, organized by country for which they explored.

37. NOVA Online: The Vikings

http://www.pbs.org/wgbh/nova/vikings/
This is a companion site to NOVA's two-hour "The Vikings" program. It contains a video, a map, a time line, information on the runes, and discussion on who the Vikings were and the secrets of Norse ships.

We highly recommend that you review our Web site for expanded information and our other product lines. We are continually updating and adding links to our Web site in order to offer you the most usable and useful information that will support and expand the value of your Annual Editions. You can reach us at:
http://www.dushkin.com/annualeditions/.

www.dushkin.com/online/

Unit Selections

1. **Once We Were Not Alone,** Ian Tattersall
2. **The Scavenging of "Peking Man",** Noel T. Boaz and Russell L. Ciochon
3. **Mapping the Past,** Adam Goodheart
4. **Japanese Roots,** Jared Diamond
5. **The Diffusionists Have Landed,** Marc K. Stengel

Key Points to Consider

❖ How did modern human beings evolve? Why did one type win the evolutionary game? Did the diversity make any difference?

❖ What is the significance of "Peking Man"?

❖ How did human beings reach the Western Hemisphere? What proof is there of this migration?

❖ What difference does it make who goes where and when? Use the Japanese as an example.

❖ What evidence do the "diffusionists" offer for proof of outside visitors? If true, did the visits make any difference?

 **Links**   # www.dushkin.com/online/

8. **The Ancient World**
   http://www.omnibusol.com/ancient.html
9. **Discussion of Evolutionism**
   http://www.arts.ubc.ca/anso/menzies/anth470h.htm
10. **Fossil Hominids**
    http://www.talkorigins.org/faqs/homs/
11. **The Origin and Evolution of Life**
    http://cmex-www.arc.nasa.gov/VikingCD/Puzzle/EvoLife.htm
12. **Peking Man**
    http://www.talkorigins.org/faqs/homs/peking.html
13. **Talk-Origins**
    http://www.talkorigins.org
14. **WWW-VL Prehistoric Web Index**
    http://easyweb.easynet.co.uk/~aburnham/database/index.htm

These sites are annotated on pages 4 and 5.

The late astronomer Carl Sagan in his famous book *The Dragons of Eden* (1979) imagined all of time compressed into a single year. New Year's Day began with the "Big Bang," a moment when the universe was created in an enormous explosion of compressed matter. Twenty-four days of his imaginary year was equal to a billion years, and thus the universe was fifteen billion years old. The Earth formed in mid-September and life began near the end of that month. In Sagan's senario humans do not evolve until 10:30 P.M. on December 31. The Akkadian Empire, the first known one, did not form until the last nine seconds of the year. When thinking in cosmic time, such as this, human existence seems both recent and fragile. It is this human story, nonetheless, that is the main concern of world history.

Although only one species of human being now occupies the planet, the evolution of *Homo sapiens* was not a straight-line descent as once thought. There were various branches in the human tree, all but one leading to a dead end. The history of human evolution, however, is incomplete and filled with mystery. What happened to the Neanderthals who shared Europe with the modern Cro-Magnons? Ian Tattersall summarizes the work of paleoanthropologists who have demonstrated that humankind evolved out of diversity. Indeed, just as this preface was being written, Meave Leakey of Kenya announced the discovery of a 3.5 million-year-old skull that was notably different from the famous fossil of "Lucy" from whom all humanity supposedly originated.

Equally fascinating is the migration of the human animal across the face of the planet. A recent reevaluation of the famous "Peking Man," thought to be a half-million years old, indicates that this humanoid may well have been hunted and eaten by hyenas. But, it is the spread of modern man that has been of primary interest to anthropologists in the past century. They have used dental patterns, language, and tools to track groups. The recent development of DNA analysis has provided an additional powerful means for following the movements of people. Adam Goodheart in his article notes the work of these new genetic historians in tracking the American Indians back to Mongolia and the Polynesians to Southeast Asia. The discovery of Kennewick Man, an 8,000-year-old skeleton found in a riverbank in Washington State in 1996, however, has raised many questions because his appearance differs from that of local Indian groups who claim to be the original people on the land. It may be possible that there have been successive migrations and from different directions.

Usually dismissed by scientists as unprofessional, a group of "diffusionists" have argued that the New World was visited by outside humans at various times. They have some proof, as discussed by Marc K. Stengel, but the majority of scholars are not yet convinced. Thoughts of possible outside influence are disturbing and leave many questions unanswered. A similar issue is raised about the Japanese, as Jared Diamond points out. Genetically the Japanese are similar to other Asians, but their language is very different. They may be related to Koreans, but this analysis is complicated by legend and prejudice. Japanese origins remain a mystery. Humankind, nonetheless, has occupied the far corners of the planet. In Carl Sagan's year this has been accomplished in less than a minute.

Once We Were Not Alone

Today we take for granted that Homo sapiens *is the only hominid on Earth.
Yet for at least four million years many hominid species shared the planet.
What makes us different?*

by Ian Tattersall

Homo sapiens has had the earth to itself for the past 25,000 years or so, free and clear of competition from other members of the hominid family. This period has evidently been long enough for us to have developed a profound feeling that being alone in the world is an entirely natural and appropriate state of affairs.

So natural and appropriate, indeed, that during the 1950s and 1960s a school of thought emerged that, in essence, claimed that only one species of hominid could have existed at a time because there was simply no ecological space on the planet for more than one culture-bearing species. The "single-species hypothesis" was never very convincing—even in terms of the rather sparse hominid fossil record of 35 years ago. But the implicit scenario of the slow, single-minded transformation of the bent and benighted ancestral hominid into the graceful

and gifted modern *H. sapiens* proved powerfully seductive—as fables of frogs becoming princes always are.

PARANTHROPUS BOISEI had massive jaws, equipped with huge grinding teeth for a presumed vegetarian diet. Its skull is accordingly strongly built, but it is not known if in body size it was significantly larger than the "gracile" australopiths.

So seductive that it was only in the late 1970s, following the discovery of incontrovertible fossil evidence that hominid species coexisted some 1.8 million years ago in what is now northern Kenya, that

the single-species hypothesis was abandoned. Yet even then, paleoanthropologists continued to cleave to a rather minimalist interpretation of the fossil record. Their tendency was to downplay the number of species and to group together distinctively different fossils under single, uninformative epithets such as "archaic *Homo sapiens*." As a result, they tended to lose sight of the fact that many kinds of hominids had regularly contrived to coexist.

Although the minimalist tendency persists, recent discoveries and fossil reappraisals make clear that the biological history of hominids resembles that of most other successful animal families. It is marked by diversity rather than by linear progression. Despite this rich history—during which hominid species developed and lived together and competed and rose and fell—*H. sapiens* ultimately emerged as the sole hominid. The reasons for this are generally unknowable, but different interactions between the last coexisting hominids—*H. sapiens* and *H. neanderthalensis*—in two distinct geographical regions offer some intriguing insights.

A Suite of Species

From the beginning, almost from the very moment the earliest hominid biped—the first "australopith"—made its initial hesitant steps away from the forest depths, we have evidence for hominid diversity. The oldest-known potential hominid is *Ardipithecus ramidus*, represented by some fragmentary fos-

---

HOMO RUDOLFENSIS was a relatively large-brained hominid, typified by the famous KNM-ER 1470 cranium. Its skull was distinct from the apparently smaller-brained *H. habilis*, but its body proportions are effectively unknown.

---

sils from the 4.4-million-year-old site of Aramis in Ethiopia [*see diagram*]. Only slightly younger is the better-known *Australopithecus anamensis*, from sites in northern Kenya that are about 4.2 million years old.

Ardipithecus, though claimed on indirect evidence to have been an upright walker, is quite apelike in many respects. In contrast, *A. anamensis* looks reassuringly similar to the 3.8- to 3.0-million-year-old *Australopithecus afarensis*, a small-brained, big-faced bipedal species to which the famous "Lucy" belonged. Many remnants of *A. afarensis* have been found in various eastern African sites, but some researchers have suggested that the mass of fossils described as *A. afarensis* may contain

---

more than one species, and it is only a matter of time until the subject is raised again. In any event, *A. afarensis* was not alone in Africa. A distinc-

---

HOMO HABILIS ("handy man") was so named because it was thought to be the maker of the 1.8-million-year-old stone tools discovered at Olduvai Gorge in Tanzania. This hominid fashioned sharp flakes by banging one rock cobble against another.

---

tive jaw, from an australopith named *A. bahrelghazali,* was recently found in Chad. It is probably between 3.5 and 3.0 million years old and is thus roughly coeval with Lucy.

In southern Africa, scientists have just reported evidence of another primitive bipedal hominid species. As yet unnamed and undescribed, this distinctive form is 3.3 million years old. At about 3 million years ago, the same region begins to yield fossils of *A. africanus*, the first australopith to be discovered (in 1924). This species may have persisted until not much more than 2 million years ago. A recently named 2.5-million-year-old species from Ethiopia, *Australopithecus garhi*, is claimed to fall in an intermediate position between *A. afarensis*, on the one hand, and a larger group that includes more recent australopiths and *Homo*, on the other. Almost exactly the same age is the first representative of the "robust" group of australopiths, *Paranthropus aethiopicus*. This early form is best known from the 2.5-million-year-old "Black Skull" of northern Kenya, and in the period between about 2 and 1.4 million years ago the robusts were represented all over eastern Africa by the familiar *P. boisei*. In South Africa, during the period around 1.6 million years ago, the robusts included the

---

distinctive *P. robustus* and possibly also a closely related second species, *P. crassidens.*

I apologize for inflicting this long list of names on you, but in fact it actually underestimates the number of australopith species that existed. What is more, we don't know how long each of these creatures lasted. Nevertheless, even if average species longevity was only a few hundred thousand years, it is clear that from the very beginning the continent of Africa was at least periodically—and most likely continually—host to multiple kinds of hominids.

The appearance of the genus *Homo* did nothing to perturb this pattern. The 2.5- to 1.8-million-year-old fossils from eastern and southern Africa that announce the earliest appearance of *Homo* are an oddly assorted lot and probably a lot more diverse than their conventional assignment to the two species *H. habilis* and *H. rudolfensis* indicates. Still, at Kenya's East Turkana, in the period between 1.9 and 1.8 million years ago, these two species were

---

HOMO ERGASTER, sometimes called "African *H. erectus,*" had a high, rounded cranium and a skeleton broadly similar to that of modern humans. Although *H. ergaster* clearly ate meat, its chewing teeth are relatively small. The best specimen of this hominid is that of an adolescent from about 1.6 million years ago known as "Turkana boy."

---

joined not only by the ubiquitous *P. boisei* but by *H. ergaster*, the first hominid of essentially modern body form. Here, then, is evidence for four hominid species sharing not just the same continent but the same landscape.

The first exodus of hominids from Africa, presumably in the form of *H. ergaster* or a close relative, opened a vast prospect for further diversification. One could wish for a better re-

known representative was *H. neanderthalensis*, a European and western Asian species that flourished between about 200,000 and 30,000 years ago. The sparse record from

ledged morphological indications of diversity, but it would be rash to claim that every hominid species that ever existed is represented in one fossil collection or another. And even if only the latter is true, it is still clear that the story of human evolution has not been one of a lone hero's linear struggle.

Instead it has been the story of nature's tinkering: of repeated evolutionary experiments. Our biological history has been one of sporadic events rather than gradual accretions. Over the past five million years, new hominid species have regularly emerged, competed, coexisted, colonized new environments and succeeded—or failed. We have only the dimmest of perceptions of how this dramatic history of innovation and interaction unfolded, but it is already evident that our species, far from being the pinnacle of the hominid evolutionary tree, is simply one more of its many terminal twigs.

TUC D'AUDOUBERT CAVE in France was entered sometime between perhaps 11,000 and 13,000 years ago by *H. sapiens*, also called Cro Magnons, who sculpted small clay bison in a recess almost a mile underground. Hominids of modern body form most likely emerged in Africa at around 150,000 years ago and coexisted with other hominids for a time before emerging as the only species of our family. Until about 30,000 years ago, they overlapped with *H. neanderthalensis* in Europe and in the Levant, and they may have been contemporaneous with the *H. erectus* then living in Java.

---

cord of this movement, and particularly of its dating, but there are indications that hominids of some kind had reached China and Java by about 1.8 million years ago. A lower jaw that may be about the same age from Dmanisi in ex-Soviet Georgia is distinctively different from anything else yet found [see "Out of Africa Again . . . and Again?," by Ian Tattersall; SCIENTIFIC AMERICAN, April 1997]. By the million-year mark *H. erectus* was established in both Java and China, and it is possible that a more robust hominid species was present in Java as well. At the other end of the Eurasian continent, the oldest-known European hominid fragments—from about 800,000 years ago—are highly distinctive and have been dubbed *H. antecessor* by their Spanish discoverers.

About 600,000 years ago, in Africa, we begin to pick up evidence for *H. heidelbergensis*, a species also seen at sites in Europe—and possibly China—between 500,000 to 200,000 years ago. As we learn more about *H. heidelbergensis*, we are likely to find that more than one species is actually represented in this group of fossils. In Europe, *H. heidelbergensis* or a relative gave rise to an endemic group of hominids whose best-

Africa suggests that at this time independent developments were taking place there, too—including the emergence of *H. sapiens*. And in Java, possible *H. erectus* fossils from Ngandong have just been dated to around 40,000 years ago, implying that this area had its own indigenous hominid evolutionary history for perhaps millions of years as well.

The picture of hominid evolution just sketched is a far cry from the "*Australopithecus africanus* begat *Homo erectus* begat *Homo sapiens*" scenario that prevailed 40 years ago—and it is, of course, based to a great extent on fossils that have been discovered since that time. Yet the dead hand of linear thinking still lies heavily on paleoanthropology, and even today many of my colleagues would argue that this scenario overestimates diversity. There are various ways of simplifying the picture, most of them involving the cop-out of stuffing all variants of *Homo* of the last half a million or even two million years into the species *H. sapiens*.

My own view, in contrast, is that the 20 or so hominid species invoked (if not named) above represent a minimum estimate. Not only is the human fossil record as we know it full of largely unacknow-

The Roots of Our Solitude

Although this is all true, *H. sapiens* embodies something that is undeniably unusual and is neatly captured by the fact that we are alone in the world today. Whatever that something is, it is related to how we interact with the external world: it is behavioral, which means that we have to look to our archaeological record to find evidence of it. This record begins some 2.5 million years ago with the production of the first recognizable stone tools: simple sharp flakes chipped from parent "cores." We don't know exactly who the inventor was, but chances are that he or she was something we might call an australopith.

This innovation represented a major cognitive leap and had profound long-term consequences for hominids. It also inaugurated a pattern of highly intermittent technological change. It was a full million years before the next significant

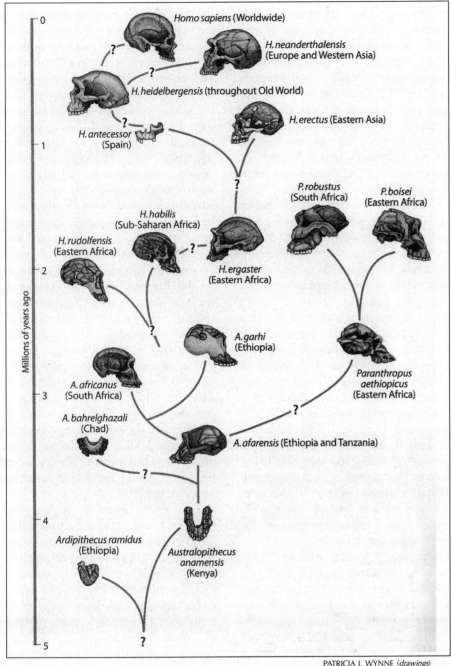

SPECULATIVE FAMILY TREE shows the variety of hominid species that have populated the planet—some known only by a fragment of skull or jaw. As the tree suggests, the emergence of *H. sapiens* has not been a single, linear transformation of one species into another but rather a meandering, multifaceted evolution.

PATRICIA J. WYNNE (*drawings*)

nology were the large-brained, big-faced and low-skulled Neanderthals, who occupied Europe and western Asia until about 30,000 years ago. Because they left an excellent record of themselves and were abruptly replaced by modern humans who did the same, the Neanderthals furnish us with a particularly instructive yardstick by which to judge our own uniqueness. The stoneworking skills of the Neanderthals were impressive, if somewhat stereotyped, but they rarely if ever made tools from other preservable materials. And many archaeologists question the sophistication of their hunting skills.

Further, despite misleading early accounts of bizarre Neanderthal "bear cults" and other rituals, no substantial evidence has been found for symbolic behaviors among these hominids, or for the production of symbolic objects—certainly not before contact had been made with modern humans. Even the occasional Neanderthal practice of burying the dead may have been simply a way of discouraging hyena incursions into their living spaces, or have a similar mundane explanation, for Neanderthal burials lack the "grave goods" that would attest to ritual and belief in an afterlife. The Neanderthals, in other words, though admirable in many ways and for a long time successful in the difficult circumstances of the late Ice Ages, lacked the spark of creativity that, in the end, distinguished *H. sapiens*.

Although the source of *H. sapiens* as a physical entity is obscure, most evidence points to an African origin perhaps between 150,000 and 200,000 years ago. Modern behavior patterns did not emerge until much later. The best evidence comes from Israel and environs, where Neanderthals lived about 200,000 years ago or perhaps even earlier. By about 100,000 years ago, they had been joined by anatomically modern *H. sapiens,* and the remarkable thing is that the tools and sites the two hominid species left behind are essentially identical. As far as can be told, these two hominids behaved in

technological innovation came along: the creation about 1.5 million years ago, probably by *H. ergaster*, of the hand axe. These symmetrical implements, shaped from large stone cores, were the first to conform to a "mental template" that existed in the toolmaker's mind. This template remained essentially unchanged for

another million years or more, until the invention of "prepared-core" tools by *H. heidelbergensis* or a relative. Here a stone core was elaborately shaped in such a way that a single blow would detach what was an effectively finished implement.

Among the most accomplished practitioners of prepared-core tech-

11

similar ways despite their anatomical differences. And as long as they did so, they somehow contrived to share the Levantine environment.

The situation in Europe could hardly be more different. The earliest *H. sapiens* sites there date from only about 40,000 years ago, and just 10,000 or so years later the formerly ubiquitous Neanderthals were gone. Significantly, the *H. sapiens* who invaded Europe brought with them abundant evidence of a fully formed and unprecedented modern sensibility. Not only did they possess a new "Upper Paleolithic" stoneworking technology based on the production of multiple long, thin blades from cylindrical cores, but they made tools from bone and antler, with an exquisite sensitivity to the properties of these materials.

Even more significant, they brought with them art, in the form of carvings, engravings and spectacular cave paintings; they kept records on bone and stone plaques; they made music on wind instruments; they crafted elaborate personal adornments; they afforded some of their dead elaborate burials with grave goods (hinting at social stratification in addition to belief in an afterlife, for not all burials were equally fancy); their living sites were highly organized, with evidence of sophisticated hunting and fishing. The pattern of intermittent technological innovation was gone, replaced by constant refinement. Clearly, these people were *us*.

In all these ways, early Upper Paleolithic people contrasted dramatically with the Neanderthals. Some Neanderthals in Europe seem to have picked up new ways of doing things from the arriving *H. sapiens*, but we have no direct clues as to the nature of the interaction between the two species. In light of the Neanderthals' rapid disappearance, though, and of the appalling subsequent record of *H. sapiens*, we can reasonably surmise that such interactions were rarely happy for the former. Certainly the repeated pattern at archaeological sites is one of short-term

replacement, and there is no convincing biological evidence of any intermixing in Europe.

In the Levant, the coexistence ceased—after about 60,000 years or so—at right about the time that Upper Paleolithic–like tools began to appear. About 40,000 years ago the Neanderthals of the Levant yielded to a presumably culturally rich *H. sapiens*, just as their European counterparts had.

The key to the difference between the European and the Levantine scenarios lies, most probably, in the emergence of modern cognition—which, it is reasonable to assume, is equivalent to the advent of symbolic thought. Business had continued more or less as usual right through the appearance of modern bone structure, and only later, with the acquisition of fully modern behavior patterns, did *H. sapiens* become completely intolerant of competition from its nearest—and, evidently, not its dearest.

To understand how this change in sensibility occurred, we have to recall certain things about the evolutionary process. First, as in this case, all innovations must necessarily arise *within* preexisting species—for where else can they do so? And second, many novelties arise as "exaptations," features acquired in one context before (often long before) being coopted in a different one. For example, hominids possessed essentially modern vocal tracts for hundreds of thousands of years before the behavioral record gives us any reason to believe that they employed the articulate speech that the peculiar form of this tract permits. Finally, we need to bear in mind the phenomenon of emergence whereby a chance coincidence gives rise to something totally unexpected. The classic example here is water, whose properties are unpredicted by those of hydrogen and oxygen atoms alone.

If we combine these various observations we can see that, profound as the consequences of achieving symbolic thought may have been,

the process whereby it came about was unexceptional. We have no idea at present how the modern human brain converts a mass of electrical and chemical discharges into what we experience as consciousness. We do know, however, that somehow our lineage passed to symbolic thought from some nonsymbolic precursor state. The only plausible possibility is that with the arrival of anatomically modern *H. sapiens*, existing exaptations were fortuitously linked by some relatively minor genetic innovation to create an unprecedented potential.

Yet even in principle this cannot be the full story, because anatomically modern humans behaved archaically for a long time before adopting modern behaviors. That discrepancy may be the result of the late appearance of some key hard-wired innovation not reflected in the skeleton, which is all that fossilizes. But this seems unlikely, because it would have necessitated a wholesale Old World–wide replacement of hominid populations in a very short time, something for which there is no evidence.

It is much more likely that the modern human capacity was born at—or close to—the origin of *H. sapiens*, as an ability that lay fallow until it was activated by a cultural stimulus of some kind. If sufficiently advantageous, this behavioral novelty could then have spread rapidly by cultural contact among populations that already had the potential to acquire it. No population replacement would have been necessary.

It is impossible to be sure what this innovation might have been, but the best current bet is that it was the invention of language. For language is not simply the medium by which we express our ideas and experiences to each other. Rather it is fundamental to the thought process itself. It involves categorizing and naming objects and sensations in the outer and inner worlds and making associations between resulting mental symbols. It is, in effect, impossible for us to conceive of thought (as we are familiar with it) in the absence of language, and it is the ability to form mental symbols that is the fount of our creativity, for only once we create such symbols can we recombine them and ask such questions as "What if . . . ?"

We do not know exactly how language might have emerged in one local population of *H. sapiens*, although linguists have speculated widely. But we do know that a creature armed with symbolic skills is a formidable competitor—and not necessarily an entirely rational one, as the rest of the living world, including *H. neanderthalensis*, has discovered to its cost.

Further Information

DARK CAVES, BRIGHT VISIONS: LIFE IN ICE AGE EUROPE. Randall White. W. W. Norton/American Museum of Natural History, 1986.

LANGUAGE AND SPECIES. Derek Bickerton. University of Chicago Press, 1990.

THE FOSSIL TRAIL: HOW WE KNOW WHAT WE THINK WE KNOW ABOUT HUMAN EVOLUTION. Ian Tattersall. Oxford University Press, 1995.

AFRICAN EXODUS: THE ORIGINS OF MODERN HUMANITY. Christopher Stringer and Robin McKie. Henry Holt, 1997.

GETTING HERE: THE STORY OF HUMAN EVOLUTION. Updated edition. William Howells. Compass Press, 1997.

THE LAST NEANDERTHAL: THE RISE, SUCCESS AND MYSTERIOUS EXTINCTION OF OUR CLOSEST HUMAN RELATIVES. Ian Tattersall. Macmillan, 1995. (Second edition by Westview Press due December 1999.)

THE ORIGIN AND DIVERSIFICATION OF LANGUAGE. Edited by Nina G. Jablonski and Leslie C. Aiello. University of California Press, 1998.

The Scavenging of "Peking Man"

New evidence shows that a venerable cave was neither hearth nor home.

By Noel T. Boaz and Russell L. Ciochon

China is filled with archaeological wonders, but few can rival the Peking Man Site at Zhoukoudian, which has been inscribed on UNESCO's World Heritage List. Located about thirty miles southwest of Beijing, the town of Zhoukoudian boasts several attractions, including ruins of Buddhist monasteries dating from the Ming Dynasty (1368–1644). But the town's main claim to fame is Longgushan, or Dragon Bone Hill, the site of the cave that yielded the first (and still the largest) cache of fossils of *Homo erectus pekinensis*, historically known as Peking man—a human relative who walked upright and whose thick skull bones and beetling brow housed a brain three-quarters the size of *H. sapiens*'s.

The remains of about forty-five individuals—more than half of them women and children—along with thousands of stone stools, debris from tool manufacturing, and thousands of animal bones, were contained within the hundred-foot-thick deposits that once completely filled the original cave. The task of excavation, initiated in 1921, was not completed until 1982. Some evidence unearthed at the site suggested that these creatures, who lived from about 600,000 to 300,000 years ago, had mastered the use of fire and practiced cannibalism.

PAINTING BY FRED F. SCHERER, JACKIE BECKETT; AMNH

Franz Weidenreich, who in the 1930s studied the fossils of *Homo erectus* unearthed in China, is caricatured along with Ralph von Koenigswald (wielding the shovel), who found fossils of *H. erectus* in Java. The fanciful setting is, according to the artist, "any place where the dead are disturbed."

But despite years of excavation and analysis, little is certain about what occurred here long ago. In the past two years we have visited the cave site, reexamined the fossils, and carried out new tests in an effort to sort out the facts.

To most of the early excavators, such as anatomist Davidson Black, paleon-

From *Natural History*, March 2001, pp. 46-51. ©2000 the American Museum of Natural History

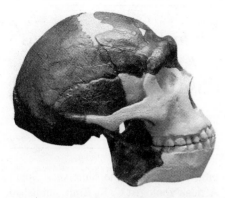

RECONSTRUCTION BY G.J. SAWYER AND IAN TATTER-
SALL. PHOTOGRAPH BY ROD MICKENS; AMNH

Above: A model of an *H. erectus* skull, based on fossils of several individuals from the Peking Man Site at Zhoukoudian. Most of the missing bones, represented in white, mirror existing parts on the opposite side of the skull.

tologist Pierre Teilhard de Chardin, and archaeologist Henri Breuil, the likely scenario was that these particular early humans lived in the cave where their bones and stone tools were found and that the animal bones were the remains of meals, proof of their hunting expertise. Excavation exposed ash in horizontal patches within the deposits or in vertical patches along the cave's walls; these looked very much like the residue of hearths built up over time.

A more sensational view, first advanced by Breuil in 1929, was that the cave contained evidence of cannibalism. If the animal bones at the site were leftovers from the cave dwellers' hunting forays, he argued, why not the human bones as well? And skulls were conspicuous among the remains, suggesting to him that these might be the trophies of headhunters. Perhaps, Breuil even proposed, the dull-witted *H. erectus* had been prey to a contemporary, advanced cousin, some ancestral form of *H. sapiens.* Most paleoanthropologists rejected this final twist, but the cannibalism hypothesis received considerable support.

In the late 1930s Franz Weidenreich, an eminent German paleoanthropologist working at Peking Union Medical College, described the *H. erectus* remains in scientific detail. A trained anatomist and medical doctor, he concluded that some of the skulls showed signs of trauma, including scars and fresh injuries from attacks with both blunt and sharp instruments, such as clubs and

stone tools. Most convincing to him and others was the systematic destruction of the skulls, apparently at the hands of humans who had decapitated the victims and then broken open the skull bases to retrieve the brains. Weidenreich also believed that the large longitudinal splits seen, for example, in some of the thighbones could only have been caused by humans and were probably made in an effort to extract the marrow.

Others held dissenting views. Chinese paleoanthropologist Pei Wenzhong, who codirected the early Zhoukoudian excavations, disagreed with Breuil and suggested in 1929 that the skulls had been chewed by hyenas. Some Western

scientists also had doubts. In 1939 German paleontologist Helmuth Zapfe published his findings on the way hyenas at the Vienna zoo fed on cow bones. Echoing Pei's earlier observations, of which he was aware, Zapfe convincingly argued that many of the bones found at sites like Longgushan closely resembled modern bones broken up by hyenas. In fact, a new term, taphonomy, was coined shortly thereafter for the field Zapfe pioneered: the study of how, after death, animal and plant remains become modified, moved, buried, and fossilized. Franz Weidenreich soon revised his prior interpretation of several *H. erectus* bones whose condition he had attributed

AMNH

The early investigations at Zhoukoudian were coordinated by the Cenozoic Research Laboratory in Beijing. Staff members there included (left to right in foreground) Teilhard de Chardin, Franz Weidenreich, Yang Zhongjian, Pei Wenzhong, and Bian Meinian.

During the 1930s, excavators dug down through the hundred-foot-thick deposits that contained the remains of "Peking man." The deposits, which also yielded animal bones, stone tools, and layers of ash, had completely filled an ancient cave.

to human cannibalistic activity, but he continued to argue that the long-bone splinters and broken skull bases must have resulted from human action.

Following disruptions in fieldwork during World War II (including the loss of all the *H. erectus* fossils collected at Longgushan up to that time, leaving only the casts that had been made of them), Chinese paleoanthropologists resumed investigation of the site. While rejecting the idea of cannibalism, they continued to look upon the cave as a shelter used by early humans equipped with stone tools and fire, as reflected in the title of paleoanthropologist Jia Lampo's book *The Cave Home of Peking Man*, published in 1975.

About this time, Western scientists began to appreciate and develop the field of taphonomy. A few scholars, notably U.S. archaeologist Lewis R. Binford, then reexamined the Longgushan evidence, but only from a distance, concluding that the burning of accumulated bat or bird guano may have accounted for the ash in the cave. With the founding in 1993 of the Zhoukoudian International Paleoanthropological Research Center at Beijing's Institute of Vertebrate Paleontology and Paleoanthropology, a new era of multidisciplinary and international research at Long gushan began. At the institute, we have been able to collaborate with paleontologists Xu Qinqi and Liu Jinyi and with other scholars in a reassessment of the excavations.

One of taphonomy's maxims is that the most common animals at a fossil site and/or the animals whose remains there are the most complete are most likely the ones to have inhabited the area in life. Standing in the Beijing institute amid row after row of museum cases filled with mammal fossils from the cave, we were immediately struck by how few belonged to *H. erectus*—perhaps only 0.5 percent. This suggests that most of the time, this species did not live in the cave. Furthermore, none of the *H. erectus* skeletons is complete. There is a dearth of limb bones, especially of forearms, hands, lower leg bones, and feet—indicating to us that these individuals died somewhere else and that their partial remains were subsequently brought to the cave. But how?

The answer was suggested by the remains of the most common and complete animal skeletons in the cave deposit: those of the giant hyena, *Pachycrocuta brevirostris*. Had *H. erectus*, instead of being the mighty hunters of anthropological lore, simply met the same ignominious fate as the deer and other prey species in the cave? This possibility, which had been raised much earlier by Pei and Zapfe, drew backing from subsequent studies by others. In 1970, for example, British paleontologist Anthony J. Sutcliffe reported finding a modern hyena den in Kenya that contained a number of human bones, including skulls, which the animals had apparently obtained from a nearby hos-

It looked as if H. erectus *had smashed open the skulls to cannibalize the brains.*

pital cemetery. In the same year, South African zoologist C. K. Brain published the findings of his extensive feeding experiments with captive carnivores, akin to those of Zapfe three decades earlier. One of Brain's conclusions was that carnivores tend to chew up and destroy the ends of the extremities, leaving, in the case of primates, very little of the hands and feet.

To test the giant hyena hypothesis, we examined all the fossil casts and the few actual fossils of *H. erectus* from Longgushan. We looked for both carnivore bite marks and the shallow, V-shaped straight cuts that would be left by stone tools (although we realized that cut marks would probably not be detectable on the casts). We also analyzed each sample's fracture patterns. Breaks at right angles indicate damage long after death, when the bone is fossilized or fossilizing; fractures in fresh bone tend to be irregular, following natural structural lines. Breakage due to crushing by cave rocks is usually massive, and the fracture marks characteristically match rock fragments pushed into the bone.

We were surprised by our findings. Two-thirds of Longgushan's *H. erectus* fossils display what we are convinced are one or more of the following kinds of damage: puncture marks from a carnivore's large, pointed front teeth, most likely the canines of a hyena; long, scraping bite marks, typified by U-shaped grooves along the bone; and fracture patterns comparable to those created by modern hyenas when they chew bone. Moreover, we feel that the longitudinal splitting of large bones—a feature that Weidenreich considered evidence of human activity—can also be attributed to a hyena, especially one the size of the extinct *Pachycrocuta*, the largest hyena known, whose preferred prey was giant elk and woolly rhinoc-

Franz Weidenreich at his laboratory at the American Museum of Natural History in the 1940s, with ape and human skulls

AMNH

eros. One of the *H. erectus* bones, part of a femur, even reveals telltale surface etchings from stomach acid, indicating it was swallowed and then disgorged.

The pattern of damage on some of the skulls sheds light on how hyenas may have handled them. Bite marks on the brow ridge above the eyes indicate that this protrusion had been grasped and bitten by an animal in the course of chewing off the face. Most animals' facial bones are quite thin, and modern hyenas frequently attack or bite the face first; similarly, their ancient predecessors would likely have discovered this vulnerable region in *H. erectus.* Practically no such facial bones, whose structure is known to us from discoveries at other sites, have been found in the Longgushan cave.

The rest of the skull is a pretty tough nut to crack, however, even for *Pachycrocuta,* since it consists of bones half again as thick as those of a modern human, with massive mounds called tori above the eyes and ears and around the back of the skull. Puncture marks and elongated bite marks around the skulls reveal that the hyenas gnawed at and grappled with them, probably in an effort to crack open the cranium and consume the tasty, lipid-rich brain. We concluded that the hyenas probably succeeded best by chewing through the face, gaining a purchase on the bone surrounding the foramen magnum (the opening in the cranium where the spinal cord enters), and then gnawing away until the skull vault cracked apart or the

opening was large enough to expose the brain. This is how we believe the skull bases were destroyed—not by the actions of cannibalistic *H. erectus.*

We know from geological studies of the cave that the animal bones found there could not have been washed in by rains or carried in by streams: the sediments in which the bones are found are either very fine-grained—indicating gradual deposition by wind or slow-moving water—or they contain angular, sharp-edged shards that would not have survived in a stream or flood. Some of the bones may have belonged to animals that died inside the cave during the course of living in it or frequenting it. Other bones were probably brought in and chewed on by hyenas and other carnivores.

Cut marks we observed on several mammal bones from the cave suggest that early humans did sometimes make use of Longgushan, even if they were not responsible for accumulating most of the bones. Stone tools left near the cave entrance also attest to their presence. Given its long history, the cave may have served a variety of occupants or at times have been configured as several separate, smaller shelters. Another possibility is that, in a form of time-sharing, early humans ventured partway into the cave during the day to scavenge on what the hyenas had not eaten and to find temporary shelter. They may not have realized that the animals, which roamed at twilight and at night, were sleeping in the dark recesses a couple of hundred feet away.

What about the ash in the cave, which has been taken as evidence that *H. erectus* used fire? Recently published work by geochemist Steve Weiner and his team at the Weizmann Institute of Science in Israel

Two-thirds of the fossils show bite marks or fractures inflicted by carnivores.

suggests that the fires were not from hearths. In detailed studies of the ash levels, they discovered no silica-rich layers, which would be left by the burning of wood. Wood (as well as grass and leaves) contains silica particles known as phytoliths—heat-resistant residues that are ubiquitous in archaeological hearth sites. The results indicate that fire was present in the cave but that its controlled use in hearths was not part of the story.

Still, a human hand may somehow be implicated in these fires. One possibility we are exploring in the next phase of our research is that Longgushan was a place where *Pachycrocuta* and *H. erectus* confronted each other as the early humans sought to snatch some of the meat brought back to the cave by the

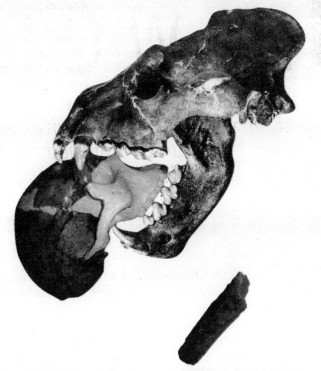

RUSSELL L. CIOCHON

A composite image of the skulls of *Pachycrocuta* and *H. erectus,* left, shows how the giant hyena may have attacked the face. Beneath is a disgorged piece of an *H. erectus* thighbone.

WILL THOMSON

Above: An artist's depiction of the cave shows hyenas consuming the remains of an *H. erectus.*

large hyenas. *Pachycrocuta* would have had the home court advantage, but *H. erectus,* perhaps using fire to hold the carnivore at bay, could have quickly sliced off slivers of meat. Although today we might turn up our noses at such carrion, it may have been a dependable and highly prized source of food during the Ice Age.

Mapping *the* Past

Adam Goodheart

Adam Goodheart, an associate editor at CIVILIZATION and author of its Lost Arts column, has also written for *The New York Times, The Washington Post* and other publications.

ANCESTORS HAVE ALWAYS been hard to keep track of. We all have them, of course, but most of us can trace our families back only four or five generations. Even the oldest lineages are fairly new on the grand scale of human history; Prince Charles, with his 262,142 recorded ancestors, has a family tree little more than 1,500 years old. (Only one reliable pedigree in the world—that of the Bagratid kings of Georgia—stretches back into classical antiquity, petering out in 326 B.C.) "As each of us looks back into his or her past," wrote E. M. Forster, "doors open upon darkness."

Writing in 1939, Forster was arguing the futility of ever tracing the genetic history of a nation. Indeed, if ancestral accounts are muddled and incomplete at the level of individual families, the genealogies of entire nations and peoples are impossibly confused. Historians who refer to "the Irish" or "the Jews" as though they were well-defined groups have only the vaguest idea of their origins, of how they fit into the family tree of the human race. And when it comes to the origins and fate of long-vanished peoples like the ancient Egyptians, the darkness is almost complete. "A common language, a common religion, a common culture all belong to the present, evidence about them is available, they can be tested," Forster wrote. "But

race belongs to the unknown and unknowable past. It depends upon who went to bed with whom in the year 1400 . . . and what historian will ever discover that?"

Yet scientists are now discovering just that—not just who went to bed with whom in 1400, but an entire family history of our species stretching far into the past. It's in an archive we've been carrying with us all along: the coiled molecules of our DNA. "Everybody alive today is a living fossil who contains their own evolutionary history within themselves," says Steve Jones, head of the genetics department at University College, London. Genetics has recently made headlines with the pronouncements of scientists looking ahead, toward medical breakthroughs and moral dilemmas. A far less publicized group of geneticists is looking backward, using new technology to analyze deoxyribonucleic acid, molecule by molecule—and trace the migrations, conquests, expansions and extinctions of ancient peoples.

Genes are often described as a blueprint. That's only a partial analogy. For besides its role in mapping out the makeup of our bodies (and perhaps our personalities), DNA serves as an internal archive handed down from generation to generation. Every individual's genetic code, though unique, contains sequences that have been passed down from parent to child, not just since the beginning of human history, but reaching back over a billion years of evolution.

Picture the human genome, then, not as a blueprint but as an elaborate medieval coat of arms, perhaps the family crest of some inbred princeling of the Holy Roman Empire. To most people,

such a heraldic device would look like a mass of meaningless symbols: dots, bars and crosshatchings, rampant lions quartered with screaming eagles. But an expert in heraldry could read in it an entire family history, tracing the prince's forebears as they married Hapsburgs, fathered bastards, conquered duchies, far back through time. Similarly, the genome

Using new genetic techniques, scientists are solving the ancient mysteries of mankind's origins and migrations

looks like gibberish: an endless repetition of four chemicals, represented by the letters *A, C, G* and *T*. But geneticists are beginning to recognize sequences that identify specific human lineages, and are using them to reconstruct the family history of the species. Recent technology is also enabling them to unearth fragments of DNA from the remains of our long-dead ancestors. Using these two approaches, one scientist says, researchers are undertaking "the greatest archaeological excavation in history."

EVER SINCE EARLY EXPLORers of the new world announced that they had discovered the lost tribes of Israel, the origin of the Native Americans has been the subject of intense debate. Experts now agree that the Indians' ancestors crossed into Alaska over a land bridge from Siberia. Yet no one knows exactly when or how. Even the vaguest legends of that time have been long forgotten, and the land that the hunters crossed, with whatever faint traces their passage left, is hidden beneath the waters of the North Pacific.

Far to the south, Connie Kolman was following the ancient immigrants' track when she drove out into western Panama in the fall of 1991. A molecular biologist with the Smithsonian Institute,

Genetic historians have begun to read the vast archive in our DNA directly, molecule by molecule

Kolman was conducting a study of the genes of some of the New World's most ancient populations. Archaeologists had known for many years that despite Panama's location on a narrow causeway between two continents, many of the tribes who lived there had been isolated from outsiders for many millenniums— perhaps almost since their hunter-gatherer ancestors arrived.

Kolman's scientific team set up their equipment in the small cinder-block schoolhouse that served an entire community of Ngöbé Indian farmers. Just past dawn, the Ngöbé started to arrive: dozens of them, coming down over the hillsides in single file, the traditional ruffled dresses of the women and girls standing out in vivid reds and purples against the tall grass. As the Indians gathered, the visitors explained their mission and asked for volunteers. A medic collected a small vial of blood from each Indian's arm. Over the next few months, back at their lab in Panama City, Kolman and her colleague Eldredge Bermingham broke down the blood cells in the samples and decoded the ancient historical text that they contained. The text, it turned out, read something like this: TGGGGAGCAC-GCTGGC . . .

The work that genetic historians like Connie Kolman have started to do— reading the DNA archive directly, molecule by molecule—relies on technology that is little more than 10 years old, so their conclusions are often controversial. Like medievalists poring over a newly unearthed manuscript, geneticists argue about every fresh interpretation, every cryptic passage and variant reading.

By the mid-1980s, scientists had begun to identify the specific genetic markers common to all Native Americans, which are similar to sequences found in present-day Asians, as one would expect. What was surprising, however, was that American Indians seemed to be divided into three distinct genetic groups. One lineage included most of the native tribes of North and South America, from northern Canada down to Patagonia. Another comprised the Eskimo and Aleut peoples of the far north. The third group included a number of tribes in northwestern Canada, as well as the Navajos and Apaches of the southwestern United States. These genetic lines corresponded with the three major Indian linguistic groups.

Some scientists, particularly a group from Emory University, have suggested that several different waves of migration crossed the Bering land bridge at different times, not the single migration most scientists envisioned. And in order to account for the genetic differences among modern Indians, these researchers maintain, their ancestors must have begun to arrive around 27,000 B.C.—more than twice as long ago as most archaeologists believe. That would mean that humans were living in North America even before the last ice age, in the days when Neanderthals and woolly rhinoceros still roamed the European continent. "Another migration about 9,000 to 10,000 years ago . . . into northwestern North America gave us the Na-Dene speaking peoples, who about 1,000 years ago went down to become the Apaches and the Navajo," says Douglas Wallace, head of the genetics department at Emory. "Finally, there was a recent migration out of Siberia to the northern part of America that gave us the Eskimos and Aleuts."

Could such a radically new version of American history be correct? This is what Kolman hoped to learn from the Ngöbé blood samples. Her research turned up an unanticipated answer: The

same kind of separation that existed among the three major Indian genetic groups also divided the Ngöbé from neighboring tribes in Panama. Yet archaeological evidence showed it was impossible that the Panamanian Indians had come over the land bridge in more than one migration. Therefore, she concluded, the genetic difference between Indian groups is the result of their separation from one another over the centuries after their arrival in the New World. Based on her own research, she says, "there doesn't appear to be any support for three waves of migration." The most likely scenario, Kolman argues, is that all of today's Native Americans, from Canada to Patagonia, are the descendants of one hardy group of prehistoric pioneers. In fact, researchers have pinpointed a region of Mongolia where the genetic patterns are similar to those of all three major Indian groups. Some modern Mongolians, then, appear to be remnants of the same population that settled the New World.

Slowly but surely, researchers like Kolman are rewriting history. In the Pacific, scientists are tracing the genetic trail left by the ancient mariners who settled Polynesia, finding evidence of a journey that began in Southeast Asia nearly 4,000 years ago—and sinking for good the widely publicized theories of Thor Heyerdahl, who sailed the balsa raft *Kon-Tiki* from Peru to the Tuamotu Archipelago to "prove" that American Indians had settled the Pacific. And in disproving Heyerdahl, the geneticists have found evidence of the Polynesians' traditional sagas, which speak of their ancestors' frequent voyages between Hawaii and Tahiti in huge oceangoing canoes. "Archaeologists kept saying it was impossible, that it was just a story people told," says Rebecca Cann, a geneticist at the University of Hawaii. "But by doing a very fine analysis of the DNA, we've seen that there is in fact one very common cosmopolitan lineage that's spread throughout the Pacific, [which] could only have happened if people were in constant physical contact. The idea that these islands were so isolated is really a foreign invention. The Polynesians used the ocean as a superhighway."

THE GREAT ARCHAEOLOGI-cal dig into the human genome began in the villages of northern Italy. In the 1950s, a young Italian geneticist named Luigi Luca Cavalli-Sforza traveled among the towns near Parma, taking blood samples in the sacristies of parish churches after Sunday Mass. He began with the prosperous communities in the river valley, then worked his way up into the smaller towns in the hills until he reached the mountain villages with 100 or fewer inhabitants. As he gathered blood samples, Cavalli-Sforza also began another investigation that, for a geneticist at least, was quite unorthodox: He pored over the parishes' manuscript books of births, marriages and deaths, records dating as far back as the 1500s.

Cavalli-Sforza was investigating the theory of genetic drift, which had never been conclusively proved. Genetic drift proposes that Charles Darwin's law of "survival of the fittest" doesn't suffice to explain all the differences among species, or among peoples. Certain changes just happen naturally over time, independent of the mechanisms of natural section—especially when populations are isolated from one another for many generations. Sometimes the changes can be quite noticeable, as in the case of remote Alpine valleys were many of the inhabitants are albinos. But more typically the effects of genetic drift are neutral and invisible: For instance, the people in an isolated region will have high percentages of an uncommon blood type. Barring extensive marriage with outsiders, every population will develop a distinctive genetic profile. (This is the same phenomenon that Connie Kolman found among the Panamanian Indians.)

In the 1950s, of course, the technology didn't exist that would allow Cavalli-Sforza to read the DNA directly. But he was able to test for blood type, and what he found confirmed the presence of genetic drift. In the large valley towns, where the parish books recorded many marriages with people from different communities, the blood-group profile was typical of that entire region of Italy. But as Cavalli-Sforza moved up into the small, isolated mountain villages, the genetic "distances" between the various settlements increased. The longer a population had been isolated, the more it differed from its neighbors. If the principle worked for villages in Italy, why shouldn't it work for the rest of the world? "My supposition was this: if enough data on a number of different genes are gathered, we may eventually be able to reconstruct the history of the entire human species," Cavalli-Sforza later wrote. And so he embarked on a decades-long project to study thousands of gene markers in hundreds of indigenous peoples around the world.

Of course, scientists had tried before to establish the relationships among the world's populations, often using methods that they claimed were based on strict Darwinian science. They traveled the world with calipers and charts, measuring the bone structure and skin color of the "natives." (One Victorian geneticist even created a "beauty map" of Britain, grading the women of various regions on a scale of 1 to 5. The low point was Aberdeen.) If you trusted such findings, the Australian aborigines, with their dark skin and flat noses, were closely related to sub-Saharan Africans. Cavalli-Sforza didn't believe it. Those visible similarities, he reasoned, might just be the result of similar adaptation to hot climates. To gauge relationships accurately, one had to measure factors that were genetically neutral, immune to the mechanisms of natural selection.

One of the most elegant aspects of Cavalli-Sforza's approach is that there is no need to sample huge numbers of people in each group under examination. Genetically, after all, each of us represents not only ourself but all of our ancestors. (Long before genome mapping, Henry Adams explained this principle quite well. "If we could go back and live again in all of our two hundred and fifty million arithmetical ancestors of the eleventh century," he wrote, speaking of those with Norman blood, "we should find ourselves . . . ploughing most of the fields of the Cotentin and Calvados; going to mass in every parish church in Normandy; [and] rendering military service to every lord, spiritual or temporal, in all this region.")

In 1994, Cavalli-Sforza, along with Paolo Menozzi and Alberto Piazza, published his magnum opus, *The History and Geography of Human Genes*—a sort of combination atlas and family tree. Cavalli-Sforza's genealogy places Africans at the root of the tree, with the Europeans and Asians branching off from them, and American Indians branching off in turn from the Asians. He finds the genetic traces of the Mongol invasions of China, the Bantus' sweep across Africa and the Arabs' spread through the Middle East under the successors of Muhammad.

In his analysis of Europe's genetic landscape, Cavalli-Sforza has shaken the foundations of conventional history. Nine thousand years ago, a technological and cultural revolution swept Europe. From the Balkans to Britain, forests sparsely dotted with the camp-fires of hunter-gatherers gave way to a patchwork of cultivated fields and burgeoning settlements. In the course of a few thousand years, as the practice of agriculture spread from southeast to northwest, Europeans abandoned the way of life they had led for tens of thousands of years. That much is agreed upon. But Cavalli-Sforza suggests that the agricultural revolution was a genetic revolution as well. It wasn't merely that the Europeans gradually learned about farming from their neighbors to the southeast. Instead, the Middle Eastern farmers actually migrated across Europe, replacing the existing population. This wasn't a case of prehistoric genocide, Cavalli-Sforza emphasizes: The farmers simply multiplied far more rapidly than the hunters, and, as they sought new land to cultivate, they pushed their frontiers to the northwest.

Today's Europeans, Cavalli-Sforza argues, are almost wholly the descendants of these interlopers—with the exception of the Basques, whose gene patterns are so anomalous that he believes they are the last close relatives of the Cro-Magnon hunters. Furthermore, Cavalli-Sforza believes, there was a *second* genetic invasion of Europe around 4000 B.C.—this time from the steppes of Central Asia. His maps show that an important component of the European gene pool spreads out from the area north of the Black Sea like ripples in a pond. Cavalli-Sforza connects this to a controversial archaeological theory: the idea that nomadic herdsmen swept in from the east, bringing with them domesticated horses, bronze weapons and the Indo-European language that would become the basis for all major European tongues.

Cavalli-Sforza's ideas have drawn criticism as well as praise. "All genetic data has a time depth of one generation back from the past," says Erik Trinkaus, an anthropologist at the University of New Mexico: Cavalli-Sforza's maps only prove that present-day Europeans demonstrate genetic divergences that occurred at some point in the past. All the rest is interpretation. Some scholars have argued that these patterns could be explained by more recent migrations, such as the barbarian invasions that toppled the Roman Empire. Even Alberto Piazza, who collaborated with Cavalli-Sforza, admits that "it's important to try to get the dates. If we find that we're talking about 6,000 or 7,000 years ago, as we believe, then it's justifiable to say that we're talking about Indo-Europeans. But if we discover instead that the dates are more recent—2,000 or 3,000 years ago—we could be talking about the Huns."

What was needed, obviously, was a more direct route into the past. As it happened, by the time Cavalli-Sforza's genetic atlas appeared, scientists were already starting to catch glimpses of the DNA in our ancestors' cells.

SINCE THE 19TH CENTURY, scientists have been studying fossils to reconstruct our past. But there was no evidence to tell them definitely whether these represented our direct ancestors or were merely dead branches on the family tree. So scientists did the logical thing: They arranged them with the oldest and most dissimilar hominids first, leading up to the most recent and close-to-human types. It was a convenient time line, familiar from textbook illustrations and museum dioramas. And then came Eve.

She debuted before the world in the winter of 1988: a naked woman holding an apple on the cover of *Newsweek*. The article explained that a team of biochemists at Berkeley had discovered the

single female ancestor of the entire human race. The scientists, led by Rebecca Cann, had done so by looking at the DNA found in a specific part of the cell called the mitochondria. Unlike other DNA, mitochondrial DNA isn't a combination of both parents' genes; it is inherited only from the mother. This means that the only changes to the mitochondrial genes, as they pass from generation to generation, are occasional mutations. By calculating the rate of these mutations, and comparing the mitochondrial DNA of people from around the world, the Berkeley researchers had come up with a surprisingly young com-

---

Genetically, each of us represents not only ourself but, in a certain sense, all of our ancestors

---

mon ancestress: Eve, as the scientists dubbed her, was only 200,000 years old. "Genetically speaking," writes James Shreeve in *The Neanderthal Enigma*, "there was not all that much difference between a [modern] New Guinean highlander, a South African !Kung tribeswoman, and a housewife from the Marin County hills. . . . Whatever appearances might suggest, they simply hadn't had time enough to diverge."

The Eve discovery shocked evolutionary historians. It meant the hominids that spread out of Africa 1.2 million years ago were not modern humans' direct ancestors. Instead they and their descendants had been supplanted by a far more recent out-of-Africa migration—perhaps only 100,000 years ago. That would mean that all the old standbys of the museum diorama—Peking Man, Java Man, Neanderthal Man—were evolutionary dead ends.

Not surprisingly, traditional paleontologists have attacked Eve with vigor, arguing that Cann's sample was skewed, her computer program flawed, and that even if all humans share a recent female ancestor, it doesn't mean there weren't other contributions to our gene pool. Eve's partisans counterattacked: A num-

ber of independent researchers have looked at different parts of the DNA and arrived at similar dates for our divergence from a common ancestor. Last fall, a geneticist at the University of Arizona claimed to have found a common male ancestor who lived 188,000 years ago.

Now scientists are tying to resolve the Eve debate by looking in the most logical place of all: ancient DNA. "If we had even one Neanderthal DNA sample we could be sure of, it would quickly emerge how closely related it was to modern *Homo sapiens*," says Sir Walter Bodmer, former president of the Human Genome Organisation. Just a few years ago, the idea of finding a sample of Neanderthal DNA would have seemed about as probable as the idea of finding a live Neanderthal living deep in some cave, since scientists believed that the fragile DNA molecule decayed rapidly after death. But now geneticist are reading DNA recovered from ancient human remains. Despite skepticism from many scientists, their results are winning acceptance.

In 1984, a group of Berkeley scientists announced that they had sequenced the DNA of a quagga, an African animal, similar to the zebra, that was hunted to extinction in the late 19th century. They had accomplished this using the polymerase chain reaction (PCR), a chemical method for amplifying tiny DNA sequences. This is the same technique that scientists like Cann and Kolman use on fresh DNA from blood samples; the Berkeley team simply applied it to a fragment of quagga skin that was preserved in a German museum.

Quickly, other researchers began applying PCR to ancient specimens—and reporting spectacular results. Scientists claimed to have cloned DNA from Egyptian mummies, woolly mammoths, even a 120-million-year-old weevil trapped in amber, à la *Jurassic Park*. There was only one problem: The PCR process is extremely vulnerable to contamination, so nearly all these results turned out to be false—the mammoth's DNA, for instance, was that of a lab technician.

However, a few ancient-DNA laboratories have started to produce credible and verifiable work. Last year, two labs independently sequenced genes from the Ice Man, the Stone Age hunter whose

---

Ancient DNA may allow scientists to establish a continuum from very early times to the present

---

frozen body was found high in the Italian Alps in 1991, and both arrived at the same results. Many of the best samples, oddly enough, have come from bones and teeth. "Now people generally accept that you can get DNA from hard tissues," says Oxford geneticist Bryan Sykes, who is generally considered one of the most careful ancient-DNA researchers. "I suppose the oldest we've ever got to was about 15,000 years— that was for some animal bones from a limestone cave in England. But I think most people wouldn't be too surprised if one were to report recovery of DNA from well-preserved bone up to maybe even 100,000 years ago."

That implies that Neanderthal DNA should be waiting to be discovered in the collections of museums around the world. The treasure hunt is now in full swing. No lab yet claims publicly to have sequenced Neanderthal genes (although Sykes, when asked if he has obtained results, hesitates and replies, "Nothing I could reveal to you"). "It's only a matter of time," says Andrew Merriwether of the University of Pittsburgh, who is looking for Neanderthal DNA in some 35,000-year-old teeth from a Croatian cave. "There are a lot of Neanderthal remains around."

Once the treasure hunters find their quarry, they'll use it to put the Eve hypothesis to a powerful test. And that's not all they'll learn. "One particularly burning question just begs to be answered," writes Walter Bodmer in *The Book of Man*. "Exactly what evolutionary advantage did Homo sapiens have over this hominid competitors, and in particular over our nearest evolutionary brothers and sisters, the Neanderthals? What genetic gifts made Homo sapiens

so special and allowed us to inherit the Earth, while other hominids conspicuously failed?"

In the meantime, scientists are using more recent ancient DNA to answer less profound questions. Scott Woodward of Brigham Young University is working with the royal mummies of Egypt's 18th dynasty, trying to chart the pharaohs' complex family tree. Sykes is using Neolithic bones from Europe to test Cavalli-Sforza's ideas about the spread of agriculture. Merriwether and Kolman are comparing DNA from ancient American specimens with that of modern Indians, hoping to resolve conclusively the history of the peopling of the New World.

Scientists hope that, bit by bit, ancient DNA samples will allow them to interpret more accurately the history encoded in modern genes. "What ancient DNA will allow us to do is establish a continuum from very early times up to the present," says Woodward. "Right now, all we can look at is a single snapshot. If we go back to 500 years ago, 1,000 years ago, 1,500 years ago, it will give us snapshots of the past. And as we fill in the gaps, soon there will be a motion picture and we'll be able to watch history unfold."

SOUTHWEST OF CAIRO, ON the edge of the great Fayum oasis, the desert sand teems with thousands upon thousands of graves. Here ancient Egyptians buried their dead, the bodies wrapped in linen cloth, with only a few possessions—a reed mat, a cup, a loaf of bread—to accompany them into the afterlife. For these were common folk, and although they lived in the shadow of the pyramids, the age of the pharaohs was already past. The Fayum cemetery was in use from the middle of the first millennium B.C. to the middle of the first millennium A.D., during the period of Greek and Roman dominion over Egypt.

Still, Scott Woodward is unearthing treasure from the simple burials: clues to the identity of the Egyptian, and to the spread of Christianity. The cemetery's history spans the time when the Egyptians abandoned paganism for the new faith, and the graves reflect the change. Until late in the first century

a.d., the dead were buried facing west. Then, suddenly, they were oriented facing east—reflecting the Christian belief that the resurrected Christ would return from the east, according to Woodward and his collaborators. Woodward is analyzing the bodies' DNA to find out just who these early Christians were—native converts or immigrants. "We're [also] trying to answer the question of how much sub-Saharan African influence there was in the ancient Egyptians," Woodward says. "Egypt was probably a very cosmopolitan place, as much of a melting pot as the United States is today. . . . My guess is that we'll see African, we'll see Asian, we'll see Caucasian markers." In time, he says, it will be possible to get a genetic picture of the entire population of the cemetery.

So far, Woodward only has results from a half-dozen burials, none of which shows the typically African DNA marker. Even so, his investigation suggests how DNA research can confirm or question disputes over the identity of a particular people, like the modern Coptic Christians, who claim that they are the sole descendants of the ancient Egyptians, or those of sub-Saharan African origin, especially in the United States, who derive ethnic pride from the theory that the pharaohs were black.

Sometimes, such research can turn up unwelcome results. "Judaism is without doubt the most genetic of all religions— it depends on descent," says Steve Jones. "Orthodox Jews are very much of the opinion that Judaism is a huge pedigree of individuals who descend from Abraham." Yet studies of Jewish DNA indicate extensive mixing with outsiders. The Yemenite Jews, Jones notes, who have been accepted without question into Israeli society, appear to be almost entirely the descendants of Arab converts. Meanwhile, members of the black Lemba tribe of South Africa, who claim to be one of the lost tribes of Israel, have never been accepted as Jews. But their genes, Jones says, seem to support their claim: They show patterns typical of Middle Eastern origin.

"The genome pushes us to redefine ourselves," says Howard University immunogeneticist Georgia Dunston. Dunston plans a major genetic study to trace the origins of American blacks back to the lands from which their ancestors were taken. "At this point in the history of African-Americans, we are seeking to make connections to roots that extend beyond slavery," she says.

OUR GENES CANNOT WHOL-ly account for our diversity. In fact, the work of genetic historians would be far easier were it not for the fact that the peoples of the world are so similar under the skin. "It is because they are external that . . . racial differ-ences strike us so forcibly, and we automatically assume that differences of similar magnitude exist below the sur-face, in the rest of our genetic makeup," Cavalli-Sforza has written. "This is simply not so: the remainder of our genetic makeup hardly differs at all." Indeed, research has shown that culture usually drives the spread of genes and not vice versa. "In the history of human development," Cavalli-Sforza says, "whenever there has been a major expansion geographically or demographically, it has been because one people has had an increase in food or power or transportation. . . . Whenever I see an expansion, I start looking for the innovation that made it." The invention of agriculture or the wheel makes history; genes only reflect it.

Even so, the story that the genes' tiny gradations tells is altering the way we think about the past. "Genetics changed something fundamental about our view of history," says Jones. "It shows us that history is largely the story of love, not war." The genetic historians suggest that it's time we started asking, with E. M. Forster: Who *did* go to bed with whom in the year 1400? And as we consider the possibilities—a Mongol chieftain and his Chinese bride, say; an Aztec woman and her husband; a fumbling pair of teenagers on a French hillside—it is pleasing to think that those ancient acts of love left their mark somewhere within each of us.

Japanese Roots

Just who are the Japanese? Where did they come from and when?
The answers are difficult to come by, though not impossible—the
real problem is that the Japanese themselves may not want to know.

By Jared Diamond

Unearthing the origins of the Japanese is a much harder task than you might guess. Among world powers today, the Japanese are the most distinctive in their culture and environment. The origins of their language are one of the most disputed questions of linguistics. These questions are central to the self-image of the Japanese and to how they are viewed by other peoples. Japan's rising dominance and touchy relations with its neighbors make it more important than ever to strip away myths and find answers.

The search for answers is difficult because the evidence is so conflicting. On the one hand, the Japanese people are biologically undistinctive, being very similar in appearance and genes to other East Asians, especially to Koreans. As the Japanese like to stress, they are culturally and biologically rather homogeneous, with the exception of a distinctive people called the Ainu on Japan's northernmost island of Hokkaido. Taken together, these facts seem to suggest that the Japanese reached Japan only recently from the Asian mainland, too recently to have evolved differences

from their mainland cousins, and displaced the Ainu, who represent the original inhabitants. But if that were true, you might expect the Japanese language to show close affinities to some mainland language, just as English is obviously closely related to other Germanic languages (because Anglo-Saxons from the continent conquered England as recently as the sixth century A.D.). How can we resolve this contradiction between Japan's presumably ancient language and the evidence for recent origins?

Archeologists have proposed four conflicting theories. Most popular in Japan is the view that the Japanese gradually evolved from ancient Ice Age people who occupied Japan long before 20,000 B.C. Also widespread in Japan is a theory that the Japanese descended from horse-riding Asian nomads who passed through Korea to conquer Japan in the fourth century, but who were themselves—emphatically—not Koreans. A theory favored by many Western archeologists and Koreans, and unpopular in some circles in Japan, is that the Japanese are descendants of immigrants

According to the earliest recorded Japanese chronicles, the emperors of Japan are descended from the sun goddess Amaterasu. Archaeology, of course, tells a different story.

from Korea who arrived with rice-paddy agriculture around 400 B.C. Finally, the fourth theory holds that the peoples named in the other three theories could have mixed to form the modern Japanese.

When similar questions of origins arise about other peoples, they can be discussed dispassionately. That is not so for the Japanese. Until 1946, Japanese schools taught a myth of history based on the earliest recorded Japanese chronicles, which were written in the eighth century. They describe how the sun goddess Amaterasu, born from the left eye of the creator god Izanagi, sent her grandson Ninigi to Earth on the Japanese island of Kyushu to wed an earthly deity. Ninigi's great-grandson Jimmu, aided by a dazzling sacred bird that rendered his enemies helpless, became the first emperor of Japan in 660 B.C. To fill the gap between 660 B.C. and the earliest historically documented Japanese monarchs, the chronicles invented 13 other equally fictitious emperors. Before the end of World War II, when Emperor Hirohito finally announced that he was not of divine descent, Japanese archeologists and historians had to make their interpretations conform to this chronicle account. Unlike American archeologists, who acknowledge that ancient sites in the United States were left by peoples (Native Americans) unrelated to most modern Americans, Japanese archeologists believe all archeological deposits in Japan, no matter how old, were left by ancestors of the modern Japanese. Hence archeology in Japan is supported by astronomical budgets, employs up to 50,000 field-workers each year, and draws public attention to a degree inconceivable anywhere else in the world.

Why do they care so much? Unlike most other non-European countries, Japan preserved its independence and culture while emerging from isolation to create an industrialized society in the late nineteenth century. It was a remarkable achievement. Now the Japanese people are understandably concerned about maintaining their traditions in the face of massive Western cultural influences. They want to believe that their distinctive language and culture required uniquely complex developmental processes. To acknowledge a relationship of the Japanese language to any other language seems to constitute a surrender of cultural identity.

What makes it especially difficult to discuss Japanese archeology dispassion-ately is that Japanese interpretations of the past affect present behavior. Who among East Asian peoples brought culture to whom? Who has historical claims to whose land? These are not just academic questions. For instance, there is much archeological evidence that people and material objects passed between Japan and Korea in the period A.D. 300 to 700. Japanese interpret this to mean that Japan conquered Korea and brought Korean slaves and artisans to Japan; Koreans believe instead that Korea conquered Japan and that the founders of the Japanese imperial family were Korean.

Thus, when Japan sent troops to Korea and annexed it in 1910, Japanese military leaders celebrated the annexation as "the restoration of the legitimate arrangement of antiquity." For the next 35 years, Japanese occupation forces tried to eradicate Korean culture and to replace the Korean language with Japanese in schools. The effort was a consequence of a centuries-old attitude of disdain. "Nose tombs" in Japan still contain 20,000 noses severed from Koreans and brought home as trophies of a sixteenth-century Japanese invasion. Not surprisingly, many Koreans loathe the Japanese, and their loathing is returned with contempt.

What really was "the legitimate arrangement of antiquity"? Today, Japan and Korea are both economic powerhouses, facing each other across the Korea Strait and viewing each other through colored lenses of false myths and past atrocities. It bodes ill for the future of East Asia if these two great peoples cannot find common ground. To do so, they will need a correct understanding of who the Japanese people really are.

JAPAN'S UNIQUE CULTURE began with its unique geography and environment. It is, for comparison, far more isolated than Britain, which lies only 22 miles from the French coast. Japan lies 110 miles from the closest point of the Asian mainland (South Korea), 190 miles from mainland Russia, and 480 miles from mainland China. Climate, too, sets Japan apart. Its rainfall, up to 120 inches a year, makes it the wettest temperate country in the world. Unlike the winter rains prevailing over much of Europe, Japan's rains are concentrated in the summer growing season, giving it the highest plant productivity of any nation in the temperate zones. While 80 percent of Japan's land consists of mountains unsuitable for agriculture and only 14 percent is farmland, an average square mile of that farmland is so fertile that it supports eight times as many people as does an average square mile of British farmland. Japan's high rainfall also ensures a quickly regenerated forest after logging. Despite thousands of years of dense human occupation, Japan still offers visitors a first impression of greenness because 70 percent of its land is still covered by forest.

Japanese forest composition varies with latitude and altitude: evergreen leafy forest in the south at low altitude, deciduous leafy forest in central Japan, and coniferous forest in the north and high up. For prehistoric humans, the deciduous leafy forest was the most productive, providing abundant edible nuts such as walnuts, chestnuts, horse chestnuts, acorns, and beechnuts. Japanese waters are also outstandingly productive. The lakes, rivers, and surrounding seas teem with salmon, trout, tuna, sardines, mackerel, herring, and cod. Today, Japan is the largest consumer of fish in the world. Japanese waters are also rich in clams, oysters, and other shellfish, crab, shrimp, crayfish, and edible seaweeds. That high productivity was a key to Japan's prehistory.

From southwest to northeast, the four main Japanese islands are Kyushu, Shikoku, Honshu, and Hokkaido. Until the late nineteenth century, Hokkaido and northern Honshu were inhabited mainly by the Ainu, who lived as hunter-gatherers with limited agriculture, while the people we know today as Japanese occupied the rest of the main islands.

In appearance, of course, the Japanese are very similar to other East Asians. As for the Ainu, however, their distinctive appearance has prompted more to be written about their origins and relationships than about any other single people on Earth. Partly because Ainu men have luxuriant beards and the most profuse body hair of any people,

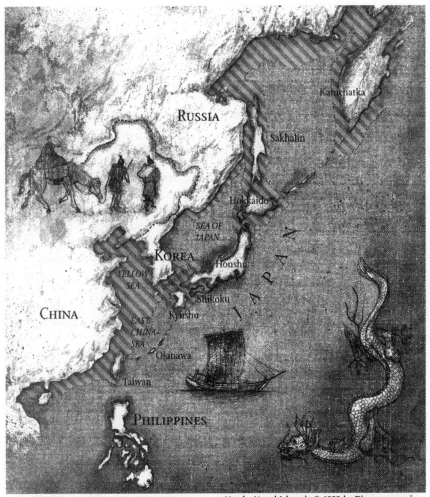

Map by Nenad Jakesevic © 1998 by Discover magazine.

During the ice ages, land bridges (striped areas) connected Japan's main islands to one another and to the mainland, allowing mammals—including humans—to arrive on foot.

they are often classified as Caucasoids (so-called white people) who somehow migrated east through Eurasia to Japan. In their overall genetic makeup, though, the Ainu are related to other East Asians, including the Japanese and Koreans. The distinctive appearance and hunter-gatherer lifestyle of the Ainu, and the undistinctive appearance and the intensive agricultural lifestyle of the Japanese, are frequently taken to suggest the straightforward interpretation that the Ainu are descended from Japan's original hunter-gatherer inhabitants and the Japanese are more recent invaders from the Asian mainland.

But this view is difficult to reconcile with the distinctiveness of the Japanese language. Everyone agrees that Japanese does not bear a close relation to any other language in the world. Most scholars consider it to be an isolated member of Asia's Altaic language family, which consists of Turkic, Mongolian, and Tun-

gusic languages. Korean is also often considered to be an isolated member of this family, and within the family Japanese and Korean may be more closely related to each other than to other Altaic languages. However, the similarities between Japanese and Korean are confined to general grammatical features and about 15 percent of their basic vocabularies, rather than the detailed shared features of grammar and vocabulary that link, say, French to Spanish; they are more different from each other than Russian is from English.

Since languages change over time, the more similar two languages are, the more recently they must have diverged. By counting common words and features, linguists can estimate how long ago languages diverged, and such estimates suggest that Japanese and Korean parted company at least 4,000 years ago. As for the Ainu lan-

guage, its origins are thoroughly in doubt; it may not have any special relationship to Japanese.

After genes and language, a third type of evidence about Japanese origins comes from ancient portraits. The earliest preserved likeness of Japan's inhabitants are statues called haniwa, erected outside tombs around 1,500 years ago. Those statues unmistakably depict East Asians. They do not resemble the heavily bearded Ainu. If the Japanese did replace the Ainu in Japan south of Hokkaido, the replacement must have occurred before A.D. 500.

Our earliest written information about Japan comes from Chinese chronicles, because China developed literacy long before Korea or Japan. In early Chinese accounts of various peoples referred to as "Eastern Barbarians," Japan is described under the name Wa, whose inhabitants were said to be divided into more than a hundred quarreling states. Only a few Korean or Japanese inscriptions before A.D. 700 have been preserved, but extensive chronicles were written in 712 and 720 in Japan and later in Korea. Those reveal massive transmission of culture to Japan from Korea itself, and from China via Korea. The chronicles are also full of accounts of Koreans in Japan and of Japanese in Korea—interpreted by Japanese or Korean historians, respectively, as evidence of Japanese conquest of Korea or the reverse.

The ancestors of the Japanese, then, seem to have reached Japan before they had writing. Their biology suggests a recent arrival, but their language suggests arrival long ago. To resolve this paradox, we must now turn to archeology.

The seas that surround much of Japan and coastal East Asia are shallow enough to have been dry land during the ice ages, when much of the ocean water was locked up in glaciers and sea level lay at about 500 feet below its present measurement. Land bridges connected Japan's main islands to one another, to the Russian mainland, and to South Korea. The mammals walking out to Japan included not only the ancestors of modern Japan's bears and monkeys but also ancient humans, long before boats had been invented. Stone tools indicate human arrival as early as half a million years ago.

Around 13,000 years ago, as glaciers melted rapidly all over the world, conditions in Japan changed spectacularly for the better, as far as humans were concerned. Temperature, rainfall, and humidity all increased, raising plant productivity to present high levels. Deciduous leafy forests full of nut trees, which had been confined to southern Japan during the ice ages, expanded northward at the expense of coniferous forest, thereby replacing a forest type that had been rather sterile for humans with a much more productive one. The rise in sea level severed the land bridges, converted Japan from a piece of the Asian continent to a big archipelago, turned what had been a plain into rich shallow seas, and created thousands of miles of productive new coastline with innumerable islands, bays, tidal flats, and estuaries, all teeming with seafood.

That end of the Ice Age was accompanied by the first of the two most decisive changes in Japanese history: the invention of pottery. In the usual experience of archeologists, inventions flow from mainlands to islands, and small peripheral societies aren't supposed to contribute revolutionary advances to the rest of the world. It therefore astonished archeologists to discover that the world's oldest known pottery was made in Japan 12,700 years ago. For the first time in human experience, people had watertight containers readily available in any desired shape. With their new ability to boil or steam food, they gained access to abundant resources that had previously been difficult to use: leafy vegetables, which would burn or dry out if cooked on an open fire; shellfish, which could now be opened easily; and toxic foods like acorns, which could now have their toxins boiled out. Soft-boiled foods could be fed to small children, permitting earlier weaning and more closely spaced babies. Toothless old people, the repositories of information in a preliterate society, could now be fed and live longer. All those momentous consequences of pottery triggered a population explosion, causing Japan's population to climb from an estimated few thousand to a quarter of a million.

The prejudice that islanders are supposed to learn from superior continentals wasn't the sole reason that record-breaking Japanese pottery caused such a shock. In addition, those first Japanese potters were clearly hunter-gatherers, which also violated established views. Usually only sedentary societies own pottery: what nomad wants to carry heavy, fragile pots, as well as weapons and the baby, whenever time comes to shift camp? Most sedentary societies elsewhere in the world arose only with the adoption of agriculture. But the Japanese environment is so productive that people could settle down and make pottery while still living by hunting and gathering. Pottery helped those Japanese hunter-gatherers exploit their environment's rich food resources more than 10,000 years before intensive agriculture reached Japan.

Much ancient Japanese pottery was decorated by rolling or pressing a cord on soft clay. Because the Japanese word for cord marking is *jomon,* the term Jomon is applied to the pottery itself, to the ancient Japanese people who made it, and to that whole period in Japanese prehistory beginning with the invention of pottery and ending only 10,000 years later. The earliest Jomon pottery, of 12,700 years ago, comes from Kyushu, the southernmost Japanese island. Thereafter, pottery spread north, reaching the vicinity of modern Tokyo around 9,500 years ago and the northernmost island of Hokkaido by 7,000 years ago. Pottery's northward spread followed that of deciduous forest rich in nuts, suggesting that the climate-related food explosion was what permitted sedentary living.

How did Jomon people make their living? We have abundant evidence from the garbage they left behind at hundreds of thousands of excavated archeological sites all over Japan. They apparently enjoyed a well-balanced diet, one that modern nutritionists would applaud.

One major food category was nuts, especially chestnuts and walnuts, plus horse chestnuts and acorns leached or boiled free of their bitter poisons. Nuts could be harvested in autumn in prodigious quantities, then stored for the winter in underground pits up to six feet deep and six feet wide. Other plant foods included berries, fruits, seeds, leaves, shoots, bulbs, and roots. In all, archeologists sifting through Jomon garbage have identified 64 species of edible plants.

Then as now, Japan's inhabitants were among the world's leading consumers of seafood. They harpooned tuna in the open ocean, killed seals on the beaches, and exploited seasonal runs of salmon in the rivers. They drove dolphins into shallow water and clubbed or speared them, just as Japanese hunters do today. They netted diverse fish, captured them in weirs, and caught them on fishhooks carved from deer antlers. They gathered shellfish, crabs, and seaweed in the intertidal zone or dove for them. (Jomon skeletons show a high incidence of abnormal bone growth in the ears, often observed in divers today.) Among land animals hunted, wild boar and deer were the most common prey. They were caught in pit traps, shot with bows and arrows, and run down with dogs.

The most debated question about Jomon subsistence concerns the possible contribution of agriculture. Many Jomon sites contain remains of edible plants that are native to Japan as wild species but also grown as crops today, including the adzuki bean and green gram bean. The remains from Jomon times do not clearly show features distinguishing the crops from their wild ancestors, so we do not know whether these plants were gathered in the wild or grown intentionally. Sites also have debris of edible or useful plant species not native to Japan, such as hemp, which must have been introduced from the Asian mainland. Around 1000 B.C., toward the end of the Jomon period, a few grains of rice, barley, and millet, the staple cereals of East Asia, began to appear. All these tantalizing clues make it likely that Jomon people were starting to practice some slash-and-burn agriculture, but evidently in a casual way that made only a minor contribution to their diet.

Archeologists studying Jomon hunter-gatherers have found not only hard-to-carry pottery (including pieces up to three feet tall) but also heavy stone tools, remains of substantial houses that show signs of repair, big village sites of 50 or more dwellings, and cemeteries—all further evidence that the Jomon people were sedentary rather than nomadic. Their stay-at-home lifestyle was made possible by the diversity of resource-rich habitats available within a short distance of one central site: inland forests, rivers, seashores, bays, and open oceans. Jomon people lived at some of the highest population densities ever estimated for hunter-gatherers, especially in central and northern Japan, with their nut-rich forests, salmon runs, and productive seas. The estimate of the total population of Jomon Japan at its peak is 250,000—trivial, of course, compared with today, but impressive for hunter-gatherers.

With all this stress on what Jomon people did have, we need to be clear as well about what they didn't have. Their lives were very different from those of contemporary societies only a few hundred miles away in mainland China and Korea. Jomon people had no intensive agriculture. Apart from dogs (and perhaps pigs), they had no domestic animals. They had no metal tools, no writing, no weaving, and little social stratification into chiefs and commoners. Regional variation in pottery styles suggests little progress toward political centralization and unification.

Despite its distinctiveness even in East Asia at that time, Jomon Japan was not completely isolated. Pottery, obsidian, and fishhooks testify to some Jomon trade with Korea, Russia, and Okinawa—as does the arrival of Asian mainland crops. Compared with later eras, though, that limited trade with the outside world had little influence on Jomon society. Jomon Japan was a miniature conservative universe that changed surprisingly little over 10,000 years.

To place Jomon Japan in a contemporary perspective, let us remind ourselves of what human societies were like on the Asian mainland in 400 B.C., just as the Jomon lifestyle was about to come to an end. China consisted of kingdoms with rich elites and poor commoners; the people lived in walled towns, and the country was on the verge of political unification and would soon become the world's largest empire. Beginning around 6500 B.C., China had de-

All through human history, centralized states with metal weapons and armies supported by dense agricultural populations have swept away sparser populations of hunter-gatherers. How did Stone Age Japan survive so long?

veloped intensive agriculture based on millet in the north and rice in the south; it had domestic pigs, chickens, and water buffalo. The Chinese had had writing for at least 900 years, metal tools for at least 1,500 years, and had just invented the world's first cast iron. Those developments were also spreading to Korea, which itself had had agriculture for several thousand years (including rice since at least 2100 B.C.) and metal since 1000 B.C.

With all these developments going on for thousands of years just across the Korea Strait from Japan, it might seem astonishing that in 400 B.C. Japan was still occupied by people who had some trade with Korea but remained preliterate stone-tool-using hunter-gatherers. Throughout human history, centralized states with metal weapons and armies supported by dense agricultural populations have consistently swept away sparser populations of hunter-gatherers. How did Jomon Japan survive so long?

To understand the answer to this paradox, we have to remember that until 400 B.C., the Korea Strait separated not rich farmers from poor hunter-gatherers, but poor farmers from rich hunter-gatherers. China itself and Jomon Japan were probably not in direct contact. In-

stead Japan's trade contacts, such as they were, involved Korea. But rice had been domesticated in warm southern China and spread only slowly northward to much cooler Korea, because it took a long time to develop cold-resistant strains of rice. Early rice agriculture in Korea used dry-field methods rather than irrigated paddies and was not particularly productive. Hence early Korean agriculture could not compete with Jomon hunting and gathering. Jomon people themselves would have seen no advantage in adopting Korean agriculture, insofar as they were aware of its existence, and poor Korean farmers had no advantages that would let them force their way into Japan. As we shall see, the advantages finally reversed suddenly and dramatically.

More than 10,000 years after the invention of pottery and the subsequent Jomon population explosion, a second decisive event in Japanese history triggered a second population explosion. Around 400 B.C., a new lifestyle arrived from South Korea. This second transition poses in acute form our question about who the Japanese are. Does the transition mark the replacement of Jomon people with immigrants from Korea, ancestral to the modern Japanese? Or did Japan's original Jomon inhabitants continue to occupy Japan while learning valuable new tricks?

The new mode of living appeared first on the north coast of Japan's southwesternmost island, Kyushu, just across the Korea Strait from South Korea. There we find Japan's first metal tools, of iron, and Japan's first undisputed full-scale agriculture. That agriculture came in the form of irrigated rice fields, complete with canals, dams, banks, paddies, and rice residues revealed by archeological excavations. Archeologists term the new way of living Yayoi, after a district of Tokyo where in 1884 its characteristic pottery was first recognized. Unlike Jomon pottery, Yayoi pottery was very similar to contemporary South Korean pottery in shape. Many other elements of the new Yayoi culture were unmistakably Korean and previously foreign to Japan, including bronze objects, weaving, glass beads, and styles of tools and houses.

While rice was the most important crop, Yayoi farmers introduced 27 new to Japan, as well as unquestionably domesticated pigs. They may have practiced double cropping, with paddies irrigated for rice production in the summer, then drained for dry-land cultivation of millet, barley, and wheat in the winter. Inevitably, this highly productive system of intensive agriculture triggered an immediate population explosion in Kyushu, where archeologists have identified far more Yayoi sites than Jomon sites, even though the Jomon period lasted 14 times longer.

In virtually no time, Yayoi farming jumped from Kyushu to the adjacent main islands of Shikoku and Honshu, reaching the Tokyo area within 200 years, and the cold northern tip of Honshu (1,000 miles from the first Yayoi settlements on Kyushu) in another century. After briefly occupying northern Honshu, Yayoi farmers abandoned that area, presumably because rice farming could not compete with the Jomon hunter-gatherer life. For the next 2,000 years, northern Honshu remained a frontier zone, beyond which the northernmost Japanese island of Hokkaido and its Ainu hunter-gatherers were not even considered part of the Japanese state until their annexation in the nineteenth century.

It took several centuries for Yayoi Japan to show the first signs of social stratification, as reflected especially in cemeteries. After about 100 B.C., separate parts of cemeteries were set aside for the graves of what was evidently an emerging elite class, marked by luxury goods imported from China, such as beautiful jade objects and bronze mirrors. As the Yayoi population explosion continued, and as all the best swamps or irrigable plains suitable for wet rice agriculture began to fill up, the archeological evidence suggests that war became more and more frequent: that evidence includes mass production of arrowheads, defensive moats surrounding villages, and buried skeletons pierced by projectile points. These hallmarks of war in Yayoi Japan corroborate the earliest accounts of Japan in Chinese chronicles, which describe the land of Wa and its hundred little political units fighting one another.

In the period from A.D. 300 to 700, both archeological excavations and frustratingly ambiguous accounts in later chronicles let us glimpse dimly the emergence of a politically unified Japan. Before A.D. 300, elite tombs were small and exhibited a regional diversity of styles. Beginning around A.D. 300, increasingly enormous earth-mound tombs called *kofun*, in the shape of keyholes, were constructed throughout the former Yayoi area from Kyushu to North Honshu. *Kofun* are up to 1,500 feet long and more than 100 feet high, making them possibly the largest earth-mound tombs in the world. The prodigious amount of labor required to build them and the uniformity of their style across Japan imply powerful rulers who commanded a huge, politically unified labor force. Those *kofun* that have been excavated contain lavish burial goods, but excavation of the largest ones is still forbidden because they are believed to contain the ancestors of the Japanese imperial line. The visible evidence of political centralization that the *kofun* provide reinforces the accounts of *kofun*-era Japanese emperors written down much later in Japanese and Korean chronicles. Massive Korean influences on Japan during the *kofun* era—whether through the Korean conquest of Japan (the Korean view) or the Japanese conquest of Korea (the Japanese view)— were responsible for transmitting Buddhism, writing, horseback riding, and new ceramic and metallurgical techniques to Japan from the Asian mainland.

Finally, with the completion of Japan's first chronicle in A.D. 712, Japan emerged into the full light of history. As of 712, the people inhabiting Japan were at last unquestionably Japanese, and their language (termed Old Japanese) was unquestionably ancestral to modern Japanese. Emperor Akihito, who reigns today, is the eighty-second direct descendant of the emperor under whom that first chronicle of A.D. 712 was written. He is traditionally considered the 125th direct descendant of the legendary first emperor, Jimmu, the great-great-great-grandson of the sun goddess Amaterasu.

JAPANESE CULTURE UNDERwent far more radical change in the 700 years of the Yayoi era than in the ten millennia of Jomon times. The contrast between Jomon stability (or conservatism) and radical Yayoi change is the most striking feature of Japanese history. Obviously, something momentous happened at 400 B.C. What was it? Were the ancestors of the modern Japanese the Jomon people, the Yayoi people, or a combination? Japan's population increased by an astonishing factor of 70 during Yayoi times: What caused that change? A passionate debate has raged around three alternative hypotheses.

One theory is that Jomon hunter-gatherers themselves gradually evolved into the modern Japanese. Because they had already been living a settled existence in villages for thousands of years, they may have been preadapted to accepting agriculture. At the Yayoi transition, perhaps nothing more happened than that Jomon society received cold-resistant rice seeds and information about paddy irrigation from Korea, enabling it to produce more food and increase its numbers. This theory appeals to many modern Japanese because it minimizes the unwelcome contribution of Korean genes to the Japanese gene pool while portraying the Japanese people as uniquely Japanese for at least the past 12,000 years.

A second theory, unappealing to those Japanese who prefer the first theory, argues instead that the Yayoi transition represents a massive influx of immigrants from Korea, carrying Korean farming practices, culture, and genes. Kyushu would have seemed a paradise to Korean rice farmers, because it is warmer and swampier than Korea and hence a better place to grow rice. According to one estimate, Yayoi Japan received several million immigrants from Korea, utterly overwhelming the genetic contribution of Jomon people (thought to have numbered around 75,000 just before the Yayoi transition). If so, modern Japanese are descendants of Korean immigrants who developed a modified culture of their own over the last 2,000 years.

The last theory accepts the evidence for immigration from Korea but denies that it was massive. Instead, highly productive agriculture may have enabled a modest number of immigrant rice farmers to reproduce much faster than Jomon hunter-gatherers and eventually to outnumber them. Like the second theory, this theory considers modern Japanese to be slightly modified Koreans but dispenses with the need for large-scale immigration.

By comparison with similar transitions elsewhere in the world, the second or third theory seems to me more plausible than the first theory. Over the last 12,000 years, agriculture arose at not more than nine places on Earth, including China and the Fertile Crescent. Twelve thousand years ago, everybody alive was a hunter-gatherer; now almost all of us are farmers or fed by farmers. Farming spread from those few sites of origin mainly because farmers outbred hunters, developed more potent technology, and then killed the hunters or drove them off lands suitable for agriculture. In the modern times European farmers thereby replaced native Californian hunters, aboriginal Australians, and the San people of South Africa. Farmers who used stone tools similarly replaced hunters prehistorically throughout Europe, Southeast Asia, and Indonesia. Korean farmers of 400 B.C. would have enjoyed a much larger advantage over Jomon hunters because the Koreans already possessed iron tools and a highly developed form of intensive agriculture.

Which of the three theories is correct for Japan? The only direct way to answer this question is to compare Jomon and Yayoi skeletons and genes with those of modern Japanese and Ainu. Measurements have now been made of many skeletons. In addition, within the last three years molecular geneticists have begun to extract DNA from ancient human skeletons and compare the genes of Japan's ancient and modern populations. Jomon and Yayoi skeletons, researchers find, are on the average readily distinguishable. Jomon people tended to be shorter, with relatively longer forearms and lower legs, more wide-set eyes, shorter and wider faces, and much more pronounced facial topography, with strikingly raised browridges, noses, and nose bridges. Yayoi people averaged an inch or two taller, with close-set eyes, high and narrow

faces, and flat browridges and noses. Some skeletons of the Yayoi period were still Jomon-like in appearance, but that is to be expected by almost any theory of the Jomon-Yayoi transition. By the time of the *kofun* period, all Japanese skeletons except those of the Ainu form a homogeneous group, resembling modern Japanese and Koreans.

In all these respects, Jomon skulls differ from those of modern Japanese and are most similar to those of modern Ainu, while Yayoi skulls most resemble those of modern Japanese. Similarly, geneticists attempting to calculate the relative contributions of Korean-like Yayoi genes and Ainu-like Jomon genes to the modern Japanese gene pool have concluded that the Yayoi contribution was generally dominant. Thus, immigrants from Korea really did make a big contribution to the modern Japanese, though we cannot yet say whether that was because of massive immigration or else modest immigration amplified by a high rate of population increase. Genetic studies of the past three years have also at last resolved the controversy about the origins of the Ainu: they are the descendants of Japan's ancient Jomon inhabitants, mixed with Korean genes of Yayoi colonists and of the modern Japanese.

Given the overwhelming advantage that rice agriculture gave Korean farmers, one has to wonder why the farmers achieved victory over Jomon hunters so suddenly, after making little headway in Japan for thousands of years. What finally tipped the balance and triggered the Yayoi transition was probably a combination of four developments: the farmers began raising rice in irrigated fields instead of in less productive dry fields; they developed rice strains that would grow well in a cool climate; their population expanded in Korea, putting pressure on Koreans to emigrate; and they invented iron tools that allowed them to mass-produce the wooden shovels, hoes, and other tools needed for rice-paddy agriculture. That iron and intensive farming reached Japan simultaneously is unlikely to have been a coincidence.

WE HAVE SEEN THAT THE combined evidence of archeology, physical anthropology, and genetics supports the transparent interpretation for how the distinctive-looking Ainu and the undistinctive-looking Japanese came to share Japan: the Ainu are descended from Japan's original inhabitants and the Japanese are descended from more recent arrivals. But that view leaves the problem of language unexplained. If the Japanese really are recent arrivals from Korea, you might expect the Japanese and Korean languages to be very similar. More generally, if the Japanese people arose recently from some mixture, on the island of Kyushu, of original Ainu-like Jomon inhabitants with Yayoi invaders from Korea, the Japanese language might show close affinities to both the Korean and Ainu languages. Instead, Japanese and Ainu have no demonstrable relationship, and the relationship between Japanese and Korean is distant. How could this be so if the mixing occurred a mere 2,400 years ago? I suggest the following resolution of this paradox: the languages of Kyushu's Jomon residents and Yayoi invaders were quite different from the modern Ainu and Korean languages, respectively.

The Ainu language was spoken in recent times by the Ainu on the northern island of Hokkaido, so Hokkaido's Jomon inhabitants probably also spoke an Ainu-like language. The Jomon inhabitants of Kyushu, however, surely did not. From the southern tip of Kyushu to the northern tip of Hokkaido, the Japanese archipelago is nearly 1,500 miles long. In Jomon times it supported great regional diversity of subsistence techniques and of pottery styles and was never unified politically. During the 10,000 years of Jomon occupation, Jomon people would have evolved correspondingly great linguistic diversity. In fact, many Japanese place-names on Hokkaido and northern Honshu include the Ainu words for river, nai or betsu, and for cape, shiri, but such Ainu-like names do not occur farther south in Japan. This suggests not only that Yayoi and Japanese pioneers adopted many Jomon place-names, just as white Americans did Native American names (think of Massachusetts and Mississippi), but also that Ainu was the Jomon language only of northernmost Japan.

That is, the modern Ainu language of Hokkaido is not a model for the ancient Jomon language of Kyushu. By the same token, modern Korean may be a poor model for the ancient Yayoi language of Korean immigrants in 400 B.C. In the centuries before Korea became unified politically in A.D. 676, it consisted of three kingdoms. Modern Korean is derived from the language of the kingdom of Silla, the kingdom that emerged triumphant and unified Korea, but Silla was not the kingdom that had close contact with Japan in the preceding centuries. Early Korean chronicles tell us that the different kingdoms had different languages. While the languages of the kingdoms defeated by Silla are poorly known, the few preserved words of one of those kingdoms, Koguryo, are much more similar to the corresponding Old Japanese words than are the corresponding modern Korean words. Korean languages may have been even more diverse in 400 B.C., before political unification had reached the stage of three kingdoms. The Korean language that reached Japan in 400 B.C., and that evolved into modern Japanese, I suspect, was quite different from the Silla language that evolved into modern Korean. Hence we should not be surprised that modern Japanese and Korean people resemble each other far more in their appearance and genes than in their languages.

History gives the Japanese and the Koreans ample grounds for mutual distrust and contempt, so any conclusion confirming their close relationship is likely to be unpopular among both peoples. Like Arabs and Jews, Koreans and Japanese are joined by blood yet locked in traditional enmity. But enmity is mutually destructive, in East Asia as in the Middle East. As reluctant as Japanese and Koreans are to admit it, they are like twin brothers who shared their formative years. The political future of East Asia depends in large part on their success in rediscovering those ancient bonds between them.

The Diffusionists Have Landed

You've probably heard of those crackpot theories about ancient Phoenicians or Chinese in the New World. Maybe it's time to start paying attention

by Marc K. Stengel

IT is arguably the biggest discovery never to have elicited any reaction whatsoever. In November of 1994 a small monthly newspaper called *Y Drych (The Mirror)*, which serves as an expatriate journal for North America's Welsh diaspora, published the following curious item among a batch of breezy tidbits:

> According to [Alan] Wilson and [Baram] Blackett ... the court of Camelot is more likely to be found in Kentucky! They claim that [King] Arthur was killed in North America by Indians after emigrating there ca. 579 A.D.

With telegraphic brevity the *Y Drych* contributor, Don John, ran through the few salient points: There were *two* Arthurs, who lived centuries apart. "It was King Arthur II who died in America. He was embalmed and taken back to Wales to be buried at Mynydd-y-Gaer, near Bridgend." Oddly, John failed to mention the discovery a few years earlier, by a man antiquing in Pennsylvania, of a two-edged sword of the Norse *spatha* type. That finding had recently been discussed in the pages of another obscure journal, *The Ancient American,* which quoted the same Alan Wilson. The sword was inscribed with seven letters of a script that Wilson identified as Coelbren y Beirdd, presumed to have

been used by ancient Welsh divines in casting lots (*coelbren* = "lots, sortilege"; *y beirdd* = "of the bards"). Wilson proposed a rough translation ("The Lord ruler well beloved, the duty of the army mutually together to you") and posited a connection between this sword and Arthurian immigrants in North America circa A.D. 570.

John's scoop has apparently remained an exclusive for *Y Drych:* the big dailies and newsweeklies have run no follow-ups; no national television crews have combed Kentucky for relics of the Once and Future King. The silence, in the United States, at least, has extended even to a book on the subject, *The Holy Kingdom,* in which the popular paranormalist Adrian Gilbert elaborates on the Wilson-Blackett proposition in exhaustive textual, photographic, and genealogical detail. The book, brought out in England in 1998, has yet to find an American publisher.

It was ever thus, judging by the sentiments of those attending a recent annual conference of the Institute for the Study of American Cultures, held in Columbus, Georgia. ISAC members are accustomed to the professional and popular disregard that greets their unorthodox inquiries into the pre-Columbian history of the Western Hemisphere—inquiries, generally known as diffusionist studies, that suppose intentional contact

with the Americas by civilizations across both the Pacific and the Atlantic, beginning sometime in the late Stone Age (7000–3000 B.C.).

Arrayed against the diffusionists stand the so-called independent inventionists—mainstream scholars who regard Western Hemisphere aboriginals as having been essentially free of cross-cultural contamination until 1492. What the inventionists and the diffusionists are fighting over is the right to propose—or, better yet, to define—the prehistory of the Americas. The two camps, it seems, agree on little before Columbus's landing. The Norwegian archaeologists Helge and Anne Stine Ingstad's famous identification, in 1961, of a Viking settlement at L'Anse aux Meadows, Newfoundland, from just after A.D. 1000 is, of course, a notable exception, no longer in dispute. But that discovery has so far gone nowhere. The Norse settlers, who may have numbered as many as 160 and stayed for three years or longer, seem to have made no lasting impression on the aboriginal skraellings that, according to Norse sagas, they encountered, and to have avoided being influenced in turn. The traditions of the Micmac people, modern-day inhabitants of the area, have not been seriously investigated; another people historically associated with this area, the reputedly fair-skinned Beothuks, have been extinct

The diffusionists have a habit of raising awkward questions. Who carved ancient Iberian script into a stone in West Virginia? Why would the Ten Commandments appear in Old Hebrew on a tablet in New Mexico?

since 1829. The Vikings came, kept to themselves, and left—that appears to be as much revision of the long-standing history of New World settlement as the hard-core academic establishment will entertain.

To many, the inventionists have clearly gained the upper hand, having marshaled shards, spearpoints, and other relics that indicate the independent cultural development of a native people whose Ice Age ancestors came overland from Northeast Asia. Still, the diffusionists have a habit of raising awkward questions—questions that even some mainstream scholars find hard to ignore, much less to explain away. Who carved Phoenician-era Iberian script into a stone found at Grave Creek, West Virginia? How did a large stone block incised with medieval Norse runes make its way to Kensington, Minnesota? Why would a rough version of the Ten Commandments appear in Old Hebrew script on a boulder-sized tablet near Los Lunas, New Mexico? Conversely, how could the sweet potato, known to be indigenous to the Americas, have become a food staple throughout Polynesia and the Pacific basin as early as A.D. 400? And why would dozens of eleventh- to thirteenth-century temple sculptures in Karnätaka, India, include depictions of what appears to be American maize?

At the ISAC gathering Mike Xu, a professor of modern languages and literatures at Texas Christian University, raised the possibility of direct Chinese influence on Mesoamerica's Olmec culture. Xu is young, quiet, and almost dif-

fident about the bold proposition he came to reveal. Drawing on linguistic scholarship in his native China, he suggested that carved stone blades found in Guatemala, dating from approximately 1100 B.C., are distinctly Chinese in pattern. Moreover, they bear ideographic writing that has uncanny resemblances to glyphs from the contemporaneous Shang Dynasty, which ruled North China from its center in the lower Yellow River valley.

Xu was candid about the skepticism, even disdain, that his proposal engenders among orthodox archaeologists. With an engaging smile, he pointed out that no less an authority than Michael Coe, a Mayan-glyph decipherer and an emeritus professor of anthropology at Yale University, considers the Shang hypothesis totally spurious. Xu remains unbowed. "The problem," he told his ISAC audience, "isn't *whether* Asians reached Mesoamerica before Columbus. The problem is *when* they arrived and what they did here." Any proposal that smacks of diffusionism in today's academic climate, Xu continued, is immediately dismissed as irresponsible at best, malevolent at worst. "Here are all these American scholars," he pointed out slyly, "speaking European languages, and they dare to say 'No, there was never any diffusion; and yes, all Western Hemisphere cultures are indigenous.'"

The two-day ISAC conference passed quietly enough for a symposium that juggled such unorthodox topics as the Bat Creek Stone—whose inscription, in what seems to be a second-century Semitic alphabet, complicates the stone's official provenance in nineteenth-century East Tennessee—and certain Native American Earth Mother symbols that resemble icons from prehistoric Europe and Asia. Gloria Farley, whose book *In Plain Sight* (1994) has become a standard reference work among diffusionists, summarized the latest inquiries into the origin and the decipherment of rock carvings at an Oklahoma site known as the Anubis Caves. A self-taught archaeologist, still dauntless in her early eighties, Farley reviewed a career in which she was among the first to posit, fifty years ago, that the caves' myriad jum-

bled symbols represent pictographs and epigraphy with proto-Celtic, Iberian, and Phoenician affinities to a time predating Jesus by centuries. The dramatic hypotheses being proposed by Farley, Xu, and other speakers stood in stark contrast to the humble setting of a small rented conference room in western Georgia.

CRANK SCIENCE

THERE is a reason, according to the academics who uphold anthropological orthodoxy at universities and research institutes, why the diffusionists have elicited nothing but enmity or disregard for their views: they are crackpots and lunatics. "Crank" is the term employed for these scientists by Stephen Williams, a retired curator of North American archaeology at the Peabody Museum of Harvard University. Williams's *Fantastic Archaeology: The Wild Side of North American Prehistory (1991)* is virtually a catalogue of outlandish theories about pre-Columbian transoceanic visits to the Americas. Williams set out to debunk them all. Wielding sarcasm like a shiv, he was relentless in attack. He scuttled the "lost continents" of Atlantis and Mu; deconstructed the latent racism that he perceives beneath the nineteenth-century fascination with Moundbuilder cultures, whose barrows freckle the great river valleys of the Ohio, the Tennessee, and the Mississippi; and squashed speculation about Norse, Semitic, and Celtic letters carved in stones from New Hampshire to New Mexico.

Similarly, for Brian Fagan, an influential professor of anthropology at the University of California at Santa Barbara, diffusionism is exasperating. "Why do such lunatic ravings persist?" he asked in his book *The Great Journey: The Peopling of Ancient America* (1987). "To read the crank literature on the first Americans is to enter a fantasy world of strange, often obsessed, writers with a complex jargon of catchwords and 'scientific' data to support their ideas." The Colgate University astronomer and anthropologist Anthony Aveni tends to be more sympathetic, perhaps because the field of archaeo-astronomy, which he has helped to ennoble, was itself an academic pariah until recent years. Nevertheless, Aveni's sympathies go only so far. "I think there is, beneath all this dialogue about diffusionism, a will to believe in bizarre ideas," he says. "This is a romantic idea that we're talking about here, after all. These are bizarre tales of an imagined era in an imagined past. And like the occult beliefs they resemble, they're really just wishful thinking. It's a belief that we can wish into existence the universe we desire and deserve."

The universe that we appear to be stuck with, however, at least as far as the peopling of the Western Hemisphere is concerned, is unromantic and fairly unambiguous. Fagan's book provides a succinct summary of establishment thinking:

> The most conservative viewpoint argues that no humans lived in the Americas before the end of the Ice Age. Tiny numbers of big-game hunters moved south of the great North American ice sheets as the glaciers retreated after 14,000 years ago. The newcomers followed large Ice Age animals into more temperate latitudes. They expanded rapidly over vast tracts of virgin hunting territory, their immediate descendants [being] the famous Clovis people, whose distinctive stone spearpoints have been found over much of North and Central America.

For decades these Clovis immigrants have been assigned a settlement date around 10,000 B.C., in what Stephen Williams, an adherent, calls "the Clovis hard-line position." Williams and other mainstream scholars contend that the wide distribution of the distinctive stone spearpoints first discovered in Clovis, New Mexico, in 1932 supports their theory that all pre-Columbian experience throughout the Western Hemisphere ultimately derives from an Ice Age monoculture with exclusively Siberian origins.

Lately, however, archaeological finds at various digs in North and South America have begun to call the Clovis-only scenario into question. For instance, the archaeologist Tom Dillehay, of the University of Kentucky at Lex-

ington, has uncovered intriguing evidence that human beings reached Monte Verde, in southern Chile, 12,500 years ago—in other words, that the extreme southern limits of the Western Hemisphere were settled at about the time that the supposed first Americans were crossing the Bering land bridge, more than 9,000 miles to the northwest. It is generally accepted that settlement across this distance would have required progressive immigrant waves over some 7,000 years. Moreover, Dillehay and his team have come across a campsite near Monte Verde that they believe may be 30,000 years old.

Less ancient but potentially more problematic for the Clovis hard-liners is the revelation in Brazil of what appear to be the oldest human remains ever found in the Western Hemisphere. Last October, Brazilian scientists announced evidence suggesting that the skull of a young woman found at Lapa Vermelha, in the state of Minas Gerais, is some 11,500 years old. Moreover, sophisticated reconstructive techniques performed on the skull in England indicate that Luzia, as the woman has been named, might have Negroid origins—or at least is not Mongoloid, as any descendant of Bering Strait pilgrims must necessarily be. Luzia's remains were discovered in 1975, but it was not until twenty years later that anthropologists examined the skull closely and thought to question the Clovis-only hypothesis on the basis of the unusual cranial features.

How might the pre-Clovis settlers have arrived? One explanation is that early immigrants floated down the western coast of North and South America in small boats. This theory, considered heretical when, nearly three decades ago, it was proposed by the archaeologist Knut Fladmark, of Simon Fraser University, has been gaining adherents of late. Researchers such as Dennis Stanford, the chairman of the anthropology department at the Smithsonian Institution; Carole Mandryk, an associate professor of anthropology at Harvard University; and Daryl Fedje, an archaeologist with Parks Canada, are urging their colleagues to consider that canoelike or skin-covered boats—prototypes of Inuit kayaks, perhaps—might

have aided migration toward the end of the last Ice Age, around 14,000 years ago. Jon Erlandson, an anthropologist at the University of Oregon, has pointed out that boats were used in Japan 20,000 years ago. By Fladmark's estimate, travelers paddling six hours a day could have made the trip from the eastern Aleutians to Chile in just four and a half years. This route might also help to explain Luzia's presence in Brazil: the anthropologist who first noted her unusual features believes that her forebears originated in Southeast Asia and migrated "northward along the coast and across the Bering Straits until they reached the Americas."

Xu, for one, is amused by this archaeological approximation of a drag race backward in time. Although he welcomes any willingness among traditional academics to question the established settlement dates, he is puzzled by their apparently exclusive fascination with older contact. "It amazes me," he told his ISAC colleagues in Columbus, "that while there are authorities who propose visits to North America by boat some twenty-five thousand years ago," most orthodox academics insist that contact across the sea in the past 3,000 years is "simply unthinkable."

THE CASE OF BARRY FELL

THE chief diffusionist culprit is the late H. Barraclough ("Barry") Fell. A Harvard biologist turned epigrapher, Fell acquired a following in 1976 with the publication of *America B.C.*, which discussed the archaeological implications of epigraphy—the study of ancient man-made markings incised in stone, clay, wood, or bone. Part adventure tale, part introductory textbook on linguistics and anthropology, *America B.C.* energized a generation with its talk of "Druids in Vermont?" and "Phoenicians in Iowa before the time of Julius Caesar?"

Despite a penchant for berets and a breezy, teasing manner, Fell was no mere dream-spinner, in the style of nineteenth-century seekers after the Lost Tribes of Israel or after survivors from

Atlantis. A scholar of high standing at one of the world's most imposing academic institutions, Fell endeavored to bring a scientist's objective discipline to the process of identifying mysterious alphabetic scripts and pictographs, translating them from their ancient languages, and interpreting their meaning in the context of their surroundings.

When Fell came across an archaeological anomaly, he gnawed at it relentlessly until an explanation issued forth. For instance, his curiosity aroused by oddities at the Comalcalco temple site, on the coast of Tabasco, in southeastern Mexico, Fell prepared reams of comparative analysis in support of a Mediterranean role in the temple's origins. The key, he insisted, was the use of fired bricks in the construction of the temple walls—an anomaly in the region. Comparing supposed masons' marks at the site with analogues from Rome, Crete, and Libya, Fell disputed mainstream assertions that this was a Classic Mayan site. With characteristic bravado he wrote that it was designed and probably built by "visitors from Europe and North Africa, trained in the manufacture of fired bricks in Roman brickyards." Moreover, these visitors came "during the first three centuries of the Christian era." Fell's absolute certainty, in this and myriad other epigraphic "explanations," inflamed mainstream scholars. But although another researcher has identified a few other instances of fired-brick construction in Mesoamerica, mysteries remain about Comalcalco and the profusion of its scripts. Fell's ghost is not easy to exorcise from this place.

For many general readers *America B.C.,* together with Fell's subsequent *Saga America* (1980) and *Bronze Age America* (1982), rewrote the cultural history of the Western Hemisphere. Fell's clear message was that Europeans, Africans, and Asians had made routine yet historically unremembered visits to North and South America for at least 3,000 years prior to Columbus's celebrated landfall.

To the academic establishment, however, Fell was a self-promoting pseudoscientist who threatened to undo more than a century of careful progress in archaeological and anthropological research. His critics charge that instead of observing protocols and rules of evidence required by traditional archaeology, Fell promoted esoteric claims to a nonspecialist—and therefore credulous—audience. A minor industry developed for the express purpose of debunking Fell.

Both before and after Fell's death, in 1994, his critics were merciless, citing a variety of errors of chronology and interpretation and also Fell's perceived distaste for peer review by specialists. Unable to trust some of his discoveries, mainstream academics have generally elected not to trust any of them. In *Fantastic Archaeology,* Stephen Williams argued that the case of Barry Fell amounted to a single question: "How many of Fell's inscriptions in North America, which now must number in the thousands, are real messages from scribes writing in non-Native American languages (Eurasian scripts)?" Williams was scathing in his answer: "The real count, I fear, is few or none."

The influential archaeologist David Kelley, of the University of Calgary, has his own concerns about Barry Fell's methods—and yet, unlike Williams and Brian Fagan, in the end he is unable simply to dismiss Fell's work. Kelley is a Harvard-trained scholar of catholic interests, which range from ancient calendrics and archaeo-astronomy to the prehistory of the Celts to the decipherment of Mayan glyphs. In conversation he seems to guide by indirection, answering questions with questions or with references to the writings of his peers. His wispy eyebrows sit above eyes undimmed by more than forty years of serious scholarship; a tight-lipped smile suggests that there are many things he will not say about himself or his accomplishments. Indeed, he is almost painfully reticent about what most scholars now consider to be a monumental achievement in the field: his having broken a century-old logjam in Mayan epigraphy. Prevailing amid a hail of academic and personal attacks, Kelley made a persuasive argument for a phonetic, as opposed to an ideographic, method of interpretation. Drawing on the work of the Russian linguist Yuri Knorosov, Kelley's work offered a way to unlock the sounds and meanings of glyphs that had stood mute for centuries—inaugurating a new age of decipherment that is transforming Mayan studies.

Kelley, who is a contributing editor to *The Review of Archaeology,* complained in a 1990 essay that "Fell's work [contains] major academic sins, the three worst being distortion of data, inadequate acknowledgment of predecessors, and lack of presentation of alternative views." Among the embarrassments that Kelley and other critics often use against Fell are a series of Celtic ogham inscriptions that were sent to Fell from McKee, Kentucky, in 1988. He dutifully translated the scripts, which later proved to be forgeries. Although Fell was the one to spot that they were fake, the damage was done.

Nevertheless, Kelley and others do credit Fell with raising the possibility of Celtic, Iberian, and North African connections to certain unexplained American inscriptions. The Grave Creek Stone, from West Virginia, is a typical example. Mainstream archaeologists, puzzled by the carvings on it, have long

---

Even some traditionalists now accept that there was overseas contact, a prominent scholar concedes. "What we doubt is the impact of the contact," he says. "These visitors simply didn't transform the societies they found."

---

dismissed it as a forgery; but Fell suggested that its symbols derive from an ancient Punic, or Phoenician, alphabet used on the Iberian Peninsula during the first millennium B.C.—a script unknown, and thus presumably unforgeable, at the time of the stone's discovery, in 1838. Kelley disagrees with Fell's theory that the Grave Creek symbols represent some sort of astronomical text. But the similarity of those symbols to obscure but undisputed Phoenician letters, he believes, is much more than coincidence—and, at the least, Fell deserves credit for emphasizing the comparison.

It is unusual to detect even this much tolerance for Barry Fell in a member of the academic mainstream. But Kelley can be more enthusiastic yet. With regard to a celebrated (or notorious) hypothesis of Fell's that the stick-figure letters carved into stones at sites ranging from Vermont to Oklahoma are Celtic in origin, Kelley wrote in his *Review of Archaeology* essay, "I have no personal doubts that some of the inscriptions which have been reported are genuine Celtic ogham." These are the very markings that most orthodox scholars dismiss as plough marks or forgeries or the figments of febrile New Age imaginations. In addition, Kelley resists joining the many of his peers who take potshots at Fell's Druids of New England. He continued,

Despite my occasional harsh criticism of Fell's treatment of individual inscriptions, it should be recognized that without Fell's work there would be no [North American] ogham problem to perplex us. We need to ask not only what Fell has done wrong in his epigraphy, but also where we have gone wrong as archaeologists in not recognizing such an extensive European presence in the New World.

The way Kelley is described by his friend Michael Coe in *Breaking the Maya Code* (1992) suggests that he might secretly revel in his controversial, if guarded, support for Fell. Coe wrote,

[Dave is] a lively mixture of Irish puckishness and New England Yankee sobriety [whose] large frame, bald head, and leprechaun smile are familiar features at [academic] meetings, where he can always be expected to present a paper that may be unusual and even outrageous, according to one's lights, but is usually grounded in the most impeccable scholarship.

In one such paper, titled "Writing in the Americas," published in October of 1998 in a special edition of the *Journal of the West,* Kelley focused on a "deci-pherment" that detractors consider to be one of Fell's most outrageous: the Peterborough Stone, in Ontario. This is a flat table rock measuring hundreds of square feet, upon which a riot of curious incised graffiti are interlaced, seemingly at random. To Fell, who made the stone the focus of his *Bronze Age America,* the layout consisted of meaningful groups of symbols and letters, carved primarily to document the visit and the commercial enterprise of a Bronze Age Nordic king whom Fell identified as Woden-lithi. "Woden-lithi, of Ringerike the great king, instructed that runes be engraved," reads one section of Fell's ambitious translation of this curious saga in stone. "A ship he took. In-honor-of-Gungnir was its name.... For ingot-copper of excellent quality came the king by way of trial."

Fell believed that Scandinavian visitors circa 1700 B.C. incised the Peterborough Stone with words and symbols that have distinctly Scandinavian pronunciations and meanings. However, the letters themselves are not depicted with recognized medieval Norse runes. In Fell's, and now Kelley's, view, a *pre*-runic alphabet was used—a little-known script called Tifinagh, preserved by a Saharan Berber people known as the Tuareg. It is as if Woden-lithi's scribe used symbols from the Classical Greek alphabet to put together English-sounding words.

In *The Review of Archaeology,* Kelley supported Fell's identification (if not his exact translation) of proto-Tifinagh at Peterborough, and he amplified this position in his *Journal of the West* article. After comparing figures at Peterborough with inscriptions found in the Bohuslän region that once encompassed parts of Norway and Sweden; in the Tassili area of Saharan Africa, near Algeria's border with Niger; and at a southern terminus of the ancient Amber Route, in the Camonica Valley of northern Italy, Kelley wrote,

I have found that the late Bronze Age of Scandinavia, corresponding to the early Iron Age of Italy and North Africa, shows a lengthy series of innovations in all areas of iconography, including apparent Proto-Tifinagh inscriptions in both Scandinavia and It-aly.... The date is about 800 B.C. (900 years later than asserted by Fell).

Kelley did not shy away from the diffusionist implications of his analysis: "It looks to me as if a single trade route united an area from the gold-mining zone along the Niger [River] to Scandinavia, and I think that oceanic voyagers from Scandinavia, linked into that route, reached Ontario."

Kelley's role in the Mayan-decipherment controversy of the 1970s has steeled him against the predictable rebukes of mainstream colleagues for his Peterborough hypothesis. "When it is clear that a 'fantastic' interpretation has many reasonable components *if the data are valid,*" he has observed, "most professional archaeologists regard that as ... adequate reason to *assume* that the data are invalid." Kelley believes that in the prevailing academic climate the challenge for diffusionists is not only to build a solid scientific case but also to win a fair hearing. "The problem I see with Barry Fell," he says, "is that the people who can evaluate him accurately are the people who are least likely to be reading him. It needs somebody with a professional understanding of linguistic evidence and a willingness to look at some quite unlikely-seeming material."

A DIFFUSIONIST REBUTTAL

THE material to which Kelley refers is not only confounding but also compelling. It ranges from small stones inscribed with ancient Semitic scripts, such as the Tennessee Bat Creek Stone and the West Virginia Grave Creek Stone, to the Phoenician-inscribed Paraiba Stone, found (and then lost) in the nineteenth century in Brazil, to Japanese-style pottery shards in Ecuador, to the "melanotic" chicken, a genetically unique strain indigenous to Southeast Asia but found in Mesoamerica as well. If Stephen Williams's *Fantastic Archaeology* gives the impression that such things are no more than a random series of strange delusions, that impression is robustly countered by the laborious research of John Sorenson and Martin Raish. Sorenson, an emeritus professor of anthropology at Brigham Young University, who also holds degrees in archaeology and meteorology, has published extensively on the topic of transoceanic contact with the Americas "before the Recognized Discoveries." Concerning Barry Fell's research, he says he is "appreciative of the enterprise but critical of the methods, logic, and resulting interpretations." Raish holds a Ph.D. in art history; he also has a master's in library and information sciences, and is an instructional librarian at Brigham Young University. It is perhaps the latter expertise on which he and Sorenson drew most heavily for the herculean task of collating, summarizing, and indexing diffusion-related texts.

Their 1,200-page, two-volume *Pre-Columbian Contact With the Americas Across the Oceans* is an annotated bibliography of more than 5,100 books, articles, dissertations, and presentations regarding the (mostly) serious scholarship devoted to matters diffusionist, pro and con. Originally published in 1990, by Research Press, of Provo, Utah, it was substantially revised and amplified in 1996. It is either a treasure trove or a refuse heap of pre-Columbian conundrums, depending on one's perspective.

There are, for example, citations of the studies of Carl Johannessen, a professor emeritus of geography at the University of Oregon, which analyze the delicately rendered carvings that look like maize—a crop known to be indigenous to the Western Hemisphere—in the Karnätaka temple sculptures. There are citations of painstaking linguistic evaluations by Richard Nielsen, a Houston-based engineer, of the inscriptions on the Kensington Rune Stone, in Minnesota. On what looks like a rough-hewn headstone are about sixty words (and some numerals) in the distinctive runic alphabet of medieval Scandinavia. They purportedly chronicle a bloody attack on a group of Swedish and Norwegian adventurers that is unmistakably dated in runes: "Year 1362." Williams has dismissed the Kensington Stone as an obvious forgery because of amateurish "mistakes" in runic orthography. How-

ever, as Sorenson and Raish point out, Nielsen "brings forward extensive evidence that what critics have called 'aberrant' features in this text are not so. They were in fact found in the old south Norwegian province and dialect of Bohuslän at least by A.D. 1200."

The bibliography also includes citations of the work of J. Huston McCulloch, a professor of economics at Ohio State University, who has written extensively on the Bat Creek Stone and collateral artifacts. A hand-sized dark-gray shard, the stone resides out of public view, in a back room at the Smithsonian Institution, to which facility it was delivered shortly after its discovery, in 1889. It bears an eight-letter script that has been identified—not without virulent controversy, of course—as a form of paleo-Hebrew from the first or second century. According to a 1970 interpretation by the prominent Semiticist Cyrus Gordon, the text fragment reads "for Judea" or "for the Judeans." Although charges of forgery or of confusion of the script with the Cherokee syllabary have been plausibly refuted by the diffusionists over the years, authorities contended that simple bracelets that were found alongside the stone amount to proof of the artifacts' Native American origin: it was presumed—without testing, as it turns out—that the bracelets were made of pure copper from the Lake Superior region. McCulloch, however, brings to light chemical analysis by the Smithsonian revealing that the "copper" bracelets are actually made of brass. Furthermore, he found, as Sorenson and Raish note, that the bracelets "have parallels in the Mediterranean world only during the first and second centuries of the Christian era, supporting the reading of the inscription as Hebrew of that period." McCulloch and other diffusionists argue that because no Native American populations are known to have smelted metals, the presence of brass—an alloy—suggests a foreign provenance, or at least a foreign influence.

To establishment charges that diffusionists are but a rabble of undisciplined intellectual guerrillas intent on archaeological anarchy, Sorenson and Raish's bibliography represents an impressive

rebuttal—a dispassionate and comprehensive summary of the most serious diffusionist research and commentary to date. However, the bibliography is the product of a publishing house with Mormon ties—a fact that establishment scholars cite with disdain. After all, the Book of Mormon identifies three main peoples as having emigrated from the Middle East to the Americas: the Jaredites, of the Book of Ether (circa 3000 B.C.); the family of Lehi, of the Book of First Nephi (circa 600 B.C.); and the people of Zarahemla, descended from King Zedekiah of the Old Testament, who escaped the destruction of Jerusalem in 586 B.C. Anything that connects ancient Mesoamerica with biblical-era Palestine lends that much more credence to the Book of Mormon—support that in itself casts doubt on the bibliography's objectivity, at least as far as most of its critics are concerned.

Explaining the criteria they used to select entries, Sorenson and Raish state that they "exclude only two categories as absolutely without redeeming scholarly value: Atlantis/Mu per se and 'extraterrestrial contacts.' " Just the same, they have drawn fire on this very point. Anthony Aveni, of Colgate, says derisively, "This diffusionist topic is, at root, Atlantean. And I think this monomyth—what you might call the Simple Solution—goes back to the Tower of Babel, to the Old Testament. It's biblical: the Lost Tribes of Israel, for example. The Mormons are still preaching that idea."

WHOSE RACE IS IT ANYWAY?

HIDDEN denominational agendas are the least of the diffusionists' problems in their ongoing struggle for academic legitimacy. Attempting to understand an archaeological outlook that he simply cannot accept, the celebrated Maya scholar Arthur Demarest, of Vanderbilt University, proposes a rather utilitarian inspiration for mid-nineteenth-century diffusionism. "That," he says, "was the period of the frontier wars with the Native Americans—a period, especially after Custer, when there was a lot of

> *"There's no effort to ask the tribes what they remember," Vine Deloria Jr. laments. "And numerous tribes do say that strange people came through our land. Or they remember that we came across the Atlantic as refugees."*

enmity and hatred toward Native Americans. So that fed into the idea that these earlier societies, not only the Maya, Aztecs, and Inca but even the ones up here—the Moundbuilders, for example—were somehow the product of some other white race that came in, was less savage, and was able to achieve these monuments and other things. I don't think contemporary diffusionists have any racist feelings, but that kind of sentiment did give diffusionism a boost back in the 1870s."

Demarest may not ascribe racist intentions to his diffusionist contemporaries, but there are some, particularly in official circles, who may. The 1996 discovery in Washington state of an ancient skeleton, designated Kennewick Man, soon sparked controversy among archaeologists, Native Americans, and the U.S. Army Corps of Engineers, because the skeleton does not appear to be of Native American origin. As the writer Mark Lasswell observed in *The Wall Street Journal,* "Scientific evidence that American Indian ancestors may not have been the first inhabitants of the Western Hemisphere is a ticklish subject, not only for Indians but also, apparently, for the Clinton administration, exquisitely attuned, as always, to the nuances of multiculturalism."

Early studies of the remains led scientists to suspect that Kennewick Man arrived here some 9,300 years ago—long after the Bering land bridge disappeared—and bore certain "Caucasoid"

features that were said to distinguish him from Native American peoples of Siberian heritage. Last fall federally appointed scientists released a report concluding that the skeleton's physiognomy is most closely linked to groups in southern and eastern Asia: the features originally described as Caucasoid are actually associated with a Japanese people known as the Ainu, they believe. If Kennewick Man is a member of the Ainu, that group's ancient maritime tradition might explain how he got here. Scientists say that more tests are needed to reach any definitive conclusions about Kennewick Man's origins; however, the government has not allowed any DNA testing of the skeleton to date, because Native Americans consider it intrusive and sacrilegious. If Kennewick Man was found on their land, area tribes insist, then he must be an ancestor, and his remains should not be disturbed. Moreover, because the religion and oral histories of these tribes hold that their people have lived in the Northwest "since the beginning of time," they are resentful of any implication that they may have ancestors who migrated from another land—whether from Siberia, Japan, or elsewhere. Archaeologists, eager to pursue the questions raised by Kennewick Man's discovery, have sued to perform DNA and other tests, and a U.S.

> *Kelley disagrees with the diffusionist theory that the Grave Creek symbols represent an astronomical text. But their similarity to undisputed Phoenician letters, he believes, is much more than coincidence.*

magistrate has set a March deadline for federal officials to decide on the matter.

Meanwhile, in implicit acknowledgment that the race card had been played successfully, in April, 1998, the Army Corps of Engineers abruptly

dumped 500 tons of rock fill over the site where Kennewick Man was discovered, beside the Columbia River. Although archaeologists often restore digging sites to their original condition after extensive studies have been completed, this action, by the corps's own admission, was meant to ensure "the protection of any additional skeletal material or cultural artifacts from further revelation."

The diffusionist cause enjoys no better political tolerance north of the border. In 1990, reacting to the prospect that some Manitoba schools might introduce discussions of pre-Columbian contact with North America into their curricula, Jack Steinbring, an anthropologist then at the University of Winnipeg, wrote to the Minister of Education at the time, Len Derkach, with a plea that he intervene. "The view that Europeans created North American Native rock art . . . is dangerous," Steinbring stated.

> Imagine Native youngsters being taught that the countless *thousands* of aboriginal rock paintings across North America were the result of the Norse, or Canaanites, or Phoenicians. The cause of this situation, and [the] implications for the strengthening of Native identity in a stressful period of acculturation are appropriately compared with apartheid or any other form of racial supremacy.

In a follow-up letter Steinbring declared, "Please understand that there is no debate on this epigraphy issue in Anthropology. Anthropology *as a profession* rejects it."

In any controversy about carvings on North American stones the name of Barry Fell inevitably surfaces. "In some rather twisted logic," Stephen Williams wrote in *Fantastic Archaeology,*

> Fell sees a failure by anthropologists to recognize that many American Indian languages are heavily larded with wholesale borrowing from Mediterranean peoples, and says that this "does a grave injustice to the cultural tradition of the Amerindian peoples.". . . . I can only suppose Fell means therefore that the only true happiness for the Amerindians is to realize that they too are a part of the great heritage of

Western civilization like ourselves. The Native Americans must want to ask, "Why have the anthropologists wanted to keep us apart?"

Why, indeed? asks Vine Deloria Jr., an outspoken Native American activist. Deloria is a member of the Standing Rock Sioux tribe of North Dakota, a former executive director of the National Congress of American Indians, and a professor of history at the University of Colorado at Boulder. His numerous books, which include *Custer Died for Your Sins* (1969), *God Is Red* (1973), and *Red Earth, White Lies* (1995), voice a thorough dissatisfaction with the standard histories of European and Native American relations since Columbus. In a 1992 paper in the academic journal *American Antiquity,* Deloria chastised the archaeological and anthropological establishment for embracing the monocultural implications of the Bering Strait hypothesis. "This migration from Siberia," he wrote, "is regarded as doctrine, but basically it is a fictional doctrine that places American Indians outside the realm of planetary human experiences."

A natural storyteller, Deloria takes obvious pleasure in drawing a listener into his tales with dramatic turns of phrase and deft modulations of his gravelly voice. He delights in irony, savors the unpredictable, and rewards surprise that is expressed at his many unexpected opinions with a mischievous "Aha!" You might think an Indian wouldn't feel such a way, he seems to be saying, but you never bothered to ask, did you?

Deloria bridles at what he sees as the reverse racism implicit in the establishment's dismissal of all things diffusionist. To him, the mainstream academic position that defends the Clovis-only hypothesis smacks of paternalism. He marvels at "the isolation of archaeologists today," and has written, "I have in the neighborhood of 80 books dealing in one way or another with Precolumbian expeditions to the Western Hemisphere." These books, he says, range from utter nonsense to some quite sophisticated reinterpretations of archaeological anomalies in light of new findings. But the archaeological establishment will have none of it, to Deloria's frustra-

tion. He laments, "There's no effort to ask the tribes what they remember of things that happened." In contrast to tribes in the area where Kennewick Man was found, he argues, "numerous tribes do say that strange people doing this or that came through our land, visited us, and so on. Or they remember that we came across the Atlantic as refugees from some struggle, then came down the St. Lawrence River, and so forth. There's a great reluctance among archaeologists and anthropologists to break centuries-old doctrine and to take a look at something new."

He continues, "As for the history of this hemisphere from, say, five thousand B.C. forward to our time, the mainstream scholars just don't want to deal with that at all. Let me give you an example. Years ago I spoke at an academic archaeological conference, and at the end of my speech I asked, 'Why don't you guys just drop the blinders and get into this diffusionist stuff?' My host, David Hurst Thomas, just about lost it and said, 'Do you know how long and hard we've fought to get members of this profession to admit that Indians could have done some of these things? And now you're saying it was Europeans!' "

BEYOND DIRT ARCHAEOLOGY

IN the end, the issues dividing the diffusionists and the independent inventionists come down to an argument about what constitutes significant historical evidence. Arthur Demarest, of Vanderbilt, touches, perhaps unconsciously, on the crux of the matter when he proffers a twig of the olive branch. "Within orthodox academics," he says, "there are a lot of people who simply dismiss the argument out of hand on the ground that the mechanics of overseas diffusion themselves are too difficult. But there are others—and I put myself in that group—who don't doubt there's been contact. I don't think that the transport problems are such that they prevented people from moving between continents. What we doubt is the transformative impact of ephemeral contact. These visitors, whoever and wherever

they were, simply didn't transform the societies they found here."

For the so-called dirt archaeologists, transformative influence is above all material, technological, and measurable. It is manifest, for example, in the distinctively fluted spearpoints left like so many business cards by the Clovis-culture immigrants who crossed the Bering land bridge. If successive waves of other visitors did reach the shores of North or South America, where is their material bequest? Where, for instance, are the wheels and keystone arches that flourished in the Old World for many centuries before Columbus but don't appear in the material record of the New World until after 1492?

The diffusionists' rebuttal is, well, diffuse; but it is thought-provoking just the same. On the one hand, the feisty George Carter, an emeritus professor of geography at Texas A&M University, points to the case of Hernando de Soto, who traipsed through the New World from 1539 to 1542. De Soto and his army came in contact with hundreds if not thousands of Native Americans, traded goods, and introduced non-native livestock—and yet, as Carter points out in the book *Across Before Columbus? Evidence for Transoceanic Contact With the Americas Prior to 1492* (1998), "of that passage virtually no trace can be found."

On the other hand, Stephen Jett, a geographer at the University of California at Davis, says that such Old World inventions as the arch and the wheel are not the sine qua non of cultural exchange, as the establishment would have us believe. In an essay in *Man Across the Sea: Problems of Pre-Columbian Contacts* (1971), Jett repeated the caution of Douglas Fraser, an art historian at Columbia University:

> If we judge West African culture by the absence of wheeled vehicles, the plow, the true arch, draft animals and milking, then the well-documented Islamic penetration of the western Sudan [which in earlier times reached from present-day Senegal to Chad] cannot have taken place. For these traits are all well known in Moslem North Africa.... the ancient Greeks also rejected [the true arch] though it

was known earlier in Sumer, Babylon, and Egypt.

For David Kelley, the wheel-and-arch conundrum is doubly perplexing. In his own contribution to *Man Across the Sea* he wondered "why neither the true arch nor the wheel [was] to be found in Egypt for more than a thousand years after Mesopotamian influences transformed Egypt from a Neolithic farming stage to a semiurban, literate society, although [those inventions] already had a long history in Mesopotamia." Moreover, the ancient riddle has significant modern ramifications. "In the light of such evidence," Kelley continued, "it is surprising to find scholars . . . arguing that the absence of the true arch and the wheel in the New World proved that there had been no contacts between New World and Old World."

In short, the diffusionists and their sympathizers contend, it is the *nature* of acceptable evidence that perpetuates the debate. "The problem," Kelley says, "is in the fact that there are influences, but they don't show up in 'dirt archaeology.' Basically, they show up in ideological materials: mythology, astronomy, calendrics. These are precisely the areas which are hardest to deal with archaeologically. And so they don't get much attention from traditional archaeologists."

Deloria echoes Kelley's concern. "There's the Stephen Jay Gould attitude out there," he says, "that believes science can do whatever it wants unless it comforts religion—because religion is considered a mere superstition. But if you look at it, most things that they're calling religious are not really religious. They're oral traditions; they're ancient memory." If mainstream archaeologists and anthropologists are unwilling or unable to consider evidence of this type, Deloria suggests, perhaps they're not the right ones for the job.

That is also the opinion of Jon Polansky, an editor of the *Epigraphic Society Occasional Papers,* a journal co-founded by Barry Fell and devoted to the study of transoceanic contact. Polansky concedes that orthodox archaeolo-

gists are certainly competent to perform excavations and to document the physical details of any artifacts they may find. He believes, however, that they are neither suitably trained nor philosophically inclined to test new hypotheses when it comes to nontraditional forms of evidence. "They're just not concerned with methods they don't use," he argues. As a result, he says, mainstream archaeology is missing—perhaps even obscuring—many opportunities for discovering transoceanic contact by limiting the academic specialties deemed fit to evaluate the evidence.

Polansky is an associate professor of medicine at the University of California at San Francisco Medical Center and the director of the laboratory that first isolated and cloned the gene responsible for glaucoma; he was a student of Barry Fell's at Harvard in the 1960s. His is an energetic, insistent, and even impatient personality; just the same, he frequently bites his lip, as if to avoid disclosing some secret or other that one has yet to earn. His quandary is this: he has an editorial responsibility to propagate the latest research about transoceanic contacts, and yet he harbors, understandably enough, a basic mistrust about how new findings will be received. Traditional academics are, he believes, less interested in new ideas than in safeguarding positions of influence and authority. In a 1998 essay in the *Journal of the West,* Polansky and his co-authors, Donal Buchanan and Norman Totten, wrote,

> Part of the scientific approach . . . is the pioneering will to follow internally consistent data to [their] logical conclusions without concern for whether or not the conclusions overturn existing idea structures. We do not favor the bias often imposed on new information, requiring "extraordinary proof" for "extraordinary ideas." Instead, we propose a level playing field in which data . . . are explored in an honest . . . application of scientific method . . . without bias as to whether [hypotheses] agree with prevailing academic thought.

The extraordinary ideas Polansky proposes include the possibility not only

of ancient contact between the hemispheres across both great oceans but also of reciprocal transfers of information and lore. It's one thing to discover evidence of travelers to the Western Hemisphere, he says. But what influences and traditions might the Native Americans have diffused among these visitors in return?

Diffusionists like Polansky and Deloria are convinced that this kind of information will be revealed only when qualified experts outside archaeology and anthropology undertake to examine the available evidence. Linguists, classicists, Asianists, specialists in comparative religion, epigraphers, archaeo-astronomers, navigation historians, ethno-botanists, and ethno-geneticists—these are the sorts of scholars who, Polansky believes, must take responsibility for evaluating the evidence that traditional academics find either meaningless or troubling.

There is no denying, of course, that the official history of the Western Hemisphere did not begin until Europeans wrote their first documents about the New World, at the close of the fifteenth century. Before then was an undoubtedly rich but largely unremembered period of habitation by the descendants of unlettered Ice Age mammoth-stalkers—people who themselves had no written language. The Western Hemisphere is unique in this respect. What we know of the hundreds of generations who lived here before Columbus staked his claim is frozen in the archaeological record. It is for the most part a mute record, consisting overwhelmingly of pottery shards, pointed flints, traces of dwellings, monuments, rock drawings—in short, of virtually every product of human imagination except alphabetic writing. How fitting, then, that the diffusionists' curious lettered stones and tablets would break the silence, inciting noisy protest from the curators of America's past even as they suggest that ancient Americans may have enjoyed the occasional conversation with visitors from afar.

Unit 2

Key Points to Consider

❖ Which comes first—the town or farming?

❖ Which was better—town life or nomad life?

❖ Which comes first—trade or farming?

❖ What is the significance of writing for societies? What is the importance of writing for the study of history?

❖ Is it possible that an isolated society could go through the same stages of development that a society with outside influences would go through, including inventions such as writing, mathematics, wheels, and calendars?

❖ Why would Mexicans be upset at the idea that the Chinese might have given cultural ideas to the Olmec? Compare this to the Japanese thoughts from Unit 1 in the article, "Japanese Roots."

❖ Can there be urban life without money as a medium of exchange? Explain.

 **Links** www.dushkin.com/online/

These sites are annotated on pages 4 and 5.

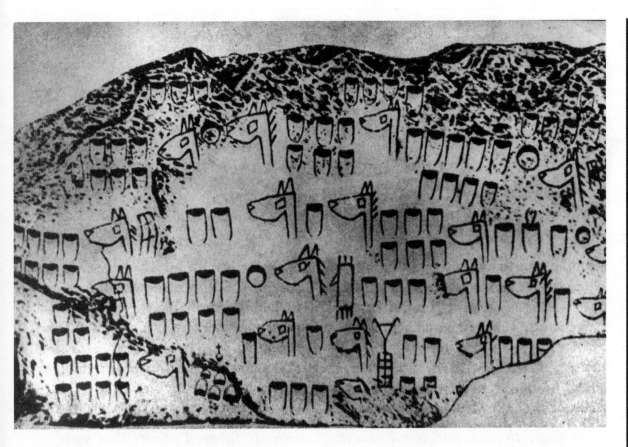

The two great leaps of humankind in technology are the discovery of agriculture and the industrial revolution. The industrial revolution, a topic of the second half of world history, is a phenomenon of the late eighteenth and early nineteenth centuries. The discovery of agriculture, however, came hand-in-hand with the establishment of the earliest cities some 10,000 years ago. Although there is evidence that nomadic peoples planted seeds that they would later harvest, as crops became a common source of food the farmers remained close by to tend the fields; thus did towns and cities evolve. The great grain crops—corn in the Western Hemisphere, wheat in the Middle East, and rice in Asia—apparently developed independently. Farming developed first, however, in the fertile crescent of the Middle East, as John Noble Wilford, a Pulitzer Prize–winning author, explains in his article on agriculture. Wilford also suggests that group dancing may have emerged at this time as a ritual to coordinate farming efforts.

In the next essay, John Noble Wilford asks, "When no one read, who started to write?" The urban Sumarians began to experiment with writing about 5,000 years ago and established the line between history and prehistory. Apparently, literacy was an important tool for governing and dealing with the economy of kingdoms and writing was invented independently in places such as China and Mesoamerica.

The independent origins of writing again brings up the idea of the diffusion of ideas, in this case, the idea of literacy. Is it possible that a visitor from the outside taught the Mesoamericans how to write? Charles Fenyvesi probes this question of cultural and technological transfer in "A Tale of Two Cultures." Were the ancient Olmec of southern Mexico influenced by the Shang Chinese? Or, did the Olmec develop their culture independently? It is an intriguing question-one that can be related to the article in Unit 1, "The Diffusionists Have Landed."

Along with writing came an advance in the sophistication of trade. Simple barter, the direct exchange of one item for another, did not work well in a marketplace of many items of different value. Thus, there was a need for some sort of money, which economists call a medium of exchange. Heather Pringle in "The Cradle of Cash" reveals that silver rings, gold, and ingots of precious metal served the purpose of cash as early as 2500 B.C.E. Agriculture and towns thus pushed humankind along the pathway of civilization.

New Clues Show Where People Made The Great Leap to Agriculture

Scientists are figuring out where and how cereal grains were domesticated during agriculture's birth in the Fertile Crescent about 10,000 years ago. Taming meant some changes for the grains like einkorn wheat, perhaps the first to be domesticated, because harvesting methods favored plants that were less able to reproduce on their own. Plants with seeds that stayed attached to sturdy stalks, even after they ripened, were more likely to be gathered and stored for another year's planting.

By John Noble Wilford

The greatest thing *before* sliced bread, to reverse the cliché, was bread itself. The first cultivation of wild grains, that is, turned hunter-gatherers into farmers, beginning some 12,000 to 10,000 years ago. In the transition, people gained a more abundant and dependable source of food, including their daily bread, and changed the world forever.

Archeologists and historians agree that the rise of agriculture, along with the domestication of animals for food and labor, produced the most important transformation in human culture since the last ice age—perhaps since the control of fire. Farming and herding led to the growth of large, settled human populations and increasing competition for productive lands, touching off organized warfare. Food surpluses freed people to specialize in crafts like textiles and sup-

ported a privileged elite in the first cities, growing numbers of bureaucrats and scribes, soldiers and kings.

Excavations at more than 50 sites over the last half-century have established the Fertile Crescent of the Middle East as the homeland of the first farmers. This arc of land, broadly defined, extends from Israel through Lebanon and Syria, then through the plains and hills of Iraq and southern Turkey and all the way to the head of the Persian Gulf. Among its "founder crops" were wheat, barley, various legumes, grapes, melons, dates, pistachios and almonds. The region also produced the first domesticated sheep, goats, pigs and cattle.

But questions persist: Where in the Fertile Crescent were the first wheat and barley crops produced? What conditions favored this region? Why was the tran-

sition from hunting and foraging to farming so swift, occurring in only a few centuries?

New genetic studies suggest possible answers. They pinpoint the Karacadag Mountains, in southeast Turkey at the upper fringes of the Fertile Crescent, as the site where einkorn wheat was first domesticated from a wild species around 11,000 years ago. Moreover, they reveal that cultivated einkorn plants, as botanists had suspected, are remarkably similar genetically and in appearance to their ancestral wild varieties, which seems to explain the relatively rapid transition to farming indicated by archeological evidence.

A team of European scientists, led by Dr. Manfred Heun of the Agricultural University of Norway in As, reported these findings in the current issue of the journal Science. The researchers ana-

Grains resemble their wild cousins, with a few crucial differences.

lyzed the DNA from 68 lines of cultivated einkorn wheat, Triticum monococcum monococcum, and from 261 wild einkorn lines, T.m. boeoticum, still growing in the Middle East and elsewhere.

In the study, the scientists identified a genetically distinct group of 11 varieties that was also most similar to cultivated einkorn. Because that wild group grows today near the Karacadag Mountains, in the vicinity of the modern city of Diyarbakir, and presumably was there in antiquity, the scientists concluded, this is "very probably the site of einkorn domestication."

Knowing the site for the domestication of such a primary crop, the scientists said, did not necessarily imply that the people living there at the time were the first farmers. "Neverthless," they wrote, "it has been hypothesized that one single human group may have domesticated all primary crops of the region."

Archeologists said that radiocarbon dating was not yet precise enough to establish whether einkorn or emmer wheat or barley was the first cereal to be domesticated. All three domestications occurred in the Fertile Crescent, probably within decades or a few centuries of each other. It was a hybrid of emmer and another species from the Caspian Sea area that produced the first bread wheat.

Dr. Bruce D. Smith, an archeobiologist at the Smithsonian Institution and author of "The Emergence of Agriculture," published two years ago by the Scientific American Library, praised the research as another notable example of new technologies' being applied in trying to solve some of archeology's most challenging problems. The einkorn findings, he said, made sense because they "fit pretty well with archeological evidence."

Not far from the volcanic Karacadag Mountains and also to the south, across the border in northern Syria, archeolo-gists have exposed the ruins of prefarming settlements and early agricultural villages that appear to have existed only a few centuries apart in time. Sifting the soil turned up seeds of both wild and cultivated einkorn wheat. The ruins of Abu Hureyra, an especially revealing Syrian site on the upper Euphrates River, contained firm evidence of einkorn farming more than 10,000 years ago.

The European research team also pointed to this archeological evidence as supporting its conclusion that the domestication of einkorn wheat began in the Karacadag area.

But some archeologists may not readily accept the new findings. They have their own favorite areas where they think the first steps in plant domestication took place, and these happen to be to the west and south of the Turkish mountains. Mud-brick ruins at the edge of an oasis in the Jordan River valley near Jericho have often been cited as from the world's first known farming village, occupied by an ancient people that archeologists call the Natufians.

Dr. Frank Hole, a Yale University archeologist who specializes in early agriculture, thinks the major center for early plant domestication was more likely in the corridor running north from the Dead Sea to Damascus. Its Mediterranean-type climate, dry summers and mild but wet winters, which prevailed at the time of agricultural origins, would have favored the growth of annual plants like barley and both einkorn and emmer wheat. The Jericho site produced early evidence of barley cultivation.

Commenting on the new research, Dr. Hole said in an interview that "the location of domestication can't be determined by the present distribution of the wild plants." For example, einkorn does not grow wild today around Abu Hureyra, though excavations show that it must have more than 10,000 years ago. So it cannot be assumed, he said, that wild einkorn was growing in southeast Turkey at the time of domestication.

But Dr. Jared Diamond, a specialist in biogeography at the University of California at Los Angeles, disagreed, noting that the Karacadag Mountains supported "stands of wild einkorn so dense and extensive that they were being harvested by hunter-gatherers even before einkorn's domestication."

An experiment more than 25 years ago by Dr. Jack Harlan, an agronomist at the University of Illinois, demonstrated the likely importance of wild einkorn in the diets of post-ice age hunter-gatherers in the region and what might have encouraged them to domesticate it. Harvesting wild einkorn by hand in southeastern Turkey, Dr. Harlan showed that in only three weeks, a small family group could have gathered enough grain to sustain them for a full year.

In reaping the wild grain over a few decades, or at most three centuries, the hunter-gatherers unwittingly caused small but consequential changes in the plants. The new DNA analysis showed that an alteration of only a couple of genes could have transformed the wild einkorn into a cultivated crop.

In the wild, brittle stems hold the einkorn grains to the plant, making it easier for them to scatter naturally and reseed the fields. But natural mutations would have produced some semi-tough stalks that held the seeds more firmly in place. People cutting the plants with sharp stone sickles would have selected the stalks more laden with grain, and these would be stored as next year's seed stock. Birds would be more apt to consume the dispersed grain from brittle stalks, leaving less of it to germinate.

As Dr. Diamond pointed out, repeated cycles of harvesting and reseeding wild einkorn stands "would have selected automatically for those mutations." Those changes included plumper, more nutritious grains in denser clusters that cling to the stem until ripe, instead of scattering before they can be harvested.

"These few, simple changes during einkorn's domestication," Dr. Diamond wrote in a separate article in Science, "contrast sharply with the drastic biological reorganization required for the domestication of Native Americans' leading cereal, maize, from its wild ancestor."

This difference alone, he said, "helps explain why densely populated agricultural societies arose so much earlier and developed so much more rapidly in the Crescent than in the New World."

It was several thousand more years before maize, or corn, would become a cultivated crop in central Mexico. There were no native wild wheats and barley in the Americas that might have led to an earlier introduction of agriculture there. Such circumstances based on geographic location have often been critical in the timing and pace of cultural and economic development for diverse societies, as Dr. Diamond argued in "Guns, Germs, and Steel: The Fates of Human Societies," published earlier this year by W. W. Norton.

Nothing in the new einkorn research seems to alter current thinking about the timing and climatic circumstances for agriculture's genesis in the Fertile Crescent.

With the end of the ice age 14,000 to 12,000 years ago, retreating glaciers left the world warmer and wetter than before. Greater rainfall in many temperate zones nourished a spread of vegetation, including many grasses like wild wheat and barley. This attracted concentrations of grazing animals. Hunter-gatherers converged on the grasses and animals, in many cases abandoning their nomadic ways and settling down to village life. Such conditions were particularly favorable in the Middle East.

Then followed a brief return of colder, drier weather more than 11,000 years ago and lasting a few centuries. Dr. Ofer Bar-Yosef, an archeologist at Harvard University, thinks the stresses of coping with the Younger Dryas, as the dry spell is called, contributed to the beginning of plant domestication. With the sudden dearth of wild food sources, hunter-gatherers began storing grain for the lean times and learning to cultivate the fields for better yields. In any case, the earliest evidence for agriculture so far comes from the period immediately after the Younger Dryas.

In his book on early agriculture, Dr. Smith of the Smithsonian wrote, "Even in the absence of such an external pressure, gradual growth in their populations and expansion of their villages may have encouraged or necessitated a variety of economic changes, including experimenting with the cultivation of wild grasses."

Whatever the factors behind its origins, Dr. Diamond said, agriculture took a firm hold in the ancient Middle East because of the diversity of plants and animals suitable for domestication. The first farmers, he said in the journal article, quickly assembled "a balanced package of domesticates meeting all of humanity's basic needs: carbohydrate, protein, oil, milk, animal transport and traction, and vegetable and animal fiber for rope and clothing."

Eurasian geography probably favored the rapid spread of agriculture out of the Middle East and throughout much of the two continents. Referring to a thesis developed in his book, Dr. Diamond pointed out that the west-east axis of the Eurasian land mass, as well as of the Fertile Crescent, permitted crops, livestock and people "to expand at the same latitude without having to adapt to new day lengths, climates and diseases."

In contrast, the north-south orientations of the Americas, Africa and the Indian subcontinent probably slowed the diffusion of agricultural innovations. And that, Dr. Diamond contends, could account for the headstart some societies had on others in the march of human history.

In Dawn of Society, Dance Was Center Stage

By JOHN NOBLE WILFORD

No one will ever know when someone first raised arms into the air, pivoted and took a few light steps this way and that—and danced.

The birds and bees, those exhibitionists, were doing it their way long before. Some mammals were already courting through an unspoken poetry of motion. Humans may have been newcomers, but dancing as self-expression probably developed early in their cultural evolution, perhaps as early as speech and language and almost certainly by the time people were painting on cave walls, making clay figurines and decorating their bodies with ornaments.

Archaeologists are at a loss to know the origins of dancing in prehistory because they lack direct evidence, nothing comparable to the art of Altamira or Lascaux. The best they have been able to do is extrapolate back from the ritual dances practiced by hunter-gatherer societies that have survived into modern times.

An Israeli archaeologist now thinks he has pieced together a significant body of evidence for dancing, if not at its beginning, at least at a decisive and poorly understood transitional stage of human culture.

Examining more than 400 examples of carved stone and painted scenes on pottery from 140 sites in the Balkans and the Middle East, Dr. Yosef Garfinkel of Hebrew University in Jerusalem has established what he says is an illustrated record of dancing from 9,000 to 5,000 years ago. This record, apparently the earliest of its kind, coincides with the

place and time hunters of wild game and gatherers of wild plant food first settled into villages and became pastoralists and farmers.

It may take imagination to see in these depictions the choreographic ancestry of Astaire and Rogers or the Bolshoi. Some show only stick figures with triangular heads, and some headless, in highly schematic scenes that appear to be dances. Others include figures in a dynamic posture, usually with bent arms and legs. Several scenes depict people in a line or completely circling an illustrated vessel, their hands linked. There is some resemblance here to current folk dancing or even a Broadway chorus line.

The prevalence of what appear to be dancing scenes in the earliest art from the ancient Middle East, Dr. Garfinkel said in a recent interview, suggests the importance of the dance in these preliterate agricultural communities.

"Dancing was a means of social communication in prestate societies," he said. "It was part of the ritual for coordinating a community's activities. 'Hey, it's time to plant the wheat or harvest it.' So everyone would gather and dance, and the next day they would go to work."

Then with the emergence of states ruled by kings and bureaucracies and the invention of writing, all occurring in the region some 5,000 years ago, dancing scenes all but disappeared from pottery. People still presumably danced, Dr. Garfinkel said, but "the dancing motif had lost its importance in society."

In the just-completed manuscript of a book on dance in the beginning of farming, Dr. Garfinkel writes: "In periods before schools and writing, community rituals, symbolized by dance, were the basic mechanisms for conveying education and knowledge to the adult members of the community and from one generation to the next.

The lengthy duration of dance depiction as a dominant artistic motif, together with its dispersion across broad geographical expanses from west Pakistan to the Danube basin testify to the efficiency of the dancing motif as one of the most powerful symbols in the evolution of human societies.

Although Dr. Garfinkel has been collecting and evaluating this evidence for eight years, his interpretation is new to many art historians and archaeologists. An early version of the idea was summarized in 1998 in an article in The Cambridge Archaeological Journal of England. Several scholars said the suggested link between dance and social communication in preliterate societies was intriguing and reasonable, though not proved.

"I think Garfinkel is on the right track," said Dr. Kent V. Flannery, an archaeologist at the University of Michigan who specializes in early agriculture.

Dr. Andrew M. T. Moore, an archaeologist and dean of liberal arts at the Rochester Institute of Technology, said he found the hypothesis interesting and worth further study. But he cautioned against any hasty acceptance of it.

"I would be skeptical of any attempt to go beyond the depictions to actually reconstruct social behavior," said Dr. Moore, who has excavated an early agricultural community in Syria. "The scenes are extremely difficult to interpret. In the absence of a written record, we must be cautious in saying what people were doing and thinking."

Both agreed that dance predated this pottery art by a great stretch of time, and that it probably had long had a social function beyond mere entertainment.

Dr. Flannery made a case for why rituals, including dancing, might have been especially important to what he called intermediate societies. (No one has seriously proposed that the availability of beer, discovered in the same period by clever barley farmers, had set off millennial bacchanals.)

For many thousands of years before they settled down, the thinking goes, people were nomadic hunter-gatherers who lived in small groups more like extended families. Once some of them in the Middle East settled into year-round camps, more than 10,000 years ago, they took up farming and congregated in village communities of as many as 200 people representing several families.

Seeking more inclusive bonds, Dr. Flannery suggested, they probably "invented a fictional common ancestor as a way to integrate the community." This practice, he noted, had been observed in the Pueblo villages of the American Southwest. The villagers believed they were all descended from a common supernatural ancestor like the Great Coyote or the Great Eagle, and so all had an obligation to one another. Their rituals and dances, often elaborate, reinforced these beliefs.

"Without strong leadership," he said, "ritual systems take on a huge burden of integrating people."

Dr. Garfinkel contends that ritual dancing may have been essential in getting the work done in early agricultural communities. Hunters and gatherers could go out and almost immediately have results they could eat. Agriculture, by contrast, created a "delayed reward economy."

"Before the harvest, there are various tasks to accomplish: land clearance, seeding and tending the fields," Dr. Garfinkel pointed out. "Thus, the beginnings of agriculture involved a cognitive revolution concerning the relationships between work investment and its final product."

The new economy had to be understood and accepted. Festivals and ceremonies, including ritual dancing, may then have invoked supernatural powers to ensure a successful harvest if everyone pulled together. Nearly all the depictions, Dr. Garfinkel said, showed dancers in groups.

Dr. Flannery said that Dr. Garfinkel was probably correct in relating the reduction in the dance motif on pottery to the rise of civilizations under kings, which occurred around 3000 B.C. with the Sumerians in Mesopotamia, a land that is now southern Iraq, and not long afterward in Egypt.

"Real authority, with people on top issuing orders that had to be obeyed, had replaced the ritual dancing in integrating the community," he said.

In time, art reflected the new official reality, portraying the king and his warriors and workers instead of dancers. Dr. Flannery offered a modern analogy. In the Soviet Union, May Day was celebrated with an official parade of arms on Red Square, a scene amply recorded on film, while faraway villages still held their peasant dances, which were not likely to be depicted in art.

In his research, Dr. Garfinkel found the earliest examples of the dancing motif in art from two 9,000-year-old sites in the Middle East.

Engraved on a stone basin, excavated at Nevali Cori in southeastern Turkey, were three human figures in a line, faces forward, legs wide and arms bent upward. The two outer figures are larger than the central one, suggesting a scene of two dancing men flanking a woman. Only in a few cases, mainly in art from early Egypt, Dr. Garfinkel said, are both sexes seen dancing together.

At Dhuweila, a small camp site in Jordan, rock carvings depict a row of four human figures holding hands. They have elongated necks and heads that appear to be nonhuman. Dr. Garfinkel thinks they are wearing masks, evidence for which has been found at other sites.

In later millenniums, most of the dance art has been found painted on pottery, usually small vessels for eating and drinking. As Dr. Garfinkel observed, the scenes emphasize dancing as a community activity. The focus is on a line or circle of identical figures moving in the same direction, indicating the importance of the group over the individual.

"Dance is thus an activity through which society instills collective discipline in its members," he concluded.

The dances also appear to take place in the open; in the few examples where some architectural elements are visible, the dance seems to be outside them. And since most of the dancing figures appear as silhouettes, it is possible the dance is being performed at night. Dr. Garfinkel expressed surprise that no musical instruments are seen in the motifs.

In his book, Dr. Garfinkel acknowledged that not every question concerning early dancing could be answered. "Only a rough general outline can be reconstructed," he wrote.

He also noted that the dancing scenes on pottery were made by local potters to be used by members of the same community. The images must have had immediate and contemporary meaning. Since the images reflected inside knowledge, he said, "it is justifiable to consider the dancing scenes as authentic documentation of dance activity."

Dr. Moore, the Rochester archaeologist, said it might take time to judge the new interpretation. Although he found "the proposition an intriguing one," he said, scholars will probably debate its pros and cons for several years until someone comes up with more research that supports or sweeps away the hypothesis.

Such is the usual practice in the scholarship of prehistory, the attempt to reconstruct a dim past from a few stones and shards, some of which may reveal people dancing in the dark through the seasons of life and toil in early agricultural communities.

When No One Read, Who Started to Write?

Ancient art might have inspired early scribblers, or maybe it was the need to keep track of livestock.

By John Noble Wilford

PHILADELPHIA—The Sumerians had a story to explain their invention of writing more than 5,000 years ago. It seems a messenger of the king of Uruk arrived at the court of a distant ruler so exhausted from the journey that he was unable to deliver the oral message. So the king, being clever, came up with a solution. He patted some clay and set down the words of his next messages on a tablet.

A Sumerian epic celebrates the achievement:

Before that time writing on clay had not yet existed,
But now, as the sun rose, so it was!
The king of Kullaba [Uruk] had set words on a tablet, so it was!

A charming just-so, or so-it-was, story, its retelling at a recent symposium on the origins or writing, held here at the University of Pennsylvania, both amused and frustrated scholars. It reminded them that they could expect little help—only a myth—from the Sumerians themselves, presumably the first writing people, in understanding how and why the invention responsible for the great divide in human culture between prehistory and history had come about.

The archeologists, historians and other scholars at the meeting smiled at the absurdity of a king's writing a letter that its recipient could not read. They also doubted that the earliest writing was a direct rendering of speech. Writing more than likely began as a separate and distinct symbolic system of communication, like painting, sculpture and oral storytelling, and only later merged with spoken language.

Yet in the story, the Sumerians, who lived in Mesopotamia, the lower valley of the Tigris and Euphrates Rivers in what is now southern Iraq, seemed to understand writing's transforming function. As Dr. Holly Pittman, director of the university's Center for Ancient Studies and organizer of the symposium, observed, writing "arose out of the need to store information and transmit information outside of human memory and over time and over space."

In exchanging interpretations and new information, the scholars acknowledged that they still had no fully satisfying answers to the most important questions of exactly how and why writing was developed. Many of them favored a broad explanation of writing's origins in the visual arts, pictograms of things being transformed into increasingly abstract symbols for things, names and eventually words in speech. Their views clashed with a widely held theory among archeologists that writing grew out of the pieces of clay in assorted sizes and shapes that Sumerian accountants had used as tokens to keep track of livestock and stores of grain.

The scholars at the meeting also conceded that they had no definitive answer to the question of whether writing was invented only once and spread elsewhere or arose independently several times in several places, like Egypt, the Indus Valley, China and among the Olmecs and Maya of Mexico and Central America.

But they criticized recent findings suggesting that writing might have developed earlier in Egypt than in Mesopotamia.

In December, Dr. Günter Dreyer, director of the German Archeological Institute in Egypt, announced new radiocarbon dates for tombs at Abydos, on the Nile about 250 miles south of Cairo. The dates indicated that some hieroglyphic inscriptions on pots, bone and ivory in the tombs were made at least as early as 3200 B.C., possibly 3400. It was now an "open question," Dr. Dreyer said, whether writing appeared first in Egypt or Mesopotamia.

At the symposium, Dr. John Baines, an Oxford University Egyptologist who had just visited Dr. Dreyer, expressed skepticism in polite terms. "I'm suspicious of the dates," he said in an interview. "I think he's being very bold in his readings of these things."

The preponderance of archeological evidence has shown that the urbanizing Sumerians were the first to develop writing, in 3200 or 3300 B.C. These are the dates for many clay tablets with a proto-cuneiform script found at the site of the ancient city of Uruk. The tablets bore pictorial symbols for the names of people, places and things for governing and commerce. The Sumerian script gradually evolved from the pictorial to the abstract, but it was probably at least five centuries before the writing came to represent recorded spoken language.

Egyptian hieroglyphics are so different from Sumerian cuneiform, Dr. Baines said, that they were probably in-

From *New York Times*, April 6, 1999, pp. D1, D4. © 1999 by The New York Times Company. Reprinted by permission.

Early Writing: Cultures Make Their First Marks

Representing spoken languages in writing grew out of the transformation of pictures and random marks into images with consistent meaning. Among the earliest cultures to do this were:

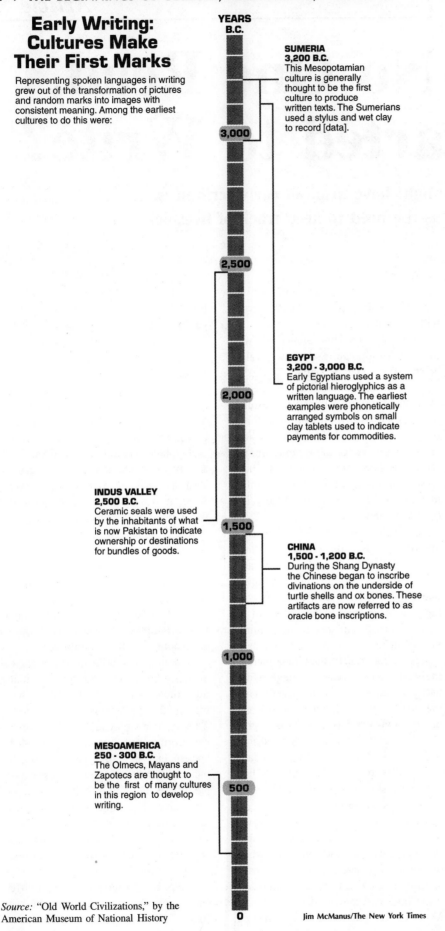

YEARS B.C.

SUMERIA 3,200 B.C.
This Mesopotamian culture is generally thought to be the first culture to produce written texts. The Sumerians used a stylus and wet clay to record [data].

3,000

2,500

EGYPT 3,200 - 3,000 B.C.
Early Egyptians used a system of pictorial hieroglyphics as a written language. The earliest examples were phonetically arranged symbols on small clay tablets used to indicate payments for commodities.

2,000

INDUS VALLEY 2,500 B.C.
Ceramic seals were used by the inhabitants of what is now Pakistan to indicate ownership or destinations for bundles of goods.

1,500

CHINA 1,500 - 1,200 B.C.
During the Shang Dynasty the Chinese began to inscribe divinations on the underside of turtle shells and ox bones. These artifacts are now referred to as oracle bone inscriptions.

1,000

MESOAMERICA 250 - 300 B.C.
The Olmecs, Mayans and Zapotecs are thought to be the first of many cultures in this region to develop writing.

500

0

Source: "Old World Civilizations," by the American Museum of National History

Jim McManus/The New York Times

vented independently not long after Sumerian writing. If anything, the Egyptians may have gotten the idea of writing from the Sumerians, with whom they had contacts in Syria, but nothing more.

In any event, the writing idea became more widespread at the beginning of the third millennium B.C. The Elamites of southern Iran developed a proto-writing system then, perhaps influenced by the proto-cuneiform of their Sumerian neighbors, and before the millennium was out, writing appeared in the Indus River Valley of what is now Pakistan and western India, then in Syria and Crete and parts of Turkey. Writing in China dates back to the Shang period toward the end of the second millennium B.C., and it dates to the first millennium B.C. in Mesoamerica.

Archeologists have thought that the undeciphered Indus script, which seemed to appear first around 2500 B.C., may have been inspired in part from trade contacts with Mesopotamia. But new excavations in the ruins of the ancient city of Harappa suggest an earlier and presumably independent origin of Indus writing.

In a report from the field, distributed on the Internet, Dr. Jonathan Mark Kenoyer of the University of Wisconsin and Dr. Richard H. Meadow of Harvard University showed pictures of marks incised on potshards that they interpreted as evidence for the use of writing signs by Indus people as early as 3300 B.C. If these are indeed proto-writing examples, the discovery indicates an independent origin of Indus writing contemporary with the Sumerian and Egyptian inventions.

Dr. Meadow, using E-mail, the electronic age's version of the king of Uruk's clay tablet, confirmed that the inscribed marks were "similar in some respects to those later used in the Indus script." The current excavations, he added, were uncovering "very significant findings at Harappa with respect to the Indus script."

At the symposium, though, Dr. Gregory L. Possehl, a Pennsylvania archeologist who specializes in the Indus civilization and had examined the pictures, cautioned against jumping to such conclusions. One had to be careful, he said, not to confuse potter's marks, graffiti and fingernail marks with symbols of nascent writing.

Of the earliest writing systems, scholars said, only the Sumerian, Chinese and Mesoamerican ones seemed clearly to be independent inventions. Reviewing the relationship between early Chinese bronze art, "oracle bones" and writing, Dr. Louisa Huber, a researcher at Harvard's Fairbanks Center for East Asian Research, concluded "Chinese writing looks to be pristine."

But few pronouncements about early writing go undisputed. Dr. Victor Mair, a professor of Chinese language at Penn, offered evidence indicating, he said, that "the Chinese writing system may well have received vital inputs from West Asian and European systems of writing and proto-writing."

Dr. Mair cited an intriguing correspondence between the Chinese script and 22 Phoenician letters and also Western-like symbols on pottery and the bodies of mummies found in the western desert of China. The recent discoveries of the mummies, wearing garments of Western weaves and having Caucasoid facial features, have prompted theories of foreign influences on Chinese culture in the first and second millennia B.C. It had already been established that the chariot and bronze metallurgy reached China from the West.

Though no one seemed ready to endorse his thesis, Dr. Mair said, "We simply do not know for certain whether the Chinese script was or was not independently created."

Dr. Peter Damerow, a specialist in Sumerian cuneiform at the Max Planck Institute for the History of Science in Berlin, said, "Whatever the mutual influences of writing systems of different cultures may be, their great variety shows, at least, that the development of writing, once it is initiated, attains a considerable degree of independence and flexibility to adapt a coding system to specific characteristics of the language to be represented."

Not that he accepted the conventional view that writing necessarily started as some kind of representation of words by pictures. New studies of Sumerian proto-cuneiform, he said, challenge this interpretation. The structures of this earliest writing, for example, did not match the syntax of a language. Proto-cuneiform seemed severely restricted, com-

Ancient writing is a field hot with controversy, and few scholarly conclusions go unchallenged.

pared with spoken language, dealing mainly in lists and categories, not in sentences and narrative.

This presumably reflects writing's origins and first applications in economic administration in a growing, increasingly complex society, scholars said. Most of the Uruk tablets were documents about property, inventory and, even then, taxes. The only texts that do not concern administrative activities, Dr. Damerow said, were cuneiform lexicons that were apparently written as school exercises by scribes in training.

For at least two decades, in fact, Dr. Denise Schmandt-Besserat, a University of Texas archeologist, has argued that the first writing grew directly out of a counting system practiced by Sumerian accountants. They used molded clay "tokens," each one specifically shaped to represent a jar of oil, a large or small container of grain, or a particular kind of livestock. When the tokens were placed inside hollow clay spheres, the number and type of tokens inside were recorded on the ball with impressions resembling the tokens. Finally, simplifying matters, the token impressions were replaced with inscribed signs, and writing was invented.

Though Dr. Schmandt-Besserat has won wide support, some linguists question her thesis and other scholars, like Dr. Pittman of Penn, think it too narrow an interpretation. They emphasized that pictorial representation and writing evolved together, part of the same cultural context that fostered experimentation in communication through symbols.

"There's no question that the token system is a forerunner of writing, and really important," Dr. Pittman said in an interview. "But I have an argument with her evidence for a link between tokens and signs, and she doesn't open up the process to include picture-making and all other kinds of information-storage practices that are as important as the tokens."

Dr. Schmandt-Besserat, who did not attend the symposium, vigorously defended herself in a telephone interview. "My colleagues say the signs on seals were a beginning of writing, but show me a single sign on a seal that becomes a sign in writing," she said. "They say that designs on pottery were a beginning of writing, but show me a single sign of writing you can trace back to a pot—it doesn't exist."

In its first 500 years, she asserted, cuneiform writing was used almost solely for recording economic information. "The first information that writing gives you is only the same information the tokens were dealing with," she said. "When you start putting more on the tablets, products plus the name of who has delivered and received them, that is where art would enter the picture. Then writing is out of the box, in all directions."

Dr. Damerow agreed that cuneiform writing appeared to have developed in two stages, first as a new but limited means of recording economic information, later as a broader encoding of spoken language for stories, arguments, descriptions or messages from one ruler to another.

Even so, it was a long way from the origin of writing to truly literate societies. At the symposium, scholars noted that the early rulers could not write or read; they relied on scribes for their messages, record keeping and storytelling. In Egypt, most early hieroglyphics were inscribed in places beyond the public eye, high on monuments or deep in tombs.

In this case, said Dr. Pascal Vernus of the University of Paris, early writing was less administrative than sacred and ideological, "a way of creating and describing the world as a dominating elite wants it to be."

Dr. Piotr Michalowski, professor of Near East civilizations at the University of Michigan, said the Uruk proto-cuneiform writing, whatever its antecedents, was "so radically different as to be a complete break with the past, a system different from anything else." It no doubt served to store, preserve and communicate information, but also was a new instrument of power.

"Perhaps it's because I grew up in Stalinist Poland," Dr. Michalowski said, "but I say coercion and control were early writing's first important purpose, a new way to control how people live."

A Tale of Two Cultures

A Beijing scholar links an ancient Chinese dynasty
to the New World's earliest civilization

Charles Fenyvesi

Abroad for the first time in his life, Han Ping Chen, a scholar of ancient Chinese, landed at Dulles International Airport near Washington, D.C., the night of September 18. Next morning, he paced in front of the National Gallery of Art, waiting for the museum to open so he could visit an Olmec exhibit—works from Mesoamerica's spectacular "mother culture" that emerged suddenly 3,200 years ago, with no apparent local antecedents. After a glance at a 10-ton basalt sculpture of a head, Chen faced the object that prompted his trip: an Olmec sculpture found in La Venta, 10 miles south of the southernmost cove of the Gulf of Mexico.

What the Chinese scholar saw was 15 male figures made of serpentine or jade, each about 6 inches tall. Facing them were a taller sandstone figure and six upright, polished jade blades called celts. The celts bore incised markings, some of them faded. Proceeding from right to left, Chen scrutinized the markings silently, grimacing when he was unable to make out more than a few squiggles on the second and third celts. But the lower half of the fourth blade made him jump. "I can read this easily," he shouted. "Clearly, these are Chinese characters."

For years, scholars have waged a passionate—and often nasty—debate over whether Asian refugees and adventurers might somehow have made their way to the New World long before Columbus, stimulating brilliant achievements in cosmogony, art, astronomy and architecture in a succession of cultures from the Olmec to the Maya and Aztec. On one side are the "diffusionists," who have compiled a long list of links between Asian and Mesoamerican cultures, including similar rules for the Aztec board game of *patolli* and the Asian pachisi (also known as Parcheesi), a theological focus in ancient China and Mesoamerica on tiger-jaguar and dragonlike creatures, and a custom, common both to China's Shang dynasty and the Olmecs, of putting a jade bead in the mouth of a deceased person. "Nativists," on the other hand, dismiss such theories as ridiculous and argue for the autonomous development of pre-Columbian civilizations. They bristle at the suggestion that the indigenous people did not evolve on their own.

Striking resemblances. For diffusionists, Olmec art offers a tempting arena for speculation. Carbon-dating places the Olmec era between 1,000 and 1,200 B.C., coinciding with the Shang dynasty's fall in China. American archaeologists unearthed the group sculpture in 1955. Looking at the sculpture displayed in the National Gallery, as well as other Olmec pieces, some Mexican and American scholars have been struck by the resemblances to Chinese artifacts. (In fact, archaeologists initially labeled the first Olmec figures found at the turn of the century as Chinese). Migrations from Asia over the land bridge 10,000–15,000 years ago could account for the Chinese features, such as slanted eyes, but not for the stylized mouths and postures particular to sophisticated Chinese art that emerged in recent millenniums.

Yet until Chen made his pilgrimage to the museum this fall, no Shang specialist had ever studied the Olmec. The scholar emerged from the exhibit with a theory: After the Shang army was routed and the emperor killed, he suggested, some loyalists might have sailed down the Yellow River and taken to the ocean. There, perhaps, they drifted with a current which skirts Japan's coast, heads for California, then peters out near Ecuador. Betty Meggers, a senior Smithsonian archaeologist who has linked pottery dug up in Ecuador to shipwrecked Japanese 5,000 years ago, says such an idea is "plausible" because ancient Asian mariners were far more proficient than they were given credit for.

But Chen's identification of the celt markings is likely to sharpen the controversy over origins even further. For example, Mesoamericanist Michael Coe of Yale University labels Chen's search for Chinese characters as "insulting to the indigenous people of Mexico." And some scholars who share Chen's narrow expertise are equally skeptical. There are only about a dozen experts worldwide in the Shang script, which is largely unrecognizable to readers of modern Chinese. Of the Americans, Profs. William Boltz of the University of Washington and Robert Bagley of Princeton recently looked at a drawing of the celts but dismissed as "rubbish" the notion that the characters could be Chinese. Those looking for a link between the two cultures, Bagley said, are Chinese, and "it no doubt gratifies their ethnic pride to

From *U.S. News & World Report*, November 4, 1996, pp. 46–48. © 1996 by U.S. News & World Report. Reprinted by permission.

discover that Mesoamerican civilization springs from China."

Others would like to see the celts before taking sides. David Keightley, University of California–Berkeley professor of history, said some characters on the celts "could, of course, be Shang, though I don't at present see it that way." His Chinese colleagues, he said "may just be onto something," and he noted that "it's important that scholars from China examine this material."

Chen, 47, is uninterested in the Mesoamericanists' war. When Prof. Mike Xu, a professor of Chinese history at the University of Central Oklahoma, traveled to Beijing to ask Chen to examine his index of 146 markings from pre-Columbian objects, Chen refused, saying he had no interest in anything outside China. He relented only after a colleague familiar with Xu's work insisted that Chen, as China's leading authority, take a look. He did and found that all but three of Xu's markings "could have come from China."

Xu was at Chen's side in the National Gallery when the Shang scholar read the text on the Olmec celt in Chinese and translated: "The ruler and his chieftains establish the foundation for a kingdom." Chen located each of the characters on the celt in three well-worn Chinese dictionaries he had with him. Two adjacent characters, usually read as "master and subjects," but Chen decided that in this context they might mean "ruler and his chieftains." The character on the line below he recognized as the symbol for "kingdom" or "country": two peaks for hills, a curving line underneath for river. The next character, Chen said, suggests a bird but means "waterfall," completing the description. The bottom character he read as "foundation" or "establish," implying the act of founding something important. If Chen is right, the celts not only offer the earliest writing in the New World but mark the birth of a Chinese settlement more than 3,000 years ago.

At lunch the next day, Chen said he was awake all night thinking about the sculpture. He talked about how he had studied Chinese script at age 5, tutored by his father, then director of the national archives. But Chen's father did not live to enjoy the honors the son reaped, such as a recent assignment to compile a new dictionary of characters used by the earliest dynasties—the first update since one commissioned by a Han emperor 2,000 years ago.

Color nuances. Chen was so taken with the Olmec sculpture that he ventured beyond scholarly caution. The group sculpture, he said, might memorialize "a historic event," either a blessing sought from ancestors or the act of founding a new kingdom or both. He was mesmerized by the tallest figure in the sculpture—made from red sandstone as porous as a sponge, in contrast to the others, which are highly polished and green-blue in hue. Red suggests higher status, Chen said. Perhaps the figure was the master of the group, a venerated ancestral spirit. The two dark blue figures to the right might represent the top noblemen, more important than the two others, carved out of pale green serpentine.

The Smithsonian's Meggers says that Chen's analysis of the colors "makes sense. But his reading of the text is the clincher. Writing systems are too arbitrary and complex. They cannot be independently reinvented."

Whether Chen's colleagues ultimately hail him or hang him, his theory yields a tale worthy of Joseph Conrad. And like Conrad, he cannot resist offering yet another footnote from the past: More than 5,000 Shang characters have survived, Chen says, even though the soldiers who defeated the Shang forces murdered the scholars and burned or buried any object with writing on it. In a recent excavation in the Shang capital of Anyang, archaeologists have found a buried library of turtle shells covered with characters. And at the entrance lay the skeleton of the librarian, stabbed in the back and clutching some writings to his breast.

The Olmec sculpture was buried under white sand topped with alternate layers of brown and reddish-brown sand. Perhaps it was hidden to save it from the kind of rage that sought to wipe out the Shang and their memory.

The Cradle of Cash

When money arose in the ancient cities of Mesopotamia, it profoundly and permanently changed civilization.

By Heather Pringle

THE SCENE IN THE SMALL, STIFLING room is not hard to imagine: the scribe frowning, shifting in his seat as he tries to concentrate on the words of the woman in front of him. A member of one of the wealthiest families in Sippar, the young priestess has summoned him to her room to record a business matter. When she entered the temple, she explains, her parents gave her a valuable inheritance, a huge piece of silver in the shape of a ring, worth the equivalent of 60 months' wages for an estate worker. She has decided to buy land with this silver. Now she needs someone to take down a few details. Obediently, the scribe smooths a wet clay tablet and gets out his stylus. Finally, his work done, he takes the tablet down to the archive.

For more than 3,700 years, the tablet languished in obscurity, until late-nineteenth-century collectors unearthed it from Sippar's ruins along the Euphrates River in what is now Iraq. Like similar tablets, it hinted at an ancient and mysterious Near Eastern currency, in the form of silver rings, that started circulating two millennia before the world's first coins were struck. By the time that

tablet was inscribed, such rings may have been in use for a thousand years.

When did humans first arrive at the concept of money? What conditions spawned it? And how did it affect the ancient societies that created it? Until recently, researchers thought they had the answers. They believed money was born, as coins, along the coasts of the Mediterranean in the seventh or sixth century B.C., a product of the civilization that later gave the world the Parthenon, Plato, and Aristotle. But few see the matter so simply now. With evidence gleaned from such disparate sources as ancient temple paintings, clay tablets, and buried hoards of uncoined metals, researchers have revealed far more ancient money: silver scraps and bits of gold, massive rings and gleaming ingots.

In the process, they have pushed the origins of cash far beyond the sunny coasts of the Mediterranean, back to the world's oldest cities in Mesopotamia, the fertile plain created by the Tigris and Euphrates rivers. There, they suggest, wealthy citizens were flaunting money at least as early as 2500 B.C. and perhaps a few hundred years before that. "There's just no way to get around it,"

says Marvin Powell, a historian at Northern Illinois University in De Kalb. "Silver in Mesopotamia functions like our money today. It's a means of exchange. People use it for a storage of wealth, and they use it for defining value."

Many scholars believe money began even earlier. "My sense is that as far back as the written records go in Mesopotamia and Egypt, some form of money is there," observes Jonathan Williams, curator of Roman and Iron Age coins at the British Museum in London. "That suggests it was probably there beforehand, but we can't tell because we don't have any written records."

Just why researchers have had such difficulties in uncovering these ancient moneys has much to do with the practice of archeology and the nature of money itself. Archeologists, after all, are the ultimate Dumpster divers: they spend their careers sifting through the trash of the past, ingeniously reconstructing vanished lives from broken pots and dented knives. But like us, ancient Mesopotamians and Phoenicians seldom made the error of tossing out cash, and only rarely did they bury their

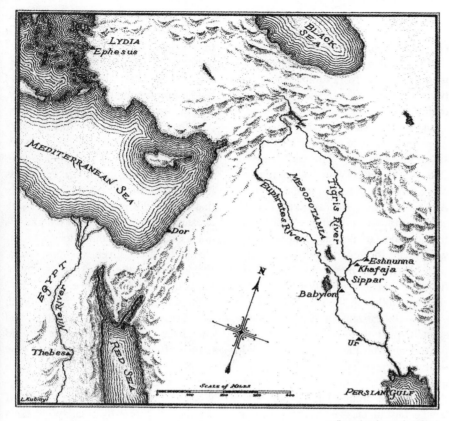

Illustrations by Laszlo Kubinyi

Cash first appeared in Mesopotamia then spread westward to the Mediterranean

most precious liquid assets in the ground. Even when archeologists have found buried cash, though, they've had trouble recognizing it for what it was. Money doesn't always come in the form of dimes and sawbucks, even today. As a means of payment and a way of storing wealth, it assumes many forms, from debit cards and checks to credit cards and mutual funds. The forms it took in the past have been, to say the least, elusive.

From the beginning, money has shaped human society. It greased the wheels of Mesopotamian commerce, spurred the development of mathematics, and helped officials and kings rake in taxes and impose fines. As it evolved in Bronze Age civilizations along the Mediterranean coast, it fostered sea trade, built lucrative cottage industries, and underlay an accumulation of wealth that might have impressed Donald Trump. "If there were never any money, there would never have been prosperity," says Thomas Wyrick, an economist at Southwest Missouri State University in Springfield, who is studying the ori-

gins of money and banking. "Money is making all this stuff happen."

Ancient texts show that almost from its first recorded appearance in the ancient Near East, money preoccupied estate owners and scribes, water carriers and slaves. In Mesopotamia, as early as 3000 B.C., scribes devised pictographs suitable for recording simple lists of concrete objects, such as grain consignments. Five hundred years later, the pictographs had evolved into a more supple system of writing, a partially syllabic script known as cuneiform that was capable of recording the vernacular: first Sumerian, a language unrelated to any living tongue, and later Akkadian, an ancient Semitic language. Scribes could write down everything from kingly edicts to proverbs, epics to hymns, private family letters to merchants' contracts. In these ancient texts, says Miguel Civil, a lexicographer at the Oriental Institute of the University of Chicago, "they talk about wealth and gold and silver all the time."

In all likelihood, says Wyrick, human beings first began contemplating cash

just about the time that Mesopotamians were slathering mortar on mud bricks to build the world's first cities. Until then, people across the Near East had worked primarily on small farms, cultivating barley, dates, and wheat, hunting gazelles and other wild game, and bartering among themselves for the things they could not produce. But around 3500 B.C., work parties started hauling stones across the plains and raising huge flat-topped platforms, known as ziggurats, on which to found their temples. Around their bases, they built street upon twisted street of small mud-brick houses.

To furnish these new temples and to serve temple officials, many farmers became artisans—stonemasons, silversmiths, tanners, weavers, boatbuilders, furniture makers. And within a few centuries, says Wyrick, the cities became much greater than the sum of their parts. Economic life flourished and grew increasingly complex. "Before, you always had people scattered out on the hillsides," says Wyrick, "and whatever they could produce for their families, that was it. Very little trade occurred because you never had a large concentration of people. But now, in these cities, for the first time ever in one spot, you had lots of different goods, hundreds of goods, and lots of different people trading them."

Just how complex life grew in these early metropolises can be glimpsed in the world's oldest accounting records: 8,162 tiny clay tokens excavated from the floors of village houses and city temples across the Near East and studied in detail by Denise Schmandt-Besserat, an archeologist at the University of Texas at Austin. The tokens served first as counters and perhaps later as promissory notes given to temple tax collectors before the first writing appeared.

By classifying the disparate shapes and markings on the tokens into types and comparing these with the earliest known written symbols, Schmandt-Besserat discovered that each token represented a specified quantity of a particular commodity. And she noticed an intriguing difference between village tokens and city tokens. In the small communities dating from before the rise of cities, Mesopotamians regularly em-

Ancient texts show that almost from its first recorded appearance in the ancient Near East, money preoccupied estate owners and scribes, water carriers and slaves.

ployed just five token types, representing different amounts of three main goods: human labor, grain, and livestock like goats and sheep. But in the cities, they began churning out a multitude of new types, regularly employing 16 in all, with dozens of subcategories representing everything from honey, sheep's milk, and trussed ducks to wool, cloth, rope, garments, mats, beds, perfume, and metals. "It's no longer just farm goods," says Schmandt-Besserat. "There are also finished products, manufactured goods, furniture, bread, and textiles."

Faced with this new profusion, says Wyrick, no one would have had an easy time bartering, even for something as simple as a pair of sandals. "If there were a thousand different goods being traded up and down the street, people could set the price in a thousand different ways, because in a barter economy each good is priced in terms of all other goods. So one pair of sandals equals ten dates, equals one quart of wheat, equals two quarts of bitumen, and so on. Which is the best price? It's so complex that people don't know if they are getting a good deal. For the first time in history, we've got a large number of goods. And for the first time, we have so many prices that it overwhelms the human mind. People needed some standard way of stating value."

In Mesopotamia, silver—a prized ornamental material—became that standard. Supplies didn't vary much from year to year, so its value remained constant, which made it an ideal measuring rod for calculating the value of other things. Mesopotamians were quick to see the advantage, recording the prices

of everything from timber to barley in silver by weight in shekels. (One shekel equaled one-third of an ounce, or just a little more than the weight of three pennies.) A slave, for example, cost between 10 and 20 shekels of silver. A month of a freeman's labor was worth 1 shekel. A quart of barley went for three-hundredths of a shekel. Best of all, silver was portable. "You can't carry a shekel of barley on your ass," comments Marvin Powell (referring to the animal). And with a silver standard, kings could attach a price to infractions of the law. In the codes of the city of Eshnunna, which date to around 2000 B.C., a man who bit another man's nose would be fined 60 shekels of silver; one who slapped another in the face paid 10.

How the citizens of Babylon or Ur actually paid their bills, however, depended on who they were. The richest tenth of the population, says Powell, frequently paid in various forms of silver. Some lugged around bags or jars containing bits of the precious metal to be placed one at a time on the pan of a scale until they balanced a small carved stone weight in the other pan. Other members of the upper crust favored a more convenient form of cash: pieces of silver cast in standard weights. These were called *har* in the tablets, translated as "ring" money.

At the Oriental Institute in the early 1970s, Powell studied nearly 100 silver coils—some resembling bedsprings, others slender wire coils—found primarily in the Mesopotamian city of Khafaje. They were not exactly rings, it was true, but they matched other fleeting descriptions of *har*. According to the scribes, ring money ranged from 1 to 60 shekels in weight. Some pieces were cast in special molds. At the Oriental Institute, the nine largest coils all bore a triangular ridge, as if they had been cast and then rolled into spirals while still pliable. The largest coils weighed almost exactly 60 shekels, the smallest from one-twelfth to two and a half shekels. "It's clear that the coils were intended to represent some easily recognizable form of Babylonian stored value," says Powell. "In other words, it's the forerunner of coinage."

The masses in Mesopotamia, however, seldom dealt in such money. It was

simply too precious, much as a gold coin would have been for a Kansas dirt farmer in the middle of the Great Depression. To pay their bills, water carriers, estate workers, fishers, and farmers relied on more modest forms of money: copper, tin, lead, and above all, barley. "It's the cheap commodity money," says Powell. "I think barley functions in ancient Mesopotamia like small change in later systems, like the bronze currencies in the Hellenistic period. And essentially that avoids the problem of your being cheated. You measure barley out and it's not as dangerous a thing to try to exchange as silver, given weighing errors. If you lose a little bit, its not going to make that much difference."

Measurable commodity money such as silver and barley both simplified and complicated daily life. No longer did temple officials have to sweat over how to collect a one-sixth tax increase on a farmer who had paid one ox the previous year. Compound interest on loans was now a breeze to calculate. Shekels of silver, after all, lent themselves perfectly to intricate mathematical manipulation; one historian has suggested that Mesopotamian scribes first arrived at logarithms and exponential values from their calculations of compound interest.

"People were constantly falling into debt," says Powell. "We find reference to this in letters where people are writing to one another about someone in the household who has been seized for securing a debt." To remedy these disastrous financial affairs, King Hammurabi decreed in the eighteenth century B.C. that none of his subjects could be enslaved for more than three years for failing to repay a debt. Other Mesopotamian rulers, alarmed at the financial chaos in the cities, tried legislating moratoriums on all outstanding bills.

While the cities of Mesopotamia were the first to conceive of money, others in the ancient Near East soon took up the torch. As civilization after civilization rose to glory along the coasts of the eastern Mediterranean, from Egypt to Syria, their citizens began abandoning the old ways of pure barter. Adopting local standards of value, often silver by weight, they began buying and selling with their own local versions of com-

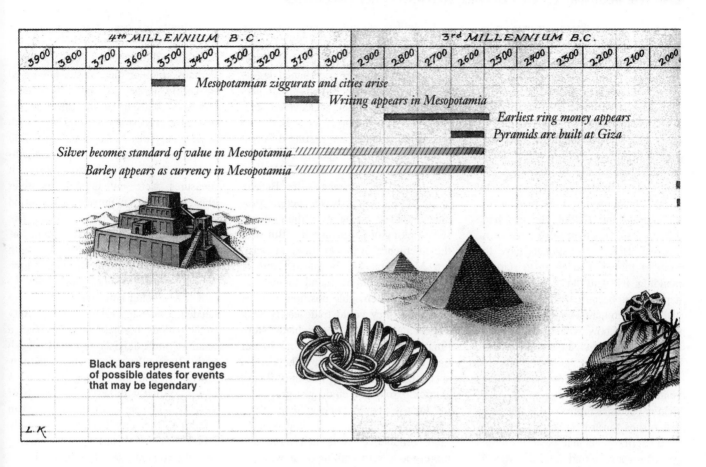

4th MILLENNIUM B.C.										3rd MILLENNIUM B.C.									
3900	3800	3700	3600	3500	3400	3300	3200	3100	3000	2900	2800	2700	2600	2500	2400	2300	2200	2100	2000

Mesopotamian ziggurats and cities arise

Writing appears in Mesopotamia

Earliest ring money appears

Pyramids are built at Giza

Silver becomes standard of value in Mesopotamia

Barley appears as currency in Mesopotamia

Black bars represent ranges of possible dates for events that may be legendary

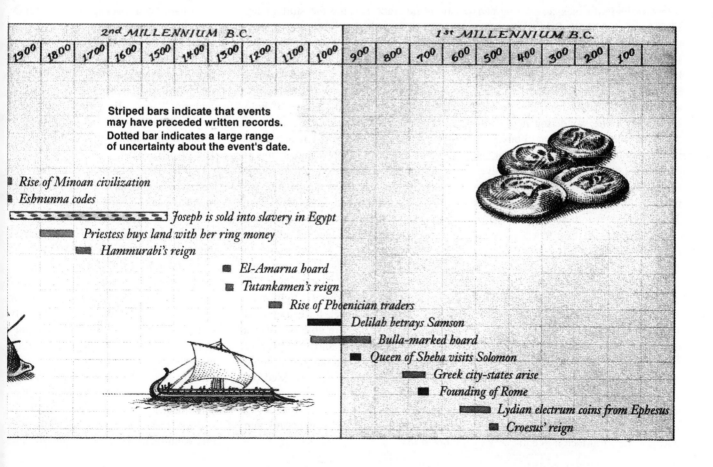

2nd MILLENNIUM B.C.										1st MILLENNIUM B.C.								
1900	1800	1700	1600	1500	1400	1300	1200	1100	1000	900	800	700	600	500	400	300	200	100

**Striped bars indicate that events may have preceded written records.
Dotted bar indicates a large range of uncertainty about the event's date.**

Rise of Minoan civilization

Eshnunna codes

Joseph is sold into slavery in Egypt

Priestess buys land with her ring money

Hammurabi's reign

El-Amarna hoard

Tutankamen's reign

Rise of Phoenician traders

Delilah betrays Samson

Bulla-marked hoard

Queen of Sheba visits Solomon

Greek city-states arise

Founding of Rome

Lydian electrum coins from Ephesus

Croesus' reign

modity moneys: linen, perfume, wine, olive oil, wheat, barley, precious metals—things that could be easily divided into smaller portions and that resisted decay.

And as commerce became smoother in the ancient world, people became increasingly selective about what they accepted as money, says Wyrick. "Of all the different media of exchange, one commodity finally broke out of the pack. It began to get more popular than the others, and I think the merchants probably said to themselves, 'Hey, this is great. Half my customers have this form of money. I'm going to start demanding it.' And the customers were happy, too, because there's more than just one merchant coming around, and they didn't know what to hold on to, because each merchant was different. If everyone asked for barley or everyone asked for silver, that would be very convenient. So as one of these media of exchange becomes more popular, everyone just rushes toward that."

What most ancient Near Easterners rushed toward around 1500 B.C. was silver. In the Old Testament, for example, rulers of the Philistines, a seafaring people who settled on the Palestine coast in the twelfth century B.C., each offer Delilah 1,100 pieces of silver for her treachery in betraying the secret of Samson's immense strength. And in a well-known Egyptian tale from the eleventh century B.C., the wandering hero Wen-Amon journeys to Lebanon to buy lumber to build a barge. As payment, he carries jars and sacks of gold and silver, each weighed in the traditional Egyptian measure, the deben. (One deben equals 3 ounces.) Whether these stories are based on history or myth, they reflect the commercial transactions of their time.

To expedite commerce, Mediterranean metalsmiths also devised ways of conveniently packaging money. Coils and rings seem to have caught on in some parts of Egypt: a mural painted during the fourteenth century B.C. in the royal city of Thebes depicts a man weighing a stack of doughnut-size golden rings. Elsewhere, metalsmiths cast cash in other forms. In the Egyptian city of el-Amarna, built and briefly occupied during the fourteenth century B.C.,

archeologists stumbled upon what they fondly referred to as a crock of gold. Inside, among bits of gold and silver, were several slender rod-shaped ingots of gold and silver. When researchers weighed them, they discovered that some were in multiples or fractions of the Egyptian deben, suggesting different denominations of an ancient currency.

All these developments, says Wyrick, transformed Mediterranean life. Before, in the days of pure barter, people produced a little bit of everything themselves, eking out a subsistence. But with the emergence of money along the eastern Mediterranean, people in remote coastal communities found themselves in a new and enviable position. For the first time, they could trade easily with Phoenician or Syrian merchants stopping at their harbors. They no longer had to be self-sufficient. "They could specialize in producing one thing," says Wyrick. "Someone could just graze cattle. Or they could mine gold or silver. And when you specialize, you become more productive. And then more and more goods start coming your way."

The wealth spun by such specialization and trade became the stuff of legend. It armed the fierce Mycenaean warriors of Greece in bronze cuirasses and chariots and won them victories. It outfitted the tomb of Tutankhamen, sending his soul in grandeur to the next world. And it filled the palace of Solomon with such magnificence that even the Queen of Sheba was left breathless.

But the rings, ingots, and scraps of gold and silver that circulated as money in the eastern Mediterranean were still a far cry from today's money. They lacked a key ingredient of modern cash—a visible guarantee of authenticity. Without such a warranty, many people would never willingly accept them at their face value from a stranger. The lumps of precious metal might be a shade short of a shekel, for example. Or they might not be pure gold or silver at all, but some cheaper alloy. Confidence, suggests Miriam Balmuth, an archeologist at Tufts University in Medford, Massachusetts, could be won only if someone reputable certified that a coin was both the promised weight and composition.

Balmuth has been trying to trace the origins of this certification. In the ancient Near East, she notes, authority figures—perhaps kings or merchants—attempted to certify money by permitting their names or seals to be inscribed on the official carved stone weights used with scales. That way Mesopotamians would know that at least the weights themselves were the genuine article. But such measures were not enough to deter cheats. Indeed, so prevalent was fraud in the ancient world that no fewer than eight passages in the Old Testament forbid the faithful from tampering with scales or substituting heavier stone weights when measuring out money.

Clearly, better antifraud devices were needed. Under the ruins of the old city of Dor along northern Israel's coast, a team of archeologists found one such early attempt. Ephraim Stern of Hebrew University and his colleagues found a clay jug filled with nearly 22 pounds of silver, mainly pieces of scrap, buried in a section of the city dating from roughly 3,000 years ago. But more fascinating than the contents, says Balmuth, who recently studied this hoard, was the way they had been packaged. The scraps were divided into separate piles. Someone had wrapped each pile in fabric and then attached a bulla, a clay tab imprinted with an official seal. "I have since read that these bullae lasted for centuries," says Balmuth, "and were used to mark jars—or in this case things wrapped in fabric—that were sealed. That was a way of signing something."

All that remained was to impress the design of a seal directly on small rounded pieces of metal—which is precisely what happened by around 600 B.C. in an obscure Turkish kingdom by the sea. There traders and perfume makers known as the Lydians struck the world's first coins. They used electrum, a natural alloy of gold and silver panned from local riverbeds. (Coincidentally, Chinese kings minted their first money at roughly the same time: tiny bronze pieces shaped like knives and spades, bearing inscriptions revealing places of origin or weight. Circular coins in China came later.)

First unearthed by archeologists early this century in the ruins of the Temple of Artemis in Ephesus, one of the Seven Wonders of the ancient world, the Lydian coins bore the essential hallmarks

---

Such wealth did the newly invented coins bring one Lydian king, Croesus, that his name became a byword for prosperity.

---

of modern coinage. Made of small, precisely measured pieces of precious metal, they were stamped with the figures of lions and other mighty beasts—the seal designs, it seems, of prominent Lydians. And such wealth did they bring one Lydian king, Croesus, that his name became a byword for prosperity.

Struck in denominations as small as .006 ounce of electrum—one-fifteenth the weight of a penny—Lydia's coinage could be used by people in various walks of life. The idea soon caught on in the neighboring Greek city-states. Within a few decades, rulers across Greece began churning out beautiful coins of varied denominations in unalloyed gold and silver, stamped with the faces of their gods and goddesses.

These new Greek coins became fundamental building blocks for European civilization. With such small change jingling in their purses, Greek merchants plied the western Mediterranean, buying all that was rare and beautiful from coastal dwellers, leaving behind Greek colonies from Sicily to Spain and spreading their ideas of art, government, politics, and philosophy. By the fourth century B.C., Alexander the Great was acquiring huge amounts of gold and silver through his conquests and issuing coins bearing his image far and wide, which Wyrick calls "ads for empire building."

Indeed, says Wyrick, the small change in our pockets literally made the Western world what it is today. "I tell my students that if money had never developed, we would all still be bartering. We would have been stuck with that. Money opened the door to trade, which opened the door for specialization. And that made possible a modern society."

Unit 3

Key Points to Consider

❖ What are the characteristics of a "civilization"? Are these reasonable? Are they useful? Is the definition necessary?

❖ What is the significance of archaeology in the study of history? Should historians rely solely on written records?

❖ What were some ways to conquer a walled city?

❖ Why has Nubia been ignored by historians?

❖ Compare the nomadic life of the Scythians with that of Nabada and Indus civilization. Can "civilization" evolve from nomadic people?

 **Links** **www.dushkin.com/online/**

These sites are annotated on pages 4 and 5.

Although the points are debatable, the characteristics of civilization include urbanization; literacy; complex economic, political, and social systems; and an advanced technology. The presence of cities, writing, and metallurgy are indications of this accomplishment. Civilization, it would seem, represents the highest level of human organization, but this strict definition can ignite arguments. If, for example, a tribe or society does not write, are they "uncivilized"? Since historians embrace written records as their main source of information, moreover, are illiterate people "prehistoric"? This can be a problem since the definition of civilization can imply a judgement about what is best or valuable. World historians usually avoid such value judgements, but they nonetheless use the history of civilizations as an organizing principle. Moreover, world historians often apply a looser definition of civilization so that a complex society, such as that of the Inca, is included as a "civilization."

A society of warring nomads like the Scythians does not meet the tighter definition of "civilization," and, moreover, with no writings and no towns, the Scythians have left little for historians to study. Therefore, they are known mainly by their elaborate gold artwork, which was fashioned by Greek artisans. The ancient Nubians are also known mainly by their artwork, but in this case a literate society existed. It has been less studied, however, even though the Nubians once controlled all of ancient Egypt. The Indus Valley civilization left behind some of the earliest planned cities at Harappa and Mohenjo-Daro, with evidence of water conduits, toilets, straight streets, and standard-sized building bricks. Urbanization, as they demonstrated, was one of the main characteristics of their civilization, but unearthing such evidence can be a daunting historical task. Most ancient cities or their civilizations did not survive into the present period. They were destroyed by war and conquest, and sometimes by nature. "Five Ways to Conquer a City" reveals the manner of Assyrian (900–600 B.C.E.) conquest. There were various ways to breach the walls of a protected city, as depicted by Assyrian wall decorations. Nabada, a lost city in northern Mesopotamia, had a circular double wall

for protection, however, and perished with no evidence of war.

Historians who normally prefer written records in cases of ancient peoples frequently must depend upon the information gathered through archaeology. Potsherds provide some technical information—they are certainly better than nothing—but yield limited insight into the mind of the maker. Hence, historians place emphasis upon literacy. Without writing there is a greater opportunity for distortion. In China there exists little information about its history from 3000–1000 B.C.E. Yet, the government would like to boast that China possesses a 5,000-year lineage of civilization, as noted in the article "In China, Ancient History Kindles Modern Doubts." There is Western speculation that such pressure will lead to exaggeration and error. This creates a problem of historiography for students of China.

The Early Civilizations to 500 B.C.E.

61

Indus Valley, Inc.

*No golden tombs, no fancy ziggurats. Four thousand years ago city builders
in the Indus Valley made deals, not war, and created a stable,
peaceful, and prosperous culture.*

By Shanti Menon

THE RAILWAY LINKING LA-
HORE TO MULTAN IN PAKISTAN
IS 4,600 YEARS OLD. In truth, the
rails were laid down in the middle of
the nineteenth century, but to build the
railway bed, British engineers smashed
bricks from crumbling buildings and
rubble heaps in a town called Harappa,
halfway between the two cities. Back in
1856, Alexander Cunningham, director
of the newly formed Archaeological
Survey of India, thought the brick ruins
were all related to nearby seventh-century Buddhist temples. Local legend told
a different story: the brick mounds were
the remnants of an ancient city, destroyed when its king committed incest
with his niece. Neither Cunningham nor
the locals were entirely correct. In small,
desultory excavations a few years later,
Cunningham found no temples or traces
of kings, incestuous or otherwise. Instead he reported the recovery of some
pottery, carved shell, and a badly damaged seal depicting a one-horned animal, bearing an inscription in an
unfamiliar writing.

That seal was a mark of one of the
world's great ancient civilizations, but
mid-nineteenth-century archeologists like
Cunningham knew nothing of it. The
Vedas, the oldest texts of the subcontinent, dating from some 3,500 years ago,
made no mention of it, nor did the Bible. No pyramids or burial mounds
marked the area as the site of an ancient
power. Yet 4,600 years ago, at the same
time as the early civilizations of Mesopotamia and Egypt, great cities arose
along the floodplains of the ancient Indus and Saraswati rivers in what is now

Pakistan and northwest India. The people of the Indus Valley didn't build towering monuments, bury their riches
along with their dead, or fight legendary
and bloody battles. They didn't have a
mighty army or a divine emperor. Yet
they were a highly organized and stu-
pendously successful civilization. They
built some of the world's first planned
cities, created one of the world's first
written languages, and thrived in an area
twice the size of Egypt and Mesopotamia for 700 years.

To archeologists of this century and
the last, Harappa and Mohenjo-Daro, a
neighboring city some 350 miles to the
southwest, posed an interesting, if un-
glamorous puzzle. Excavations revealed
large, orderly walled cities of massive
brick buildings, with highly sophisticated sanitation and drainage systems
and a drab, institutional feel. The streets
of Harappa, remarked British archeologist Mortimer Wheeler, "however impressive quantitatively, and significant
sociologically, are aesthetically miles of
monotony." The archeologist and popular author Leonard Cottrell, a contemporary of Wheeler's, wrote in 1956,
"While admiring the efficiency of
Harappan planning and sanitary engineering, one's general impression of
Harappan culture is unattractive....
One imagines those warrens of streets,
baking under the fierce sun of the Pun-
jab, as human ant heaps, full of disciplined, energetic activity, supervised and
controlled by a powerful, centralized
state machine; a civilization in which
there was little joy, much labor, and a
strong emphasis on material things."

Superior plumbing and uniform
housing, no matter how well designed,
don't fire the imagination like ziggurats
and gold-laden tombs. "But there's more
to society than big temples and golden
burials," argues Jonathan Mark Kenoyer,
an archeologist at the University of Wisconsin in Madison. "Those are the worst
things that ancient societies did, because
they led to their collapse. When you
take gold and put it in the ground, it's
bad for the economy. When you waste
money on huge monuments instead of
shipping, it's bad for the economy. The
Indus Valley started out with a very different basis and made South Asia the
center of economic interactions in the
ancient world."

Kenoyer, who was born in India to
missionary parents, has been excavating
at Harappa for the past 12 years. His
work, and that of his colleagues, is
changing the image of Harappa from a
stark, state-run city into a vibrant, diverse metropolis, teeming with artisans
and well-traveled merchants.

"What we're finding at Harappa, for
the first time," says Kenoyer, "is how
the first cities started." Mesopotamian
texts suggest that cities sprang up
around deities and their temples, and
once archeologists found these temples,
they didn't look much further. "People
assumed this is how cities evolved, but
we don't know that for a fact," says
Kenoyer. At Harappa, a temple of the
glitzy Mesopotamian variety has yet to
be found. Kenoyer's archeological evidence suggests that the city got its start
as a farming village around 3300 B.C.
Situated near the Ravi River, one of sev-

eral tributaries of the ancient Indus River system of Pakistan and northwestern India, Harappa lay on a fertile floodplain. Good land and a reliable food supply allowed the village to thrive, but the key to urbanization was its location at the crossroads of several major trading routes.

Traders from the highlands of Baluchistan and northern Afghanistan to the west brought in copper, tin, and lapis lazuli; clam and conch shells were brought in from the southern seacoast, timber from the Himalayas, semiprecious stones from Gujarat, silver and gold from Central Asia. The influx of goods allowed Harappans to become traders and artisans as well as farmers. And specialists from across the land arrived to set up shop in the new metropolis.

The city had room to expand and an entrepreneurial spirit driven by access to several sources of raw materials. "You had two sources of lapis, three of copper, and several for shell," says Kenoyer. "The way I envision it, if you had entrepreneurial go-get-'em, and you had a new resource, you could make a million in Harappa. It was a mercantile base for rapid growth and expansion." Enterprising Harappan traders exported finely crafted Indus Valley products to Mesopotamia, Iran, and Central Asia and brought back payment in precious metals and more raw materials. By 2200 B.C., Harappa covered about 370 acres and may have held 80,000 people, making it roughly as populous as the ancient city of Ur in Mesopotamia. And it soon had plenty of neighbors. Over the course of 700 years, some 1,500 Indus Valley settlements were scattered over 280,000 square miles of the subcontinent.

Unlike the haphazard arrangement of Mesopotamian cities, Indus Valley settlements all followed the same basic plan. Streets and houses were laid out on a north-south, east-west grid, and houses and walls were built of standard-size bricks. Even early agricultural settlements were constructed on a grid, "People had a ritual conception of the universe, of universal order," says Kenoyer. "The Indus cities and earlier villages reflect that." This organization, he believes, could have helped the growing city avoid conflicts, giving newcomers their own space rather than leaving

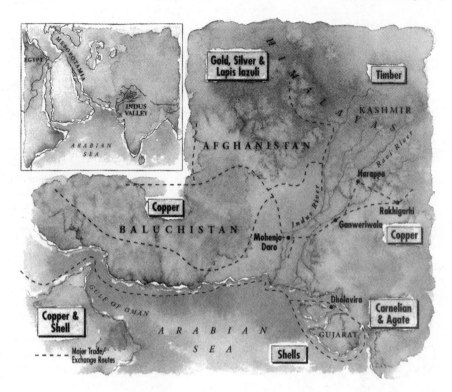

MAP BY BETTE DUKE

Indus Valley cities lay along major trade routes.

them to elbow their way into established territories.

Part of that ritual conception included a devotion to sanitation. Nearly every Harappan home had a bathing platform and a latrine, says Kenoyer, and some Indus Valley cities reached heights of 40 feet in part because of concern about hygiene. Cities often grow upon their foundations over time, but in the Indus Valley, homes were also periodically elevated to avoid the risk of runoff from a neighbor's sewage, "It's keeping up with the Joneses' bathroom," he quips, "that made these cities rise so high so quickly." Each neighborhood had its own well, and elaborate covered drainage systems carried dirty water outside the city. By contrast, city dwellers in Mesopotamian cities tended to draw water from the river or irrigation canals, and they had no drains.

The towering brick cities, surrounded by sturdy walls with imposing gateways, reminded early researchers of the medieval forts in Delhi and Lahore. But Kenoyer points out that a single wall, with no moat and with no sudden turns to lead enemies into an ambush, would have been ill-suited for defense. He

thinks the walls were created to control the flow of goods in and out of the city. At Harappa, standardized cubical stone weights have been found at the gates, and Kenoyer suggests they were used to levy taxes on trade goods coming into the city. The main gateway at Harappa is nine feet across, just wide enough to allow one oxcart in or out. "If you were a trader," he explains, "you wanted to bring goods into a city to trade in a safe place, so bandits wouldn't rip you off. To get into the city, you had to pay a tax. If you produced things, you had to pay a tax to take goods out of the city. This is how a city gets revenues."

THE IDENTITY OF THE TAX collectors and those they served remains a mystery. Unlike the rulers of Mesopotamia and Egypt, Indus Valley rulers did not immortalize themselves with mummies or monuments. They did, however, leave behind elaborately carved stone seals, used to impress tokens or clay tabs on goods bound for market. The seals bore images of animals, like the humped bull, the elephant, the rhinoceros, and the crocodile, which were probably emblems of

Unlike Mesopotamian cities, Indus Valley cities all followed the same basic plan, reflecting the people's ritual conception of universal order.

powerful clans. The most common image is the unicorn, a symbol that originated in the Indus Valley.

Frustratingly, though, those seals carry inscriptions that no one has been able to decipher. Not only are the inscriptions short, but they don't resemble any known language. From analyzing overlapping strokes, it is clear that the script reads right to left. It is also clear that the script is a mix of phonetic symbols and pictographs. Early Mesopotamian cuneiform, which used only pictographs, was thought to be the world's first written language, says Kenoyer, but the Indus Valley script emerged independently around the same time—at least by around 3300 B.C.

As long as the language remains a mystery, so too will the identities of the Indus Valley elites. Kenoyer thinks each of the large cities may have functioned as an independent city-state, controlled by a small group of merchants, landowners, and religious leaders. "They controlled taxation, access to the city, and communication with the gods," he says. While the balance of power may have shifted between these groups, they seem to have ruled without a standing army. Sculptures, paintings, and texts from Egypt and Mesopotamia clearly illustrate battles between cities and pharaonic wars of conquest. But in the Indus Valley, not a single depiction of a military act, of taking prisoners, of a human killing another human has been found. It's possible these acts were illustrated on cloth or paper or some other perishable and simply did not survive. Yet none of the cities show signs of battle damage to buildings or city walls, and very few weapons have been recovered.

Human remains show no signs of violence either. Only a few cemeteries have been found, suggesting that burial of the dead may have been limited to high-ranking individuals (others may have been disposed of through cremation or river burials). The bones from excavated burials show few signs of disease or malnourishment. Preliminary genetic studies from a cemetery in Harappa have suggested that women were buried near their mothers and grandmothers. Men do not seem to be related to those near them, so they were probably buried with their wives' families. There is evidence that people believed in an afterlife: personal items like amulets and simple pottery have been recovered from a few burials. But true to their practical, businesslike nature, the Harappans didn't bury their dead with riches. Unlike the elites of the Near East, Harappans kept their valuable items in circulation, trading for new, often extraordinary ornaments for themselves and their descendants.

In spite of this practice, excavators have turned up some hints of the wealth an individual could accumulate. Two decades ago, in the rural settlement of Allahdino, near modern Karachi in Pakistan, archeologists stumbled upon a buried pot filled with jewelry, the secret hoard of a rich landowner. Among the silver and gold necklaces and gold bands, beads, and rings was a belt or necklace made of 36 elongated carnelian beads interspersed with bronze beads. Shaping and drilling these long, slender beads out of hard stone is immensely difficult and time-consuming. Indus craftsmen made a special drill for this purpose by heating a rare metamorphic rock to create a superhard material. Even these high-tech drills could perforate carnelian at a rate of only a hundredth of an inch per hour. Kenoyer estimates that a large carnelian belt like the one at Allahdino would have taken a single person 480 working days to complete. It was most likely made by a group of artisans over a period of two or three years.

Such intensive devotion to craftsmanship and trade, Kenoyer argues, is what allowed Indus Valley culture to spread over a region twice the size of Mesopotamia without a trace of military domination. Just as American culture is currently exported along with goods and media, so too were the seals, pottery styles, and script of the Indus Valley spread among the local settlements. Figurines from the Indus Valley also testify to a complex social fabric. People within the same city often wore different styles of dress and hair, a practice that could reflect differences in ethnicity or status. Men are shown with long hair or short, bearded or clean-shaven. Women's hairstyles could be as simple as one long braid, or complex convolutions of tresses piled high on a supporting structure.

Eventually, between 1900 and 1700 B.C., the extensive trading networks and productive farms supporting this cultural integration collapsed, says Kenoyer, and distinct local cultures emerged. "They stopped writing," he says. "They stopped using the weight system for taxation. And the unicorn motif disappeared." Speculation as to the reasons for the disintegration has ranged from warfare to weather. Early archeologists believed that Indo-Aryan invaders from the north swept through and conquered the peaceful Harappans, but that theory has since been disproved. None of the major cities show evidence of warfare, though some smaller settlements appear to have been abandoned. There is evidence that the Indus River shifted, flooding many settlements and disrupting agriculture. It is likely that when these smaller settlements were abandoned, trade routes were affected. In the Ganges River valley to the east, on the outskirts of the Indus Valley sphere of influence, the newly settled Indo-Aryans, with their own customs, grew to prominence while cities like Harappa faded.

But the legacy of the ancient Indus cities and their craftspeople remains. The bead makers of Khambhat in India continue to make beads based on Harappan techniques—though the carnelian is now bored with diamond-tipped drills. Shell workers in Bengal still make bangles out of conch shells. And in the crowded marketplaces of Delhi and Lahore, as merchants hawk the superiority, of their silver over the low-quality ore of their neighbors, as gold and jewels are weighed in bronze balances, it's hard to imagine that a 4,000-year-old Harappan bazaar could have been terribly different.

In China, Ancient History Kindles Modern Doubts

By ERIK ECKHOLM

BEIJING, Nov. 9— Everyone here knows that Chinese civilization has 5,000 years of uninterrupted history, a truism proudly repeated by schoolchildren and President Jiang Zemin alike. But as serious scholars have long conceded, hard proof of the first 2,000 years is missing.

Today, scholars announced the results of an urgent government-sponsored research program that—using "the superiority of socialism to develop a multidisciplinary approach"—has filled in key gaps in the ancient record of China's first kings and dynasties. The project, which mobilized more than 200 scholars for five years, has been hailed for shedding light on the murky origins of Chinese civilization. But it has also raised questions about the role of nationalism in scholarship.

Ample evidence does exist of early cultures in the Yellow River Valley, where legend holds that the Chinese language and imperial system took form under a mythical Yellow Emperor 5,000 years ago. But no firmly documented chronology of rulers, reigns and conquests—of the sort that exists for ancient Egypt and Mesopotamia—actually goes back beyond 841 B.C.

"This has been a major regret for Chinese history and world history," said Li Xueqin, a prominent historian, today at a news conference to disclose the results of the project.

Mr. Li, the project's director, was certainly understating the despair that many scholars and officials have felt about the history problem. China is a country obsessed with its past, as a source of national worth and an explanation for every foible.

Mr. Li announced that the Xia-Shang-Zhou Chronology Project, named for the three early dynasties under study, "has been able to solve a series of long-standing questions about early Chinese civilization." He said the project had yielded the most reliable time line yet for these dynasties, the earliest of which is said to date back more than 4,000 years.

He also said scholars in disciplines including archaeology, astronomical history, early manuscripts and the parsing of inscriptions on bronze vessels and divination bones had made many new discoveries and synthesized the sketchy evidence. Project leaders hope their newly detailed dating of early emperors will soon enter the world's textbooks and museum exhibits.

Tonight the report was featured in television news and newspapers, which ran headlines like "Chinese History Pushed Back 1,229 Years."

But the project has been questioned by other scholars, here and abroad, who say its authors, driven by a political urge to document Chinese culture's primacy and uniqueness, have tried to leapfrog the slow, disorderly march of science. Project researchers resolutely deny anyone told them what to find, but critics say they have forced an illusion of consensus in some cases.

"There's a chauvinistic desire to push the historical record back into the third millennium B.C., putting China on a par with Egypt," said Edward L. Shaughnessy, a historian at the University of Chicago. "It's much more a political and a nationalistic urge than a scholarly one."

A time line officially documents three murky dynasties.

Several Chinese historians and archaeologists have argued with the project leaders or refused to take part, said one scholar, who spoke on condition of anonymity. But today Mr. Li and others were adamant about the conclusions' having been drawn fairly and cautiously, through a form of "academic democracy."

The research enterprise was begun in 1995 by Song Jian, a senior official overseeing China's science policies.

"A history without chronology is no history at all," Mr. Song wrote in a newspaper article this fall. "It can only be called rumor or myth."

Li Tieying, a member of the Communist Party Politburo as well as president of the Chinese Academy of Social

Sciences, has said: "The project is an important scientific study and also has major political and cultural significance. Explicating Chinese civilization will necessarily strengthen our national cohesiveness and raise our national self-confidence and pride."

From the outset, the scholars acknowledged that they were unlikely to stretch history all the way back to the fabled Yellow Emperor. Instead they set out to enrich knowledge of three dynasties that they say reigned from about 2070 B.C., the beginning of the reputed Xia Dynasty, to 771 B.C., when the Zhou Dynasty fell. All are believed to have been agricultural societies with elaborate rituals of divination and sacrifice.

Evidence for the very existence of a Xia Dynasty remains slender. Though it is mentioned in history books centuries later, the name does not appear on archaeological finds from the period, or even in inscriptions from the centuries that followed its supposed demise. Some Western scholars feel it remains more legend than fact.

Still, the project takes as already proven the existence of the Xia as a precursor empire to the better-established Shang, pointing to a site uncovered at Erlitou, Henan Province, in 1959 as the probable capital.

Today the presumed palace walls at Erlitou lie under farmland. After the site was excavated and documented, it was covered for protection and local farmers moved in. A few hundred yards away, trained villagers dig in a related excava-tion, and a few yards beyond them, new buildings are being built.

The report today concludes that the Xia ruled from around 2070 B.C. to 1600 B.C., though it does not try to date the reign of each Xia ruler.

The scholars were able to muster new findings about the Shang Dynasty, which is believed to have reigned in the Yellow River area centered on present-day Henan and Shaanxi Provinces for the following 550 years, but fixed rulers' exact dates only for the later Shang era, after 1300 B.C.

Early in the 20th century, many scholars doubted traditional claims of a Shang Dynasty, too. But then discoveries of "oracle bones"—animal bones bearing inscriptions used to decipher the future—proved its existence. There was also evidence that the Shang engaged in human sacrifice and may have held slaves.

By all accounts, the project has also helped clarify the formerly confused chronology of the early Zhou Dynasty, which produced beautiful bronzes seen in world museums.

But one of the most contentious and important questions involves the timing of the Zhou conquest of the Shang. The event's date is vital to chronology before and after, but scholars must sort out contradictory signs from early inscriptions, reports of Jupiter's position in the sky and accounts in ancient documents of disputed authenticity.

The project's decision to settle on 1046 B.C. as the probable date for the fall of the Shang—the date became widely known when draft reports were circulated —angered some scholars.

One historian, Jiang Xiaoyuan of Jiaotong University in Shanghai, complained in an interview that his published conclusions about the conquest year, developed under project auspices, had been set aside by project leaders to support the date they preferred. But Mr. Jiang also acknowledged that the project had brought fresh funding and modern equipment to starved disciplines and had "vastly advanced the study of China's ancient history."

David S. Nivison, emeritus professor of Chinese studies at Stanford University, said he was outraged by the selection of 1046, which he said contradicted research he had submitted to the project. His favored date is 1040, but whoever is right, he says, insisting on a single date now is intellectually dishonest.

"It's going to be a mess," Mr. Nivison said, adding that international scholars were likely to tear the report "to pieces."

"These are going to be seen as the dates pronounced to be correct by the Chinese government," Mr. Nivison said. "For the government of China to be in this position may poison scholarship for generations."

Mr. Li, the project director, replied today: "Our findings are, I believe, the best that can be obtained at present. That doesn't mean there can't be further progress."

Five Ways
to Conquer a City

Erika Bleibtreu

In the spring of 1843, Paul-Emile Botta, the French consul at Mosul in present-day Iraq, invited Austen Henry Layard, then 26 years old and the British ambassador's secretary in Constantinople, to join him at a site Botta thought was ancient Nineveh: "Come, I pray you," Botta wrote, "and let us have a little archaeological fun at Khorsabad!"

Although Layard's notes indicate he was "anxious to visit" the site, he did not actually do so until August 1846. He found it an unhealthy place: "During M. Botta's excavations, the workmen suffered greatly from fever, and many fell victims to it."[1] He was also somewhat critical of Botta's excavation methods and was not very impressed with the remains.

For himself, Layard chose the site of Nimrud, about 35 miles south of Khorsabad. He began excavating Nimrud in 1845 and was soon as handsomely rewarded as Botta with monumental sculptures and other Assyrian treasures—now on display at the British Museum in London.

In 1849 Layard turned his attention to the ruins of Kuyunjik, on the other side of the Tigris River, opposite modern Mosul. Ironically, Botta had been here earlier, in 1842, but he had abandoned the site after a few months without discovering any remarkable remains.[2]

It turned out that Layard's site of Kuyunjik, not Botta's site at Khorsabad, was actually Nineveh. But when Botta published the results of his excavations at Khorsabad, it was under the title *Monument de Ninive* (five volumes, 1849–1850). Actually Khorsabad was Dur-Sharrukin, literally "town of Sargon" or "Sargonsburg"; Botta had excavated the capital of Sargon II of Assyria, who reigned from 722 to 705 B.C. In 1849, 1850 and 1853, Layard published his own volumes on Nineveh containing most of the reliefs he had excavated at Kuyunjik and at Nimrud (*The Monuments of Nineveh* [two volumes, 1849 and 1853], *Nineveh and Its Remains* [two volumes, 1850] and *Discoveries in the Ruins of Nineveh and Babylon* [1853]).

Despite their stupendous finds, Botta and Layard both left much to be desired in excavation technique. Botta was an Italian-born physician turned diplomat, not a trained excavator at all. By modern standards, Layard was only marginally better. He excavated by tunneling along the walls of halls revealed by the discovery of sculptured slabs.

Nevertheless, at all three sites, the two men made discoveries still in many ways unsurpassed—monumental palaces, huge sculptures, major libraries of cuneiform texts and, most important for purposes of this article, miles of sculptured slabs that formed the decorations on the walls of the palaces.

At the real Nineveh, for example, Layard recovered almost two miles of sculptured slabs made of Mosul alabaster, in addition to 27 pairs of colossal, human-headed, winged bulls and lions that flanked the entrances to the Southwest Palace. The sculptured slabs formed the wall decorations of a palace with more than 70 rooms and courts. It was built for Sennacherib (704–681 B.C.), who led a major military campaign against Judah in the late eighth century B.C. By his own account, he destroyed 46 Judean cities including Lachish[3] and even besieged Jerusalem, although for some reason failed to conquer it. (The Bible describes all this in 2 Kings 18.) Sennacherib decorated several rooms of his palace at Nineveh to celebrate his victory in this campaign. He called it "Palace Without Equal" and intended it to surpass the palaces of all his predecessors.

At Nimrud, Layard discovered two other palaces: one built by Ashurnasirpal II (883–859 B.C.), covering about 6.5 acres, and the other built by Tiglath-pileser III (744–727 B.C.).

Soon thereafter, another palace was excavated at Nineveh by Hormuzd Rassam and William Kennett Loftus. Called the North Palace, it was constructed during the reign of Sennacherib's grandson, Ashurbanipal (668–627 B.C.), who probably moved there from his grandfather's palace.

All together, these 19th-century excavations uncovered six Assyrian kings' palaces decorated with wall reliefs, dating from the early ninth to the late seventh centuries B.C.:

Ashurnasirpal II	883–859 B.C.
Tiglath-pileser III	744–727 B.C.
Sargon II	722–705 B.C.
Sennacherib	704–681 B.C.
Esarhaddon	680–669 B.C.
Ashurbanipal	668–627 B.C.

Before this period, palace walls had simply been painted. However, during this period, palace walls in most of the capital cities of Assyria were decorated with sculptured slabs of alabaster and

Assyrian Palaces Where Wall Reliefs Were Found

Ancient Name of Site	Modern Name of Site	Assyrian Ruler	Excavators*	Date of Excavation
Dur-Sharrukin (Botta thought it was Nineveh. The city was founded by Sargon II and named after him.)	Khorsabad	Sargon II (721–705 B.C.) Palace	**Paul-Emile Botta and** **Eugène Flandin** Victor Place Henri Frankfort Gordon Loud Directorate General of Antiquities, Baghdad, Iraq	**1843–44** 1852–54 1929–32 1938–39
Kalhu (Calah of the Bible— see Genesis 10:11–12)	Nimrud	Ashurnasirpal II (883–859 B.C.) Northwest Palace	**Austen Henry Layard** **Hormuzd Rassam** Sir Max Mallowan Directorate General of Antiquities, Baghdad, Iraq Janusz Meuszynski	**1845–47, 1849–51** **1853–54** 1949–53 1959–60, 1969–74 1974–75
Kalhu	Nimrud	Tiglath-pileser III (744–727 B.C.) Central Palace	**Austen Henry Layard** **Hormuzd Rassam** **William Kennett Loftus** **Hormuzd Rassam** Sir Max Mallowan Janusz Meuszynski	1845–47, 1849–51 **1853–54** **1854** **1878–79** 1952 1975–1976
Kalhu	Nimrud	Esarhaddon (680–669 B.C.) Southwest Palace (Slabs sculptured for the Northwest Palace of Ashurnasirpal II and for the Central Palace of Tiglath-pileser III were found here ready to be reused and recarved.)	**Austen Henry Layard** **William Kennett Loftus** George Smith Sir Max Mallowan	**1845–47, 1849–51** **1854** 1873 1951
Nineveh Citadel	Kuyunjik	Sennacherib (704–681 B.C.) Southwest Palace (partly redecorated under the reign of his grandson Ashurbanipal)	**Austen Henry Layard** Henry Ross Christian Rassam **Austen Henry Layard** Christian Rassam **and his** **brother Hormuzd** **William Kennett Loftus** George Smith **Hormuzd Rassam** and his nephew Nimroud E. A. Wallis Budge Leonard William King R. Campbell Thompson Tariq Madhloom	**1846–47** 1847–48 1848 **1849–51** **1851–54** **1854** 1873–74 **1878** 1889–91 1903–05 1904–05, 1927, 1931–32 1965–67
Nineveh Citadel	Kuyunjik	Ashurbanipal (668–627 B.C.) North Palace	**Hormuzd Rassam William** **Kennett Loftus** and William Boutcher Christian Rassam E. A. Wallis Budge R. Campbell Thompson	**1853–54** **1854** 1854–55 1889–91 1904–05

* Excavators in boldface are mentioned in the accompanying article.

limestone. These slabs were carved in flat relief and then, for the most part, painted and finally aligned along the walls constructed of unbaked brick.

Botta and Layard managed to send some hundreds of tons of Assyrian sculptures back to Paris and London. Even so, only the most magnificent and better-preserved pieces were selected for transport. Many of the smaller fragments—which were less important from the 19th-century treasure-hunting perspective—found their way to the antiquities market, eventually coming to reside in more than 50 museums and galleries on three continents.

Some of the major pieces were lost in transport. Botta's first shipment from

Sargon's palace at Khorsabad, intended for the Louvre, sank in the Tigris River when the rafts upon which it had been loaded overturned in treacherous rapids on the way to the Persian Gulf.

Fortunately, we have in public museums not only the pieces that survived, but also the original drawings made on the spot by superb artists who were both talented and careful.

A young artist named Eugène Napoléon Flandin copied the sculptures found at Khorsabad. Between May and October 1844, he made about 150 drawings of the wall reliefs of Sargon's palace. These drawings are undoubtedly the best ever made of Assyrian wall reliefs, and were published as engravings in Botta's *Monument de Ninive*. Recently, in 1986, Flandin's original drawings—now kept in the Bibliothèque de l'Institut de France in Paris—were published for the first time in Pauline Albenda's *The Palace of Sargon, King of Assyria* (Paris, 1986).

In addition, the Department of Western Asiatic Antiquities in the British Museum has about 500 original drawings of Assyrian wall reliefs from the ninth to the seventh centuries B.C. Layard himself probably made about half of these. Although Layard was not a professional artist, he was a very gifted amateur. His drawings are of a high standard and very faithful.

Many of the drawings illustrate remains that have since disappeared. Most of the slabs not chosen for transport to a European museum by the 19th-century excavators were reburied in the rubbish of the site.

The slabs that decorated the walls are masterpieces of Assyrian art. It took enormous effort and talent to create them. The slabs first had to be transported from the quarries to the capital cities of the Assyrian empire, then carried through courts and corridors to the rooms in which they were to be used. The slabs were attached to the walls of the palaces by sinking them partly below floor-level. Clamps were probably used to tie them to the walls at the top.

To decorate the slabs, outlines of the scenes were first sketched on the flattened stone, probably following a model in clay that had been approved by the king. Thereafter a team of artisans executed the main scenes by carving away the background around the figures. Another group of stonemasons probably added the minor details, such as the mountain-scale pattern and the pattern of foliage on the trees. Still another team of artisans painted certain details in the reliefs; traces of red and black paint can still be seen on some of the slabs, for example on the shoes of the king and his courtiers in the Nimrud Gallery of the British Museum.

The result was a massive pictorial record of major events in the kings' reigns and the illustration of important ritual activities in which the kings took part.

Pictorial means of communication were more immediately effective than oral or even written storytelling. Pictures could reach illiterate people and people who spoke languages other than the Akkadian used by their Assyrian overlords. We do not know who was allowed to enter the palace, apart from the king's family and his courtiers. Therefore, we cannot say whether these wall decorations served as a kind of political propaganda to impress foreign visitors, or whether they were meant as a kind of religious demonstration to show that the will of the gods was being continually fulfilled in glorious Assyrian victories.

Scenes of warfare and Assyrian victory provide the themes of the reliefs—the conquest of foreign peoples, the deportation of prisoners, the inspection of spoil and booty and its transportation to Assyria. But above all was the superiority of the Assyrian army, whose victory was ordained by her gods, according to whose command the Assyrian kings led their campaigns.

The realistic representations on the wall reliefs depict various units of the Assyrian army—infantry, chariotry and cavalry. We see well-trained Assyrian soldiers fighting alongside auxiliaries from all parts of the Near East. We see too the enemies of the Assyrians. The wall reliefs also depict the tactics and strategies employed in order to conquer so many fortified cities.

Obviously, there is an enormous amount to be learned from these extraordinary reliefs. Here we shall concentrate on one aspect of them—what they teach us about the means by which walled, strongly fortified cities were conquered.

Five different methods can be distinguished. However, a combination of two or more of these methods can usually be observed at each site of attack.

We will describe these methods generally and illustrate them more particularly from the Assyrian palace reliefs:

1. One way to penetrate a fortified walled city was to use ladders to get over the top of the wall and inside the city. Scaling ladders were used to break the resistance of the defenders who fought from the city's towers and parapets. By this method, at least some of the attackers could enter the city from the top of the fortifications. Prior to the attack, however, trees had to be cut and ladders constructed to a suitable height for the walls surrounding the besieged city.

In some of the reliefs, archers and spearmen are shown climbing up the ladders. Helmets, shields and different kinds of body armour protect the attackers from the missiles that the defenders throw from above. Soldiers on the ground, shooting arrows, provided additional protection to those on the ladders.

2. A second method of attack involved penetration through a city wall or a city gate, the latter being the weakest point in the fortification. The wooden doors of a city gate could be easily demolished by setting them on fire, even when they were sheathed with bronze.

A wall or gate could also be forcibly penetrated by means of battering rams. In the Judahite cities Sennacherib says he conquered, he claims to have used battering rams, a claim consistent with the portrayal of the conquest of Lachish depicted on his palace walls, where several battering rams can be seen.

Battering rams from the ninth century B.C. are depicted as being heavy, six-wheeled engines. Later they became lighter and more mobile. The later battering rams were covered with raw hides to protect them against fire.

Before a battering ram could be used, a path had to be created to get it to the appropriate place at the appropriate height in the wall. To accomplish this, a siege ramp had to be built so that the battering rams could be rolled up it to the upper part of the wall.

Several carvings on the reliefs show different methods of building these ramps. In some cases they were built of rows of bricks. In others, regularly shaped stones appear to have been used with branches of trees as fillers between the layers. The quantity of stones needed to build a siege ramp was enormous. That is why bricks had to be used in Mesopotamia, which is a largely stoneless area. In some cases wooden tracks were used on the surface of siege ramps, as the ramps had to be smooth for the wheels of the battering rams.

3. It was possible for an attacker to go not only over the wall and through the wall, but also under the wall. To penetrate the city wall from underground was less dangerous for the attacker, but it was technically more difficult. Iron implements were used to dig what was in effect a tunnel from which the wall could be undermined. At the beginning of this effort, it was especially important to protect the diggers from attacks from above. Shield-bearers provided this protection. The great body-shields with curving tops, as shown in the reliefs, proved particularly useful in this regard.

4. A city could also be conquered without having its walls attacked by force. To conquer a strongly fortified city without attacking its walls by force, it was necessary to lay siege to it for as long as required. A siege could last several months or even years. Much depended on the supply of water and food inside the besieged city. Outside the city, the besieging army established its own fortified camp (or camps). The site of the besiegers' camp was on raised ground whenever this was available. This offered some security from counterattack by foraging city defenders.

The siege camps are always shown in the reliefs in a maplike representation. In the ninth century B.C., the groundplans are generally circular, square or rectangular; in the seventh-century reliefs, they all have oval shapes and are surrounded by their own fortified walls.

The reliefs depict two different types of tents inside the siege camps. The more elaborate are closed tents that are open to the sky in the middle. This type was used by the king, or by the chief commander of the army, or by high-ranking officers. The soldiers used ordinary tents with open sides. In the reliefs, we see inside these tents and thus observe the daily life of the soldiers—slaughtering animals or cooking and baking. In one fragment of a slab, a returning Assyrian archer is seen drinking beside his open bed.

5. The final method of conquering a fortified city involved cutting off its water supply. A scene from the palace of Ashurnasirpal II probably depicts the cutting off of the water supply of a city under siege. (It is certainly not so easy to illustrate ruses that were sometimes used to conquer a city.)

Once a city was conquered, much of it was destroyed, especially its fortifications. Soldiers of various units are seen in the reliefs systematically demolishing city walls. Then the city itself was put to the torch.

Once the battle was over, the Assyrians boasted of their prowess and bravery by delivering severed heads to a scribe, who registered the heads for a special reward. Usually a pair of scribes is illustrated, one using a two-part writing board covered with wax, and the other using a scroll of leather or papyrus. Thus, Assyrian valor was recorded for posterity and for the gods.

Notes

1. Austen H. Layard, *Nineveh and Its Remains* (London, 1850), p. 148.
2. The reason was that a deep accumulation of rubbish from later occupations covered the most impressive Assyrian remains.
3. See Hershel Shanks, "Destruction of Judean Fortress Portrayed in Dramatic Eighth-Century B.C. Pictures," **BAR**, March/April 1984.

Bleibtreu wrote her doctoral thesis on Neo-Babylonian inscriptions and later studied under Sir Max Mallowan at Oxford. Since 1963, she has worked as research assistant at the Oriental Institute of Vienna University, where she has also served, since 1978, as senior lecturer in ancient Near Eastern art history and archaeology. Her excavations include sites in eastern Anatolia (Turkey) and in Austria. In collaboration with Geoffrey Turner and the late Richard D. Barnett, she is preparing a catalogue titled *The Sculptures of Sennacherib (705–681 B.C.) and Ashurbanipal (668–627 B.C.) from the Southwest Palace at Nineveh.*

NABADA:
The Buried City

JOACHIM BRETSCHNEIDER

Palace ruins

Excavations in northern Syria reveal the metropolis of Nabada, founded 4,500 years ago. Its elaborate administration and culture rivaled those of the fabled cities of southern Mesopotamia

The "tell," or mound, at Nabada

Aerial view of ruins

JOACHIM BRETSCHNEIDER (*top*); TEAM DRIESSEN-CUNNINGHAM (*bottom*)

The Cities of Northern Mesopotamia

by Joachim Bretschneider

Since the end of the 19th century, archaeologists have strived to uncover the ancient history of the Near East and to trace the region's biblical roots. They focused on the Fertile Crescent between the rivers Euphrates and Tigris in Iraq, where lie the ruins of the ancient city-states of Assur, Babylon, Ur and Uruk. The architecture, tablets and other artifacts of these cities illustrate a tumultuous history that began more than 5,000 years ago. Scholars assumed that only here, in southern Mesopotamia, were the earliest centers of power and the origins of civilization.

Until quite recently, the steppes of northern Mesopotamia (in present-day Syria) were largely neglected. But when the war between Iraq and Iran closed access to southerly sites in the 1980s, archaeologists were forced to pay more attention to peripheral areas. A research team led by Marc Lebeau of the European Center for Upper Mesopotamian Studies and Antoine Suleiman of the Directorate-General of Antiquities and Museums (Syria) began to excavate Tell Beydar, a large mound—or "tell"—rising out of the flat steppes near the Khabur River. The team also consists of the universities of Leuven (Karel Van Lerberghe), Venice (Philippe Talon), Brussels (Lucio Milano) and Münster (Bretschneider). In these steppes, a tell indicates a long-buried city; after eight years of intensive research, we can now say that Beydar did not disappoint.

Inside the 28-meter-high circular hill archaeologists found a complex almost as large as the citadel of ancient Troy. The city, known in ancient times as Nabada, evidently enjoyed its greatest prosperity during the early Bronze Age, between 2800 and 2200 B.C., and the excavation concentrates on this period. Our aim is to understand the birth of city-states—the metropolises that ruled the surrounding countryside and, sometimes, other cities—in northern Mesopotamia. Complex administration, as evinced by written tablets and seals, evolved at this time.

In places the Bronze Age strata are right at the surface, whereas at others they lie several meters deep. Almost all

The steppes of northern Mesopotamia near the Khabur River in present-day Syria are home to the ruins of numerous ancient cities, including Nabada. Nabada reached its peak of prosperity in the third millennium B.C., when political and economic power in the region were being concentrated in a few large centers: Kish, Lagash, Umma, Ur and Uruk in modern Iraq; and Chuera, Ebla, Mari, Nagar, Nabada and Tuttul in northern Syria.

Nabada and nearby cities probably served as relay stations for caravans traveling the ancient routes *(black lines)* between Anatolia (present-day Turkey) and Babylonia or between Egypt and Mesopotamia.

Archaeologists have uncovered a variety of artifacts at Nabada that reflect the city's route as a cultural and trade center (see photographs on next page). —*J.B.*

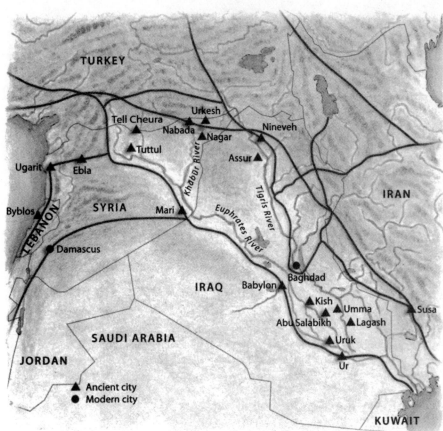

PATRICIA J. WYNNE AND BRYAN CHRISTIE

of the scientific staff and students work for free, and so the summer holidays at European universities dictate the length of an excavation campaign; from the end of August until the end of October. Strenuous work under a ferocious sun, as well as occasional sandstorms and scorpions, fall to our lot. The day begins at 5 A.M. and continues in a miasma of sweat and dust until 1 P.M., when we retire to the shadows to process, record and analyze the objects we have uncovered. Digging resumes in the late afternoon; when the sun sets quickly at 6 P.M. we have to work by electric light or occasionally by candles. At night a cloak

of unearthly silence falls on the ancient site.

Early in this century German archaeologist Max Freiherr von Oppenheim demonstrated that the vast and now abandoned spaces of northern Syria were densely inhabited in ancient times. Today archaeologists know of almost 300 tells rising conspicuously from the flat plains. In one of these, Tell Halaf, von Oppenheim found exquisitely shaped and painted pottery dating back to the fifth millennium B.C. He also surveyed some of the more conspicuous circular tells, which cluster around the upper course of the Khabur River. Such

Ivory furniture inlay, 1400 B.C.

Ceremonial vase, 1400 B.C.

PHOTOGRAPHS BY JOACHIM BRETSCHNEIDER

a tell, which he described as "Kranz-hügel," or "wreath hill," is surrounded by a ring, the decomposed mud brick of a circular fortification wall. Von Oppenheim suggested that the lower levels of these towns were all created at around the same time and formed a single political or cultural unit, the so-called Kranzhügel culture.

Another explorer in the Khabur region, Englishman Max E. L. Mallowan, excavated at Tell Brak, a mountain now known to hide the city of Nagar, and at Tell Chagar Bazar, a much smaller site. In 1958 a small team led by Anton Moortgat of the Free University of Berlin began a systematic study of Tell Chuera, a circular hill with a diameter of almost a kilometer. Later excavations at Tell Chuera revealed an urban complex dating to the first half of the third millennium. Although Chuera is made of sundried mud brick, as was common in the metropolises of southern Mesopo-

tamia, its temples were constructed on monumental stone terraces.

Who built Tell Chuera or where these people came from remains a mystery. Curiously, Tell Beydar, the only other circular tell to be systematically investigated, is turning out to be quite different.

In Tell Beydar we discerned three main phases of occupation. Researchers date these phases by a combination of techniques: comparing trends in pottery design; measuring the occurrence of radioactive carbon in ashes and other debris of organic origin; and relating names occurring on tablets with those known from other sources. In my view, the dates are uncertain by only about 50 to 100 years, although other scholars differ.

Wreath City

The first and most significant phase began with the founding of Nabada around 2800 B.C. Apparently following a set plan, the builders constructed a circular settlement with a diameter of 600 meters. They protected it by a wall five meters thick, built on a raised embankment. Four gates, now seen as gaps in the buried outer ring, penetrated this wall. Peasants' dwellings and artisans' quarters clung to its inner side as in Europe's medieval cities. About 20 tombs have so far been excavated near the wall, whose elevated base apparently served as a cemetery.

The tombs, some of which also lie beneath the houses, provide a clue to the

people's religious beliefs. In one case, a shaft led to the burial chamber, constructed of mud brick and sealed. The dead man, apparently an important official, lay in a fetal position surrounded by weapons, jewelry and pottery to ease his passage to the afterlife. Another grave was supplied with a bronze ax, ceramic jars filled with wheat and many other objects. Whereas soldiers were buried with their weapons, artisans were interred with their work tools; social stratification is evident in the varying richness of the burial gifts.

Some later Babylonian sources describe a tomb as an entrance to the underworld, a place of damnation from which there is no return. The offerings of food and drink by the relatives appeased the spirits of the dead in this dark and gloomy realm. Evidently the citizens of Nabada adhered to a similar belief.

An inner wall 300 meters in diameter protected the heart of the settlement. It is very likely that traders were allowed to spend the night between the two walls, safe from highway robbers but not themselves posing a danger to the sleeping citizens of Nabada. The double wall may also have let peasants from surrounding regions take refuge in the city in times of trouble. From the gates, radiating streets led to the central mound, on which rose a palace. Lining the city's streets were blocks of houses, filling the space between the palace and the inner city wall. Drainage systems evacuated water from houses and courtyards into channels underlying the paved streets and alleys.

In the eastern section of the city stood a remarkable 27-meter-long building whose walls still rise up to three meters. Wide, arched doorways connected the structure's four rooms, a sign of advanced architecture. Low sockets in the walls show that the rooms were fitted with elevated wooden floors for storing grain or wool; the supplies stayed dry thanks to the ventilation underneath them. Storehouses of such size suggest a complex economy.

For its size, the city inside Tell Beydar had surprisingly few houses: most of it consisted of a palace, rising like a fortress on the central, 20-meter-high acropolis. (That is, at least 20 meters of cultural levels and the ruins of several palaces, all from the early Bronze Age, underlie the present excavation.) The royal complex covered about 50 by 60 meters, comprising almost 50 rooms on the ground floor alone. Many of the mud-brick walls are excellently preserved, being up to four meters high and having intact doorways frequently spanned by a vault. A number of rooms boast a fine, white lime plaster on their walls.

A large central courtyard provided easy access to the palace's many rooms. Friezes with clay rosettes decorated the walls of the main rooms, and stairways led up to a throne room (where the king met his subjects) and ceremonial chambers at a higher level. These rooms, which archaeologists recognize by their altars and other characteristic features, had annexes supplied with terracotta shafts up to 20 meters deep. The small rooms may well have been used for ritual washing and purification, with the shafts providing drainage.

From this large courtyard a smaller one toward the southeast could be reached. From here other staircases led to a higher level, where the living quarters of the ruler may have been situated. All around the perimeter of the palace are storage rooms, still filled with huge ceramic jars that once brimmed with goods. The southern part of the palace featured elaborate wall niches and altar platforms. The ruler may even have been interred here beneath the floor, following an old Syrian practice.

Last year excavators uncovered an intriguing set of terraces. These suggest that this year we are likely to find giant stairways leading up to the palace from the southern gate of the outer wall. They would have formed a steep ramp or stepped pyramid, lined with temples, the whole probably creating a monumental entrance for visiting dignitaries and the elaborate processions accompanying them.

Accounts of Nabada

In 1993 and 1994 excavators made a surprising discovery: a collection of clay tablets with a meticulous record of the palace's daily accounts. Since then, we have found 170 tablets inscribed

Life inside Nabada's Walls

Nabada was founded around 2800 B.C., with the construction of a circular settlement 600 meters in diameter. The early inhabitants protected their town with a wall five meters thick built on a raised embankment (*illustration below*). Even before the mound, or tell, was excavated, the remains of the city's outer walls and the central mound were evident in the Syrian desert. About 20 tombs have been excavated from this embankment; in one tomb, a shaft led to the burial chamber, which was made of mud brick and then sealed. The dead man, apparently an important official, lay in a fetal position surrounded by gifts such as weapons, jewelry and pottery, which were thought to ease his passage to the after life (*see photograph on next page*). An inner wall 300 meters in diameter protected the heart of this settlement: rising from a central 20-meter-high mound stood Nabada's palace. The royal complex covered about 50 by 60 meters, comprising almost 50 rooms on the ground floor alone. A large central courtyard provided easy access to the palace's many rooms.
—*J.B.*

PATRICIA J. WYNNE

with a cuneiform script familiar from southern Mesopotamia. Most of the tablets were part of the floor of a house; they had evidently been discarded and reused as building material. Recently we have come across a heap of trash thrown over the palace wall, including many tablets. These written documents date to 2350 B.C., their age making them an important key to the culture.

The tablets are curious in one aspect: the script is Sumerian, but the language is Semitic. Philologists assume that Semites migrated into Mesopotamia around the end of the fourth millennium

B.C., intermingling with Sumerians and finally dominating Mesopotamian civilization. They adopted the Sumerian script—the only one available—to express their own language. The tablets of Tell Beydar represent the largest collection of Old Semitic texts found in the Khabur area.

The Semitic royal cities of Mari and Ebla had yielded archives of this period. Mari, discovered in the 1930s, lay halfway between southern and northern Mesopotamia and formed a link between the two cultures. Around 2400 B.C. it ruled much of the region to its

JOACHIM BRETSCHNEIDER

Burial chamber near city wall

north. Ebla, in western Syria, was discovered in 1968 by an Italian team led by Paolo Matthiae of the University of Rome "La Sapienza." Here the archaeologists found an extensive archive of cuneiform tablets, which describe trade relations with Nagar and Mari. Nagar was said to lie on an international trade route between the mountains, which were rich in ores, and southern Mesopotamia, with its major center at Kish.

Some of the tablets, deciphered by Walther Sallaberger of the University of Munich, speak of neighboring hamlets administered by Nabada. One group of texts informs us of the care taken of travelers, recording precisely the rations for people and animals. At one time, 11 teams of 44 onagers—a subspecies of the wild ass now found mainly in the north of Iran—had to be taken care of for four days, costing the city a considerable amount of grain. From other texts, Sallaberger concluded that onagers of high quality were bred in the region of Nabada and traded over hundreds of kilometers—as far as the city of Ebla.

Another text mentions the king of Nagar, who apparently ruled Nabada around 2350 B.C. This king visited the "province"—that is, Nabada—on occasions such as council meetings and ritual celebrations. A recently unearthed tablet lists delicacies provided to a woman named Paba, possibly the queen of Mari and spouse of King Iblul-il. Her visit illustrates the city's far-reaching political connections.

Daily activity in this ancient city is also revealed in the impressions made by seals. High officials in the palace possessed finely carved stone cylinders that they rolled over gobs of clay to seal doors, containers and documents [*see illustration on next page*]. We found many such seal impressions in Tell Beydar, on pots and doors of storage rooms and also at the entrances of the throne room and the temple. These rooms may have been opened only on special occasions. Many of the sealings are miniature masterpieces depicting celebrations, lively traffic on trade routes, war and diplomatic activity.

Historians now know that during the first half of the third millennium B.C., political and economic power in Mesopotamia were being concentrated in a few large centers. Thus, cities such as Kish, Lagash, Umma, Ur and Uruk in present-day Iraq and Chuera, Ebla, Mari, Nagar, Urkesh, Nabada and Tuttul in northern Syria came into being. (The earliest levels of Troy in northwestern Asia Minor and the early occupation of Byblos on the Lebanese coast also belong to this era.) Each of these cities contained fortification walls, palaces, storage areas and temple complexes.

The economic and political structure of southern Mesopotamia is relatively well understood. Burgeoning agricultural production allowed livestock to be raised communally. The surplus of food enabled specialized artisanal and administrative skills to flower, and a flourishing trade in raw materials such as copper spurred the evolution of centralized authority and power—as well as warfare. Perhaps the most far-reaching innovation was the craft of writing.

It is not clear that the northern cities followed a similar pattern. As in the south, the larger cities probably controlled extensive regions with vital trade routes. Nabada and its neighboring cities seem to have functioned as relay stations for caravans traveling the ancient routes between Anatolia (present-day Turkey) and Babylonia or between Egypt and Mesopotamia. Important families and a council of elders ruled, as in the south, and offered sacrifices to local and regional deities. A growing number of settlements also led to armed disputes over water rights, agricultural and pasture land, and control of trade routes.

Many questions remain. Historians would like to know who founded Nabada and other northern cities, where they came from, what language they spoke, and around what political and moral principles their society was organized. Moreover, Nabada appears to be quite distinct from the other circular tell that was examined, Tell Chuera. (Tell Chuera is, however, older than the levels so far excavated at Tell Beydar, and so a direct comparison cannot be made.) Chuera had monumental stone architecture (not just mud brick as in Nabada), and, more significantly, 15 years of digging have as yet yielded no evidence of writing. Nabada was probably more allied with southern Mesopotamia than with Tell Chuera, which had closer links with the civilization in Turkey.

After 500 years of prosperity, Nabada was abandoned around 2350 B.C. Why, we do not know; the other known cities of northern Mesopotamia declined at the same time. Perhaps the kings of Akkad, who conquered many of the city-states of Mesopotamia, burned Nabada as they did Ebla. At Nabada, however, no indications of fire or other destruction have been found.

Writings from Nabada

A picture of what life was like in Nabada can be found in the impressions made by seals. To produce a seal, palace officials rolled a finely carved stone cylinder over wet clay; when the clay dried, it sealed shut pots, documents, even doors. Many of the seals depict celebrations, lively traffic on trade routes, war or diplomatic activity. The photograph at the right shows a seal illustrating the use of wagons in both religious ceremonies and in war. —J.B.

Seal found on a container at Nabada

Carving a stone cylinder

Rolling a seal onto a jar

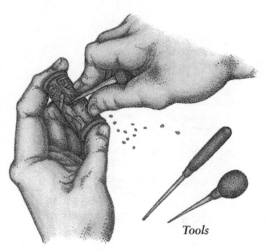

Tools

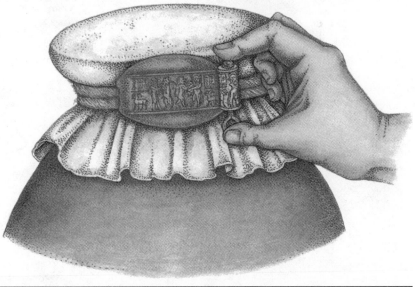

Some architectural changes may provide a clue to this mystery. Shortly before deserting the palace at Nabada, its inhabitants added a sanctuary and renovated several of the ritual rooms. Could this religiously motivated activity have been prompted by some natural event, such as a drought? Or do the deep fissures and cracks in the palace walls suggest a phase of intense earthquakes? Hartmut Kühne of the Free University of Berlin has suggested that a large increase in population caused the natural resources of the region to be overexploited, forcing a migration. It may simply be that a reduction in the number of

caravans traveling the trade routes made the northern cities uneconomical.

Tell Beydar was briefly reoccupied a few hundred years later. Around 2250 B.C., however, it suffered from plundering, decline and erosion. In the next millennium the Hurrians, a people who originated in the mountains of East Anatolia, arrived in the region, founding new royal cities such as Urkesh (excavated by Giorgio and Marilyn Buccellati at Tell Mozan). Around 1600 B.C. a Hurrian empire called the kingdom of Mitanni developed in the Khabur area. At its apex, around 1400 B.C., it extended all the way from the Mediterranean coast to the Zagros Moun-

tains. The Hurrians settled amid the ruins of Nabada, 1,000 years after the fall of the early Bronze Age metropolis.

In the lower town surrounding the abandoned palace of Nabada, outside and to the west of the fortification wall, some preliminary excavations have located remains of the Mitanni period. We came across a ceremonial vase decorated with rams' heads and a collection of ivory reliefs depicting lions and bulls that were probably once used as inlays for furniture. The Hurrians did not, however, build a palace, and overall Tell Beydar was far less important at this time than in its heyday as Nabada.

A New Language

The writings found at Nabada are unusual: the script is Sumerian, but the language is Semitic. The tablets of Tell Beydar (an example is shown below) represent the largest collection of Old Semitic texts found in the Khābūr area. Language experts have translated the symbols; a sample dictionary is shown below. —J.B.

Carving a clay tablet

Tablet written in a Semitic language, with Sumerian script

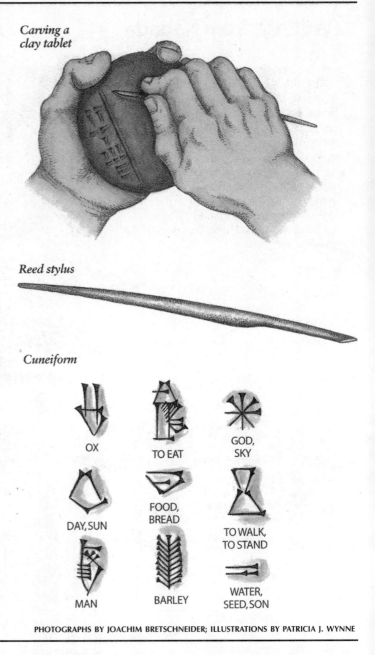

Reed stylus

Cuneiform

OX	TO EAT	GOD, SKY
DAY, SUN	FOOD, BREAD	TO WALK, TO STAND
MAN	BARLEY	WATER, SEED, SON

PHOTOGRAPHS BY JOACHIM BRETSCHNEIDER; ILLUSTRATIONS BY PATRICIA J. WYNNE

The empire of Mitanni perished in its turn, and in the eighth century B.C. Assyrians conquered the Khabur region. From Assur, their capital city to the northwest of Babylon, these warlike people increased in influence after 1100 B.C. For a brief period, they even advanced as far as Egypt. The Assyrians were feared by their enemies: they are said to have deported entire populations and slaughtered opponents without respect to sex or age.

The invaders settled on top of the earlier Hurrian occupation in the lower regions of Tell Beydar. Their stay was brief; Babylonians and Medes (from what was then Persia) combined their forces and attacked them. "All who hear the news of you clap their hands at your downfall," wrote the prophet Nahum in the Old Testament when Nineveh, the last and greatest capital of the Assyrian Empire, was reduced to ashes in 612 B.C.

With the fall of the Assyrian empire, Tell Beydar once again returned to dust and silence.

Further Information

EARLY MESOPOTAMIA: SOCIETY AND ECONOMY AT THE DAWN OF HISTORY. J. N. Postgate. Routledge, 1994.

THE STORY OF WRITING: ALPHABETS, HIEROGLYPHS AND PICTOGRAMS. Andrew Robinson. Thames and Hudson, 1999.

JOACHIM BRETSCHNEIDER studied archaeology and Oriental studies at the Westfälische Wilhelms University in Münster, Germany. He is an assistant professor at the Catholic University in Leuven. Bretschneider is leading the German team—from the Altorientalische Seminar of the University of Münster—of the Euro-Syrian excavations at Tell Beydar.

Out of Africa:
The superb artwork
of ancient Nubia

*The rich heritage and tradition of this venerable, long-neglected civilization
beside the Nile is now celebrated in four great Western museums*

David Roberts

David Roberts' latest book, Once They
Moved Like the Wind: Cochise, Geroni-
mo and the Apache Wars, *is published
by Simon & Schuster.*

To the ancient Greeks and Romans,
Nubia was one of the foremost civilizations of the world. Because its domain
lay on the edge of the unknown—south
of Egypt, along the tortured cataracts of
the upper Nile, where few Greek or Roman travelers had ventured—Nubia
shimmered with legend. But there was
no mistaking the area's might or wealth.

For centuries, exotic goods had
flowed north in an inexhaustible stream
from this African font: gold, frankincense, ebony, ivory, panther skins, giraffe tails and hippopotamus teeth.
Brave mercenary soldiers, virtuosos of
the bow and arrow, also traveled north
out of the storied land. Herodotus described Nubians as the "tallest and hand-
somest" people in the world, adding that
they reputedly lived to an age of 120,
thanks to a diet of boiled meat and milk.
Roman chroniclers reported that the
southern empire was ruled by queens.
From their own artwork, we know that
the Nubian ideal of female beauty put a
premium on fatness. Indeed, the sar-
donic Juvenal claimed that the breasts

of Nubian women were bigger than their
chubbiest babies. Writing in the third
century A.D., a romantic biographer of
Alexander the Great insisted that in Nubia there were whole temples carved
from a single stone, and houses with
translucent walls; the queen traveled in
a mobile palace on wheels drawn by 20
elephants.

Although these accounts veered into
the fabulous, Nubia was no mere phan-
tasm of the poets, no El Dorado. Within
Nubia, stretching along the Nile from
present-day Aswan in Egypt to Khar-
toum in the Sudan, at least six distinct,
supremely accomplished cultures
evolved between 3800 B.C. and A.D. 600.
Nubian civilizations lasted far longer
than either classical Greece or Rome.
Always a rival to the kingdom to its
north, Nubia conquered Egypt around
730 B.C. and ruled it for the following
60 years.

TA-SETI OR YAM OR WAWAT

Why is it, then, that most of us today
have barely heard of Nubia?

One reason is semantic. Over millennia, Nubia was known under many different names. To the early Egyptians, it
was Ta-Seti or Yam or Wawat. Later it

appears as Meroe. The Greeks and Romans called it Aethiopia (today's Ethiopia being Abyssinia to them). In the
Bible it appears as Kush.

Another reason has to do with prejudice. Nubia has always been exceed-
ingly remote and difficult of access.
From its Christianization in the 6th century A.D. all the way down to the 19th,
the kingdom vanished from the European record: only the glowing reports of
the classical authors kept its memory
alive. This neglect had everything to do
with race—for Nubia had been an African empire, and a black African one at
that. Even the Greeks perpetrated the
prejudice. An early biographer of Alexander the Great records the queen of
Nubia responding to an inquisitive letter
from the youthful conqueror in the following words: "Do not despise us for
the color of our skin. In our souls we
are brighter than the whitest of your
people."

The first archaeologists to document
the glory that was Nubia succumbed to
a kindred bias. Even as he dug the remarkable royal cemeteries of El Kurru
below the Fourth Cataract, George A.
Reisner, working for Harvard University
and the Boston Museum of Fine Arts,
concluded that the rulers whose tombs

he unearthed must have been an offshoot of a dynasty of Libyan (thus, white-skinned) pharaohs. For decades, everything Nubian was regarded as derived from the Egyptian, hence "decadent" and "peripheral."

Only now, perhaps, is the Western world beginning to acknowledge the achievements of ancient Nubia, as signaled by four dazzling new exhibitions at major North American museums. At the Boston Museum of Fine Arts (MFA)—which, thanks to Reisner and his colleagues, owns one of the finest collections of Nubian treasures in the world—a permanent display opened in 1992. Another permanent installation was unveiled the year before at the Royal Ontario Museum in Toronto. Through September 1993, the Oriental Institute Museum in Chicago will host "Vanished Kingdoms of the Nile: The Rediscovery of Ancient Nubia." And at the University of Pennsylvania's Museum of Archaeology and Anthropology, "Ancient Nubia: Egypt's Rival in Africa" recently opened. After closing in Philadelphia in October 1993, the exhibition will travel to seven other museums around the country, through 1996.

The exhibitions have had strong attendance, particularly among African-Americans, many of them in school groups. And there's evidence that awareness of Nubia is seeping into the popular culture. A new comic-book character called "Heru: Son of Ausar," which was created by cartoonist Roger Barnes, is a Nubian hero. A rap band out of New York City calls itself Brand Nubian.

The surge of interest in Nubia did not arise in a vacuum. For the past 30 years, scholars in Europe and the United States have been piecing together a vivid but tantalizing picture of the neglected civilization. Yet it took the building of a dam to stimulate this new appraisal of ancient Nubia.

Reisner, the pioneer of Nubian archaeology, was an Egyptologist working on the lower Nile in 1906 when the Egyptian government decided to raise the dam at Aswan by 16.5 feet. Before the resultant flooding could drown forever many unexcavated sites, Reisner was invited to survey and dig upriver. Thus was launched what one scholar calls the "earliest program of extensive salvage archaeology" in the world.

Close on Reisner's heels came two British archaeologists working for the University of Pennsylvania, David Randall-MacIver and Leonard Woolley. The rich collections existing today in Boston and Philadelphia derive from the seminal fieldwork of these scholars. Yet so strong was the lingering condescension toward Nubia as a kind of second-rate Egypt, that as late as 1960 only one American scholar—Dows Dunham, Reisner's protégé and successor at the MFA—was working in Nubian studies.

In 1959 Egypt announced plans to build a huge new dam at Aswan. The waters of the Nile would create Lake Nasser, stretching 300 miles south to the Second Cataract, just across the border in the Sudan. UNESCO launched an all-out appeal to the archaeologists of the world, who responded with scores of energetic expeditions, sowing the seeds of our current understanding of ancient Nubia.

The disruption wrought by the dam was tragic. Nubians whose ancestors had lived along the middle Nile for as long as the oldest tales could testify gathered their belongings and made their exodus north to the planned villages that would replace their own. They kissed the graves of their ancestors; many filled their pockets with sand, their only keepsake of the lost homeland.

LOSING ONE'S WAY COULD MEAN LOSING ONE'S LIFE

On the face of it, Nubia seems an unlikely place for a major civilization to sprout. It lies in the middle of the hottest and driest area on Earth's surface; in much of Nubia, rain never falls. Farther north, in classical Egypt, the Nile creates a generous floodplain up to 15 miles wide, but in Nubia the fertile land bordering the river comes only in intermittent patches rarely exceeding 1,600 yards in width. The cataracts—canyons seamed with big rapids—as well as long, tormented passages such as Batn el Hajar, the "Belly of Rocks"—make continuous navigation up and down the Nile impossible. In the Sudan, where the river makes two great loops in the shape of an S, the ancient trade routes struck off on bold shortcuts across the empty desert. To lose one's way often meant to lose one's life. Even today, travel here remains as difficult and as dangerous as anywhere in Africa.

As Reisner plunged into this archaeologically pristine wilderness, where he worked tirelessly from 1907 to 1932, he slapped provisional names on the various cultures he began to identify. Unfortunately, these temporary labels have stuck. Thus we still allude to some Nubian cultures—each as complex and impressive as, say, that of the Hittites or the Etruscans—as the A-Group, the C-Group and the X-Group.

With the emergence of the A-Group around 3800 B.C., Nubia takes its place on the prehistoric stage. We still know relatively little about this early civilization, which became a serious rival to Pre-Dynastic Egypt. The A-Group's most distinctive artifact is a handsome "eggshell" pottery, named for its thin walls. Crisscross hatches and geometric patterns in red and cream seem to conjure up weaving; it is as if the potters were celebrating the discovery of the vessel that worked better than basketry.

Toward the end of its thousand-year sway, the A-Group emerges also in the written record, as the Egyptians invented their hieroglyphic script. The domain of the blacks in the Lower Nubia was known as Egypt as Ta-Seti—the "Land of the Bow." Eventually the pharaohs waged war with Ta-Seti. A great victory around 2600 B.C. was won by the pharaoh Sneferu, who bragged that he took 7,000 Nubians and 200,000 domestic animals captive.

Bruce Williams of Chicago's Oriental Institute believes that the earliest definite evidence anywhere in the world of the institution of kingship may be among the A-Group of Nubia. Williams' argument hinges upon a handful of extraordinary objects found in royal A-Group graves. During my own visit to the Oriental Institute, Williams showed me a beautiful stone incense burner found at Qustul (just north of the Sudanese border), dated to around 3300 B.C.

The cylindrical burner is encircled by a frieze of incised figures.

Peering through the display glass, I followed Williams' pointing finger. "The falcon means a god," he said. "That's definitely a representation of a king, and he's wearing a crown. The bound prisoner is going to be bashed in the head in front of the god. The burner is definitely a typical Nubian, not an Egyptian, object."

Other scholars, however, reject Williams' theory. Says David O'Connor of the University of Pennsylvania, "I think there may well have been an elite group in Nubia at the time, in charge of a complex chiefdom. But the objects Williams' argument depends on are almost certainly Egyptian, not Nubian-traded to Nubia in early pharaonic times. The kings he sees were Egyptian kings."

One of the most formidable obstacles to an appreciation of ancient Nubia is that, in terms of the written record, we learn about the civilization almost entirely in the words of its enemies—Egyptians above all, but also Hebrews, Assyrians, Persians and Romans. Thus, for the Egyptians, Nubia is always "vile," "miserable," "wretched." The pharaohs had images of Nubians carved on their footstools and on the bottom of their sandals so that they could trample on their enemies daily.

The aggression of Egypt throughout the third millennium B.C. seems to have driven A-Group survivors south into the little-known lands above the Second Cataract. Around 2300 B.C., a pair of new cultures springs into view. One, appearing in Lower Nubia, was called by Reisner the C-Group. Elaborate tombs suggest these people were skilled pastoralists, raising huge herds of livestock and perhaps worshiping their gods through a cattle cult.

The C-Group kept peace with the kingdom to the north for centuries, during which time trade flourished and ideas flowed both ways. Then, in the 19th century B.C., the pharaohs turned belligerent again. Their motive may have been to control the gold mines that were being opened in the eastern desert. Thrusting above the Second Cataract, Egyptian armies built a series of colossal fortresses along the tortuous Belly of Rocks. These fortresses were placed so that line-of-sight signals could be flashed from one to the next.

Meanwhile, 170 miles beyond the southernmost Egyptian fortress, the most powerful empire Nubia had yet seen was flourishing. Named the Kerma culture by Reisner, who in 1913 excavated tombs close to the modern town of that name, it was known to the Egyptians as the Kingdom of Kush. An ancillary motive for erecting the Egyptian fortresses, with their intensely defensive character, was no doubt fear of Kush.

A FLAMBOYANT AND GRANDIOSE GLORY

After 1700 B.C., racked by internal struggles, Egypt retreated from Nubia, abandoning its fortresses along the Belly of Rocks. In the void, Kerma grew magnificently. Nothing declares the flamboyant, even grandiose glory of Kerma more forcefully than its royal tombs. The king was buried under a huge tumulus—a circular mound—with the diameter nearly the length of a football field. He was laid on a gold-covered bed, and the finest objects wrought of gold, bronze, ivory and faience were placed beside him. Into the tomb's central corridor crowded a host of followers and concubines (400 of them in one king's tomb), who, dressed in their best clothes, came willingly to be buried alive in honor of their master.

All through Nubia, from Reisner until the present day, burial sites have monopolized archaeologists' attention. This has been true in part because the remains of habitation sites are so hard to find; houses were made of perishable stuff, but tombs were built to last. Only two large villages from the C-Group, for instance, have ever been excavated. Consequently we know much more about the rulers of Nubia than about the commoners.

At Kerma, however, for the past 28 years an international team under Charles Bonnet, of the University of Geneva, has carried out one of the most ambitious digs in Africa. In the process, they have revealed not only the palaces and cemeteries but the main town of Kerma.

When I visited Bonnet in Geneva last fall, he showed me the plan of the settlement. Tapping an outlying area with his pencil, he said, "Just last year we found a whole new section of houses here. It goes on and on!" Bonnet's work documents the oldest city that has ever been found in Africa outside Egypt.

Many of the houses Bonnet's team excavated were rectangles of mud bricks, but the most characteristic domicile was a circular hut made of wood (always a rare substance along the Nile), topped with a thatched roof. Each hut was ingeniously designed to allow the prevailing north wind to blow through it during the desperate heat of summer; in winter, a temporary wall blocked the same breeze. Small neighborhoods of huts were bordered by fields and gardens where crops (chiefly wheat and barley) were raised, and cattle and goats pastured. No general plan governed the shape of the sprawling city, but a defensive palisade surrounded it.

Once more the tides of empire shifted. Around 1550 B.C., a newly invigorated Egypt invaded Nubia. The struggle against Kerma lasted 100 years, but at last the pharaohs conquered all but the southernmost reaches of Nubia. Their sway lasted another 350 years, during which the Nubian upper class became thoroughly Egyptianized, decorating their tombs with images of workers on date palm plantations and with performing dancers and musicians.

But the tides shifted again. At the end of the New Kingdom, about 1080 B.C., Egypt was torn by conflict between the pharaohs and the priesthood. The country began to fragment into city states, among them several in Nubia that became all but autonomous. What happened after 1080 remains a great mystery.

According to Timothy Kendall of the MFA, "the greatest gap in our knowledge of ancient Nubia is the period from 1000 to 850 B.C. We know almost nothing about it. Only one or two sites in Nubia can be dated to this period, and then, only to the latter part of it. Some experts believe Nubia was growing stronger and politically independent; others think that Egyptian enclaves and temple estates persisted. But these are theories spun out of thin air. Nobody really has a clue, except that a series of elaborate tombs began to be built in 850 B.C."

When Nubia emerged from this historical void in the eighth century B.C., it did so dramatically, achieving the greatest triumph in all its long history. By this time the center of power lay at Napata, which was just below the Fourth Cataract. Here a holy mountain called Jebel Barkal was believed to be the home of the ram-headed god Amun, who spoke oracles through statues and even selected the country's rulers.

Whatever their motive, after 750 B.C. the Napatan kings pushed boldly north. Around 730, a great army under a king named Piye conquered all of Egypt. He and his successors became the pharaohs of the 25th Dynasty, the later kings moving from Napata to Memphis to govern. The Nubian empire now stretched all the way from the junction of the Blue and White Niles to the delta (present-day Alexandria)—1,200 miles as the crow flies.

Although the inscribed victory stela Piye erected to proclaim his triumph alludes to him in Egyptian hieroglyphs as "raging like a panther" and bursting upon his enemies "like a cloudburst," the Nubian pharaohs of the 25th Dynasty ruled with an enlightened benevolence. They were Medicis, rather than Caesars, who awoke Egypt to the artistic and cultural splendor of its own past as they patronized artists, revived lost learning and rebuilt derelict temples.

Piye was also a great lover of horses, the first of four successive pharaohs to have whole chariot teams buried near his grave. The horses, interred in a standing position, were decked with bead nets and brilliant jewelry. When Piye conquered Hermopolis, the defeated King Nemlot opened his harem. But Piye averted his eyes from the women and demanded to see the king's horses instead. These he found nearly starved to death. "That my horses were made to hunger," he thundered at Nemlot (as recorded on Piye's stela), "pains me more than any other crime you committed in your recklessness. Do you not know God's shadow is above me?"

The brilliance of the Napatan empire speaks in many of the objects now on display in Boston, Philadelphia, Chicago and Toronto. In the MFA, I gazed at haunting rows of *shawabtis*, part of a cache of 1,070 found in the tomb of King Taharqo, Piye's son. Figurines carved out of alabaster and gray or black granite, ranging from seven inches to two feet in height, these sober-looking humans with arms crossed were "answerers" who would perform for the deceased king the work the gods commanded of him. (Here, I thought, was a humane alternative to the retainers buried alive at Kerma!)

One of the most exquisite objects ever recovered from Nubia is also on display in Boston. It is a small pendant from the tomb of one of Piye's wives, a gold head of Hathor, goddess of beauty, mounted on a ball of rock crystal, thought to have magical properties.

The Napatan supremacy was short-lived. By 667 B.C. the Nubian pharaohs had abandoned Egypt to another raging panther, King Esarhaddon of Assyria. Once again, we learn of a profoundly pivotal moment in Nubian history only in the contemptuous boasts of its enemies: "I tore up the root of Kush," crowed Esarhaddon, "and not one therein escaped to submit to me."

Gradually through the next four centuries, the Nubian political and cultural center shifted south beyond the Fourth Cataract. In isolation and relative obscurity, the last Nubian empire evolved. Its center was the town of Meroe, halfway between the Fifth Cataract and the junction with the Blue Nile.

Meroe, which flourished from about 270 B.C. to A.D. 350, is in many respects the most intriguing of all the incarnations of Nubian greatness. Cambyses of the Persians, as well as Petronius among the Romans, sent out armies to conquer the distant country, without success. Even Nero contemplated the possibility of an attack. Despite all this contact, the veil of mystery that clung to the legendary southern land never really lifted.

One reason was linguistic. In their isolation from Egypt, the Meroites lost the use of Egyptian hieroglyphs. By 170 B.C. they had developed their own written language, a quasi-cursive script now called Meroitic. Stelae and plaques covered with this writing abound. By 1909 scholars had proved that it was an alphabetic script (unlike the hieroglyphs, which are part ideographic, part phonetic and part alphabetic). Thanks to a few parallel inscriptions, they had learned the sound values for each of the 23 Meroitic letters. Yet more than eight decades later, the language remains undeciphered.

At first, scholars were confident that Meroitic would turn out to be a cognate of the Nubian tongues spoken today along the Nile. That hope faded, and all that the experts can now assert is that Meroitic seems to be related to no other known language. Decipherment must await the discovery of a Nubian Rosetta Stone—a stela with lengthy parallel texts in Meroitic and Egyptian or Meroitic and Greek.

A ROYAL OFFERING TO AMUN

In the MFA, I walked around and around a five-foot-tall stela found at Jebel Barkal; covered on all sides with writing, the stone bears the longest known inscription in Meroitic. We know the text has something to do with an offering by King Tanyidamani to the god Amun, and we can see places where lines have been deliberately erased. The rest is enigma.

Timothy Kendall tantalized me further by describing the second-longest Meroitic inscription known, found on a stela now in the British Museum. "If we could read it," he sighed, "we'd have the Meroitic version of the war against Petronius and the Romans in 24 B.C."

In its drift away from Egyptian culture over the centuries, Meroitic art developed its own idiosyncratic genius. At the Oriental Institute, Emily Teeter explained to me its quirks. "It becomes a very spontaneous art, full of free-flowing improvisation," she said, pausing before a Meroitic pot. "You see that?" She pointed to a curling snake painted on the vessel, holding in its mouth a drooping flower. "The flower is obviously an *ankh*."

I gasped in sudden recognition. I had seen many an *ankh* on Egyptian objects: a cross-shaped symbol topped with an oval, which is the hieroglyph for the verb "to live." In Egyptian art, the *ankh* appears alone or in rows of declarative rigidity. On the Meroitic pot, the snake stings the world to life with a flower. "The Egyptians are too staid for this," Teeter said. "They don't like loopy things."

At the University of Pennsylvania museum, David O'Connor guided me through several hundred Meroitic objects from the provincial capital of Karanog, excavated by MacIver and Wooley in 1907–08. The same freedom—a set of wild variations on Egyptian themes—graced these priceless objects. In Egypt, O'Connor explained, the *ba* statue, which represents a dead person's spirit, is a formal-looking bird with a human head; in Meroe, the *ba* becomes a human with wings. The pots dance with two-legged crocodiles, with giraffes ranging from the lordly to the comic, with deer darting through shadows. There are abstract designs made of endless waves of draped festoons and floral curlicues.

The sheer exuberance of Meroitic art proclaims a civilization that believed in pleasure and playfulness. The pots were largely used for wine drinking. At certain Meroitic sites, whole barrooms have been excavated.

At the end of the fourth century A.D., Meroe declined. The distinctive script fell out of use, and no new temples were built. It has long been the fashion to regard the 250-year interim before Christianity, whose culture Reisner called the X-Group, as a Nubian Dark Age; but recent scholars point to the continued excellence of pottery and jewelry, to a flowering of brilliant work in bronze and iron, as well as to the magnificent royal tombs at Ballana and Qustul, as signs of a healthy culture, original in its own right.

Although the Meroitic language seems to have been lost forever, scholars who travel in the Sudan have been struck by the remarkable survival in living cultures of traits and belongings they know also from archaeology. The wood-and-palm-fiber bed a Sudanese sleeps on today looks very much like ones found in royal tombs in Kerma. The throw-stick, a proto-boomerang still used for hunting today, is identical to ones retrieved by Reisner from a Kerma tomb. Even current Sudanese fashions in hairstyle and facial scarification find their counterparts in ancient paintings of Nubians.

Thus the discipline of ethnoarchaeology, still in its infancy, may yield new insights into Nubia, as scholars ask living informants to comment on ancient relics. Emily Teeter told me of a pair of small revelations. Shortly after the Oriental Institute's exhibition opened, she met Awad Abdel Gadir, a Sudanese teaching in Texas. He took her aside, pointed to a stone object and said politely, "That's not an incense burner. We have those in our village. It's a receptacle for a liquid offering." Teeter changed the label. He paused before a "thorn-removal kit" from the X-Group—a kind of Swiss Army Knife of iron tools on a chain, including tweezers, picks and scrapers. "I remember," said Abdel Gadir, "my grandmother used to wear a set like that on her belt."

Meanwhile, the archaeological surface of ancient Nubia has barely been scratched. The sites that lie in lower Nubia, north of the Egypt-Sudan border, are gone forever, swallowed by Lake Nasser. In the Sudan, the 1989 coup that brought Islamic fundamentalists to power, as well as the civil war that continues to rage in the country's south,

have made it harder than ever for Western archaeologists to work there.

Yet, in the Sudan, a French survey has counted one million ancient mounds, only a fraction of which have been excavated. There are more royal pyramids in the Sudan than in all of Egypt. I asked Timothy Kendall, who has done breakthrough work at Jebel Barkal, where he would dig if he had carte blanche to choose among the Sudan's best Nubian sites.

He leaned back in his chair, put his hands behind his head and smiled. "I'd go to Naga," he said, "although it's just a pipe dream, because the Sudanese Antiquities Service is saving it for themselves."

I knew Naga as a Meroitic site that, uncharacteristically, lay inland in the Butana Desert, some 25 miles south of the Nile. "Why Naga?"

"It's a complete Meroitic city founded about the first century A.D., with important temples, a settlement and a cemetery," Kendall answered. "The residents built an artificial reservoir of water. Not a single spadeful of earth has ever been turned there.

"Of course," he added, gazing off into space at the eternal dilemma that bedevils archaeologists, "you'd need a lot of money, a big team, a lot of cooperation, extreme physical endurance." He paused. "And a very, very long life."

ADDITIONAL READING

Nubia: Corridor to Africa by William Y. Adams, Princeton University Press, 1977

Meroe by Peter L. Shinnie, Praeger (New York), 1967

Nubia Under the Pharaohs by Bruce G. Trigger, Westview Press (Boulder, Colorado), 1983

The African Origin of Civilization: Myth or Reality by Cheikh Anta Diop, Lawrence Hill, 1974

Scythian Gold

An exhibition of treasures from ancient Ukraine illuminates a great warrior culture, notable for its relentless ferocity and remarkable art

By Doug Stewart

SOMEWHERE UP IN THE SWEET HEREAFTER, a grave gobber is cursing his eternal rotten luck for having plied his trade before the days of metal detectors. When he tunneled into a fifth-century B.C. Scythian burial chamber near a tributary of Ukraine's Dnieper River, he pocketed a goodly trove of gold artifacts scattered about the bones of a one-time Scythian strongman. But how was he to know that hidden under just a few inches of dirt next to the deceased were priceless masterpieces of solid gold: an ornate finial covered with a furious orgy of snarling, thrashing animals, a braided-gold necklace and an exquisite drinking cup with six horse heads patterned in a tight, whirling hexagon, their gold reins radiating from a disk of Baltic amber?

The owners of these treasures were violent, hard-living horsemen who dominated the European steppe from the seventh to the third century B.C. Like the Huns and the Mongols, who thundered across the same open grasslands centuries later, the Scythians lived in the saddle and traveled light. At the same time, oddly enough, they were among the ancient world's most extravagant art patrons. Nearly all their treasure, most of it finely wrought gold, was small enough to wear, befitting a people on the move.

"The elite within this nomadic culture were able to amass an incredible amount of wealth," says Gerry D. Scott III, curator of ancient art at the San Antonio Museum of Art, "and I guess, like the Egyptians, they believed they could

BRUCE WHITE

The charmingly rendered golden boar (above) likely served as the handle of a wooden cup.

take it with them, so fortunately we've been able to learn about their culture from their burials."

The three objects near the Dnieper that the looter missed remained hidden until 1990, when a team of Ukrainian archaeologists uncovered them. They are now highlights of a sumptuous new traveling exhibition, "Gold of the Nomads: Scythian Treasures from Ancient Ukraine," at Baltimore's Walters Art Gallery from March 7 to May 28. The show includes a number of other recently unearthed pieces, many of which have never before left Ukraine. With more than 170 artifacts—fanciful and attention-getting jewelry, weapons and ritual objects—this is the most comprehensive exhibition of Scythian gold ever assembled. It opened last fall at the San Antonio Museum of Art and will move from Baltimore to the Los Angeles County Museum of Art on July 2 and to the Brooklyn Museum of Art on October 29. Next year, it travels to Toronto's Royal Ontario Museum, Kan-

sas City's Nelson Atkins Museum of Art and the Grand Palais in Paris.

Neither Greek nor Asian, Scythian art arose from the creative interplay of nomadic Central Asia and the classical Mediterranean world, says archaeologist Ellen D. Reeder. Now deputy director for art at the Brooklyn Museum, Reeder curated the exhibition while at the Walters Art Gallery, in collaboration with Gerry Scott in San Antonio and experts on Scythian culture in Ukraine. Reeder also has edited the companion volume from Harry N. Abrams, Inc., *Scythian Gold: Treasures from Ancient Ukraine.* "There's a common idea that nomads are longhaired and unwashed, so they must be primitive, but that's not true," she says. The Scythians had a discriminating eye for good design, and the wealth to indulge it. By the fifth century B.C., the steppe-dwelling horsemen were important patrons of master goldsmiths living in Greek cities on the northern shores of the Black Sea. "It was a symbiotic relationship. The Greeks, who didn't want to leave their cities on the Black Sea, were happy to work with the Scythians, who didn't want to abandon their nomadic life." The result, she says, was "a wonderful new artistic amalgamation."

To traditional art historians, the Scythians are little more than a footnote. The neglect is due in part to the Scythians' lack of a written language and in part to their disdain for building houses, fortresses, temples, or monu-

 From *Smithsonian* magazine, March 2000, pp. 89, 90-94. © 2000 by Doug Stewart.

LYNTON GARDINER (2)

Left: A disk of hammered gold bearing a spotted leopard attacking a stag adorns the top of a fifth-century B.C. finial; the life-size limestone stele of a warrior once marked a Scythian burial mound. Right: This modern reconstruction of a Scythian warrior's battle dress, complete with iron-plated armor, is based on remains found in fifth- and fourth-century B.C. tombs.

BRUCE WHITE

Scythia was less a nation than a group of related, warring nomadic tribes. During the first millennium B.C., what was sometimes called Greater Scythia stretched from the Carpathian Mountains in eastern Europe to Mongolia, more than 4,000 miles away. The Scythians who roamed this vast sweep of grasslands were probably of Indo-European stock and may have spoken a language related to Persian. The new exhibition focuses on finds from tombs of the most powerful and sophisticated of these nomad groups, which the ancient Greeks called the Royal Scythians. Having swept into present-day Ukraine from Central Asia sometime after 700 B.C., they soon dominated the flat, fertile pastures from the Danube to the Don and viewed all other Scythians as their slaves.

These nomads had a fearsome reputation throughout the ancient world. At a time when the horse had not been domesticated for very long, the Scythians fielded the first truly effective mounted cavalry. The sight of Scythian warriors on horseback could have inspired the Greek myth of the centaur. And a biblical allusion to a horde threatening Babylon, in the Book of Jeremiah, possibly referred to a Scythian penetration into the Near East in the seventh century B.C.: "Behold, a people comes from the north.... They lay hold of bow and spear; they are cruel, and have no mercy. The sound of them is like the roaring of the sea; they ride upon horses, arrayed as a man for battle against you, O daughter of Babylon!"

Suddenly, wild-eyed horsemen broke ranks and galloped recklessly across the plain.

ments other than graves. The few eyewitness reports on the Scythians' ways were usually written by Greeks, who tended to be condescending if not hostile. The fifth-century B.C. physician Hippocrates reported that Scythians were "bloated" and "sweaty." His contemporary Aristophanes wrote them into his plays as stock comic characters who dressed outlandishly, spoke mangled Greek and drank to excess. More charitable was the fourth-century B.C. historian Ephorus. Some of the Scythians, he maintained, "excel all men in justice.... They not only are orderly towards one another ... but also remain invincible and unconquered by outsiders."

Following a fact-finding mission to the northern Black Sea coast in the fifth century B.C., Herodotus devoted much of Book IV of his *Histories* to tabloid-worthy tales of the Scythians' gruesome exploits. Wealthy Scythians, he reported, gilded the insides of their enemies' skulls and used them as drinking cups. "They treat the skulls of their kinsmen in the same way, in cases where quarrels have occurred." Though Herodotus professed not to admire the Scythians, he saluted their military success. "A people without fortified towns, living, as the Scythians do, in wagons which they take with them wherever they go, accustomed, one and all, to fight on horseback with bows and arrows, and dependent for their food not

LYNTON GARDINER

Left: One of the 16 Greek-made bronze vessels found in a peat bog with the remains of a shipwrecked trader, this fifth-century B.C. hydria bears the image of a siren. Right, gold boat-shaped earrings were derived from Greek prototypes, but modified to respond to Scythian taste. Below: A scene from a hammered gold gorytos cover reflects the interplay of Greek and Scythian artistry.

BRUCE WHITE

Darius the Great of Persia learned this to his regret when he invaded the Scythian heartland in 513 B.C. at the head of a 700,000-man army. The Scythians' use of "tactical retreat"—staying tauntingly just out of reach, while poisoning wells and burning fields as they withdrew—confounded the king and exhausted his troops. After several weeks, the Scythian army at last approached the Persian camp, ready to do battle. Suddenly, reported Herodotus, boisterous whoops arose from the Scythian lines as wild-eyed horsemen broke ranks and galloped recklessly across

upon agriculture but upon their cattle: how can such a people fail to defeat the attempt of an invader not only to subdue them, but even to make contact with them?"

BRUCE WHITE

"The sunlight would have jumped off all of this gold—it would have been fabulous."

---

the plain—in pursuit of a hare. "These fellows have a hearty contempt for us," Darius was said to mutter to an aide. Humiliated, the Persians began their retreat under cover of darkness that night.

On their home ground, the Scythians were invincible for four centuries. "Using the speed of their horses, these people in essence practiced an ancient form of blitzkrieg," Gerry Scott tells me as he and Ellen Reeder take me around the exhibition at the San Antonio Museum of Art. On display is a suit of reconstructed armor—leather covered with tiny, scalelike iron plates—based on archaeological finds. Nearby is a lavish gold cover for a gorytos, a combination bow-and-arrow holder that the Scythians apparently invented; its intricate gilded design suggests it was either ceremonial or belonged to a paramount chieftain. Next to it is an impressive array of arrowheads, used in hunting as well as combat.

"The Scythians were incredible archers," Scott says, "and they chose their weapons depending on what they were hunting. If they were after birds, they'd choose a delicate arrowhead because they aimed for the eye." Warriors might carry more than 200 needle-sharp arrows into battle. Several of the arrowheads, I notice, are barbed. "These were designed to do as much damage coming out as going in," Scott explains. Moreover, wrote Ovid of the Scythians' favored weapon, "a poisonous juice clings to the flying metal"—a juice brewed from snake venom, putrefied human blood and dung (to hasten infection). The Greeks dubbed the mixture "scythicon." Could there be any doubt that these people reveled in warfare?

Other than the weapons on display, however, most of the pieces in the exhibition exude a sense not of violence but of ostentatious refinement and even

charm. There are hammered-gold headdresses, decorative gold scabbards, elaborately wrought jewelry and embossed gold plaques the size of postage stamps that were sewn onto their clothing.

Though they were technically homeless nomads, the Scythians of the European steppe were nonetheless at the top of their world's pecking order. "The area north of the Black Sea was a breadbasket of the ancient Mediterranean world," Reeder says. "Grain exported from this region kept ancient Greece alive." The Scythians who ruled the area weren't farming the grain; more likely, they exacted tribute from those who did. They also commandeered a lively north-south trade in fur, timber and, perhaps, slaves. "They went from a pastoral culture to a military culture to the international import-export business," Reeder continues. "You have to admire their adaptability." In the process, they grew immensely wealthy, which allowed them to buy caravans' worth of gold (probably from the Urals or Central Asia) and to pay for artisans to shape it to their taste.

Scythians were fond of three pictorial motifs, which recur obsessively in their artwork: the leopard, the eagle and the stag. Most likely, these animals were cherished memories from the Scythians' origins in the mountainous wilds of Central Asia. Burial sites in the Altai Mountains, near Mongolia, have yielded artifacts with much the same imagery. The three animals, along with other beasts, appear as stylized, almost abstract forms. Worn on a gorytos or tunic, images of predators and prey might have served as good-luck charms for a hunter or a fighter. Often, the antlers and hooves of stags mutate fancifully into bird heads or spiral motifs. On one plaque, a tiny spotted leopard munches on a severed human head.

Oddly, horses rarely figure in the Scythians' animal-style art. Perhaps horses were too ordinary and too tame to merit immortality in art. One important exception is a pair of sixth-century B.C. cheekpieces carved in bone, with a horse head at one end and a single hoof at the other. The Scythians themselves are also notably absent from most of the objects on display, but here, too, there

are exceptions. One is a fourth-century B.C. solid-gold helmet on which long-haired warriors with embroidered tunics, tight-fitting leggings and tasseled scabbards menace one another with swords and spears. That all the combatants are dressed Scythian-style suggests a bit of internecine strife. "Herodotus records that these people did take scalps," Scott says, referring to one scene on the helmet. "The fact that the man on the ground is being grabbed by the hair is probably significant here."

Gold being a soft metal, this extravagant headgear was no doubt intended for show, not protection. Indeed, showiness seems central to the Scythian aesthetic. Nomads or no, these bold horsemen must have prided themselves on the lavishness as well as the sheer volume of their goldwork. "This makes sense," Scott says, "when you consider they were living in yurtlike structures that they took down and moved along with their livestock. In that situation, you can't put in a swimming pool to show you're elite." Better, he says, to concentrate on personal displays. One buried Scythian male was found wearing a gold earring, a heavy bronze torque, and gold beads, buttons and plaques on his clothing. Both men and women were buried with mirrors, possibly to admire themselves in the afterlife.

I take in a pair of earrings that would make a belly dancer blush, each an exaggerated boat hull from which dense clusters of golden ducks dangle on gold chains. Yes, Reeder says, an Athenian aesthete would have sneered at these as tacky gewgaws for nouveau riche barbarians. "The Scythians took a Greek design and made it bigger, made it fatter, made it louder," she explains.

Louder in more ways than one. Noisemaking pendants were a favorite of well-to-do Scythian women. A particularly elaborate pair of cascading headdress pendants would have jingled distractingly next to the wearer's ears. "When you move these, the pendants make a mesmerizing tinkle and rattle," Reeder says. "And when a woman walked through an encampment, the sunlight would have jumped off all of this gold—it would have been fabulous."

The imposing image of a horned lion-griffin and a frieze of battling animals enliven a fourth-century B.C. sword and scabbard.

One of the show's centerpieces is a very different kind of noisemaker. A mysterious bronze ornament, possibly a cap for a tent pole or a staff, consists of a set of curved branches with a nude goateed male (most likely a deity) in the center. Perched on his head, or maybe carrying him off, is an eagle with wings outstretched. "This was probably an important ritual object," Reeder says. "The sound it makes when it moves is just magical." A ritual use would help explain its jarringly different feel from the more refined, clearly secular objects in the show. Its form may hark back to homegrown Asian archetypes.

Later objects increasingly show the influence of Greek and Near Eastern figurative art. A golden scabbard from the late fourth century B.C. features a winged griffin. Another boasts a boar with a tightly curled mane, calling to mind the almost heraldic figures on Assyrian reliefs. Both these and a spectacular gorytos cover include the Scythians' favorite motif, animals in deadly combat. The gorytos, however, also offers a rare tableau of human figures interacting in some long-forgotten drama. The figures are Greek in style, but aspects of the scene are decidedly un-Greek. "Notice that each of the nude males has some strategically placed drapery," says Scott. Scythians were evidently prudes. And everyone's hands are almost comically busy, Reeder points out, unlike the classic Greek poses of effortless ease. Moreover, for reasons unknown, two of the women are perched on overturned stools.

Archaeologists have found the remains of a number of heavily armed Scythian women.

The routines of a dusty, windswept Scythian camp were certainly a world apart from the existence of a well-heeled urbanite in Athens or Babylon. Scythians spent their days and nights amid cattle, sheep, goats and, above all, horses. They drank fermented mare's milk, made mare's-milk cheese and ate horsemeat, along with other meat, domestic and wild. In lieu of bathing, Herodotus reported, Scythians crowded into tightly sealed woolen tents and tossed hemp seeds onto red-hot stones inside: "The Scythians enjoy it so much that they howl with pleasure." The historian seems to have been unfamiliar with the mood-altering properties of cannabis. The nomads also consumed huge quantities of wine, drinking it uncut with water (which the disapproving Greeks called "Scythian style").

The role of women and family is largely a mystery. A tale passed on by Herodotus recounted how a marauding band of Amazons clashed repeatedly with a Scythian contingent near the Sea of Azov. Discovering their foes were female, the Scythians dispatched their most virile young horsemen to make love, not war. The goal, according to

Herodotus, was to breed new warriors. The women were easily seduced but not so easily domesticated. Rebuffing the Scythians' marriage proposals, the Amazons explained: "We are riders; our business is with the bow and the spear... but in your country... women stay at home in their wagons occupied with feminine tasks, and never go out to hunt, or for any other purpose." Ultimately, Herodotus reported, the two groups rode off together and founded their own tribe. The women continued to dress as men and to hunt and fight. Although Herodotus' tale has long been taken as fiction, archaeologists in recent years have found the remains of a number of heavily armed Scythian women. Their weapons could be ceremonial, yet the graves are numerous enough, writes Esther Jacobson of the University of Oregon, a leading expert on Scythian art, "to allow one to conclude that there was in Scythian society a place for women to take up a warrior's role."

In any case, woman's work in a Scythian encampment held its own challenges. Herodotus wrote in amazement of the nomads' approach to cooking a feast on the steppe. "This has called for a little inventiveness, because there is no wood in Scythia to make a fire with." Thus a butchered animal would be simmered using its own paunch as a pot and its bones as fuel.

The Scythians didn't always travel so light, especially in later years. As early as the fifth century B.C., Greek traders were venturing far into the steppe north of the Black Sea. The exhibition in-

LYNTON GARDINER

This ritualistic staff ornament with pendant bells was designed to appeal to the Scythians' predilection for sound and movement.

cludes eight of the large bronze vessels uncovered by chance in 1961 in a peat bog along a tributary of the Dnieper. Greek in form and superbly ornamented, the containers were found with the remains of a capsized boat, hewn from the trunk of a massive oak, along with the bones of the boatman or trader. "These say a lot about the extensiveness of the Greek trade and the affluence of the Scythian customers," Reeder says. "You don't sail expensive things like these 300 treacherous miles upstream unless you're fairly confident they're going to be sold."

The Scythians' ever-growing possessions eventually undercut their mobile lifestyle. Inevitably, they began to settle down and intermarry with other groups. In the second century B.C. a new tribe of ruthless horsemen, the Sarmatians, swept across the steppe. In time, the displaced Scythians faded from history.

Although the Scythians' culture disappeared, their burial mounds, or kurhans, remained in Ukraine for millennia as mysterious holy sites. In place of grave markers, crudely carved stone figures stood at the top. Though the

European steppe has now been sliced by canals, factories and farms, thousands of these mounds still punctuate the table-flat Ukrainian landscape. The largest are the height of a six-story building and more than 300 feet across.

"The Scythians didn't just heap up whatever was around," Scott says. "They had layers of sod brought in, maybe to provide pasturage in the afterlife for the horses that were buried with their owners." Equine sacrifice was a staple of Scythian funerals. In one kurhan in 1898, archaeologists found the remains of more than 400 horses arrayed geometrically around the fallen warrior. The outside perimeter of another tomb yielded enough bones and amphora shards to suggest a knockout wake for about 1,000 people. Some mourners suffered more than hangovers. Herodotus reported that the funeral of important Scythians included the strangling and co-burial of consorts and retainers. Though the Father of History's credibility has often been challenged—Aristotle himself called him a "legend-monger"—archaeologists have dug up support for

many of his claims, including evidence of human sacrifice.

Many kurhans were looted almost immediately, perhaps by local peasants who'd been recruited to build them. Burial chambers, however, are hazardous sites. "Some of the tomb robbers weren't too clever and ended up part of the archaeological record," says Scott. With Scythian grave robbing a cottage industry by the early 1700s, Peter the Great ordered that looters be arrested and that the gold and other finds be added to the Russian imperial collections.

Methodical investigation of Scythian kurhans began only in the 19th century. The tombs have yielded not only gold but also pottery, wagons, remnants of clothes, even residues of cosmetics. With independence in 1991, Ukraine is looking to Scythian history, and that of the new nation's other legendary horsemen, the Cossacks, as it seeks to flesh out its own national heritage. These days, though, the government has little money for archaeological digs. "In Soviet times, there were more than 50 teams working in Ukraine on Scythian archaeology," says Denis Kozak, deputy director of the country's national archaeological institute. "For now, there are only two teams still working."

Wonderful finds continue to surface, nonetheless; a spectacular gold necklace and a pair of headdress pendants in the exhibition were unearthed only in 1998. Kozak and others in Ukraine and the United States hope the current tour will spark new interest in Ukrainian history and new support for Scythian archaeology. Herodotus wrote of a remote place called Gerrhi, where the richest Scythian tombs were said to be clustered. Some scholars believe Herodotus was misinformed. Others believe Gerrhi can be found. If the optimists are right, and the looters haven't gotten there first, look for a grander and even more dazzling exhibition of Scythian gold a few years hence.

The author, a regular contributor, wrote about American designers Charles and Ray Eames in the May 1999 SMITH-SONIAN.

Unit 4

Key Points to Consider

❖ What can be learned about Inca civilization from 500-year-old mummies?

❖ Where are the places in modern life that serve the purpose of an agora?

❖ What do sports, such as those of Rome and Greece, tell you about the interests of a society?

❖ Why have people throughout time been interested in Cleopatra? What are the historical problems in finding the truth about this woman?

❖ Compare life in the cities of Rome and Petra. Which would you choose? Was it better in Athens?

 **Links**   # www.dushkin.com/online/

These sites are annotated on pages 4 and 5.

Life in the ancient world was likely to be short and brutal. Poor nutrition, disease, hazards of childbirth, warfare, and violence all took their toll. In the Roman Empire, for example, only one child in eight could expect to reach 40 years of age. Since people were often judged by their usefulness, long life was not necessarily a blessing. Women were often subservient and mistreated, criminals and slaves were publicly slaughtered, and unwanted children were abandoned to die. Yet, at the same time, humankind built splendid cities, formed empires, wrote history, invented sports, and created great art. Aspects of this growing diversity are examined in this section.

In the New World, civilization evolved later than in the Old World, perhaps due to the pattern of migration to that hemisphere and the later development of agriculture. The Aztecs, Maya, and Inca, nonetheless, constructed magnificent stone cities and developed complex social and economic institutions. Unfortunately, most of these accomplishments were destroyed during the Spanish invasion. In addition, many of the native people died due to the widespread disease brought by the Europeans (see Unit 7, "How Many People Were Here Before Columbus?"). The achievements of Inca civilization, a nonliterate society, have been seen in the ruins of their cities and road system, but recently young sacrificial victims, frozen for 500 years on high Andean peaks, have been recovered. The mummies of these children should reveal more about the Inca people.

Athens, in the Old World, developed into one of the most interesting of the ancient Greek city-states and was important for the origin of modern ideas about government, art, sport, and philosophy. At the center of the city was the agora, a plaza surrounded by civic and religious buildings. In Athens, the agora served as meeting place for merchants and scholars, as John Fleischman points out in his article, "In Classical Athens, a Market Trading in the Currency of Ideas."

From the decorations on Athenian pots, modern sports historians have found illustrations of Greek athletics. The Greeks represent the highest level of development in ancient sports, but other peoples—Minoans, Egyptians, Etruscans, Romans—also enjoyed sporting events. Allen Guttmann, one of the leading scholars of sports history, reviews this sporting interest in his article, "Old Sports." The most significant development was the Olympic Games of Greece that lasted 1,100 years. Although it was based upon military and survival skills, this was the event that inspired the Olympic Games of the present time.

The Romans absorbed Greek culture, including the ideas about Greek sports. Life in ancient Rome, as examined by Lewis Lord in "The Year One," was nonetheless likely to be brutal, unhappy, and brief. Even for Cleopatra, the queen of Egypt, life ended at age 39. Barbara Holland, with wry skepticism, relates what happened to Cleopatra's history at the hands of entertainment and pop culture.

Although the Roman Empire encircled the Mediterranean Sea, its influence reached throughout Europe and northern Africa. At Petra, an oasis city established by the Nabataeans for caravans traveling across the Middle Eastern deserts, a happier life flourished until the Romans altered the trade routes. As explained in the article, "Secrets of a Desert Metropolis," Petra withered in the sun and now remains only as a tourist attraction for the country of Jordan.

The Later Civilizations to 500 C.E.

Tiny Sacrifices at 22,000 Feet

Archaeologists find mummified Incan children on an Andean peak

By Jonah Blank

At the peak of an Andean volcano, three children were found cold, with gold—and 500 years old. They certainly didn't look their age: The ice mummies unveiled in Argentina last week may be the best-preserved ancient human remains ever discovered. The bodies, two girls and one boy, ages between 8 and 15, were probably left at this towering height as sacrificial victims offered to Incan deities. One wore a white feather headdress and a yellow mantle with ornate geometric patterns.

Gasping for breath in the oxygen-poor atmosphere 22,057 feet above sea level, nine archaeologists, workers, and guides spent nearly two weeks battling adverse conditions, including ferocious blizzards and 70-mph winds. For three days the team members were trapped in their tents under about 3 feet of snow, with the temperature at times 20 degrees below zero. "Even taking off my gloves to write notes was a major ordeal," expedition co-director Maria Constanza Ceruti recalled from Argentina. The altitude of the summit—only 6,971 feet lower than that of Mount Everest—can cause the brain to swell and the lungs to fill with fluid.

Johan Reinhard, primary organizer of the American-Argentine-Peruvian expedition sponsored by the National Geographic Society, had been scouting out this mountain peak since 1983 and had already brought 16 ice mummies down

from other Andean summits. He knew the Incas were inclined to offer human sacrifices on the highest possible spots. "You feel like you're on the top of the world there," he said, after bringing the mummies down last week.

The weight of history. After using picks and shovels to dig through 5 feet of rock and frozen earth, the crew had to lower a graduate student into the pit by his ankles to lift the mummies out of their sanctuary. The team wrapped the bodies in protective foam and ice and carried the 80-pound burdens down the mountain in backpacks. Ceruti said she knew the find was remarkable when she saw the children's fingernails and the fine hairs on their arms, still preserved after five centuries. But the discovery's full import wasn't clear until CT scans revealed all the internal organs in two of the bodies to be intact.

David Hunt, a biological anthropologist at the Smithsonian Institution, said the find would probably prove to be even more impressive than "Juanita," the Incan "Ice Maiden" Reinhard discovered in Peru four years ago.

Unlike most mummies found elsewhere, the children's bodies have been in near-perfect states since the time of their deaths: The permafrost of ice-packed rock and dirt kept the internal organs and bodily fluids frozen rather than freeze-dried. Normally, the fluids in a corpse quickly bring about decay.

Embalmers of Pharaonic Egypt and other ancient cultures painstakingly removed fluids to ensure preservation in hot, dry climates.

"Accidental" mummies have survived when nature served as an embalmer instead. The Ice Maiden Juanita—whom President Bill Clinton once jokingly said he might be tempted to ask out on a date—and the famous 5,300-year-old "Ice Man" discovered in the Italian Alps in 1991 were desiccated by exposure or repeated cycles of thawing and refreezing. The 1,000-year-old Bog People found at various sites in Northern Europe were turned to leather by the tannic acid of the peat into which they'd been cast. The newly discovered ice mummies, however, were saved from dehydration by the perpetual cold of their high-altitude burial site.

The fact that these mummies have not been desiccated makes them a particularly valuable source of information: Scientists can examine the corpses the same way that a coroner would perform an autopsy on a murder victim. Arthur Aufderheide, a University of Minnesota-Duluth expert on New World mummies who also worked as a pathologist, says the plasma of these bodies might reveal what diseases were present in the pre-Columbian Andes.

"This is the sort of thing folks like me dream about," says Aufderheide, whose research on 1,000-year-old mum-

From *U.S. News & World Report*, April 19, 1999, pp. 60-61. © 1999 by U.S. News & World Report. Reprinted by permission.

mies proved that tuberculosis was present in the New World 500 years before its widespread distribution by Europeans. Studying historical patterns of disease, Aufderheide says, can help predict future outbreaks, and the DNA of ancient microbes could assist doctors fighting their modern descendants.

Keys to kinships. DNA fingerprinting of the mummies might also help trace genetic links between the Incas and other societies. "Blood serum can show relations between distant populations," says the Smithsonian's Hunt. Analysis of samples drawn from modern individuals is complicated by the social mobility and subsequent genetic intermingling of the past five centuries. The DNA of a pre-Columbian population would be more homogeneous. "If we found a rare genetic marker shared with a group as far off as the Arctic Circle or Asia," Hunt says, "that could tell us a lot about how and when South America was settled."

For cultural anthropologists, the discovery provides striking details about the ritual life of the Incas. For nearly a century prior to the Spanish conquest of 1532, the Incan empire encompassed much of what is now Peru, Ecuador, Bolivia, Chile, and Argentina. That period remains shrouded in mystery: Unlike earlier Central American peoples such as the Maya, the Incas had no written language. Highly skilled as mathematicians and builders, they kept the records of a vast kingdom with a complex system of knots tied in strings of varying lengths and colors. Apart from archaeological artifacts, the only evidence modern scholars have about the culture of the Incas comes from accounts written during the time of the Spanish invasion. Those accounts often focused solely on recording "idolatrous" practices as a prelude to obliterating them.

The Incas' most controversial custom was human sacrifice. They did not practice it nearly as often as did the Maya, Aztecs, and Toltecs (the Incas preferred to slaughter llamas or guinea pigs). But on occasions of special importance such as coronations or natural disasters, young children were offered up in a rite called *capac cocha*. The Incas also gave their gods the most valuable gifts they could—the burial site unearthed last week included statuettes made of gold, silver, and rare shells from the far-distant ocean—so the sacrifice of an unblemished, aristocratic child was seen as a particularly auspicious offering. "This find could answer many questions about the *capac cocha* ritual," says Richard Burger, a specialist in Peruvian archaeology at Yale University.

The Incas considered mountains sacred: The higher the mountain, the closer to divinities represented by the sun and the moon. "It was almost a spiritual moment when we saw the face of the first girl," said Ceruti. "At the summit, I looked at her and tried to imagine her last moments." For Ceruti, Reinhard, and the rest of the team, however, the search is far from over. They know the high Andes have many secrets left to tell. The day after announcing their find, the crew set out again for Mount Llullaillaco to continue their search.

In Classical Athens, a market trading in the currency of ideas

For 60 years, archaeologists have pursued secrets of the Agora, where Socrates' society trafficked in wares from figs to philosophy

John Fleischman

John Fleischman, who wrote about the excavation of the legendary site of Troy in a past Smithsonian, *braved Athens' summer heat on the trail of his story.*

Athens on an August afternoon: the clear radiant light of Greece suffuses every stone and walkway. From my vantage point, I squint upward to the outcropping of the Acropolis, crowned by Athena's temple, the Parthenon; hordes of tourists lay constant siege to the site. Standing at the base of that fabled rampart, I begin to traverse a quiet, heat-baked square, crisscrossed by gravel paths, dotted with the stubs of ancient walls and scrubby pomegranate and plane trees.

This dusty archaeological park, a sanctuary amid the roar of overmotorized Athens, is in fact one of the most remarkable sites in Classical archaeology. I am crossing the Agora—or central marketplace—of ancient Athens. That this place still exists seems nothing short of miraculous. I am walking in Socrates' footsteps.

The gadfly philosopher frequented this very square—as did his compatriots in the extraordinary experiment that was Classical Athens. Shades of Pericles, Thucydides, Aristophanes, Plato. They

all strolled in this place—the Agora, where philosophy and gossip were retailed along with olive oil. And where Classical Athens actually lived, traded, voted and, of course, argued. The Agora was the city's living heart. Here, politics, democracy and philosophy (their names, after all, are Greek) were born.

For every ten tourists who climb to the Parthenon, only one discovers the precincts of the serene archaeological site at its base. Those visitors are in fact missing an excursion into history made palpable, as well as a glimpse into what must be acclaimed as one of this century's most triumphant urban archaeology undertakings.

Since 1931, the American School of Classical Studies has been digging here, unearthing a dazzling array of artifacts from the layers of history compacted under this earth: Neolithic, Mycenaean, Geometric, Classical, Hellenistic, Roman, Byzantine and more—all collected from this 30-acre site. Still, it is the objects from Classical Athens that seem to speak with greatest resonance.

And fortunately for those of us unable to make it to Athens anytime soon, we have a chance to see for ourselves some of the Agora's most celebrated artifacts. The occasion of this opportunity

is a striking anniversary: 2,500 years ago, the Athenian reformer Cleisthenes renounced tyranny and proclaimed the birth of a radically new form of government, democracy. His genius was to offer a straightforward plan. To diffuse powerful political factions, Cleisthenes reshuffled the Athenian city-state into ten arbitrary tribes and called 50 representatives from each to a senate, or boule, of 500. This, then, was the beginning of democracy, however imperfect and subject to subversion and strife it might have been.

Hence the arrival of the exhibition "The Birth of Democracy," which opened recently in the rotunda of the National Archives in Washington, D.C. and continues there through January 2, 1994. A few steps from our own Declaration of Independence, Constitution and Bill of Rights lie the humble tools of Athenian self-government, nearly all of them unearthed in the Agora over the past 60 years by American excavators.

You can look upon actual fourth-century B.C. Athenian jurors' ballots, discovered still inside a terra-cotta ballot box. The ballots, stamped "official ballot," look like metal tops. Each juror was handed two; the spindle shafts designated the vote, solid for acquittal and hollow for guilty. Taking the spindle ends between thumb and forefinger, an Athenian juror was assured that no one could see which spindle he deposited in the ballot box.

FOR THE TOO POWERFUL, A DECREE OF EXILE

Also on view are ostraca, pottery fragments on which Athenians inscribed the names of persons they felt too powerful for the good of the city and deserving of ostracism, or ten years' exile, a procedure formalized by Cleisthenes. More than 1,300 ostraca, condemning many famous figures—Pericles, for instance, and Aristides and Themistocles—have been found in the Agora. Looking closely at the sherds, you can spell out the names straight from the history books and realize that these ostraca were written out by contemporaries who knew these men personally. And in some cases hated them.

Ostracism was not the worst punishment the democracy could decree. The National Archives also displays a set of distinctive pottery vials uncovered from the fifth-century B.C. Athenian state prison. These tiny vials were used to hold powerful drugs, such as lethal doses of hemlock. Socrates swallowed just such a dose, voted for him in 399 B.C. by his fearful fellow citizens. Archaeologists say the death scene of Socrates described in Plato's *Phaedo* fits the layout of a precise location in the Agora—a building near the southwest corner of the market square.

Plato recounts that after Socrates took the poison, he walked about, then lay down, telling his friends to stop weeping "for I have heard that one ought to die in peace." When the numbness spread from his legs upward to his abdomen, he covered his face. His last words were, as always, ironic. Socrates claimed he had a debt to the god of medicine. "I owe a cock to Asclepius," he informed a companion, "do not forget, but pay it."

The exhibition contains several other objects associated with Socrates, including part of a small marble statue, thought to be of the philosopher, that

was also recovered from the prison. Visitors can find, as well, actual hobnails and bone eyelets from the Agora shop of one Simon the cobbler. Socrates is known to have met at such a shop with young students and prominent Athenians alike.

The boundaries of the Agora were clearly marked, and entrance was forbidden to Athenian citizens who had avoided military service, disgraced themselves in the field—or mistreated their parents. Around the open square, but outside its actual boundaries, lay the key civic buildings—courts, assembly halls, military headquarters, the mint, the keepers of the weights and measures, commercial buildings and shrines to the city gods. One such shrine, the Altar of the Twelve Gods, stood within the Agora and marked the city's center.

On business days, the square was filled with temporary wicker market stalls, grouped into rings where similar wares were offered. There was a ring for perfume, for money changing, for pickled fish, for slaves. The Agora was a constantly changing mix of the mundane and the momentous—pickled fish and the world's first democracy. The comic poet Eubulus described the scene: "You will find everything sold together in the same place at Athens: figs, witnesses to summonses, bunches of grapes, turnips, pears, apples, givers of evidence, roses, medlars, porridge, honeycombs, chickpeas, lawsuits, beestings-puddings, myrtle, allotment machines, irises, lambs, water clocks, laws, indictments."

"The Agora was a place for hanging out," according to archaeologist John M. Camp, who is my patient guide this afternoon. "You'd have men of affairs doing a little business, conducting a little politics and stirring up a little trouble." Camp has spent most of his adult life digging here, and he's tireless even in the heat. (He's also the author of *The Athenian Agora*, an erudite and delightful guide to the site, written for a general audience.) The real pleasure of studying this site, he says, is the shock of recognition. "Our own ideas, our own concepts originated right *here*," he told me, gesturing toward the bright open square of the Agora. "It's not only democracy, it's virtually all of Western

drama, law—you name it. Over and over again, you find the only thing that's really changed is the technology. Everything else, they thought of it before. They did it before, and it all happened *here*."

IN THE BEGINNING, ARCHAEOLOGISTS BANKED ON HOPE

The open Agora at midday is suited only for mad tourists and foreign archaeologists, both on tight schedules. The tourists can see the Agora today because American archaeologists (funded in large part by American philanthropists—principally John D. Rockefeller jr. and the David and Lucile Packard Foundation) saved the site from total obliteration. At the outset, the archaeologists who began nosing around here in the late 1920s were banking on educated hope. Although the memory of the Agora was preserved by sources such as Plato and the historian Xenophon, tantalizing description was all that remained. That celebrated site had vanished at least 1,400 years before, lost to waves of pillaging barbarians, buried under layers of settlement from medieval times on.

In short, no one knew for sure where the ancient Agora really was. (Greek and German archaeologists had made some tentative beginnings in the 19th century, but their efforts had shed little light on the actual location.) The most likely site, authorities agreed, was at the foot of the northwestern slopes of the Acropolis. That area, however, was buried beneath a dense neighborhood of 19th-century houses and shops.

The debate remained largely academic until 1929, when the Greek government offered to the American School of Classical Studies a dig-now-or-forever-hold-your-peace deal. The Americans would have to demolish 300 houses and relocate 5,000 occupants. The Greek government required that a permanent museum be built for any finds and that the Agora be landscaped as a park.

The American School finally commenced excavations in 1931. As archaeologists have labored here for more than

60 years, we can read the life and times of Classical Athens in the spaces they have cleared and excavated.

Take the Panathenaic Way, for example, a diagonal street running uphill to the Acropolis. The roadway is packed gravel today, as it was in the days of the Panathenaia, the city's great religious festival. The celebrations began with the Athenian cavalry leading a procession of priests, sacrificial animals, chariots, athletes and maidens across the Agora to the temples of the gods above. All of Athens would have gathered along this route to witness the splendid parade wending across the marketplace. One Panathenaic event, the *apobates* race, in which a contestant in full armor leapt on and off a moving chariot, continued in the Agora well into the second century B.C.

With or without armor, walking uphill is not a recommended Athenian summer-afternoon activity. But taking your time and picking your shade, you can cut across the square to the base of a sharply inclined hill and look upward at a large Doric temple just beyond the western limit of the Agora. This is the Hephaisteion—a temple dedicated to Hephaestus, the god of the forge, and to Athena, patron deity of the city and of arts and crafts. Excavations have shown that it was once surrounded by shops where bronze sculpture, armor and fine pottery were made. Today the world's best-preserved Classical temple, it is a marvel unto itself. Somehow it has survived from Pericles' time onward, a marble monument to the miracle of Athens.

The temple's friezes are carved with scenes that spoke to the imagination of every Athenian. Theseus battling the Minotaur, the labors of Hercules, the Battle of the Centaurs—all images from a world where gods and men resided in a kind of rarefied complicity.

Below the Hephaisteion stood the most important buildings of the Athenian city-state. Here was the Bouleuterion where the 500 representatives of the tribes met. (An older assembly hall stood next door.) Nearby was the round, beehive-shaped Tholos where the 50 members of the executive committee of the Boule served 35- or 36-day terms of continuous duty, living and dining in the Tholos at state expense. (Those early practitioners of democracy apparently subsisted on simple fare—cheese, olives, leeks, barley, bread and wine. No lavish state dinners yet.)

In front of the Bouleuterion stood the statues of the Eponymous Heroes, the ten tribal namesakes chosen by the Delphic Oracle (and the source of our word for a group or thing named after a real or mythical person). Athenians tended to throng before this monument—not out of piety but because this was the site of the city's public notice board, a kind of proto-daily-paper for ancient news junkies. Nearby lay the Strategeion where the ten military leaders of the tribes made their headquarters (and gave us a Greek word for military planning).

North of the Bouleuterion complex rose the Stoa, or covered colonnade, of Zeus, a religious shrine but apparently an excellent place to practice philosophy. Both Plato and Xenophon said that the Stoa of Zeus was a favorite teaching post of Socrates. No one is more closely associated with the Agora than Socrates. He lived his life here. He met his death here. Xenophon remembered his former teacher moving among the market tables and stoas: "he was always on public view; for early in the morning he used to go to the walkways and gymnasia, to appear in the agora as it filled up, and to be present wherever he would meet with the most people."

As much as Socrates enjoyed the public scene in the Agora, he made it clear, according to Plato, that he was not a "public" person, that is, he was not interested in politics. This was a scandalous opinion to hold in Athens, where the real work of every Athenian citizen was just that—being a citizen. In Plato's *Apology,* Socrates rounded on his critics: "Now do you really imagine that I could have survived all those years, if I had led a public life, supposing that . . . I had always supported the right and had made justice, as I ought, the first thing?"

He had learned the hard way. Allotted to a turn in the Bouleuterion in 406–05 B.C., he was assigned to the Tholos as a member of the executive committee. And thus it fell to Socrates to preside over a wild meeting of the mass Athenian Assembly when word arrived of the sea battle at Arginusae. It was an Athenian win, but the victorious generals were accused of leaving their own dead and dying behind. The majority moved to condemn the generals to death as a group without individual trials. Socrates resisted. "Serving in the Boule and having sworn the bouleutic oath [to serve in accordance with the law], and being in charge of the Assembly, when the People wished to put all nine [actually eight of the ten] generals to death by a single vote, contrary to the laws, he refused to put the vote," according to Xenophon. "He considered it more important to keep his oath than to please the People by doing wrong."

That was the sort of behavior that could earn you a great many enemies. Eventually, three citizens brought charges against Socrates for mocking the gods and corrupting Athenian youth. The exact location of the courtroom where Socrates stood trial still eludes identification, but the place of his indictment, the Royal Stoa, has been excavated. As for the place of his death, if you hunt carefully on the rising slope beyond the Tholos, you can find the low precinct of exposed stones that archaeologists believe was the site of his demise.

The precise forces and circumstances that led to the jury's death sentence have never been elucidated completely. What is clear is that the questions raised by that trial so long ago are not dead letters. Dissent versus consent, public good versus private conscience, they still buzz about the ears of modern democracies. "I am the gadfly which the god has given the state," Socrates told his jury in the *Apology,* "and all day long and in all places am always fastening upon you, arousing and persuading and reproaching you."

The Athenian Agora still buzzes with surprises and mysteries. In 1981, on the northern edge of the Agora, Princeton archaeologist T. Leslie Shear jr. hit the corner of one of the most famous buildings of ancient Athens, the Poikile, or Painted, Stoa. This discovery was stunning good news for Agora archaeology. The structure had been renowned throughout the ancient world for its spectacular wall paintings. The glowing images, covering enormous wooden panels, lionized Athenian victories both mythological (over the Amazons, for instance) and historical (over the Persians at Marathon).

The fabled paintings were removed by the Romans in the fourth century A.D. but survived long enough to have been described by the second-century A.D. chronicler Pausanias. "The last part of the painting," he recorded, "consists of those who fought at Marathon.... In the inner part of the fight the barbarians are fleeing and pushing one another into the marsh; at the extreme end of the painting are the Phoenician ships and the Greeks killing the barbarians who are tumbling into them."

For Athenians, the Painted Stoa was the arena of their triumphs made visible. It was also a hotbed of philosophical speculation, eventually turning up as the gathering place of the third-century B.C. followers of Zeno of Citium. Zeno preached that the wise man should remain indifferent to the vanities of the transient world. The people of Athens associated the school of thought with the building, calling Zeno's disciples Stoics and their philosophy Stoicism. And 2,300 years later, so do we.

Stoicism is a necessity in Agora archaeology. As Leslie Shear explains, his father had, in some ways, an easier time of it here. The elder Shear supervised the original excavations during the 1930s. He had a squad of colleagues and 200 paid workmen to take down a whole neighborhood at a time. This summer, Shear has John Camp, his coinvestigator and colleague of 25 years, a nine-week season, and 33 student volunteers (American, Canadian and British) in addition to a small crew of Greek workmen who handle the heavy machinery and earthmoving. And he has his wife, Ione, a highly trained archaeologist in her own right, who has also worked at the site for 25 years.

Pursuing the Agora in the present Athens real estate market is tedious and expensive. It is house-to-house archae-ology—negotiation, demolition and then excavation. While he has been busy elsewhere on the site, Shear is still waiting patiently to acquire the five-story building that is standing on the rest of the Painted Stoa.

Meanwhile, every water jug, bone or loom weight excavated anywhere in the Agora must receive a numbered tag. Every number goes into the dig's records, meticulously kept in special 4-by-6-inch clothbound notebooks. When in use in the field, these notebooks reside in an old, cheap suitcase that sits on a rough wooden desk that looks even older and cheaper. With a folding umbrella for shade, this is the nerve center for the dig. The senior archaeologists sit here, drawing tiny diagrams of the strata and the find location for every tagged item.

MAY 28, 1931: "H. A. THOMPSON COMMENCED . . ."

It is, as Camp puts it, "dinosaur-age" archaeology in the era of field computers, but it works. Completed notebooks go into filing cabinets in offices inside the Stoa of Attalos. (This colonnade, originally a great commercial arcade in the second century B.C., was completely reconstructed in the 1950s to house the excavation's museum, laboratories, offices and storage vaults.) There the records march back in unbroken order through the decades to May 28, 1931, and the very first entry: "In the afternoon, H. A. Thompson commenced the supervision of Section A."

Looking back over more than 60 years, from the other side of the Atlantic, Homer Thompson smiled when he heard again that clipped description of the first day. He was a young, relatively inexperienced archaeologist then. Today he is a vigorous professor emeritus at the Institute for Advanced Study in Princeton, New Jersey. He oversaw the Agora excavations from 1947 to 1967.

Back in the '30s, he recalls, it took seven years to find the first boundary stone that used the word "Agora." It wasn't a thrill so much as a relief, says Thompson, who was in charge of the crew that uncovered the marker, wedged in by the wall of Simon the cobbler's shop. "We believed we were working in the Agora, but we had so little to show for it—in inscriptions—that some of our colleagues would come by and ask 'How do you know that you're in the Agora?' Well, this settled it."

Finding the second boundary stone took another 30 years. The marker lies on the southwest corner of the square. Ione Shear uncovered it one afternoon in 1967.

It is a very ordinary marble block. The faintly visible lettering runs across the top and then down one side. The important thing, says Leslie Shear, is that this block and the one found near Simon's shop have not been moved in 2,500 years. Other boundary stones have been found uprooted, buried in rubble fill. "But these two stand where they've stood since the sixth century B.C.," he observes. "They were set out at about the time the democracy was founded. In a very real sense, democracy as we understand it was invented in the Agora of Athens." He leaned down to trace the letters.

Stones can speak, although they rarely speak in the first person. This one spoke loud and clear: "I am the boundary of the Agora." There was no dispute after that. This was the word. This was the place.

ADDITIONAL READING

The Athenian Agora: Excavations in the Heart of Classical Athens by John M. Camp, Thames and Hudson (London), 1986
The Birth of Democracy: An Exhibition Celebrating the 2500th Anniversary of Democracy, edited by Josiah Ober and Charles W. Hedrick, American School of Classical Studies at Athens (Princeton, New Jersey), 1993
The Athenian Agora: A Guide to the Excavation and Museum, American School of Classical Studies at Athens, 1990
The Agora of Athens, The Athenian Agora, Volume XIV by H. A. Thompson and R. E. Wycherley, American School of Classical Studies at Athens, 1972

Old Sports

The Olympic Games were not the earliest athletic rituals in the eastern Mediterranean

Allen Guttmann

Guttman has completed an English translation of Sports and Games of Ancient Egypt, *by Wolfgang Decker. A professor of English and American studies at Amherst College, he has also examined the diffusion of modern sports from England and America as a case of cultural imperialism*

Every four years at Olympia, the athletes of ancient Greece paid homage to Zeus by demonstrating their *arete*, their excellence of mind and body. According to Hippias of Elis, the nearby city-state that organized the competitions, the Olympic Games began in 776 B.C. with a simple footrace, and other events were subsequently added. But the list of victors Hippias compiled, sometime about 400 B.C., exaggerated the age of the games, apparently to aggrandize the glory of his native city. Plutarch admonished that Hippias "had no fully authoritative basis for his work," and historians now believe that the games began, with as many as five different sports, about 600 B.C., more or less at the same time as the sacred games at Delphi, Corinth, and Nemea, which rounded out the four-year cycle of Greek athletics. (Isaac Newton anticipated modern scholars, estimating the games' later origin by recalculating the duration of royal reigns and accurately dating eclipses referred to by ancient astronomers.)

The true precursors of the sixth-century games remain elusive, but we do know that the Greeks were not the only people of the eastern Mediterranean to emphasize athletic ritual as a religious and political statement. In ancient Egypt, for example, from at least 3000 B.C., physical prowess was a necessary sign of a pharaoh's fitness to rule. As a representative of divinity on earth, his role required him to maintain order against the forces of chaos. A pharaoh commemorating the thirtieth anniversary of his enthronement would formally prove his fitness by executing a ceremonial run in the jubilee known as the Festival of Sed. The course, from one mark to another and back, symbolized the boundaries of the kingdom he protected. The earliest known turn markers, at the pyramid of Djoser (ca. 2600 B.C.), lie about sixty yards apart.

There were numerous other occasions for a pharaoh to display his strength and stamina. Inscriptions and reliefs testify to almost superhuman demonstrations of hunting skill, events that may or may not have actually occurred. Tuthmosis III, for example, one of the monarchs of the Eighteenth Dynasty (1552–1306 B.C.), boasted, "In an instant I killed seven lions with my arrows." Similarly, he and several other monarchs of that dynasty were said to have so mastered the composite bow (made of hardwood, softwood, and horn) that their arrows were able to transfix sheets of copper "three fingers thick." (Modern attempts to replicate this feat have failed.) The pharaoh had to be seen as the mightiest archer, most successful hunter, and swiftest runner. An American president can lose a tennis match without unleashing the forces of chaos, but Tuthmosis III was required to surpass all mortal achievements.

In the biography of Cheti, prince of Siut, who lived during the Eleventh Dynasty (2134–1991 B.C.), we read that "he learned to swim together with the children of the pharaoh." But despite the central role of the Nile in Egyptian life, there is no evidence that the pharaoh was expected to demonstrate his prowess at swimming. Or perhaps Egyptian artists considered the physical movements too undignified to show in a representation of divinity. There is, however, an inscription telling of the amazing boating exploits of the Eighteenth Dynasty monarch Amenophis II, who was said to have steered his "falcon ship" for three *itrw* (about 18.6 miles), when others gave up in exhaustion after a mere half *itrw*. And according to Egyptian legend, the gods Horus and Seth, both of whom claimed the right to rule the universe, agreed to settle their dispute with a diving contest.

If the quantity of visual evidence is any indication, wrestling was among the most popular Egyptian sports. Murals discovered in the eleventh-century tombs at Beni Hasan depict nearly every hold known to modern wrestlers. Although the sport has a religious character in many cultures, including those of Africa south of the Sahara, for the ancient Egyptians it seems to have been a purely secular contest. A pharaoh thrown roughly to the ground would have been a terrifying portent of disaster.

The pharaohs most celebrated for their athletic achievements were the martial monarchs of the Eighteenth Dynasty, especially Tuthmosis III, Amenophis II, Tuthmosis IV, and Amenophis III. These were the immediate successors of the Hyksos, a seminomadic people whose warriors swept from the northeast into the valley of the Nile about 1650 B.C. Their war chariots spread terror among the Egyptians of the time, for whom this was an unknown weapon. For more than a century, the Hyksos usurpers ruled Egypt; once they were expelled, more emphasis than ever was placed on the pharaoh's physical prowess. Even Queen Hatshepsut, an Eighteenth Dynasty monarch who ruled as if she were a man, had to prove her fitness with the time-honored ceremonial run. A relief discovered at Karnak depicts her in the middle of the ceremony, accompanied by the bull-god Apis. The great exception was the pacific Amenophis IV (who ruled as Akheneten), best remembered for his heretical monotheistic religious views.

The Hyksos were expelled; the chariot remained. It was used for hunting as well as for waging war, and pharaohs were often portrayed wielding spears or drawing bows from the basket of a chariot. Chariot races as such were not part of ancient Egyptian culture, despite the suitability of the terrain. But later, during the Hellenistic age (fourth to first centuries B.C.), when Alexander the Great and his successors spread Greek culture throughout the eastern Mediterranean, chariot races became immensely popular in Alexandria and elsewhere in Egypt.

The Egyptians seem never to have been as passionate about horses as were the Hyksos, the Hittites (of what is now central Turkey), the Assyrians of Mesopotamia (modern Iraq), and other peoples of the Near East, who devoted enormous amounts of time and energy to their care and breeding. An obscure fourteenth-century Hittite named Kikkuli has left us a detailed account of these matters in writings sometimes referred to as *The Book of Horses*. The later Persian empire, which came close to overwhelming Greek civilization in 490 B.C., had similar roots. As Xenophon and other Greek historians made clear, equestrianism was an essential aspect of the education of a Persian prince, whose skill as a rider and hunter was a warranty of fitness to rule.

We know little about the role of sports in the great Minoan civilization, which reached its height on the island of Crete between 2200 and 1400 B.C.

The written language remains mostly a mystery. But few frescoes have engendered more speculation than the one excavated at the Palace of Minos in Knossos, which shows adolescents, a boy and two girls, seizing the horns of a charging bull and somersaulting over its back. Ever since Arthur Evans discovered the image in 1900, scholars have wondered whether people really performed this dangerous stunt and, if so, what it signified. Was it a contest in which youths competed against each other, like modern gymnasts, or was the bull their adversary, as in a Spanish *corrida de toros?* Another fresco from Knossos, now at the National Museum in Athens, depicts a group of male and female spectators arranged on terraces, or tiers. Whether the audience consists of assembled worshipers or sports enthusiasts is not clear, but some scholars believe they are attending a bull-vaulting performance.

Vases, statuettes, coins, and other remains of Minoan culture attest to the popularity of hunting, boxing, and wrestling. Among the most tantalizing discoveries is a fresco from the island of Thera, a Minoan outpost, that shows two boys wearing some kind of boxing gloves, squaring off as if in a modern ring. The guides in Thera call them the "boxing princes," but whether they really were princes proving their fitness for rule or merely two boys at play remains the artist's secret.

The Etruscans, whose civilization flourished during the seventh century B.C. in the region north and west of Rome, were enthusiastic about sports, perhaps as a result of Greek influence. The murals inside the so-called Tomb of the Monkey and other burial sites feature Etruscan wrestling and boxing, while chariots race across the walls of the Tomb of the Olympics, Tomb of the Two-Horse Chariots, and others. The murals of the chariot races include the spectators and perhaps the officials, at least one of whom seems to have been female. Jean-Paul Thuillier, the leading authority on Etruscan sports, argues that these types of murals represented funeral games, traditionally held to honor the dead. This is plausible for many sports, but one wonders about the scenes

in the Tomb of Hunting and Fishing, which include a fine picture of a man diving.

A mysterious Etruscan sport appears in the Tomb of the Augurs and Tomb of the Olympics. Known as the Phersu combat, from a word inscribed in the latter tomb, it pitted a masked man against a dog held on a leash by a second man. It may have inspired the later Roman combats of men and animals (*venationes*).

Scholars once believed that the Etruscans also gave the Romans the idea for their *munera*, combats between pairs of armed gladiators. An origin in Campania, south of Rome, or Samnia, east of Rome, now seems more likely. The precedent may have been a deadly funeral contest that had evolved from a still earlier ritual of human sacrifice. Such sacrifices would have been made to provide dead heroes with an entourage and appease the gods of the underworld. Eventually, death in combat might have been deemed a better offering than the less thrilling sacrifice of a passive victim. The Romans took the ultimate step of making a fight to the death a gruesome form of entertainment. (The religious trappings of Rome's pagan games, incidentally, were what horrified Christian theologians like Tertullian, who deplored idolatry more than the martyrdom of his fellow believers.)

Funeral games may also have been the chief precursors of the Greek Olympics. Our best early source is not visual art or archeology but literature: Homer's *Iliad*, a ninth-century account of the Trojan War, which probably occurred in the thirteenth century B.C. In Book XXIII, the Greeks, who have not yet captured the city of Troy, celebrate funeral games for Patroklos, who has been slain by the Trojan hero Hektor. Lavish prizes are offered by the great Achilles, Patroklos's bosom friend.

The first event of the games is a chariot race, for which Achilles offers five prizes, chief of which is "a woman skilled in fair handiwork." Although Greece was not the ideal place to breed horses, chariot races were apparently common in Attica, Thessaly, and other places where the terrain was not too forbidding. The plain before "the topless towers of Ilium" provides a suitable course, but the race is a rough one, with the goddess Athene intervening to assure victory for her favorite, Diomedes. (Fair play, which requires that everyone compete under the same rules, is as much a nineteenth-century concept as the nearly defunct amateur rule of the modern Olympics.)

The chariot race is followed by the boxing and wrestling contests. The first is won by Epeius, who fells his opponent with a mighty blow to the cheek. The second is declared a draw when neither Odysseus nor Ajax can throw the other. Then comes the footrace, in which Athene again intervenes, this time to favor Odysseus, whose limbs she lightens. The oafish Ajax she causes to slip and fall on offal left from the ritual slaughter of oxen.

When Ajax recovers, he is matched against Diomedes in potentially deadly armed combat, but the spectators stop the fight when Diomedes thrusts fiercely at Ajax's throat. Ajax has apparently suffered enough for a single day. The games conclude with the hurtling of the discus and with an archery contest in which the target is a dove tethered to a ship's mast. (The javelin contest, which was supposed to end the games, is canceled when Achilles, deciding that Agamemnon is certain to win anyway, gives him the prize.)

In Homer's dramatization, we can see that the games were a form of religious ritual, an appropriate way to worship the gods and to honor a fallen warrior. The contests also emphasized the skills and accomplishments of warriors. Both themes were eventually incorporated in the Greek Olympics, although the nature of the contestants changed somewhat. At first they were aristocratic warriors, but later, ordinary Greek men also competed and the role of the full-time athlete grew.

Pelops, a local hero said to be buried at Olympia, may have been honored by funeral games, and subsequent commemorative contests may explain why the site was chosen when the official games were instituted about 600 B.C. Originally, the Olympics probably consisted of a number of events, foremost of which was the short-distance race, or stade, from one end of the field to the other (a stadium for the footrace built later at Olympia may still be visited). The other events may have included a chariot race and the pentathlon or its constituents—a footrace, the discus, long jump, javelin, and wrestling. Other contests added over the years included longer footraces, a race in armor, and boys' events.

Neither the *Iliad*'s archery contest nor its armed combat were a part of the Olympic Games. Nor, despite the location of most Greek cities on the shores of the Aegean or on the banks of a river, were there swimming events at Olympia or any of the other sacred games. This was true even of the Isthmian Games, held at Corinth in honor of Poseidon, god of the sea.

Although the Greek athletic festivals were not the only, or even the earliest, ritualized sports of antiquity, they, more than any others, characterized an entire culture and embodied many of its people's highest aspirations. When, nearly a century ago, Pierre de Coubertin championed ancient Greece as an inspiration for modern games, he chose his model wisely. Amenophis II proved his divinity by his superhuman (and probably imaginary) athletic performance. Olympic victors, true exemplars of human physical excellence, won their immortality the hard way.

Cleopatra: What Kind of a Woman Was She, Anyway?

Serpent of the Nile? Learned ruler? Sex kitten? Ambitious mom? African queen? History is still toying with the poor lady's reputation

Barbara Holland

Barbara Holland, who often writes wryly about history and politics for the magazine, is the author of several books, including Endangered Pleasures *(Little, Brown).*

Until now, everyone has had pretty much the same fix on Cleopatra: passion's plaything, sultry queen, a woman so beautiful she turned the very air around her sick with desire, a tragic figure whose bared bosom made an asp gasp when she died for love. Inevitably, the best-known incarnation of her is Hollywood's: Theda Bara, Claudette Colbert, Elizabeth Taylor, telling us what fun it was to be filthy rich in the first century B.C., spending days in enormous bathtubs and nights in scented sheets. Drinking pearls dissolved in vinegar. (Do not try this at home; it doesn't work.) Lounging around on a barge, being waited on hand and foot.

Sometimes the asp looks like a small price to pay.

Hollywood's queen rests less on George Bernard Shaw's Cleopatra, who is a clever sex kitten, than on William Shakespeare's; in the Bard's *Antony and Cleopatra* she's a fiercer soul, downright unhinged by love for Mark Antony. Of course, they both had to leave out her children. Everyone does. It's tough being the world's top tragic lover with four kids underfoot. Even if you can get a sitter, it doesn't look right.

The latest version, part of the current debate about the possible influences of Africa on Greek and Roman culture, suggests that she was black. The last time we looked she was a Macedonian Greek, but the black-Cleopatra advocates like to point out that since nobody knows anything about her paternal grandmother except that she wasn't legally married to Ptolemy IX, it is possible that she was black.

Most classical scholars disagree. Some note that though Ptolemy II, more than a century earlier, had an Egyptian mistress, the Ptolemies were wicked snobs, so proud of their bloodline, not to mention the line of succession to their throne, that they tended to marry their brothers and sisters to keep it untainted. When they picked mistresses, they customarily chose upper-class Greeks. They felt so superior to the Egyptians, in fact, that after 300 years in Alexandria, they couldn't say much more than "good morning" to the locals in their native tongue; Cleopatra was the first in her family to learn the language.

Nobody should be surprised at such claims, however. For the fact is that for purposes political and otherwise, people have been fooling around with Cleopatra's image to suit themselves for centuries. In *All for Love* John Dryden gives us a traditional Cleo less a queen and a ruler than an addictive substance. Shaw

From *Smithsonian magazine*, February 1997, pp. 57–62, 64. © 1997 by Barbara Holland. Reprinted by permission of the author.

made her stand for everything unBritish and thus deplorable. In the course of his *Caesar and Cleopatra* she evolves from a superstitious, cowardly little girl into a vengeful, bloodthirsty little girl. To underline his point he lops five years off her actual age and leaves her under the thumb of a sturdy Roman governor, forerunner of the wise and kindly British administrators of later colonies full of childish foreigners.

Of course, nearly everyone's story goes back to Plutarch, the first-century Greek biographer, who included two versions of Cleo. He knew the writings and stories of people in her part of the world who remembered her as a scholar in their own refined tradition, so unlike the ignorant, loutish Romans; a mothering goddess; a messiah sent to liberate the East from under the jackboots of Rome. On the other hand, he had the Roman story, largely attributed to her enemy in war, and conqueror, Octavian (who later became the emperor Augustus—portrayed as the clueless husband of the evil Livia in the television series *I, Claudius*). Octavian worked hard to set her up as everything scheming, treacherous, female, foreign and, most of all, sexually rapacious. His Queen Cleopatra was a drunken harlot, the wickedest woman in the world.

Actually, where we can reasonably deduce them, the facts are more interesting than these exotic scenarios.

Cleopatra VII was born in 69 B.C, the third child of Ptolemy XII, called Auletes, known as the Flute Player. Egypt was still rich, then, but its ancient empire had been nibbled away, and the natives, unfond of their Macedonian masters, were restless. The Flute Player kept going to Rome to get help in holding onto his throne. He may have taken Cleopatra along when she was 12; she may have watched the Roman loan sharks charge him 10,000 talents, or nearly twice Egypt's annual revenue, for services to be rendered.

Not only couldn't he control his subjects, he couldn't do a thing with his children. While he was away his eldest daughter, Tryphaena, grabbed the throne. After she got assassinated, second daughter Berenice grabbed it next—until Ptolemy came back with Roman

help and executed her. Cleopatra, now the eldest, had cause to ponder. She knew Egypt needed Roman help, but paying cash for help was beggaring the state. She knew she had to watch her back around her family. I suppose you could call it dysfunctional.

She seems to have found herself an education. Cicero, like most Romans, couldn't stand her, but he grudgingly admits she was literary and involved like him in "things that had to do with learning." The Arab historian Al-Masudi tells us she was the author of learned works, "a princess well versed in the sciences, disposed to the study of philosophy." According to Plutarch she spoke at least seven languages.

In 51 B.C., when Cleopatra was 18, the Flute Player died and left the kingdom to her and her 10-year-old brother (and fiancé) Ptolemy XIII. The reign got off on the wrong foot because the Nile refused to flood its banks to irrigate the yearly harvest. A court eunuch named Pothinus reared his ugly head; he'd got himself appointed regent for little Ptolemy, squeezed Cleopatra clear out of town and began giving orders himself.

Cleopatra's looks are one of the burning issues of the ages.

Rome, meanwhile, was in the process of shedding its republican privileges to become an empire. An early phase involved the uneasy power-sharing device called the First Triumvirate, with Caesar, Pompey and Crassus (a money man) jointly in charge. It wasn't Rome's brightest idea. Caesar and Pompey quarreled, Caesar defeated Pompey in Greece, Pompey took refuge in Egypt.

Not wanting to harbor a loser, the Egyptians had him murdered and cut off his head and presented it to victorious Caesar when he sailed into Alexandria to collect the defunct Flute Player's debts. Pothinus had reason to hate and fear Rome. He was very likely plotting to do in Caesar, too, who took over the palace and stayed on with a guard of 3,000 Roman soldiers. He couldn't take his ships and go home; the winds were unfavorable.

Cleopatra needed a secret word with him, so as we've all heard, she got herself rolled up in some bedding and had herself delivered to Caesar as merchandise. According to Plutarch, Caesar was first captivated by this proof of Cleopatra's bold wit, and afterward so overcome by the charm of her society that he made a reconciliation between her and her brother. Then he killed Pothinus. So there was Cleopatra, at the price of being briefly half-smothered in bedding, with her throne back. And of course, sleeping with Caesar, who was in his 50s and losing his hair.

How did she do it? Cleopatra's looks are one of the burning issues of the ages. European painters tend to see her as a languishing blue-eyed blonde with nothing to wear but that asp. However, there's a coin in the British Museum with her profile on it, and she looks more like Abraham Lincoln than a voluptuous queen. Most people who have written about her agree that she commissioned the coins herself and, being a woman, was vain of her looks, so even this profile could have been downright flattering. In any case, it launched a lot of cracks about her proboscis. Had Cleopatra's nose been shorter, according to 17th-century French writer Blaise Pascal, the whole face of the world would have been changed. However, there's no evidence that Antony was unhappy with her nose the way it was.

Or maybe it wasn't so long. Maybe she thought more of her kingdom than her vanity and wanted to scare off possible enemies by looking fierce. Considering the speed with which she corrupted Rome's top commanders—both of them widely traveled, experienced married men—it's possible she looked more like a woman and less like Mount Rushmore than she does on the coins. Besides, the second-century Greek historian Dio Cassius says Cleopatra seduced Caesar because she was "brilliant to look upon . . . with the power to subjugate everyone." (She knew a few things about fixing herself up, too, and wrote a book on cosmetics full of ingredients unknown to Estee Lauder, like burnt mice.) And Plutarch reports that "It was a pleasure merely to hear the sound of her voice, with which, like an instrument of many strings, she could pass from one language to another. . . ."

She bowled Caesar over, anyway, and when reinforcements came he squelched the rebellious Egyptian army for her. In the process he had to burn his own ships, and the fire spread and took out part of Alexandria's famous library, which housed most of what had been learned up to the time—Shaw called it "the memory of mankind." When the smoke cleared they found Ptolemy XIII drowned in the Nile in a full suit of golden armor, but as far as we know, his sister hadn't pushed him. Caesar then married her to her youngest brother, Ptolemy XIV, age 12, whom she ignored. When Caesar left, she was pregnant. Anti-Cleopatrans scoff at the notion that Caesar was the father, claiming he never admitted it himself, but there was plenty he never admitted, including his whole Egyptian fling, and somehow it seems likely. Giving the childless Caesar a son was a much shrewder move than getting pregnant by your 12-year-old brother; as policy it might have done wonders for Egypt. She named her son Ptolemy Caesar, always referred to him as Caesarion, and took him with her to Rome in 46 B.C. Mindful of her father's mistake, she took Ptolemy XIV, too, so she could keep an eye on him.

In Rome she was Caesar's guest. They gave fabulous parties together. He put up a golden statue of her in the temple of Venus Genetrix, causing a scandal that made him more vulnerable to the people who were plotting to kill him, as they did in March of 44. After he got stabbed, it turned out that he hadn't named Caesarion as his heir, but his great-nephew Octavian, so Cleopatra had to pack up and go home. When brother Ptolemy XIV conveniently died,

she appointed the toddler Caesarion as coruler.

Here the record loses interest in her for several years, between lovers, but she must have been busy. She'd inherited a country plagued by civil wars, Egypt was broke, and twice more the Nile floods misfired. Somehow, though, by the time the West began to notice her again, peace reigned even in fractious Alexandria. She'd played her cards deftly with Rome and her subjects loved her. According to the first-century A.D. Jewish historian Josephus, she'd negotiated a sweetheart real estate deal with the Arabs and in general managed the economy so well that Egypt was the richest state in the eastern Mediterranean. So rich that Mark Antony came calling in 41 B.C. in search of funds to finance an attack on the Parthians.

. . . like any Washington lobbyist with a pocketful of Redskins tickets, she was putting her time and money where they mattered most.

By then the Romans were pigheadedly pursuing the triumvirate notion again, this time with Octavian, Lepidus and Antony. If you believe Plutarch, Antony was simple, generous and easygoing, though a bit of a slob. Cicero says his orgies made him "odious," and there's a story that, after an all-night party, he rose to give a speech and threw up into the skirt of his toga while a kindly friend held it for him. Still, he was doing all right until Cleopatra came along, when he was, as Dryden laments, "unbent, unsinewed, made a woman's toy."

Plutarch's description of their meeting on her barge makes poets and movie producers salivate. Who could resist those silver oars and purple sails, those

flutes and harps, the wafting perfumes, the costumed maidens, and the queen herself dressed as Venus under a canopy spangled with gold? Not Antony, certainly. She knew what he'd come for and planned to drive a hard bargain. Naturally, they became lovers; they also sat down to deal; she would pay for his Parthian campaign, he would help fight her enemies and, for good measure, kill her sister Arsinoe, her last ambitious sibling.

Antony came for money and stayed to play. A sound relationship with Rome was tops on the whole world's agenda at the time. So, like a perfect hostess, Cleopatra lowered her standards of decorum and encouraged her guest in rowdy revels that have shocked the ages. The ages feel that all that frivoling means she was a frivolous woman, and not that, like any Washington lobbyist with a pocketful of Redskins tickets, she was putting her time and money where they mattered most.

She drank and gambled and hunted and fished with him. Sometimes they dressed as servants and roamed the town teasing the natives. Plutarch's grandfather knew a man who knew one of her cooks and reported that each night a series of banquets was prepared. If Antony wanted another round of drinks before dinner, the first banquet was thrown out and a second was served up, and so on. Anyone standing outside the kitchen door must have been half-buried in delicacies.

Back in Rome, Antony's third wife, Fulvia, and his brother raised an army against Octavian. (Lepidus, like Crassus, fizzled out early.) She got whipped, and Antony had to bid the fleshpots farewell and go patch things up. Then Fulvia died, and Antony sealed a temporary peace by marrying Octavian's sister, Octavia. Within weeks of that ceremony in Rome, Cleopatra had twins, Alexander Helios and Cleopatra Selene.

At the news of Antony's marriage, Shakespeare's queen has hysterics and tries to stab the messenger, but the Bard is guessing. The real queen probably took it in stride. She could recognize a political move when she saw it; she had Antony's alliance and a son to prove it, and a country to run besides.

SHE HAD NO TIME TO LOLL IN ASS'S MILK

No one suggests that she had a prime minister, and after Ponthinus, who would? No one denies, either, that Egypt was in apple-pie order. So there sits our drunken harlot, with Caesarion and the twins in bed, working late by oil light, signing papyri, meeting with advisers, approving plans for aqueducts, adjusting taxes. Distributing free grain during hard times. Receiving ambassadors and haggling over trade agreements. She may hardly have had time to put eyeliner on, let alone loll in ass's milk, and apparently she slept alone.

Antony finally got it together enough to invade Parthia. He needed help again, so he sent for Cleopatra to meet him at Antioch and she brought the children. Some see this as strictly business, but Plutarch insists his passion had "gathered strength again, and broke out into a flame." Anyway, they were rapturously reunited, and she agreed to build him a Mediterranean fleet and feed his army in exchange for a good deal of what is now Lebanon, Syria, Jordan and southern Turkey.

Did she really love him, or was it pure ambition? Ambition certainly didn't hurt, but it seems she was fond of him, though he probably snored after parties. Sources say she tried to introduce him to the finer things in life and dragged him to learned discussions, which at least sounds affectionate.

After a happy winter in Antioch, he went off to attack Parthia and she was pregnant again. The Parthian campaign was a disaster, ending with the loss or surrender of nearly half his army.

But for Cleopatra it was another boy, Ptolemy Philadelphus. When she'd recovered, she went to Antony's rescue with pay and warm clothes for the survivors. Presently Octavia announced that she, too, was coming to bring supplies. Antony told her to forget it and stay home. Octavian felt his sister had been dissed and suggested to the Romans that Antony was a deserter who planned to move the capital of the empire to Alexandria and rule jointly with his queen from there.

You could see it that way. In a public ceremony in Alexandria, Antony assembled the children, dressed to the teeth and sitting on thrones, and proclaimed Cleopatra "Queen of Kings" and Caesarion "King of Kings." He made his own three kids royalty, too, and gave them considerable realms that weren't, strictly speaking, his to give. Worst of all, he announced that Caesarion, not Octavian, was Julius Caesar's real son and the real heir to Rome.

Then he divorced Octavia.

All hands prepared for war. If the lovers had been quick off the mark, they might have invaded Italy at once and won, but instead they retired to Greece to assemble their forces, including Cleopatra's fleet. She insisted on sailing with it, too; her national treasury was stowed in the flagship. The upshot was that in 31 B.C. they found themselves bottled up at Actium, facing Octavian across the Ambracian Gulf. The standard version of the Battle of Actium is that while the fight hung in the balance, Cleopatra took her ships and left, because, being a woman, she was a coward and deserted in battle. The besotted Antony, we're told, followed her like a dog, and the fight turned into a rout.

With battles, the winner gets to tell the tale. Octavian was the winner, and he saw Cleopatra as a threat to Rome, a lascivious creature, and himself as a noble Roman able to resist her Eastern blandishments. All we really know is that it was a bloody mess, from which she managed to retreat with the treasury intact, enough to build another fleet with change left over. Octavian wanted that money to pay his troops. She wanted Egypt for her children. Perhaps deals could be made. Antony even suggested killing himself in trade for Cleopatra's life, but Octavian was bound for Egypt and he wouldn't deal.

Thus threatened, the queen swiftly stuffed a big mausoleum with treasure, along with fuel enough to burn it down if all else failed, and locked herself in with her serving maids. It's unclear whether Antony was told she was dead or he just felt depressed, but anyway he disemboweled himself. He botched the job—it's harder than you'd think—and lingered long enough to be hauled to the mausoleum and hoisted through the upstairs window, where presumably he expired in Cleopatra's arms. Victorious Octavian marched into town. He sent his henchmen to the queen, and they tricked their way in, snatched away her dagger, taking her—and her treasure—prisoner.

> *. . . she and her ladies dressed up in their best finery and killed themselves. Octavian did the handsome thing and had her buried with Antony.*

According to Plutarch, at 39 "her old charm, and the boldness of her youthful beauty had not wholly left her and, in spite of her present condition, still sparkled from within." It didn't help, so she and her ladies dressed up in their best finery and killed themselves. Octavian did the handsome thing and had her buried with Antony. Then he tracked down and killed Caesarion and annexed Egypt as his own personal colony.

The best-remembered Cleo story is the asp smuggled in with the basket of figs. Plutarch, who saw the medical record, mentions it as a rumor, wrestles with the evidence and concludes that "what really took place is known to no one, since it was also said that she carried poison in a hollow comb . . . yet there was not so much as a spot found, or any symptom of poison upon her body, nor was the asp seen within the monument. . . ."

Later it was suggested—probably by Octavian—that she'd tried various substances on her slaves and, so the story usually goes, opted for the asp, but in truth its bite is even less fun than disemboweling. Maybe she used a cobra, whose effects are less visible. But where did it go? Some people claimed there were two faint marks on her arm, but they sound like mosquito bites to me. Others insist they saw a snake's trail on the sand outside; fat chance, with all those guards and soldiers and distressed citizens milling around shouting and trampling the evidence.

It looks likelier that she'd brewed up a little something to keep handy. She was clever that way; remember the second brother. Octavian's men had patted her down—"shook out her dress," Plutarch says—but she was smarter than they were. And why gamble on the availability of snakes and smugglers when you could bring your own stuff in your suitcase? When Octavian led his triumph through Rome, lacking the actual queen, he paraded an effigy of her with her arm wreathed in snakes, and the asp theory slithered into history. Maybe he'd heard the rumor and believed it, or maybe he started it himself. It would have played well in Rome. In Egypt the snake was a symbol of royalty and a pet of the goddess Isis, but in Rome it was strictly a sinuous, sinister reptile, typical of those Easterners, compared with a forthright Roman whacking out his innards.

History has always mixed itself with politics and advertising, and in all three the best story always carries the day. But why did the man who was now undisputed ruler of the known world work so hard to ruin a dead lady's reputation? Maybe she'd been more formidable than any of our surviving stories tell. We do know she was the last great power of the Hellenistic world, "sovereign queen of many nations" and the last major threat to Rome for a long time. She might have ruled half the known world or even, through her children, the whole thing, and ushered in the golden age of peace that she believed the gods had sent her to bring to the Mediterranean.

At least she would have left us her own version of who she was, and maybe it would be closer to the truth than the others. And then again, given the human urge to tell good stories, maybe not.

The Year One

Life was nasty, brutish, and short 2,000 years ago,
but the issues of the day were surprisingly modern

By Lewis Lord

Two thousand years ago this week, the Year One arrived. But no one knew it, either then or for several centuries thereafter. The 12 months we call A.D. 1 came and went as just another year. To the Romans who ruled what was considered the civilized world—and whose civilization would one day be the basis for our own—the year was 754 A.U.C. (*ab urbe condita*—"from the foundation of the city")—754 being the number of years since Romulus and Remus, the legendary orphans suckled by a she-wolf, were said to have founded Rome. Among Rome's Greek subjects, who marked time in four-year units between Olympic Games, the year was merely the first quarter of the 195th Olympiad. Meanwhile, the Chinese saw it as nothing more than "the second year of the reign period of P'ing-ti," the boy emperor who would die five years later at the age of 13.

But to a sixth-century monk in Rome, the year ranked as the greatest in all history. According to Dionysius Exiguus's reckonings, it was "Anno Domini"—the first full "year of our Lord"—the year that began a week after the birth of Christ. All time prior to A.D. 1 would be counted as so many years B.C., "before Christ." With papal support, Dionysius's chronological system gradually won almost universal acceptance—even though it miscalculated the Nativity by several years: Scholars believe that Jesus was probably 5, 6, or 7 years old in A.D. 1.

Now and then. The people of the Year One shared concerns that exist to-

AKG-LONDON

{ LOVE, ROMAN STYLE }

Men and women married young: Girls were deemed ready at 12 and boys at 14. Augustus penalized men still single at 25 and women at 20. Engagements were sealed with an iron ring placed on the bride's third finger. Wedding parties started with the sacrifice of a pig, followed by cake. Amid dirty songs, the couple left for their new home, where the bride greased the door posts before being carried across the threshold.

day—child rearing, social behavior, faith—but did so in ways now impossible to understand. Historian John Evans tells his first-year students at the University of Minnesota they would find it easier to "deal with a star-faring race that showed up from Betelgeuse than to cross the divides of time and space and deal with the Romans on their own terms."

In the political world of 2,000 years ago, Ronald Reagan would never have made it in politics. Romans ranked actors on a level with prostitutes. Nor would Al Gore have won support by kissing Tipper. Men in love were considered laughable, so much so that one senator was stripped of his seat for embracing his wife in public. But George W. Bush would have stood tall. In Rome, every "young nobleman" was dutybound "to avenge any humiliations suffered by his father," wrote historian Florence Dupont in her book *Daily Life in Ancient Rome*. "Not to be avenged was the worst misfortune that could befall a father and the deepest shame that could sully a son's name."

In the Year One, the world's most powerful politician—a man who unintentionally paved the way for Christianity's rise—was a 63-year-old, 5-foot-5 hypochondriac with gallstones, dirty teeth, and a knack for climbing to the top and staying there. The emperor Augustus, grandnephew and adopted son of the murdered Julius Caesar, was in the 27th year of his 41-year reign as the unquestioned leader of the world's biggest empire.

Those years found Augustus pondering very modern issues: law and order, welfare, family values, and moral decay, including sexual transgressions in his own household. Augustus would boast that he found Rome brick and made it marble, but more lasting by far than his monuments was the influence of his reign, which helped shape life and thought in much of the world for the next 2,000 years. The Age of Augustus would create a framework of government and society that would transform Western Europe—and hence America—with Rome's laws, its institutions, its language, and what eventually would become its state religion, Christianity.

Without the good roads and widespread order of the Pax Romana—the two centuries of peace that Augustus introduced—the "good news" of Christ might never have spread. Yet the stability was wafer-thin. In the decades just before A.D. 1, Augustus had conned the Roman people into scrapping their cherished but ultimately unworkable republic and its freedoms for the security and efficiency of an imperial dictatorship. Beneath the grandeur of empire lay a decaying social system peopled overwhelmingly by the poor and the left out. It was there that Christianity, offering hope in a hopeless world, would take root, grow, and eventually flower.

Indeed, the teachings of Christ were spread in a world of unrelenting cruelty. Who today could condone the sight of men and women being fed to beasts as people of all classes shrilled their delight? To the Romans, the spectacle was a just punishment for lawbreakers. What's to be made of a superpower that conquered cities by enslaving the men and killing the women and children? Owning or killing people, Romans believed, was as natural as water running downhill. Who can comprehend a father's tossing an infant into the village dung heap for being female, sick, or a surplus mouth to feed? The Romans were not offended, especially if the father followed the law and invited five neighbors to examine the baby before he left it to die.

Why not? In the Year One, questioning such behavior would have drawn blank stares. "The Romans saw the world as it was," says Sarah Pomeroy, a classics professor at New York's Hunter College who wrote *Goddesses, Whores, Wives, and Slaves: Women in Classical Antiquity*. "They didn't think of whether anything was unjust."

In the world of the Romans, the cure for stomachache was a dose of water in which feet had been washed. Hawkers in the town squares offered amulets conferring power from gods for every need, from giving sight to the blind to raising a child (among the baby gods: Wailer, Breastfeeder, Eater, and Stander). Children, until they walked and talked, were not considered humans. Citizens didn't use soap but cleansed themselves with olive oil and a scraping tool. A stick with a wet sponge on the tip did what toilet paper does today. (Indeed, paper as we know it did not exist until a hundred years later in China.)

Centuries of rough existence had bred a Roman acceptance of savagery and the conviction that life was a series of bleak choices. How, for instance, might a poor family acquire a slave? If it had food to spare, it could pluck a child from the dung heap and raise it in servitude. "Nothing was wasted in the ancient world: not an abandoned baby, not the cloth that kept the ragpicker in business . . . not even the grains of barley in horse manure on the streets," writes Yale historian Ramsay MacMullen in his book *Roman Social Relations, 50 B.C. to A.D. 284*. "There were always people poor enough to fight over another's leavings."

Political and social influence was reserved for a tiny group: the senators and knights who owned most of the land and the bulk of the wealth. By one estimate, these elites—essentially the guys in togas in the Hollywood epics—made up less than one tenth of 1 percent of the population. Rome's upper-middle class—prosperous but not immensely rich—ranked socially only a notch above the vast citizenry that was poor. Many of the not-rich-enough contented themselves with a few well-cultivated acres where, amid kin and slaves, they lived relatively comfortable lives, going barefoot, sleeping on straw, and eating pork, vegetables, and bread.

The colossally rich, like the patrician who gave his pet eel a jeweled bracelet, retained their unsalaried political offices by treating supporters to gigantic parties. But in the century leading up to the Year One, fewer and fewer politicians could afford the soaring costs of feasts, theater shows, and gladiatorial combats that the public had come to expect. Many officeholders turned to bribes. By the first century A.D., venality was rampant. Even officers in the army expected payoffs from their soldiers.

Home and away. The Romans had a propensity for rewarding the wrong people. In the two centuries before the Year One, a long series of wars kept untold thousands of farmers in the army and away from their farms. To prevent their families from starving, many soldiers sold their neglected land to rich landowners. Once out of the legions, multitudes sought refuge in Rome, swelling the city's population in A.D. 1 to nearly 1 million people. It wasn't a promise of good jobs that drew the dispossessed veterans to Rome, however. Slaves did nearly all the work, not just the menial but also such important tasks as operating stores, delivering mail, practicing medicine, and tutoring the children of the wealthy. What pulled the ex-soldiers to Rome was "bread and circuses," specifically free food and free entertainment financed by taxes and tributes from conquered territories.

The government, since Caesar's rule, had given daily wheat rations to most citizens of Rome, the plebeians who included all adults except foreigners, slaves, and women. Even farmers who still owned land were abandoning it and flocking to the city to live on the dole. Rome's elites scorned the newcomers as rabble—"the bloodsuckers of the treasury," Cicero called them—and Caesar tried belatedly to curb the giveaway. But his welfare reform was short-lived. Augustus, Caesar's successor, reversed the cuts in 5 B.C. and extended the benefits to boys as well as men.

In the Year One, to keep his citizenry happy and grievance-free, Augustus was delivering a lavish array of religious ceremonies, festivals, and *ludi*, "the games in honor of the gods." Chariot races drew crowds of 200,000 or more to the Circus Maximus, where the most popular scene—a mass littering of overturned chariots, squealing horses, and maimed men—was known as a "shipwreck." A day at the Forum often began with fans savoring Augustus's wild-beast matches, although the regulars had a good idea which animals would win. Packs of hounds always beat herds of deer, bears withstood bulls, and lions usually finished off tigers. But not even the ferocious charge of the rhinoceros could penetrate the thick hide of the elephant.

The afternoon brought more variety: animals vs. humans. Some of the men, trained and equipped with spears, lived to fight another day. But for others, the outcome was never in doubt. They were the *bestiarii*—condemned criminals who later would include Christian men and women—thrown into the arena with no training and no weapons. The carni-

GRANGER COLLECTION

{ WORLDLY ROMANS }

To feed itself, Rome relied on its empire, which stretched from the English Channel to North Africa and from Syria to Spain. The Romans built deep-water harbors like this one to get wheat from Egypt and Sicily, wine from Spain, and olive oil from Africa. One observer reported that Rome "seems like a common warehouse of the world. . . .The arrival and departure of ships never ceases."

ROD LITTLE—*USN&WR*

Source: The Metropolitan Museum of Art, *The Year One*

vore often was a quick-killing lion; many fans preferred smaller beasts that did more dragging and tearing.

By the Year One, the *ludi* were part of everyday Roman life. "One might even say that they pervaded life," wrote the French historian Roland Auguet in *Cruelty and Civilization: The Roman Games.* "They imposed their rhythm on existence and provided nourishment for the passions." Augustus, ever a stickler for order, tried to regulate the gore. If two gladiators still stood after dueling long and hard, he decreed, both should receive the palm of victory. But the mob preferred blood. For centuries, *ludi* sponsors would ignore Augustus's law and force the faceless men—helmets hid their features—to fight until one became a corpse in the sand.

A decree telling spectators where to sit was part of Augustus's most ambitious project, his campaign to restore public morality. The best seats went to patrician couples, the Vestal Virgins, soldiers, and married men. Why favor married men? Augustus had the notion that Rome's population was shrinking because too many men were visiting prostitutes, keeping concubines, and avoiding marriage. If more men would take wives, he believed, Rome would have what Cicero termed "less lust and larger families."

To promote family values, Augustus hatched a system of rewards and punishments. Husbands who fathered three children were put on fast tracks for promotions. Mothers of three won a voice in property questions. Bachelors and spinsters, on the other hand, saw their inheritances restricted. Scrapped was an old law that let husbands kill adulterous wives. But any man who refused to divorce such a woman, the emperor decreed, should be prosecuted. Wives could divorce their husbands, but at a risk: Fathers apparently always got the children.

The men of Rome had griped about their women for nearly two centuries, ever since the Senate agreed in 195 B.C. to let ladies wear dyed clothes and ride in carriages. Wives were expected to keep the hearth burning, fetch water, cook, spin, weave, and bear children. They weren't supposed to drink—a sure sign of sexual aberrations. (The reason men kissed their female kin, Cato the Elder reported, was to check for wine on their breath.) Nor, in the presence of males, were they to appear very smart. Wives who discussed history and poetry and used correct grammar, the writer Juvenal observed, were "really annoying."

No romance. Romans married for duty, specifically to preserve family lines and replenish the citizenry. Fathers decided who wed whom. Until Augustus decreed that engaged girls be at least 10, some Roman daughters, including his own, were betrothed in infancy. Teenage boys, like their fathers, could have their way with prostitutes or slaves of either sex. But first-time brides were expected to be virgins. One of Julius Caesar's wives no doubt passed the test: She was only 11. Affection was rarely a factor in Roman engagements. "But it was taken for granted that if the husband and wife treated each other properly, love would develop and emerge, and by the end of their lives it would be a deep, mutual feeling," says David Konstan, a classics professor at Brown University.

Few people, ancient or modern, made a bigger mess of family life than did the family-values leader of Rome. Augustus ditched his first wife, Scribonia, because of a "moral perversity of hers," namely her contempt for his mistress. A year later, the randy emperor fell for Livia, who happened to be six months pregnant and married to another man. Three days after the baby arrived, Augustus and Livia wed. Livia's freshly divorced husband, posing as her father, obligingly gave her away.

AKG-LONDON

{ GORE TRIUMPHANT }
In a single season, Augustus financed spectacles that saw as many as 10,000 gladiators fighting—and many dying. He built a lake for a battle involving 30 ships and 3,000 combatants. In his wild-beast shows, 3,500 animals perished, including elephants and rhinoceroses. "Let us go back to Rome," one fan wrote from abroad. "It might be rather nice, too, to see somebody killed."

{ A FEW GOOD VIRGINS }
Elite families proposed preadolescent daughters for 30-year jobs as Vestal Virgins—seen here as statues in Rome's Forum—who kept the Temple of Vesta's fire burning. The perks were excellent: posh parties, meals of sow's udders and thrushes, and prime seats at gladiatorial shows. But the risks were great for some: Lose your virginity, and you'd be buried alive.

Livia kept Augustus content, critics would claim, by sending slave girls to his chamber and looking the other way as he dallied with politicians' wives. Whatever the cause, the emperor would ultimately laud his marriage as 51 years of happiness. But his opinion of his only child, Julia, was less felicitous.

Julia was born just before Augustus divorced her mother, the strait-laced Scribonia. As a newborn, she was betrothed to a son of her father's ally, Mark Antony. When friend turned foe, Augustus had her young fiancé killed. When she was 14, Augustus wed her to his nephew Marcellus, who would die two years later. She then married another cousin's husband, Agrippa, and consequently gave Augustus four grandchildren. But the emperor was not satisfied. When Agrippa died, Augustus matched Julia with Livia's son Tiberius, even though Tiberius was happily married to someone else.

The result was the greatest sex scandal of the Augustan Age. Tiberius, craving the wife he was forced to divorce, withdrew to an island and brooded. The abandoned Julia, meanwhile, took her first stab at enjoying life on her terms. She had lovers—not just a few, it was said, but many. She got drunk in revels at the Forum, informants reported, and offered herself as a prostitute on the street.

In 2 B.C., word of his daughter's transgressions reached Augustus. In a blaze of publicity, he terminated Julia's marriage, wrote the Senate a letter detailing her alleged debaucheries, and banished her, at 37, to an island in the Tyrrhenian Sea.

Ten years later, an identical charge hit Julia's daughter, also named Julia, and she, too, was sent into exile. For good measure, Augustus struck back at one perceived cause of his progeny's lax morals. The emperor had long endured the poems of Ovid, whose *Art of Love* seduction manual

flew in the face of the official family-values campaign. For corrupting his kin, the monarch expelled Rome's most popular poet to a Black Sea town so backward that men wore trousers.

Slippery slope. Augustus never understood that a force far more pervasive than Ovid's poems was fueling Rome's moral slide. It was wealth that rotted out the Roman character. With trade and tribute pouring in from the provinces, the rich grew richer, lazier, and more indulgent. Nor did the doles and free spectacles strengthen the moral fiber of the city's idle mob. As time went on, the disparities between the rich and the wretched widened in every respect. Housing costs in the cities soared, chasing the impoverished into attics and one-room hovels with no water and no hearth. In the countryside, land increasingly fell into the hands of a few patrician families that now owned thousands of acres tended by hundreds of disinherited, indigent workers.

By the third century A.D., to meet the rising costs of defending its frontier, Rome was soaking the poor. The Romans never imagined anything like today's graduated income tax, which places the heaviest burden on those best able to bear it. Rome's system was the opposite: The richer and more politically connected a man was, the less he paid.

The fifth-century collapse of the empire that began just before the Year One had many perceived causes, from exhaustion of topsoil to poisonous lead in the pipes of an otherwise splendid plumbing system. No claim has been more controversial than Edward Gibbon's. His five-volume *History of the Decline and Fall of the Roman Empire* (1776–88) blamed Christianity, asserting that it had wrecked the old religions that had sustained the Roman soul and stabilized the Roman state. But Will Durant, the 20th-century philosopher, noted that the old religions were breaking up long before Jesus was born. Romans lost faith in their leaders, Durant wrote in *Caesar and Christ*, "because the state defended wealth against poverty, fought to capture slaves, taxed toil to support luxury, and failed to protect its people from famine, pestilence, invasion, and destitution."

As for the spread of Christianity—now the world's largest religion with roughly 2 billion followers—sources from antiquity suggest an important role by the emperor who reigned during Jesus's childhood. Thanks to Augustus's Pax Romana, Christ's revolutionary message was able to spread from one generation to the next in a world made stable by the hegemony of Rome, developing, as the apostle Paul described it, "in the fullness of time."

"A peace was prevalent which began at the birth of Christ," the Christian teacher Origen wrote in the second century. "For God prepared the nations for his teaching so that they should be under one prince, the king of the Romans, and that it might not . . . be more difficult for the apostles to carry out the task laid on them by their Master when he said, 'Go and teach all nations.'"

AROUND THE WORLD

Meanwhile, in other lands . . .

Not all roads led to Rome in A.D.1. Though he never saw it, China's Han dynasty would have humbled even Augustus: A detailed census taken in A.D. 2 counted nearly 60 million souls under the emperor's rule, protected from northern barbarians by a garrisoned wall stretching hundreds of miles.

At the heart of Han power was trade, with far-reaching and well-regulated routes on sea and land. Silk, along with other manufactured goods like lacquer boxes and iron, tied the empire to almost every corner of the ancient world, as trade pulsed along the route travelers today still call the Silk Road. (The secrets of cultivating the sild-worm were closely guarded by the imperial government.) Goods moved form the Chinese heartland east to the islands of Japan, south to the kingdoms of India, and west all the way to Rome. To keep track of this trade and manage the rest of the empire, the Han refined what was to become their most lasting legacy: bureaucracy. A rigid hierarchy of provincial and local officials reported to the emperor; a wide-ranging network of roads with special lanes reserved for official use and a sophisticated post system kept them in touch with the capital. Officials studied administration, Confucianism, and archery at a national university that taught as many as 30,000 students at once. They wrote on silk or wood, though in the Year One the invention of paper was just a few decades away.

Strong Han. The Han's success in controlling such a huge empire left such an impact on the Chinese that they still call themselves "people of Han" today. The Han gave "recognizable shape . . . to the culture, social structure, political system, and economy of China," historians Joseph Levenson and Franz Schurmann write. " . . .It was the political system of Han that gave China its unique stamp."

Already vast, the Han seem to have been less interested in expansion than the Romans. The Chinese fought constantly with northern nomads and despite military campaigns and diplomatic efforts never managed to consolidate control over the Central Asian merchant kingdoms, preventing any substantive direct links between the Han and Rome. Still, profits on the Silk Road flowed in one direction: east. With nothing much to offer the Chinese in the way of trade goods, Rome paid dearly for its indulgence in silk. Pliny the Elder, writing in the first century A.D., estimated Rome paid 100 million sesterces (or 22,000 gold pounds) for its imports from the east.

The Han legacy, like that of the Romans, is still visible today. Not all the peoples of the Year One were as lucky. On the other side of the world, an empire was forming that would dominate Central America for seven centuries—and then virtually vanish.

The pyramids of Teotihuacán still tower over the valley floor near modern-day Mexico City. These massive structures are remnants of a thriving metropolis that once housed as many as 200,000 people, making it one of the largest cities in the world at its peak in the fifth century A.D.

City living. Building Teotihuacán scholar Esther Pasztory. "It's more practical for people to live dispersed, especially in preindustrial society." Though the city's setup was less efficient for farming, organization enabled the city to become a trading powerhouse. The city's workshops turned out millions of blades and scrapers crafted from green volcanic glass. Thriving exports, perhaps facilitated by foreign delegations living in the city, spread Teotihuacán's distinctive obsidian tools and pottery all over Central America.

But today, much about Teotihuacán remains mysterious. There are no written records and no accounting for the city's collapse. Around A.D. 700, some sort of political conflict broke out, and the population slowly dispersed over several decades. By the time of the Aztecs seven centuries later, the abandoned city's origins were shrouded in myth. Even the city's original name was lost; Teotihuacán is Aztec for "City of the Gods," Pasztory says, because "the Aztecs thought it was so impressive only the gods could have made it."

—Andrew Curry

Secrets of a Desert Metropolis

The Hidden Wonders of Petra's Ancient Engineers

BY EVAN HADINGHAM

TODAY, PETRA IS A VAST EMPTY CANYON encircled by astonishing tombs. Their magnificent facades, carved into sandstone cliffs, overlook a chaos of eroded ruins on the valley floor. Until recently, so little of the 2,000-year-old city had been explored that some scholars had branded Petra a "city of the dead" or a "tent city"—an occasional metropolis settled only seasonally by wandering peddlers and pilgrims.

Recent excavations reveal a very different city. The archaeological jewel of Jordan was, in fact, a fabulously wealthy hub of merchants and traders known from Rome to China. Surrounded by a brutal desert, some 30,000 people thrived in a city that for centuries lavished precious water on public pools, baths, and fountains. Petra in its prime virtually ruled the incense trade.

The city's rulers enjoyed a reputation as canny diplomats and generals skilled in outwitting more powerful neighbors. By the first century A.D., the city boasted graceful temples, a broad avenue lined with shops, public gardens, and water brought through more than six kilometers (3.7 miles) of ceramic pipes. The canyon walls that encircled the city were crowded with more than 800 tombs that awe today's visitors as completely as they must have amazed travelers two millennia ago.

The Treasury is the most famous of more than 800 rock-cut tombs at Petra, nearly all concealing simple, undecorated burial chambers.

Archaeologists finally are discovering and fitting critical pieces into the abiding puzzles of Petra: How could scattered desert nomads have created so mighty a citadel? And what finally caused their prosperity to falter and their wondrous city to fade?

Investigations built on satellite imagery, aerial photography, and extensive ground surveys have banished old theories of Petra and its founders, who were known to the ancient world as Nabataeans.

Once visualized as little more than wandering, camel-borne traders, the Nabataeans are now known to have deliberately planted year-round settlements throughout the arid wilderness of southern Jordan and northern Saudi Arabia. In a region that tastes barely 10 centimeters (3.9 inches) of rain annually, these outposts were succored with the same ingeniously engineered water systems recently revealed at Petra.

And while the city's demise has been blamed on everything from the Romans to a series of devastating earthquakes, new evidence suggests a completely unexpected scenario for Petra's final centuries.

NOMADIC ORIGINS

History's first notice of the Nabataeans is in a fourth-century B.C. account by the Greek historian Hieronymus. He describes nomadic bands—wandering traders and herders of sheep and camels—who forbade the growing of grain or the con-

From *Scientific American Discovering Archaeology*, September/October 2000, pp. 70-77. © 2000 by Scientific American Discovering Archaeology.

struction of houses on pain of death. The archaeological picture of Nabataean origins remains obscure, although some argue their ancestors were pastoralists in the deserts of northeast Arabia.

The first Nabataean sites appear abruptly during the first century B.C. Within 100 years, they had exploded all over what is now southern Jordan and northern Saudi Arabia, including such hostile environments as the Negev and Hisma deserts.

Four centuries after Hieronymus, another Greek historian, Strabo, describes a radically different Nabataean culture. Strabo discovered a pleasure-loving people who lived in fine, stone houses and cultivated fruit and vines. The king, the historian contended, presided over lavish banquets with female singers and poured wine into his guests' golden cups. Strabo also reported that the king answered to a popular assembly.

This image of a fun-loving, populist monarchy may well be as mythical as Hieronymus' hardy, nomadic shepherds. Nonetheless, Nabataean society doubtless underwent extraordinary changes that drove its explosive growth during the first century B.C.

By that time, Nabataeans were the primary transporters of frankincense and myrrh from their sources in the southern Arabian desert. These aromatic resins were prized throughout the known world for cosmetic, medicinal, and spiritual uses, as their prominence in the Chris-

tian Nativity story implies. (Some early Christian sources suggest the Three Magi may have been Nabataean merchants.)

CAMELS AND CARAVANS

The precious gums were harvested from spindly trees grown mainly in a narrow coastal region of Oman and Yemen. Petra's position at the crossroads of the incense trade produced the city's extraordinary wealth. Strabo describes caravans of as

A pair of rock-cut tombs reveal the varied cultures that influenced Petra's builders, from miniature Egyptian obelisks on the top tomb to the Hellenistic columns on the lower one.

many as 2,000 camels that crossed the desert from southern Arabia to Petra and then on to Mediterranean ports or Egypt.

"These vast caravans must have needed protection from thieves and numerous stops for refreshment as they crossed the desert. There were probably lots of opportunities for Nabataean camel guides and merchants to line their

Nabataeans some 2,000 years ago climbed steep stairways hewn into the cliffs to worship at sacrificial alters perched on mountain tops high above the splendid metropolis of Petra.

©Wolfgang Kaehler/CORBIS

The magnificent Roman-style amphitheater carved from Petra's sandstone cliffs once seated as many as 4,000 spectators.

The Scrolls of Petra

A Great City's Last Decades are Deciphered from Charred Papyrus

At first glance, one of the great document discoveries of the Near East resembles little more than charred fragments like those you might find amid the ashes of a backyard barbecue. But apply a strong, raking light, and you suddenly begin picking out faint, spidery lines. Fragments of Greek text show up in glossy contrast against the blackened surface of the papyrus.

The crushed papyrus rolls were found under the rubble of Petra's ruined Byzantine church in 1993 by Zbigniew Fiema of the American Center of Oriental Research, then conserved by Jaakko Frösén and his team from the University of Helsinki in Finland. The team teased apart thousands of burned papyrus scraps and fit the charred scraps back together like a daunting jigsaw puzzle.

By 1995, 152 rolls were reconstituted, of which about a third are legible. They represent one of the most significant document finds in the region since the Dead Sea scrolls.

The scrolls and pieces of scrolls reside now between glass plates in a lab at the American Center for Oriental Research in Amman, Jordan. Ludwig Koenen, Frösén, and their colleagues from Michigan and Helsinki universities are deciphering the texts and fitting more loose scraps into place.

The texts, mostly contracts relating to the management of property throughout the sixth century A.D., have rewritten the story of Petra's final decades.

Far from being deserted in the wake of devastating earthquakes, as historians always assumed, Petra was evidently still flourishing in this era. The production of wine, wheat, and fruit is noted in the scrolls. Orchards, farmlands, and vineyards clearly indicate that the city's complex irrigation systems were still intact just a few decades before the Muslim conquest in A.D. 631 closed another chapter in Petra's long saga. □ EH

COURTESY OF JAAKKO FRÖSÉN

pockets along the way," says University of Miami historian David Graf.

An eloquent relic of the camel-borne trade was unearthed in 1997, when archaeologists with the Petra National Trust began removing tons of sand and debris from the bottom of the Siq—a narrow gorge that provided a winding, kilometer-long (.6-mile) route into the city. There, alongside ancient paving stones that once floored the Siq, archaeologists found the stumps of larger-than-life relief sculptures carved into the cliff wall. They depict a pair of robed men, each leading a camel. One appears to be facing toward the city, while the other seems to be departing—symbols, perhaps, of the camel traffic that once echoed through this towering ravine.

If camel caravans were the bedrock of Nabataean wealth, did Petra's population live like desert nomads in roomy tents of woven camel hair, as traditional Bedouin families still do today? Little more than a decade ago, some scholars still visualized Petra as a seasonal tent city, Occupied only for rituals connected with the great tombs. Such notions held as long as archaeologists mostly confined their attention to imposing tombs and temple ruins.

'STONE TENTS'

Then in 1988, a joint team from Switzerland and Liechtenstein led by Rolf Stucky launched the first systematic effort to explore the urban heart of Petra. In the years since, they have discovered what Stucky describes as "a city of stone tents." The tent platforms that marked Petra's early days were replaced by substantial stone houses that were scattered informally (as tents might be) across the landscape.

In one house, excavations revealed a bowl still bearing traces of fish sauce. Another yielded a bear paw that probably came from an imported fur rug. One house even preserved traces of a multicolored wall painting from the first century A.D. It depicts architectural motifs similar to the elaborately carved tomb entrances that line the surrounding canyon.

Broken remnants of once-mighty columns that supported the front of the Great Temple were toppled, probably by earthquakes that plagued Petra.

The style of Petra was heavily influenced by the classic Greek architecture that Nabataean merchants encountered on trading visits around the Mediterranean. Local craftsmen freely adapted the Hellenistic designs to their own tastes to produce a unique blend. Both on their massive tombs and inside their homes, the people of Petra invoked the urban sophistication of the Greek and Roman world as evidence of their wealth.

High above the ruins of these prosperous homes are mountain shrines that crown the peaks around Petra. They are connected to the valley floor by broad stairways, carved in the cliff face at enormous labor by the Nabataeans. It is easy to visualize them, robed and in solemn procession, toiling slowly up these stairways to the rock-carved altars and receptacles for sacrificial blood—which at least one Nabataean inscription implies was sometimes human.

Other inscriptions—written in a precursor of today's Arabic script—identify the chief Nabataean deities as Dushara (a male god of fertility, vegetation, and everlasting life) and Al-'Uzza (a mother goddess often identified with Aphrodite of the Greeks or Isis of the Egyptians.).

Ceremonies invoking these deities occurred not only on mountaintops but also in at least four freestanding temples on either side of Petra's main street. One temple, excavated for nearly three decades by Phillip C. Hammond, was probably dedicated to Al-'Uzza or another female deity. A small, carved idol bears the tantalizing, but fragmentary inscription: "Goddess of . . . "

AN AMAZING TEMPLE

One of the biggest surprises from recent work at Petra came in 1997, when Brown University archaeologists unearthed an amphitheater at the heart of a sprawling ruin dubbed the "Great Temple." The entrance to this building, erected in the first century B.C., was framed by a massive portico some 18 meters (60 feet) high, supported by four huge columns, and vividly decorated with red and white stucco and delicate floral sculptures.

The purpose of this structure in the center of the temple is a mystery. Could it be that the great temple was not really a temple at all, but the "popular assembly" mentioned by Strabo, the Greek historian?

"There are quite a few possibilities," says Martha Sharp Joukowsky, leader of the Brown team. "It could be that we're looking at a kind of temple/theater, or a law court, or a *curia*—a Roman [style] political meeting place. In future seasons, we'll search for evidence to test these various possibilities."

Barely a year after the amphitheater was found, an even more startling discovery—a true measure of Petra's extravagance—came from the area long assumed to be a marketplace. This area was, in fact, a public garden with a promenade surrounding an open-air pool, says Pennsylvania University archaeologist Leigh-Ann Bedal. A little island at the center of the pool supported a lavishly decorated structure interpreted by Bedal as a recreational pavilion.

The pool was nearly identical in size to a modern Olympic pool—50 meters (165 feet) across. An elaborate network of ceramic pipes channeled water to it from the Ain Musa gorge over six kilometers (nearly four miles) away. The pipeline carried water through the Siq to the city center, then branched off to supply the pool, the Great Temple, public baths, fountains, and other luxurious amenities.

In the middle of a blazing, barren desert, what better symbol of Petra's opulence could there be than such an extravagant use of water?

REMOTE OUTPOSTS

The great city was unique only in scale. Much smaller Nabataean settlements reveal traces of elaborate waterworks, temples, and bathhouses. University of Victoria archaeologist John P. Oleson, excavating a remote outpost called Humeima in southern Jordan, found a roofed, stone aqueduct 27 kilometers (17 miles) long —a remarkable feat of planning and construction.

Oleson believes that Petra's first-century monarchs actively encouraged the spread of a more settled way of life throughout their realm, building water channels and bathhouses even in the parched canyons of the Hisma desert. "We're not sure what lay behind this wide-scale settlement planning," Oleson says, "but one idea is that new villages and towns helped discourage attacks by desert nomads on the caravan routes. Also, the Nabataean kings probably wanted to encourage the growth of a new economy in case the incense trade faltered."

The classic tale of Petra's demise begins with the city's annexation by the Romans in A.D. 106. The Romans, in this telling, gradually drained Petra's wealth by diverting caravans northward to new centers, notably Palmyra in Syria. Then, in A.D. 363, a devastating earthquake supposedly finished off the impoverished Nabataeans.

New work by David Graf and others, however, indicates that Nabataean sites and the old caravan routes still prospered well into the Roman era. Petra, in fact, was given the Roman title *metropolis,* while the governor of Rome's Arabian province chose to be buried in one of Petra's fanciest tombs.

PETRA'S DEMISE

The spectacular discovery in 1993 of the Petra scrolls proves that as late as the sixth century A.D., when these papyrus records were compiled, Petra's traditional systems of land ownership and irrigation were still in place. Indeed, fragments of old Nabataean beliefs and values may well have lingered until the coming of Islam in A.D. 631.

Skillfully exploiting their position as middlemen on the fringes of the classical world, the Nabataeans blended the comforts and style of Greece and Rome with their Arabian roots. This exotic cultural mixture captivates both researchers and visitors to Petra. Yet even more remarkable was the Nabataeans' command of water, a mastery that enabled them to colonize the desert and protect the caravans that had brought them so much wealth and greatness.

EVAN HADINGHAM is Science Editor of NOVA, the PBS science series, and author of Lines to the Mountain Gods *and other books on prehistory.*

Unit Selections

Key Points to Consider

❖ What is the purpose of religion in human life? What has been the role of religion in history?

❖ Why make a fuss about the historical aspects of a religion? What difference can it make?

❖ Why do people of one faith often mistrust people of another religion?

❖ Why is it difficult to study religion in a scientific manner?

❖ On what points are the major religions alike and different?

 **Links**   **www.dushkin.com/online/**

These sites are annotated on pages 4 and 5.

According to the *World Almanac, 2001,* there are 2 billion Christians, 1.2 billion Muslims, 800 million Hindus, 356 million Buddhists, 14 million Jews, and 6 million Confucians in the world. Many people profess some sort of religion. Although it is often difficult to ascribe religious motivation to people and events, the world religions, nonetheless, provide a moral foundation for human interaction. In some instances the role of religion is obvious, such as in the current conflicts between Jews and Muslims in Israel, Protestants and Catholics in Ireland, and Muslims and Hindus in India. In other situations the role of religion is subtle, but in any historical analysis religious motivation should not be ignored.

The great world religions were developed in premodern times, and since they began a long time ago there are many unanswered historical questions. In the story of their development, however, there are common themes—the relationship of one person to another and the relationship of people to a greater entity.

Religion permeates the history and culture of India, and T. R. Sundaram in "Ancient Jewel" outlines the significant religious ideas of Indian civilization. Indian civilization, among the oldest in the world, created not only Hinduism, but also Buddhism. The religion of Buddha, however, left India and migrated into Asia.

The search for historical data about the religious founders has gone on, but this has proven offensive to some believers. The Koran, the basic sacred text of Islam, is considered the unchanged word of God by orthodox followers. Yet, comparison with earlier versions, as noted by Toby Lester in "What Is the Koran?" reveals changes. This is threatening to orthodox believers. History presents a threat regarding the control of Jerusalem, a city sacred to Muslims, Jews, and Christians. Walid Khalidi, in "The Dome of the Rock," provides a tour through these sacred places. The Christians' site of the Crucifixion, the Jews' Wailing Wall, and the Muslims' rock from which Muhammad ascended into heaven are all in close proximity. It is no wonder that there is stress created by who controls these holy places.

Christianity, the world's most popular religion, has had vast influence in art, culture, politics, and war not only in the West, but also elsewhere in the world. Kenneth L. Woodward summaries the historical influence—good and bad—of Christianity in "2000 Years of Jesus." It is interesting to ask what other religions think about Jesus. Kenneth L.

Woodward surveys the answers of Muslims, Jews, Hindus, and Buddhists. With others, there is particular difficulty with the pain and death of crucifixion. They wonder why God would allow that to happen.

Confucius, in comparison to the other religious leaders, was much less concerned about spirituality. He was involved with the relationships between people and with the government. His ideas from the fifth century B.C.E. endure and still influence Chinese thinking. Jonathan Spence, a Chinese scholar, comments on why Confucius is worthy of study.

Comparisons between faiths or beliefs are not easy. Yet, spiritual matters have long been of interest to humankind and they cannot be lightly dismissed or cynically disregarded in the study of world history. Even in nations that profess religious freedom and emphasize the separation of religion from government, such as the United States, religion has a permeating influence. Therefore, in evaluating any nation or society, this dimension of human interest demands consideration.

Ancient Jewel

From early Greece to the modern civil rights movement, Indian thought and philosophy have had a wide-ranging influence on Western culture.

T. R. (Joe) Sundaram

T. R. (Joe) Sundaram is the owner of an engineering research firm in Columbia, Maryland, and has written extensively on Indian history, culture, and science.

The very word *India* conjures up exotic images in one's mind. Yet this name for the south Asian subcontinent is of Western making, mediated by the Persians and the Arabs. The name used in ancient Sanskrit texts is *Bharat* (for the land of Bharatha, a legendary king), which is also the official name of the modern republic. Other familiar Western words such as *Hindu, caste,* and *curry* are also totally foreign to India. The general knowledge that exists in the West about India, its early history, philosophy, and culture is, at best, superficial. Nevertheless, since it would be impossible in a brief article to do justice to even one of these topics, I shall provide a brief, accurate glimpse into each.

India covers about 1.2 million square miles and is home to a population of 895 million; in comparison, the United States covers 3.6 million square miles and has 258 million residents. Thus, the population density of India is nearly 10 times that of the United States. (The size of classical India—which includes modern-day India, Pakistan, Bangladesh, and parts of Afghanistan—is about two-thirds that of the continental United States.)

But statistics about India can be misleading. For example, while only about one-quarter of the population is "literate," able to read and write, this has to be viewed in light of the strong oral traditions present in India since antiquity. Therefore, while a "literate" American may often be unaware of the collective name of the first 10 amendments to the U.S. Constitution, an "illiterate" Indian peasant would be aware of the history of his ancestors from antiquity to the present day.

Not only is India one of the oldest civilizations in the world, being more than 6,000 years old, but also it may be the oldest continuing civilization in existence; that is, one without any major "gaps" in its history. As the renowned historian A. L. Basham has pointed out,

Until the advent of archeologists, the peasant of Egypt or Iraq had no knowledge of the culture of his forefathers, and it is doubtful whether his Greek counterpart had any but the vaguest ideas about the glory of Periclean Athens. In each case there had been an almost complete break with the past. On the other hand, the earliest Europeans to visit India found a culture fully conscious of its own antiquity.

India is a land of many ancient "living" cities, such as, for example, Varanasi. Even at sites like Delhi, many successive cities have been built over thousands of years. Among old buried cities that have been unearthed in modern times by archaeologists are Mohenjo-Daro and Harappa.

Of these cities, the renowned archaeologist Sir John Marshall writes that they establish the existence

in the fourth and third millennium B.C., of a highly developed city life; and the presence in many houses, of wells and bathrooms as well as an elaborate drainage system, betoken a social condition of the citizens at least equal to that found in Sumer, and superior to that prevailing in contemporary Babylonia and Egypt.

Thus, India was the "jewel of the world" long before the Greek and Roman civilizations.

Nor was classical India isolated from developing civilizations in other parts of the world. Clay seals from Mohenjo-Daro have been found in Babylonia and

Embassy of India

Continuous civilization: Excavations at Mohenjo-Daro and Harappa reveal well-planned towns and a sophisticated urban culture dating back to 2500 B.C.

vice versa. Ancient Indian artifacts such as beads and bangles have been found in many parts of the Middle East and Africa. India and Indian culture were known to the Greeks even before the time of Alexander the Great. The Greek historian Herodotus wrote extensively about India during the sixth century B.C. Also, during this period many Greeks, including Pythagoras, are known to have traveled to India.

Sixth century B.C. was a period of great religious and philosophical upheaval in India. Hinduism was already an established, "old" religion, and re-

Crucible of Learning

- *India's may be the oldest continuing civilization in existence.*

- *To avoid misunderstanding India, it is essential to appreciate three central tenets of Indian thinking: assimilating ideas and experiences, a belief in cycles, and the coexistence of opposites.*

- *India has made numerous contributions to contemporary Western understanding of mathematics, science, and philosophy.*

form movements were beginning to appear, such as one by a prince known as Siddhartha Gautama, who later came to be known as the Buddha. The religion that was founded based on his teachings spread not only throughout Asia but also to many parts of the world, including Greece, and it helped spread Indian culture in the process.

In Alexander the Great's campaign to conquer the world, his ultimate goal was India; he died without achieving that objective. When Seleucus Nicator, Alexander's successor, tried to follow in Alexander's footsteps, he was soundly defeated by Indian emperor Chandragupta Maurya. A peace treaty was signed between the two, and Seleucus sent an ambassador, Megasthenes, to the court of Chandragupta. Megasthenes sent glowing reports back to Greece about India, and he pronounced Indian culture to be equal or superior to his own, a high compliment indeed, since Greece was then near its zenith.

For the next 1,500 years or so, India—rich in material wealth, scientific knowledge, and spiritual wisdom—enjoyed the reputation of being at the pinnacle of world civilizations. Arab writers of the Middle Ages routinely re-

ferred to mathematics as *hindsat*, the "Indian science."

And as is well known now, it was Columbus' desire to reach India that led to the discovery of America. Indeed, the explorer died thinking that he had discovered a new sea route to India, while he had merely landed on a Caribbean island. Columbus' mistake also led to the mislabeling of the natives of the land as "Indians," a label that survived even after the mistake had been discovered.

THE UPANISHADS

Indian philosophy is almost as old as Indian civilization, and its zenith was reached nearly 3,000 years ago with the compilation, by unknown sages, of 108 ancient philosophical texts known as the Upanishads. These texts reflect even older wisdom, which was passed down from generation to generation through oral transmission. A Western commentator has remarked that in the Upanishads the Indian mind moved from cosmology to psychology, and that while most other contemporary civilizations were still asking the question "What am I?" the Indian mind was already asking, "Who am I?"

When translations of the Upanishads first became available in the West in the nineteenth century, the impact on European philosophers such as Goethe and Schopenhauer and on American writers such as Emerson and Whitman was profound. "In the whole world," wrote Schopenhauer emotionally, "there is no study as beneficial and as elevating as the Upanishads." Emerson wrote poems based on the texts.

One of the principal underlying themes in the Upanishads is the quest for a "personal reality." This quest began with the conviction that the limitations of our sensory perceptions give us an imperfect model to comprehend the real world around us; this is known as the concept of *maya*. Since individual perceptions can be different, different people can also have different "realities."

For example, a happy event for one individual may be an unhappy one for another. Recognition and perfection of our personal reality is the quintessential goal of Indian philosophy and is also the basic principle behind yoga. Indeed, the literal meaning of the Sanskrit word *yoga* is "union," and the union that is sought is not with any external entity but with one's self. This is, of course, also the principal tenet of modern psychoanalysis.

From a Western perspective, to avoid misunderstanding India in general, and Indian philosophy in particular, it is essential to appreciate three central tenets of the Indian way of thinking. These are:

Assimilation. In the Indian way of thinking, new experiences and ideas never replace old ones but are simply absorbed into, and made a part of, old experiences. Although some have characterized such thinking as static, in reality such thinking is both dynamic and conservative, since old experiences are preserved and new experiences are continually accumulated.

Belief in cycles. Another central tenet of the Indian character is the belief that all changes in the world take place through cycles, there being cycles superimposed on other cycles, cycles within cycles, and so on. Inherent in the concept of cycles is alternation, and the Upanishads speak of the two alternating states of all things being "potentiality" and "expression."

Acceptance of the coexistence of opposites. Early Western readers of the Upanishads were puzzled by the apparent inherent ability of the Indian mind to accept the coexistence of seemingly diametrically opposite concepts. Belief in, and acceptance of, contradictory ideas is a natural part of the Indian way of life, and the logical complement to the tenets already mentioned. It is an indisputable fact that birth (creation) must necessarily be eventually followed by death (destruction). Creation and destruction are inseparable alternations. Even concepts such as "good" and "evil" are complementary, as each of us may have within us the most lofty and divine qualities and at the same time the basest qualities. We ourselves and the whole world can be whatever we want to make of them.

These three tenets are responsible for the amazing continuity of the Indian civilization, its reverence for the elderly, and the acceptance of the aging process without a morbid fear of death.

Ironically, the culture that taught of the need to renounce materialistic desires also produced some of the most pleasurable things in life. The intricacies and highly developed nature of Indian art, music, dance, and cuisine are examples. And the Kama Sutra is perhaps the oldest, and best known, manual on the pleasures of love and sex.

FROM PYTHAGORAS TO KING

Throughout history, India's contributions to the Western world have been considerable, albeit during the Middle Ages they were often felt only indirectly, having been mediated by the Middle Eastern cultures.

After the early contacts between Greece and India in the sixth and fifth centuries B.C., many concepts that had been in use in India centuries earlier made their appearance in Greek literature, although no source was ever acknowledged. For example, consider the so-called Pythagorean theorem of a right triangle and the Pythagorean school's theory of the "transmigration of souls"; the former was in use in India (for temple construction) centuries earlier, and the latter is merely "reincarnation," a concept of Vedic antiquity. There was also a flourishing trade between the Roman Empire and the kingdoms in south-

Embassy of India

A terra-cotta toy cow: Ancient Indian civilizations featured highly talented artisans and craftsmen.

ern India, through which not only Indian goods but also ideas made their journey westward.

During the Middle Ages, the Arabs translated many classical Indian works into Arabic, and the ideas contained in them eventually made their way to Europe. A principal mission of the "House of Wisdom" that was established by the caliph in Baghdad in the eighth century was the translation of Indian works.

Among the major Indian ideas that entered Europe through the Arabs are the mathematical concept of zero (for which there was no equivalent in Greek or Roman mathematics) and the modern numerical system we use today. Until the twelfth century, Europe was shackled by the unwieldy Roman numerals. The famous French mathematician Laplace has written: "It is India that gave us the ingenious method of expressing all numbers by ten symbols, each receiving a value of position as well as an absolute value, a profound and important idea which appears so simple to us now that we ignore its true merit."

India's contributions to other areas of science and mathematics were equally important. The seventh-century Syrian astronomer Severus Sebokht wrote that "the subtle theories" of Indian astronomers were "even more ingenious than those of the Greeks and the Babylonians."

The scientific approach permeated other aspects of Indian life as well. For example, classical Indian music has a highly mathematical structure, based on divisions of musical scales into tones and microtones.

In modern times, Indian music has had a considerable influence on Western music. Starting in the 1960s, the famous Indian sitar virtuoso Ravi Shankar popularized sitar music in the West, and now the melodic strains of the sitar, as well as the beat of the Indian drum known as tabla, can be heard in the works of many pop-music artists, ranging from the Beatles to Michael Jackson. The movies of the Indian filmmaker Satyajit Ray have also made a significant impact on the West.

The contributions of many modern Indian scientists have been important to the overall development of Western sci-

Khorrum Omer/The World & I

Indian music has influenced Western artists, particularly in modern times. The beat of the tabla can be heard in pop music ranging from the Beatles to Michael Jackson.

ence. The mathematical genius Srinivasa Ramanujan, who died in 1920, has been called "the greatest mathematician of the century" and "the man who knew infinity." The discovery by the Nobel Prize–winning Indian physicist Chandrasekhara Venkata Raman of the effect (which bears his name) by which light diffusing through a transparent material changes in wavelength has revolutionized laser technology. The theoretical predictions by the Nobel Prize-winning astrophysicist Subrahmanyan Chandrasekhar on the life and death of white-dwarf stars led to the concept of "black holes."

In the literary area, the poetry of Nobel laureate Rabindranath Tagore and the philosophical interpretations of the scholar (and a former president of India) Sarvepalli Radhakrishnan have inspired

the West. Albert Einstein was one of the admirers of the former and corresponded with him on the meaning of "truth."

In terms of our daily dietary habits, many vegetables such as cucumber, eggplant, okra, squash, carrots, many types of beans, and lentils were first domesticated in India. Rice, sugarcane, and tea, as well as fruits such as bananas and oranges, are of Indian origin. The name *orange* is derived from the Sanskrit word *narangi*. Chicken and cattle were also first domesticated in India, albeit the latter for milk production and not for meat consumption. Cotton was first domesticated in India. The process of dying fabrics also was invented in India. Indian fabrics (both cotton and silk) have been world renowned for their quality since antiquity. The game of

Khorrum Omer/The World & I

Melodic inspiration: Performing traditional dance and music in Orissa.

chess was invented in India, and the name itself derives from the Sanskrit name Chaturanga.

India's most popular modern exports have been yoga and meditation. Hatha yoga, the exercise system that is a part of yoga, is now taught widely in America, in institutions ranging from colleges to hospitals. Many scientific studies on the beneficial effects of yoga practice are now under way. A similar state of affairs is true of Indian meditation techniques, which people under stress use for mental relaxation.

Finally the Rev. Martin Luther King, Jr., repeatedly acknowledged his debt to Mahatma Gandhi for the technique of nonviolent civil disobedience, which he used in the civil rights movement. For all India's material contributions to the world, it is its spiritual legacy that has had the widest impact. The ancient sages who wrote the Upanishads would have been pleased.

ADDITIONAL READING

A. L. Basham, *The Wonder That Was India,* Grove Press, New York, 1959.

——, *Ancient India: Land of Mystery,* Time-Life Books, Alexandria, Virginia, 1994.

Will Durant, *the Story of Civilization: Part I, Our Oriental Heritage,* Simon and Schuster, New York, 1954.

What Is the Koran?

Researchers with a variety of academic and theological interests are proposing controversial theories about the Koran and Islamic history, and are striving to reinterpret Islam for the modern world. This is, as one scholar puts it, a "sensitive business"

By Toby Lester

IN 1972, during the restoration of the Great Mosque of Sana'a, in Yemen, laborers working in a loft between the structure's inner and outer roofs stumbled across a remarkable gravesite, although they did not realize it at the time. Their ignorance was excusable: mosques do not normally house graves, and this site contained no tombstones, no human remains, no funereal jewelry. It contained nothing more, in fact, than an unappealing mash of old parchment and paper documents—damaged books and individual pages of Arabic text, fused together by centuries of rain and dampness, gnawed into over the years by rats and insects. Intent on completing the task at hand, the laborers gathered up the manuscripts, pressed them into some twenty potato sacks, and set them aside on the staircase of one of the mosque's minarets, where they were locked away—and where they would probably have been forgotten once again, were it not for Qadhi Isma'il al-Akwa', then the president of the Yemeni Antiquities Authority, who realized the potential importance of the find.

Al-Akwa' sought international assistance in examining and preserving the fragments, and in 1979 managed to interest a visiting German scholar, who in turn persuaded the German government to organize and fund a restoration project. Soon after the project began, it became clear that the hoard was a fabulous example of what is sometimes referred to as a "paper grave"—in this case the resting place for, among other things, tens of thousands of fragments from close to a thousand different parchment codices of the Koran, the Muslim holy scripture. In some pious Muslim circles it is held that worn-out or damaged copies of the Koran must be removed from circulation; hence the idea of a grave, which both preserves the sanctity of the texts being laid to rest and ensures that only complete and unblemished editions of the scripture will be read.

Some of the parchment pages in the Yemeni hoard seemed to date back to the seventh and eighth centuries A.D., or Islam's first two centuries—they were fragments, in other words, of perhaps the oldest Korans in existence. What's more, some of these fragments revealed small but intriguing aberrations from the standard Koranic text. Such aberrations, though not surprising to textual historians, are troublingly at odds with the orthodox Muslim belief that the Koran as it has reached us today is quite simply the perfect, timeless, and unchanging Word of God.

The mainly secular effort to reinterpret the Koran—in part based on textual evidence such as that provided by the Yemeni fragments—is disturbing and offensive to many Muslims, just as attempts to reinterpret the Bible and the life of Jesus are disturbing and offensive to many conservative Christians. Nevertheless, there are scholars, Muslims among them, who feel that such an effort, which amounts essentially to placing the Koran in history, will provide fuel for an Islamic revival of sorts—a reappropriation of tradition, a going forward by looking back. Thus far confined to scholarly argument, this sort of thinking can be nonetheless very powerful and—as the histories of the Renaissance and the Reformation demonstrate—can lead to major social change. The Koran, after all, is currently the world's most ideologically influential text.

LOOKING AT THE FRAGMENTS

THE first person to spend a significant amount of time examining the Yemeni fragments, in 1981, was Gerd-R. Puin, a specialist in Arabic calligraphy and Koranic paleography based at Saarland University, in Saarbrücken, Germany. Puin, who had been sent by the German government to organize and oversee the restoration project, recognized the antiquity of some of the parchment fragments, and his preliminary inspection also revealed unconventional verse orderings, minor textual variations, and rare styles of orthography and artistic embellishment. Enticing, too, were the sheets of the scripture

The effort to reinterpret the Koran, thus far confined to scholarly argument, could lead to major social change. The Koran, after all, is currently the world's most ideologically influential text.

written in the rare and early Hijazi Arabic script: pieces of the earliest Korans known to exist, they were also palimpsests—versions very clearly written over even earlier, washed-off versions. What the Yemeni Korans seemed to suggest, Puin began to feel, was an *evolving* text rather than simply the Word of God as revealed in its entirety to the Prophet Muhammad in the seventh century A.D.

Since the early 1980s more than 15,000 sheets of the Yemeni Korans have painstakingly been flattened, cleaned, treated, sorted, and assembled; they now sit ("preserved for another thousand years," Puin says) in Yemen's House of Manuscripts, awaiting detailed examination. That is something the Yemeni authorities have seemed reluctant to allow, however. "They want to keep this thing low-profile, as we do too, although for different reasons," Puin explains. "They don't want attention drawn to the fact that there are Germans and others working on the Korans. They don't want it made public that there is work being done *at all*, since the Muslim position is that everything that needs to be said about the Koran's history was said a thousand years ago."

To date just two scholars have been granted extensive access to the Yemeni fragments: Puin and his colleague H.-C. Graf von Bothmer, an Islamic-art historian also based at Saarland University. Puin and Von Bothmer have published only a few tantalizingly brief articles in scholarly publications on what they have discovered in the Yemani fragments. They have been reluctant to publish partly because until recently they were more concerned with sorting and classifying the fragments than with systematically examining them, and partly because they felt that the Yemeni authorities, if they realized the possible implications of the discovery, might refuse

them further access. Von Bothmer, however, in 1997 finished taking more than 35,000 microfilm pictures of the fragments, and has recently brought the pictures back to Germany. This means that soon Von Bothmer, Puin, and other scholars will finally have a chance to scrutinize the texts and to publish their findings freely—a prospect that thrills Puin. "So many Muslims have this belief that everything between the two covers of the Koran is just God's unaltered word," he says. "They like to quote the textual work that shows that the Bible has a history and did not fall straight out of the sky, but until now the Koran has been out of this discussion. The only way to break through this wall is to prove that the Koran has a history too. The Sana'a fragments will help us to do this."

Puin is not alone in his enthusiasm. "The impact of the Yemeni manuscripts is still to be felt," says Andrew Rippin, a professor of religious studies at the University of Calgary, who is at the forefront of Koranic studies today. "Their variant readings and verse orders are all very significant. Everybody agrees on that. These manuscripts say that the early history of the Koranic text is much more of an open question than many have suspected: the text was less stable, and therefore had less authority, than has always been claimed."

COPYEDITING GOD

By the standards of contemporary biblical scholarship, most of the questions being posed by scholars like Puin and Rippin are rather modest; outside an Islamic context, proposing that the Koran has a history and suggesting that it can be interpreted metaphorically are not radical steps. But the Islamic context—and Muslim sensibili-

ties—cannot be ignored. "To historicize the Koran would in effect delegitimize the whole historical experience of the Muslim community," says R. Stephen Humphreys, a professor of Islamic studies at the University of California at Santa Barbara. "The Koran is the charter for the community, the document that called it into existence. And ideally—though obviously not always in reality—Islamic history has been the effort to pursue and work out the commandments of the Koran in human life. If the Koran is a historical document, then the whole Islamic struggle of fourteen centuries is effectively meaningless."

The orthodox Muslim view of the Koran as self-evidently the Word of God, perfect and inimitable in message, language, style, and form, is strikingly similar to the fundamentalist Christian notion of the Bible's "inerrancy" and "verbal inspiration" that is still common in many places today. The notion was given classic expression only a little more than a century ago by the biblical scholar John William Burgon.

> The Bible is none other than *the voice of Him that sitteth upon the Throne!* Every Book of it, every Chapter of it, every Verse of it, every word of it, every syllable of it . . . every letter of it, is the direct utterance of the Most High!

Not all the Christians think this way about the Bible, however, and in fact, as the *Encyclopaedia of Islam* (1981) points out, "the closest analogue in Christian belief to the role of the Kur'ān in Muslim belief is not the Bible, but Christ." If Christ is the Word of God made flesh, the Koran is the Word of God made text, and questioning its sanctity or authority is thus considered an outright attack on Islam—as Salman Rushdie knows all too well.

The prospect of a Muslim backlash has not deterred the critical-historical study of the Koran, as the existence of the essays in *The Origins of the Koran* (1998) demonstrate. Even in the aftermath of the Rushdie affair the work continues: In 1996 the Koranic scholar Günter Lüling wrote in *The Journal of Higher Criticism* about "the wide extent to which both the text of the Koran and the learned Islamic account of Islamic origins have been distorted, a deformation unsuspectingly accepted by Western Islamicists until now." In 1994 the journal *Jerusalem Studies in Arabic and Islam* published a posthumous study by Yehuda D. Nevo, of the Hebrew University in Jerusalem, detailing seventh- and eighth-century religious inscriptions on stones in the Negev Desert which, Nevo suggested, pose "considerable problems for the traditional Muslim account of the history of Islam." That same year, and in the same journal, Patricia Crone, a historian of early Islam currently based at the Institute for Advanced Study, in Princeton, New Jersey, published an article in which she argued that elucidating problematic passages in the Koranic text is likely to be made possible only by "abandoning the conventional account of how the Qur'an was born." And since 1991 James Bellamy, of the University of Michigan, has proposed in the *Journal of the American Oriental Society* a series of "emendations to the text of the Koran"—changes that from the orthodox Muslim perspective amount to copyediting God.

Crone is one of the most iconoclastic of these scholars. During the 1970s and 1980s she wrote and collaborated on several books—most notoriously, with Michael Cook, *Hagarism: The Making of the Islamic World* (1977)—that made radical arguments about the origins of Islam and the writing of Islamic history. Among *Hagarism*'s controversial claims were suggestions that the text of the Koran came into being later than is now believed ("There is no hard evidence for the existence of the Koran in any form before the last decade of the seventh century"); that Mecca was not the initial Islamic sanctuary ("[the evidence] points unambiguously to a sanctuary in northwest Arabia . . . Mecca was secondary"); that the Arab conquests preceded the institutionalization of Islam ("the Jewish messianic fantasy was enacted in the form of an Arab conquest of the Holy Land"); that the idea of the *hijra*, or the migration of Muhammad and his followers from Mecca to Medina in 622, may have evolved long after Muhammad died ("No seventh-century source identifies the Arab era as that of the *hijra*"); and that the term "Muslim" was not commonly used in early Islam ("There is no good reason to suppose that the bearers of this primitive identity called themselves 'Muslims' [but] sources do . . . reveal an earlier designation of the community [which] appears in Greek as 'Magaritai' in a papyrus of 642, and in Syriac as 'Mahgre' or 'Mahgraye' from as early as the 640s").

Hagarism came under immediate attack, from Muslim and non-Muslim scholars alike, for its heavy reliance on hostile sources. ("This is a book," the authors wrote, "based on what from any Muslim perspective must appear an inordinate regard for the testimony of infidel sources.") Crone and Cook have since backed away from some of its most radical propositions—such as, for example, that the Prophet Muhammad lived two years longer than the Muslim tradition claims he did, and that the historicity of his migration to Medina is questionable. But Crone has continued to challenge both Muslim and Western orthodox views of Islamic history. In *Meccan Trade and the Rise of Islam* (1987) she made a detailed argument challenging the prevailing view among Western (and some Muslim) scholars that Islam arose in response to the Arabian spice trade.

Gerd-R. Puin's current thinking about the Koran's history partakes of this contemporary revisionism. "My idea is that the Koran is a kind of cocktail of texts that were not all understood even at the time of Muhammad," he says. "Many of them may even be a hundred years older than Islam itself. Even within the Islamic traditions there is a huge body of contradictory information, including a significant Christian substrate; one can derive a whole Islamic *anti-history* from them if one wants."

Patricia Crone defends the goals of this sort of thinking. "The Koran is a scripture with a history like any other—except that we don't know this history and tend to provoke howls of protest when we study it. Nobody would mind the howls if they came from Westerners, but Westerners feel deferential when the howls come from other people: who are you to tamper with *their* legacy? But we

Islamicists are not trying to destroy anyone's faith."

Not everyone agrees with that assessment—especially since Western Koranic scholarship has traditionally taken place in the context of an openly declared hostility between Christianity and Islam. (Indeed, the broad movement in the West over the past two centuries to "explain" the East, often referred to as Orientalism, has in recent years come under fire for exhibiting similar religious and cultural biases). The Koran has seemed, for Christian and Jewish scholars particularly, to possess an aura of heresy; the nineteenth-century Orientalist William Muir, for example, contended that the Koran was one of "the most stubborn enemies of Civilisation, Liberty, and the Truth which the world has yet known." Early Soviet scholars, too, undertook an ideologically motivated study of Islam's origins, with almost missionary zeal: in the 1920s and in 1930 a Soviet publication titled *Ateist* ran a series of articles explaining the rise of Islam in Marxist-Leninist terms. In *Islam and Russia* (1956), Ann K. S. Lambton summarized much of this work, and wrote that several Soviet scholars had theorized that "the motive force of the nascent religion was supplied by the mercantile bourgeoisie of Mecca and Medina"; that a certain S. P. Tolstov had held that "Islam was a social-religious movement originating in the slave-owning, not feudal, form of Arab society"; and that N. A. Morozov had argued that "until the Crusades Islam was indistinguishable from Judaism and . . . only then did it receive its independent character, while Muhammad and the first Caliphs are mythical figures." Morozov appears to have been a particularly flamboyant theorist: Lambton wrote that he also argued, in his book *Christ* (1930), that "in the Middle Ages Islam was merely an off-shoot of Arianism evoked by a meteorological event in the Red Sea area near Mecca."

Not surprisingly, then, given the biases of much non-Islamic critical study of the Koran, Muslims are inclined to dismiss it outright. A particularly eloquent protest came in 1987, in the *Muslim World Book Review*, in a paper titled "Method Against Truth: Orientalism and

Qur'ānic Studies," by the Muslim critic S. Parvez Manzoor. Placing the origins of Western Koranic scholarship in "the polemical marshes of medieval Christianity" and describing its contemporary state as a "cul-de-sac of its own making," Manzoor orchestrated a complex and layered assault on the entire Western approach to Islam. He opened his essay in a rage.

> The Orientalist enterprise of Qur'ānic studies, whatever its other merits and services, was a project born of spite, bred in frustration and nourished by vengeance: the spite of the powerful for the powerless, the frustration of the "rational" towards the "superstitious" and the vengeance of the "orthodox" against the "non-conformist." At the greatest hour of his worldly-triumph, the Western man, coordinating the powers of the State, Church and Academia, launched his most determined assault on the citadel of Muslim faith. All the aberrant streaks of his arrogant personality—its reckless rationalism, its world-domineering phantasy and its sectarian fanaticism—joined in an unholy conspiracy to dislodge the Muslim Scripture from its firmly entrenched position as the epitome of historic authenticity and moral unassailability. The ultimate trophy that the Western man sought by his dare-devil venture was the Muslim mind itself. In order to rid the West forever of the "problem" of Islam, he reasoned, Muslim consciousness must be made to despair of the cognitive certainty of the Divine message revealed to the Prophet. Only a Muslim confounded of the historical authenticity or doctrinal autonomy of the Qur'ānic revelation would abdicate his universal mission and hence pose no challenge to the global domination of the West. Such, at least, seems to have been the tacit, if not the explicit, rationale of the Orientalist assault on the Qur'ān.

Despite such resistance, Western researchers with a variety of academic and theological interests press on, applying modern techniques of textual and historical criticism to the study of the Koran. That a substantial body of this scholarship now exists is indicated by the recent decision of the European firm Brill Publishers—a long-established publisher of such major works as *The Encyclopaedia of Islam* and *The Dead Sea Scrolls Study Edition*—to commission the first-ever *Encyclopaedia of the Qur'an.* Jane McAuliffe, a professor of Islamic studies at the University of Toronto, and the general editor of the encyclopedia, hopes that it will function as a "rough analogue" to biblical encyclopedias and will be "a turn-of-the-millennium summative work for the state of Koranic scholarship." Articles for the first part of the encyclopedia are currently being edited and prepared for publication later this year.

The *Encyclopaedia of the Qur'an* will be a truly collaborative enterprise, carried out by Muslims and non-Muslims, and its articles will present multiple approaches to the interpretation of the Koran, some of which are likely to challenge traditional Islamic views—thus disturbing many in the Islamic world, where the time is decidedly less ripe for a revisionist study of the Koran. The plight of Nasr Abu Zaid, an unassuming Egyptian professor of Arabic who sits on the encyclopedia's advisory board, illustrates the difficulties facing Muslim scholars trying to reinterpret their tradition.

"A MACABRE FARCE"

THE Koran is a text, a *literary* text, and the only way to understand, explain, and analyze it is through a literary approach," Abu Zaid says. "This is an essential theological issue." For expressing views like this in print—in essence, for challenging the idea that the Koran must be read literally as the absolute and unchanging Word of God—Abu Zaid was in 1995 officially branded an apostate, a ruling that in 1996 was upheld by Egypt's highest court. The court then proceeded, on the grounds of an Islamic law forbidding the marriage of an apostate to a Muslim, to order Abu Zaid to divorce his wife, Ibtihal Yunis (a ruling that the shocked and happily married Yunis described at the time as coming "like a blow to the head with a brick").

Abu Zaid steadfastly maintains that he is a pious Muslim, but contends that the Koran's manifest content—for example, the often archaic laws about the treatment of women for which Islam is infamous—is much less important than its complex, regenerative, and spiritually nourishing latent content. The orthodox Islamic view, Abu Zaid claims, is stultifying; it reduces a divine, eternal, and dynamic text to a fixed human interpretation with no more life and meaning than "a trinket . . . a talisman . . . or an ornament."

For a while Abu Zaid remained in Egypt and sought to refute the charges of apostasy, but in the face of death threats and relentless public harassment he fled with his wife from Cairo to Holland, calling the whole affair "a macabre farce." Sheikh Youssef al-Badri, the cleric whose preachings inspired much of the opposition to Abu Zaid, was exultant. "We are not terrorists; we have not used bullets or machine guns, but we have stopped an enemy of Islam from poking fun at our religion. . . . No one will even dare to think about harming Islam again."

Abu Zaid seems to have been justified in fearing for his life and fleeing: in 1992 the Egyptian journalist Farag Foda was assassinated by Islamists for his critical writings about Egypt's Muslim Brotherhood, and in 1994 the Nobel Prize—winning novelist Naguib Mahfouz was stabbed for writing, among other works, the allegorical *Children of Gabalawi* (1959)—a novel, structured like the Koran, that presents "heretical" conceptions of God and the Prophet Muhammad.

Deviating from the orthodox interpretation of the Koran, says the Algerian Mohammed Arkoun, a professor emeritus of Islamic thought at the University of Paris, is "a *very* sensitive business" with major implications. "Millions and millions of people refer to the Koran daily to explain their actions and to justify their aspirations," Arkoun says. "This scale of reference is much larger than it has ever been before."

MUHAMMAD IN THE CAVE

MECCA sits in a barren hollow between two ranges of steep hills in the west of present-day Saudi Arabia. To its immediate west lies the flat and sweltering Red Sea coast; to the east stretches the great Rub' al-Khali, or Empty Quarter—the largest continuous body of sand on the planet. The town's setting is uninviting: the earth is dry and dusty, and smolders under a relentless sun; the whole region is scoured by hot, throbbing desert winds. Although sometimes rain does not fall for years, when it does come it can be heavy, creating torrents of water that rush out of the hills and flood the basin in which the city lies. As a backdrop for divine revelation, the area is every bit as fitting as the mountains of Sinai or the wilderness of Judea.

The only real source of historical information about pre-Islamic Mecca and the circumstances of the Koran's revelation is the classical Islamic story about the religion's founding, a distillation of which follows.

In the centuries leading up to the arrival of Islam, Mecca was a local pagan sanctuary of considerable antiquity. Religious rituals revolved around the Ka'ba—a shrine, still central in Islam today, that Muslims believe was originally built by Ibrahim (known to Christians and Jews as Abraham) and his son Isma'il (Ishmael). As Mecca became increasingly prosperous in the sixth century A.D., pagan idols of varying sizes and shapes proliferated. The traditional story has it that by the early seventh century a pantheon of some 360 statues and icons surrounded the Ka'ba (inside which were found renderings of Jesus and the Virgin Mary, among other idols).

Such was the background against which the first installments of the Koran are said to have been revealed, in 610, to an affluent but disaffected merchant named Muhammad bin Abdullah. Muhammad had developed the habit of periodically withdrawing from Mecca's pagan squalor to a nearby mountain cave, where he would reflect in solitude. During one of these retreats he was visited by the Angel Gabriel—the very same angel who had announced the coming of Jesus to the Virgin Mary in Nazareth some 600 years earlier. Opening with the command "Recite!," Gabriel made it known to Muhammad that he was to serve as the Messenger of God. Subsequently, until his death,

the supposedly illiterate Muhammad received through Gabriel divine revelations in Arabic that were known as *qur'an* ("recitation") and that announced, initially in a highly poetic and rhetorical style, a new and uncompromising brand of monotheism known as *Islam*, or "submission" (to God's will). Muhammad reported these revelations verbatim to sympathetic family members and friends, who either memorized them or wrote them down.

Powerful Meccans soon began to persecute Muhammad and his small band of devoted followers, whose new faith rejected the pagan core of Meccan cultural and economic life, and as a result in 622 the group migrated some 200 miles north, to the town of Yathrib, which subsequently became known as Medina (short for Medinat al-Nabi, or City of the Prophet). (This migration, known in Islam as the *hijra*, is considered to mark the birth of an independent Islamic community, and 622 is thus the first year of the Islamic calendar.) In Medina, Muhammad continued to receive divine revelations, of an increasingly pragmatic and prosaic nature, and by 630 he had developed enough support in the Medinan community to attack and conquer Mecca. He spent the last two years of his life proselytizing, consolidating political power, and continuing to receive revelations.

The Islamic tradition has it that when Muhammad died, in 632, the Koranic revelations had not been gathered into a single book; they were recorded only "on palm leaves and flat stones and in the hearts of men." (This is not surprising: the oral tradition was strong and well established, and the Arabic script, which was written without the vowel markings and consonantal dots used today, served mainly as an aid to memorization.) Nor was the establishment of such a text of primary concern: the Medinan Arabs—an unlikely coalition of ex-merchants, desert nomads, and agriculturalists united in a potent new faith and inspired by the life and sayings of Prophet Muhammad—were at the time pursuing a fantastically successful series of international conquests in the name of Islam. By the 640s the Arabs possessed most of Syria, Iraq, Persia,

and Egypt, and thirty years later they were busy taking over parts of Europe, North Africa, and Central Asia.

In the early decades of the Arab conquests many members of Muhammad's coterie were killed, and with them died valuable knowledge of the Koranic revelations. Muslims at the edges of the empire began arguing over what was Koranic scripture and what was not. An army general returning from Azerbaijan expressed his fears about sectarian controversy to the Caliph 'Uthman (644–656)—the third Islamic ruler to succeed Muhammad—and is said to have entreated him to "overtake this people before they differ over the Koran the way the Jews and Christians differ over their Scripture." 'Uthman convened an editorial committee of sorts that carefully gathered the various pieces of scripture that had been memorized or written down by Muhammad's companions. The result was a standard written version of the Koran. 'Uthman ordered all incomplete and "imperfect" collections of the Koranic scripture destroyed, and the new version was quickly distributed to the major centers of the rapidly burgeoning empire.

During the next few centuries, while Islam solidified as a religious and political entity, a vast body of exegetical and historical literature evolved to explain the Koran and the rise of Islam, the most important elements of which are *hadith*, or the collected sayings and deeds of the Prophet Muhammad; *sunna*, or the body of Islamic social and legal custom: *sira,* or biographies of the Prophet: and *tafsir*, or Koranic commentary and explication. It is from these traditional sources—compiled in written form mostly from the mid eighth to the mid tenth century—that all accounts of the revelation of the Koran and the early years of Islam are ultimately derived.

"FOR PEOPLE WHO UNDERSTAND"

ROUGHLY equivalent in length to the New Testament, the Koran is divided into 114 sections, known as *suras,* that vary dramatically in length and form. The book's organizing principle is neither chronological nor thematic—for the most part the *suras* are arranged from beginning to end in descending order of length. Despite the unusual structure, however, what generally surprises newcomers to the Koran is the degree to which it draws on the same beliefs and stories that appear in the Bible. God (*Allah* in Arabic) rules supreme: he is the all-powerful, all-knowing, and all-merciful Being who has created the world and its creatures; he sends messages and laws through prophets to help guide human existence; and, at a time in the future known only to him, he will bring about the end of the world and the Day of Judgement. Adam, the first man, is expelled from Paradise for eating from the forbidden tree. Noah builds an ark to save a select few from a flood brought on by the wrath of God. Abraham prepares himself to sacrifice his son at God's bidding. Moses leads the Israelites out of Egypt and receives a revelation on Mount Sinai. Jesus—born of the Virgin Mary and referred to as the Messiah—works miracles, has disciples, and rises to heaven.

The Koran takes great care to stress this common monotheistic heritage, but it works equally hard to distinguish Islam from Judaism and Christianity. For example, it mentions prophets—Hud, Salih, Shu'ayb, Luqman, and others—whose origins seem exclusively Arabian, and it reminds readers that it is "A Koran in Arabic,/ For people who understand." Despite its repeated assertions to the contrary, however, the Koran is often extremely difficult for contemporary readers—even highly educated speakers of Arabic—to understand. It sometimes makes dramatic shifts in style, voice, and subject matter from verse to verse, and it assumes a familiarity with language, stories, and events that seem to have been lost even to the earliest of Muslim exegetes (typical of a text that initially evolved in an oral tradition). Its apparent inconsistencies are easy to find: God may be referred to in the first and third person in the same sentence; divergent versions of the same story are repeated at different points in the text; divine rulings occasionally contradict one another. In this last case the Koran anticipates criticism and defends itself by asserting the right to ab-rogate its own message ("God doth blot out/Or confirm what He pleaseth").

Criticism did come. As Muslims increasingly came into contact with Christians during the eighth century, the wars of conquest were accompanied by theological polemics, in which Christians and others latched on to the confusing literary state of the Koran as proof of its human origins. Muslim scholars themselves were fastidiously cataloguing the problematic aspects of the Koran—unfamiliar vocabulary, seeming omissions of text, grammatical incongruities, deviant readings, and so on. A major theological debate in fact arose within Islam in the late eighth century, pitting those who believed in the Koran as the "uncreated" and eternal Word of God against those who believed in it as created in time, like anything that isn't God himself. Under the Caliph al-Ma'mum (813–833) this latter view briefly became orthodox doctrine. It was supported by several schools of thought, including an influential one known as Mu'tazilism, that developed a complex theology based partly on a metaphorical rather than simply literal understanding of the Koran.

By the end of the tenth century the influence of Mu'utazili school had waned, for complicated political reasons, and the official doctrine had become that of *i'jaz* or the "inimitability" of the Koran. (As a result, the Koran has traditionally not been translated by Muslims for non-Arabic-speaking Muslims. Instead it is read and recited in the original by Muslims worldwide, the majority of whom do not speak Arabic. The translations that do exist are considered to be nothing more than scriptural aids and paraphrases.) The adoption of the doctrine of inimitability was a major turning point in Islamic history, and from the tenth century to this day the mainstream Muslim understanding of the Koran as the literal and uncreated Word of God has remained constant.

PSYCHOPATHIC VANDALISM?

GERD-R. Puin speaks with disdain about the traditional willingness, on the part of Muslim and Western scholars, to accept the conventional understanding of the Koran. "The Koran claims for itself that it is *'mubeen,'* or 'clear.' " he says. "But if you look at it, you will notice that every fifth sentence or so simply doesn't make sense. Many Muslims—and Orientalists—will tell you otherwise, of course, but the fact is that a fifth of the Koranic text is *just incomprehensible*. This is what has caused the traditional anxiety regarding translation. If the Koran is not comprehensible—if it can't even be understood in Arabic—then it's not translatable. People fear that. And since the Koran claims repeatedly to be clear but obviously is not—as even speakers of Arabic will tell you—there is a contradiction. Something else must be going on."

Trying to figure out that "something else" really began only in this century. "Until quite recently," Patricia Crone, the historian of early Islam, says, "everyone took it for granted that everything the Muslims claim to remember about the origin and meaning of the Koran is correct. If you drop that assumption, you have to start afresh." This is no mean feat, of course; the Koran has come down to us tightly swathed in a historical tradition that is extremely resistant to criticism and analysis. As Crone put it in *Slaves on Horses,*

> The Biblical redactors offer us sections of the Israelite tradition at different stages of crystallization, and their testimonies can accordingly be profitably compared and weighed against each other. But the Muslim tradition was the outcome, not of a slow crystallization, but of an explosion; the first compilers were not redactors, but collectors of debris whose works are strikingly devoid of overall unity; and no particular illuminations ensue from their comparison.

Not surprisingly, given the explosive expansion of early Islam and the passage of time between the religion's birth and the first systematic documenting of his history, Muhammad's world and the worlds of the historians who subsequently wrote about him were dramatically different. During Islam's first century alone a provincial band of pagan desert tribesmen became the guardians of a vast international empire of institutional monotheism that teemed with unprecedented literary and scientific activity. Many contemporary historians argue that one cannot expect Islam's stories about its own origins—particularly given the oral tradition of the early centuries—to have survived this tremendous social transformation intact. Nor can one expect a Muslim historian writing in ninth- or tenth-century Iraq to have discarded his social and intellectual background (and theological convictions) in order accurately to describe a

engaged in the critical study of the Koran today must contend with Wansbrough's two main works—*Quranic Studies: Sources and Methods of Scriptural Interpretation* (1977) and *The Sectarian Milieu: Content and Composition of Islamic Salvation History* (1978).

Wansbrough applied an entire arsenal of what he called the "instruments and techniques" of biblical criticism—form criticism, source criticism, redaction criticism, and much more—to the Koranic text. He concluded that the Koran evolved only gradually in the seventh

cles, but many Muslims understandably have found them deeply offensive. S. Parvez Manzoor, for example, has described the Koranic studies of Wansbrough and others as "a naked discourse of power" and "an outburst of psychopathic vandalism." But not even Manzoor argues for a retreat from the critical enterprise of Koranic studies; instead he urges Muslims to defeat the Western revisionists on the "epistemological battlefield," admitting that "sooner or later [we Muslims] will have to approach the Koran from methodological assumptions and parameters that are radically at odds with the ones consecrated by our tradition."

The Koran is a scripture with a history like any other," one scholar says, "except that we tend to provoke howls of protest when we study it. But we are not trying to destroy anyone's faith."

deeply unfamiliar seventh-century Arabian context. R. Stephen Humphreys, writing in *Islamic History: A Framework for Inquiry* (1988), concisely summed up the issue that historians confront in studying early Islam.

If our goal is to comprehend the way in which Muslims of the late 2nd/8th and 3rd/9th centuries [Islamic calendar/Christian calendar] understood the origins of their society, then we are very well off indeed. But if our aim is to find out "what really happened" in terms of reliably documented answers to modern questions about the earliest decades of Islamic society, then we are in trouble.

The person who more than anyone else has shaken up Koranic studies in the past few decades is John Wansbrough, formerly of the University of London's School of Oriental and African studies. Puin is "re-reading him now" as he prepares to analyze the Yemeni fragments. Patricia Crone says that she and Michael Cook "did not say much about the Koran in *Hagarism* that was not based on Wansbrough." Other scholars are less admiring, referring to Wansbrough's work as "drastically wrongheaded," "ferociously opaque," and a "colossal self-deception." But like it or not, anybody

and eighth centuries, during a long period of oral transmission when Jewish and Christian sects were arguing volubly with one another to the north of Mecca and Medina, in which are now parts of Syria, Jordan, Israel and Iraq. The reason that no Islamic source material from the first century or so of Islam has survived, Wansbrough concluded, it that it never existed.

To Wansbrough, the Islamic tradition is an example of what is known to biblical scholars as a "salvation history": a theologically and evangelically motivated story of a religion's origins invented late in the day and projected back in time. In other words, as Wansbrough put it in *Quranic* Studies, the canonization of the Koran—and the Islamic traditions that arose to explain it—involved the

attribution of several, partially overlapping, collections of *logia* (exhibiting a distinctly Mosiac imprint) to the image of a Biblical prophet (modified by the material of the Muhammadan *evangelium* into an Arabian man of God) with a traditional message of salvation (modified by the influence of Rabbanic Judaism into the unmediated and finally immutable word of God).

Wansbrough's arcane theories have been contagious in certain scholarly cir-

REVISIONISM INSIDE THE ISLAMIC WORLD

Indeed, for more than a century there have been public figures in the Islamic world who have attempted the revisionist study of the Koran and Islamic history—the exiled Egyptian professor Nasr Abu Zaid is not unique. Perhaps Abu Zaid's most famous predecessor was the prominent Egyptian government minister, university professor, and writer Taha Hussein. A determined modernist, Hussein in the early 1920s devoted himself to the study of pre-Islamic Arabian poetry and ended up concluding that much of that body of work had been fabricated well after the establishment of Islam in order to lend outside support to Koranic mythology. A more recent example is the Iranian journalist and diplomat Ali Dashti, who in his *Twenty Three Years: A Study of the Prophetic Career of Mohammed* (1985) repeatedly took his fellow Muslims to task for not questioning the traditional accounts of Muhammad's life, much of which he called "myth-making and miracle-mongering."

Abu Zaid also cites the enormously influential Muhammad 'Abduh as a precursor. The nineteenth-century father of Egyptian modernism, 'Abduh saw the potential for a new Islamic theology in the theories of the ninth-century Mu'tazilis. The ideas of the Mu'tazilis gained popularity in some Muslim circles early in this century (leading the important

Egyptian writer and intellectual Ahmad Amin to remark in 1936 that "the demise of Mu'tazilism was the greatest misfortune to have afflicted Muslims; they have committed a crime against themselves"). The late Pakistani scholar Fazlur Rahman carried the Mu'tazilite torch well into the present era: he spend the later years of his life, from the 1960s until his death in 1988, living and teaching in the United States, where he trained many students of Islam—both Muslims and non-Muslims— in the Mu'tazilite tradition.

Such work has not come without cost, however: Taha Hussein, like Nasr Abu Zaid, was declared an apostate in Egypt: Ali Dashti died mysteriously just after the 1979 Iranian revolution; and Fazlur Rahman was forced to leave Pakistan in the 1960s. Muslims interested in challenging orthodox doctrine must tread carefully. "I would like to get the Koran out of this prison," Abu Zaid has said of the prevailing Islamic hostility to reinterpreting the Koran for the modern age, "so that once more it becomes productive for the essence of our culture and the arts, which are being strangled in our society." Despite his many enemies in Egypt, Abu Zaid may well be making progress toward this goal: there are indications that his work is being widely, if quietly, read with interest in the Arab world. Abu Zaid says, for example, that his *The Concept of the Text* (1990)—the book largely responsible for his exile from Egypt—has gone through at least eight underground printings in Cairo and Beirut.

Another scholar with a wide readership who is committed to re-examining the Koran is Mohammed Arkoun, the Algerian professor at the University of Paris. Arkoun argued in *Lectures du Coran* (1982), for example, that "it is time [for Islam] to assume, along with all of the great cultural traditions, the modern risks of scientific knowledge," and suggested that "the problem of the divine authenticity of the Koran can serve to reactivate Islamic thought and engage it in the major debates of our age." Arkoun regrets the fact that most Muslims are unaware that a different conception of the Koran exists within their own historical tradition. What a re-examination of Islamic history offers Muslims, Arkoun and others argue, is an opportunity to challenge the Muslim orthodoxy from within, rather than having to rely on "hostile" outside sources. Arkoun, Abu Zaid, and others hope that this challenge might ultimately lead to nothing less than an Islamic renaissance.

The gulf between such academic theories and the daily practice of Islam around the world is huge, of course—the majority of Muslims today are unlikely to question the orthodox understanding of the Koran and Islamic history. Yet Islam became one of the world's great religions in part because of its openness to social change and new ideas. (Centuries ago, when Europe was mired in its feudal Dark Ages, the sages of a flourishing Islamic civilization opened an era of great scientific and philosophical discovery. The ideas of the ancient Greeks and Romans might never have been introduced to Europe were it not for the Islamic historians and philosophers who rediscovered and revived them.) Islam's own history shows that the prevailing conception of the Koran is not the only one ever to have existed, and the recent history of biblical scholarship shows that not all critical-historical studies of a holy scripture are antagonistic. They can instead be carried out with the aim of spiritual and cultural regeneration. They can, as Mohammed Arkoun puts it, demystify the text while reaffirming "the relevance of its larger intuitions."

Increasingly diverse interpretations of the Koran and Islamic history will inevitably be proposed in the coming decades, as traditional cultural distinctions between East, West, North and South continue to dissolve, as the population of the Muslim world continues to grow, as early historical sources continue to be scrutinized, and as feminism meets the Koran. With the diversity of interpretations will surely come increased fractiousness, perhaps intensified by the fact that Islam now exists in such a great variety of social and intellectual settings— Bosnia, Iran, Malaysia, Nigeria, Saudi Arabia, South Africa, the United States, and so on. More than ever before, anybody wishing to understand global affairs will need to understand Islamic civilization, in all its permutations. Surely the best way to start is with the study of the Koran—which promises in the years ahead to be at least as contentious, fascinating, and important as the study of the Bible has been in this century.

Toby Lester is the executive editor of Atlantic Unbound, the *Atlantic Monthly* Web site.

The Dome of The Rock: Jerusalem's Epicenter

Written By Walid Khalidi

Islam is the third great monotheistic religion of the world. Its followers, about a billion people, constitute the majority of the population in some 50 countries. Like Judaism and Christianity, Islam has rich and deep associations with the city of Jerusalem.

Islam is an Arabic word which means "submission"; in its religious context it means submission to the will of God alone. The message of Islam was delivered by the Prophet Muhammad, who was born in Makkah, in present-day Saudi Arabia, in the year 570 and died in 632. Such was the power of the divine message he preached that, within 100 years of his death in Madinah, Islam had spread across North Africa, into Spain and across the borders of France in the West, and to the borders of India and China in the East. (See *Aramco World*, November/December 1991.)

Very early in this period—in 637—the forces of Islam won Jerusalem from the Byzantine Empire, whose capital was in Constantinople, signing a treaty by which the holy city was surrendered to 'Umar ibn al-Khattab, the second caliph, or successor, of Muhammad. For the following 1280 years, except for the period between 1109 and 1187, during the Crusades, Jerusalem remained in Muslim hands: In 1917, during World War I, the British took control of the city Muslims call al-Quds, "The Holy."

To understand Jerusalem's position in Islam, we need to look at how Islam sees itself in relation to Judaism and Christianity, to which of course Jerusalem is also sacred.

Islamic doctrine states that God has, since creation, revealed His teachings repeatedly to humankind through a succession of prophets and scriptures. The first of this line was the prophet Noah, according to many Muslim scholars; others believe Adam must be considered the first. But in this line of succession, Muhammad is the last, or "seal" of the prophets, and the teachings revealed to him are the culmination of all the previous messages. Muslims believe that the Qur'an, the literal word of God revealed to Muhammad, follows the Torah and the Gospels as God's final revelation. Thus the Qur'an accords great reverence to the Hebrew prophets, patriarchs and kings who received revelations from God and are associated with Jerusalem. Similarly, Jesus Christ is revered as one of God's most dedicated messengers, and Jerusalem, as the locus of much of his teaching, is further blessed by that association.

To Islam, then, Jerusalem is sacred for many of the reasons it is sacred to Judaism and Christianity, but in addition, it is sacred for specifically Muslim reasons. The most important of these is the Prophet Muhammad's miraculous nocturnal journey, or *isra'*, to *Bayt al-Maqdis*, "the house of holiness," in Jerusalem and his ascent from there to heaven—the *mi'raj*. These events are mentioned in a number of verses of the Qur'an, most clearly in the first verse of Chapter 17, titled *Al-Isra'*. Accounts of the Prophet's life supply the details. Led by the angel Gabriel, Muhammad traveled in one night from Makkah to the

site of *al-masjid al-aqsa*, "the furthest mosque," on Mount Moriah, called the Temple Mount, in Jerusalem. The site derives its name from the temples and houses of worship built there over the millennia, including the temple of the prophet Solomon, the temple of Jupiter, the Herodian temple and the al-Aqsa Mosque.

There, Muhammad led Abraham, Moses, Jesus and other prophets in prayer. Then, from a rock on the Temple Mount, Muhammad was taken by Gabriel to heaven itself, to "within two bowlengths" of the very throne of God.

The spot from which the Prophet's ascent began was sanctified in the eyes of Muslims by the *mi'raj*; the Qur'an refers to the prayer site as *al-masjid al-aqsa*. From Muhammad's journey evolved a vast body of Muslim devotional literature, some authentic and some uncanonical, that places Jerusalem at the center of Muslim beliefs concerning life beyond the grave. This literature is in circulation in all the diverse languages spoken by the world's one billion Muslims, most of whom to this day celebrate the anniversary of the *mi'raj*.

Jerusalem is also uniquely linked to one of the "pillars" of the Muslim faith, the five daily prayers. The earliest Muslims, for a time, turned toward Jerusalem to pray. A later revelation transferred the *qibla*, the direction of prayer, to Makkah, but to this day Jerusalem is known as "the first of the two *qiblas*." And according to Muhammad's teachings, it was during the *mi'raj* that Muslims were ordered by God to pray,

From *Aramco World*, September/October 1996, pp. 2-17. © 1996 Walid Khalidi and Tom McNeff. Reprinted by permission of Aramco World.

THE NOBLE SANCTUARY

(Continued on next page)

Watercolor by Tom McNeff.
Copyright © 1996 Aramco Services Company.

and that the number of the daily prayers was fixed at five.

The center of Muslim power shifted, through the centuries, from one great capital to the next: from Madinah to Umayyad Damascus to Abbasid Bagh-dad to Mamluk Cairo and to Ottoman Constantinople. But after Jerusalem became part of the Muslim state in 637, whichever dynasty was in control of that city lavished it with care and attention in the form of public monuments: mosques, colleges for the study of the Qur'an and the traditions of the Prophet, hospitals, hospices, fountains, orphanages, caravansarais, baths, convents for mystics, pools and mausolea. This is why Jerusalem's Old City, within the

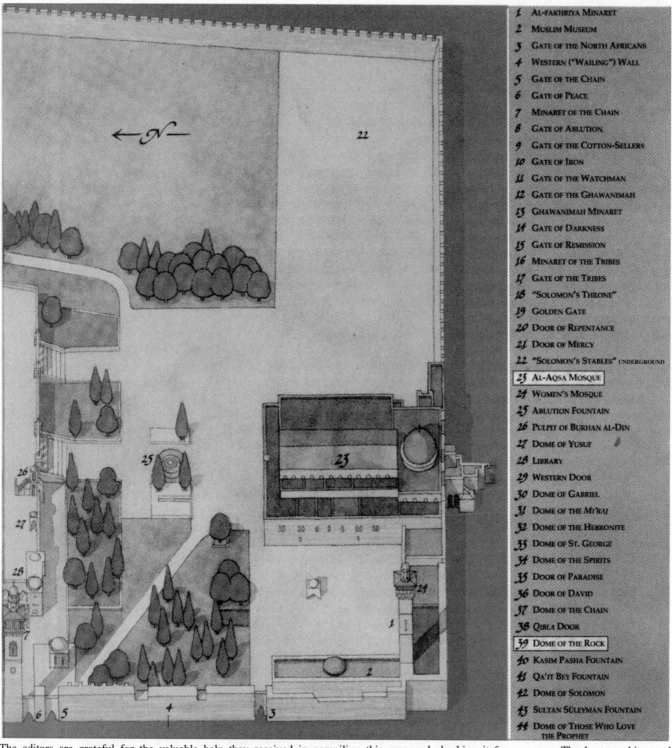

1 AL-FAKHRIYA MINARET
2 MUSLIM MUSEUM
3 GATE OF THE NORTH AFRICANS
4 WESTERN ("WAILING") WALL
5 GATE OF THE CHAIN
6 GATE OF PEACE
7 MINARET OF THE CHAIN
8 GATE OF ABLUTION
9 GATE OF THE COTTON-SELLERS
10 GATE OF IRON
11 GATE OF THE WATCHMAN
12 GATE OF THE GHAWANIMAH
13 GHAWANIMAH MINARET
14 GATE OF DARKNESS
15 GATE OF REMISSION
16 MINARET OF THE TRIBES
17 GATE OF THE TRIBES
18 "SOLOMON'S THRONE"
19 GOLDEN GATE
20 DOOR OF REPENTANCE
21 DOOR OF MERCY
22 "SOLOMON'S STABLES" UNDERGROUND
23 AL-AQSA MOSQUE
24 WOMEN'S MOSQUE
25 ABLUTION FOUNTAIN
26 PULPIT OF BURHAN AL-DIN
27 DOME OF YUSUF
28 LIBRARY
29 WESTERN DOOR
30 DOME OF GABRIEL
31 DOME OF THE MI'RAJ
32 DOME OF THE HEBRONITE
33 DOME OF ST. GEORGE
34 DOME OF THE SPIRITS
35 DOOR OF PARADISE
36 DOOR OF DAVID
37 DOME OF THE CHAIN
38 QIBLA DOOR
39 DOME OF THE ROCK
40 KASIM PASHA FOUNTAIN
41 QA'IT BEY FOUNTAIN
42 DOME OF SOLOMON
43 SULTAN SÜLEYMAN FOUNTAIN
44 DOME OF THOSE WHO LOVE THE PROPHET

The editors are grateful for the valuable help they received in compiling this map and checking it for accuracy. Thanks to architectural photographer Saïd Nuseibeh, whose book *The Dome of The Rock,* was published by Rizzoli (1996); to Jeff Spurr of the Aga Khan Program for Islamic Architecture and the Visual Collections of the Fine Arts Library at Harvard University; to Ahmad Nabal of the Aga Khan Visual Archives, Rotch Visual Collection, Massachusetts Institute of Technology; and to Dr. Walid Khalidi.

16th-century walls built by the Ottoman sultan Süleyman, strikes the modern-day visitor with its predominantly Muslim character.

Caliph 'Umar personally came to Jerusalem to accept the city's surrender from the Byzantines, and visited the site of *al-masjid al-aqsa,* known to some Muslims today as *al-Haram al-Maqdisi al-Sharif,* "the Noble Sanctuary of Jerusalem," or simply *al-Haram al-Sharif.* The site lay vacant and in ruins; 'Umar ordered it cleaned, and, tradition says, took part in the work himself, carrying dirt in his own robe. When the site had been cleansed and sprinkled with scent, 'Umar and his followers prayed there, near the rough rock from which Muhammad had ascended to heaven.

Two generations later, about 691, the Umayyad caliph 'Abd al-Malik ibn Marwan's Syrian craftsmen built in the same location the earliest masterpiece of Islamic architecture, the Dome of the Rock *(Qubbat al Sakhra)*—the octago-nal sanctuary, centered on the rock, whose golden dome still dominates the skyline of Old Jerusalem. 'Abd al-Malik's son al-Walid, who ruled from 705 to 715, built the second major monument, the al-Aqsa Mosque, also on the Temple Mount.

The octagonal plan of the Dome of the Rock may not have been accidental. Cyril Glassé, in his *Concise Encyclopedia of Islam,* points out that "the octagon is a step in the mathematical series going from square, symbolizing the fixity of earthly manifestation, to circle, the natural symbol for the perfection of heaven.... In traditional Islamic architecture this configuration symbolizes the link between earth . . . and heaven...." Nor is it coincidence that the elegant calligraphy that encircles the structure inside and out—240 meters, or 785 feet, of it—includes all the Qur'anic verses about the prophet Jesus. "The calligraphic inscriptions," writes Glassé, "recall the relationship between Jerusalem and Jesus . . . ; and the architecture, above all the octagonal form supporting a dome, is symbolic of the . . . ascent to heaven by the Prophet, and thus by man." Mount Moriah, with the Dome of the Rock at its center, is thus "the place where man, as man, is joined once more to God. . . ."

History, tradition and symbolism intersect in this building, whose presence suffuses Jerusalem.

Dr. Walid Khalidi was educated in London and Oxford and has taught at Oxford University, the American University of Beirut and Harvard University. Since 1982, he has been a senior research fellow at Harvard's Center for Middle Eastern Studies. Members of his family have served Jerusalem as scholars, judges, diplomats and members of parliament since the late 12th century.

2000 Years of Jesus

For believers, he is the hinge of history. But even by secular standards, Jesus is the dominant figure of Western culture. How Christian ideas shaped the modern world—for good and, sometimes, for ill.

By Kenneth L. Woodward

Historians did not record his birth. Nor, for 30 years, did anyone pay him much heed. A Jew from the Galilean hill country with a reputation for teaching and healing, he showed up at the age of 33 in Jerusalem during Passover. In three years, he was arrested, tried and convicted of treason, then executed like the commonest of criminals. His followers said that God raised him from the dead. Except among those who believed in him, the event passed without notice.

Two thousand years later, the centuries themselves are measured from the birth of Jesus of Nazareth. At the end of this year, calendars in India and China, like those in Europe, America and the Middle East, will register the dawn of the third millennium. It is a convention, of course: a fiction and function of Western cultural hegemony that allows the birth of Jesus to number the days for Christians and non-Chris-

tians alike. For Christians, Jesus is the hinge on which the door of history swings, the point at which eternity in-

---

LAMB OF GOD

For every time and place, we reimagine and reimage Jesus," says Thomas Lucas, professor of fine arts at the University of San Francisco. But some imagery—such as the agony of crucifixion, a symbol of the redemptive power of suffering—has had special resonance over the last two millennia.

---

tersects with time, the Savior who redeems time by drawing all things to himself. As the second millennium draws to a close, nearly a third of the

world's population claims to be his followers.

But by any secular standard, Jesus is also the dominant figure of Western culture. Like the millennium itself, much of what we now think of as Western ideas, inventions and values finds its source or inspiration in the religion that worships God in his name. Art and science, the self and society, politics and economics, marriage and the family, right and wrong, body and soul—all have been touched and often radically transformed by Christian influence. Seldom all at once, of course—and not always for the better. The same Jesus who preached peace was used to justify the Crusades and the Inquisition. The same gospel he proclaimed has underwritten both democracy and the divine right of kings. Often persecuted—even today—Christians have frequently persecuted others, including other Christians. As Pope John Paul II

MIRACLE WORKER

One of the most important functions of religious art throughout the ages has been to bring Jesus' story alive for the many unlettered believers who would never hold a Bible in their own hands. Depictions of miracles like the healing of the sick, the raising of the dead and the story of the loaves and fishes are a reminder of the transformative power with which God endowed his son—and the compassion that first endeared him to humanity.

has repeatedly insisted, Christians cannot welcome the third millennium without repenting of their own sins.

This millennial moment invites historical reflection: how has Christianity shaped the way we think about God, about ourselves, about how individuals ought to live and the way that societies are to be organized? As scholars have long realized, there was little in the teachings *of* Jesus that cannot be found in the Hebrew Scriptures he expounded. From this angle, says theologian Krister Stendahl of Harvard Divinity School, "Christianity became a Judaism for the Gentiles." But the New Testament is primarily Scripture *about* Jesus—the Risen Christ as Lord. This message was something altogether new. Like a supernova, the initial impact of Christianity on the ancient Greco-Roman world produced shock waves that continued to register long after the Roman Empire disappeared.

A NEW CONCEPTION OF GOD

THE FIRST CHRISTIANS WERE JEWS WHO preached in the name of Jesus. But Jesus wasn't all that they preached. As Jewish

monotheists, they believed in one God—the father to whom Jesus was obedient unto death. But they also worshiped Jesus as his "only begotten Son" conceived through the power of the Holy Spirit. This experience of God as three-in-one was implicit in the New Testament, but defied efforts to fit into the traditional monotheistic mold. By "asking Greek questions of Hebrew stories," says theologian David Tracy of the University of Chicago Divinity School, the early church fathers developed a doctrine of God that was—and remains—unique among world religions. "All monotheists tend to make God into a transcendent individual standing outside time and outside all relationships," Tracy observes. "Now, as in modern physics, we are coming to see that all of reality is interrelated. The doctrine of the Trinity says that even the divine reality in all its incomprehensible mystery is intrinsically relational." In short, Christianity bequeathed to Western culture a God who revealed himself definitively in the person of Jesus, and who continues to redeem the world by the work of the Holy Spirit. Time itself was

What is your religious preference?

PERCENT RESPONDING

62	Protestant
20	Roman Catholic
7	No religion
4	Non-Christian
3	Jewish

Do you think Jesus Christ ever actually lived?

PERCENT RESPONDING "YES"

93	Christians
68	Non-Christians

SON OF MAN

While the earliest depictions of Jesus often presented a distant, almost imperial Christ, artists later came to focus on the humanity of God's only son. "Everyone understands what a baby is about," says Professor Lucas. "There is no more vivid way of showing God's vulnerability in the person of Jesus than a tender scene of the infant in the manger."

transformed: where the Greeks and Romans thought of the universe as fixed and eternal, Christianity—building on the Hebrew prophets—injected into Western consciousness the notion of the future as the work of God himself.

BREAKING THE BOUNDARIES

TO A WORLD RULED BY FATE AND THE whims of capricious gods, Christianity brought the promise of everlasting life. At the core of the Christian faith was the assertion that the crucified Jesus was resurrected by God and present in the church as "the body of Christ." The message was clear: by submitting to death, Jesus had destroyed its power, thereby making eternal life available to everyone. This Christian affirmation radically changed the relationship between the living and the dead as Greeks and Romans understood it. For them, only the gods were immortal—that's what made them gods. Philosophers might achieve immortality of the soul, as Plato taught, but the view from the street was that human consciousness survived in the dim and affectless underworld of Hades. "The Resurrection is an enormous answer to the problem of death," says Notre Dame theologian John Dunne. "The idea is that the Chris-

How important is it to you that non-Christians convert to Christianity?

PERCENT RESPONDING "VERY IMPORTANT"

72	Evangelical Protestants
25	Other Protestants
17	Catholics

Do you believe that Jesus Christ rose from the dead after dying on the cross?

PERCENT RESPONDING "YES"

88	Christians
32	Non-Christians

tian goes with Christ through death to everlasting life. Death becomes an event, like birth, that is lived through."

Once death lost its power over life, life itself took on new meaning for believers. Sociologist Rodney Stark of the University of Washington sees dramatic evidence of this in the high Christian survival rates during the plagues that repeatedly hit the citizens of the ancient Roman Empire. "The Romans threw people out into the street at the first symptoms of disease, because they knew it was contagious and they were afraid of dying," says Stark. "But the Christians stayed and nursed the sick. You could only do that if you thought, 'So what if I die? I have life eternal'."

Indeed, those who were martyred for the faith were revered as saints and heavenly "friends of God" who could intercede for the faithful below. Their bones became sacred relics, their tombs the sites of pilgrimage. Thus was the Christian cult of the saints born, a reverencing of the dead and their bodies that confounded Rome's elites. "You keep adding many corpses newly dead to the corpse [Christ] of long ago," complained Emperor Julian, a fourth-century persecutor of Christians. "You have filled the whole world with tombs and sepulchers." Eventually, churches were built over the tombs of saints (the Vatican's Basilica of St. Peter is the most famous example) and cemeteries were turned into cities.

INVERSION OF VALUES

AS THE SIGN OF THE NEW RELIGION, THE cross signified much more than Christ's victory over death. It also symbolized an inversion of accepted norms. Suffering was noble rather than merely pathetic when accepted in imitation of the crucified Christ. Forgiveness—even of one's enemies—became the sign of the true Christian. More radically, Jesus taught that in the kingdom of God the last would be first, the first last. "In the New Testament, you find Jesus more among the beggars than the rulers, the sick than the healthy, the women and children than the conquerors, the prostitutes and lepers than the holy people," says Martin Marty, director of the Public Religion Project at the University of Chicago.

Christianity also challenged prevailing notions of the virtuous life. Where Aristotle had touted prudence, justice, courage and temperance as the virtues proper to the good life, Jesus emphasized the blessedness of humility, patience and peacemaking in his crowning Sermon on the Mount. Where the Buddha taught compassion as an *attitude* of the Enlightened, Jesus demanded deeds: "In truth I tell you, in so far as you did this to one of the least of these brothers of mine, you did it to me." In Roman times, Christian compassion was manifest in special concern for widows, orphans, the aged and infirm. When Saint Lawrence, an early Christian martyr and deacon of the nascent church, was ordered by Roman authorities to reveal the church's treasures, he showed them the hungry and the sick. Twenty centuries later, the same attitude can be seen in the work of exceptional contemporary figures (usually women) like Dorothy Day and Mother Teresa. "The idea," says Marty, is "the poor are my masters."

DISCOVERING THE INDIVIDUAL

IF, AS HAROLD BLOOM HAS LATELY ARgued, Shakespeare "invented the human," it can be said—with equal hyperbole—that Christianity "discovered" the individual. In the ancient world, individuals were recognized as members of tribes or nations or families, and conducted themselves accordingly. For Jews, this means—as now—that one's relationship with God depends upon the prior covenant he has made with Israel as his chosen people. But the Gospels are replete with scenes in which Jesus works one on one, healing this woman's sickness, forgiving that man's sins and calling each to personal conversion. He invites Jews and Gentiles alike to enter God's kingdom. "Christianity discovers individuality in the sense that it stresses personal conversion," says Bernard McGinn, professor of historical theology at the University of Chicago Divinity School. "This is a crucial contribution to Western civilization because it releases the individual from the absolute constraints of family and society."

The sense of self deepened. Prayer became more personal. As Jesus himself taught, God could be addressed as "Abba"—the equivalent of "Dad." But as the possibility of intimacy with God increased, so did the interior sense of personal unworthiness. As a moralist, Jesus had set the bar high: those who even looked on another's wife with sexual desire, he declared, committed "adultery in the heart." With the evolution of the Roman Catholic Church came the practice of personal confession and repentance. And in the Confessions of Saint Augustine (354–430), we have the first great document in the history of what Stendahl has called "the introspective conscience of the West." A towering figure whose shadow stretched

LIGHT OF THE WORLD

How do you show the power of God—the divinity of Jesus that set him apart, which made him more than a man? Many painters used an unearthly glow to remind their viewers that Jesus was indeed not of this world; even the crudest early mosaics and the darkest crucifixion scenes are suffused with a glow that shines out of the body of Christ: the light of God shining through our humanity.

THE GLOBAL JESUS

As believers—and artists—all over the world can attest, the image and ideal of Jesus belongs to everybody. "The Christ of faith is so much bigger than his three decades in Judea at the beginning of the first millennium," says Professor Lucas. "Look at an African crucifixion scene, or a Chinese nativity. Jesus is constantly being remythologized according to the needs and longings of the times."

across the Middle Ages and touched a tormented Martin Luther, Augustine remains to this day the father of autobiography, the first great psychologist and the author who anticipated—by a millennium and a half—the modern novel's explorations of individual self-consciousness.

REDEFINING MALE AND FEMALE

IN ROMAN AS IN JEWISH SOCIETY, WOMEN were regarded as inherently inferior to men. Husbands could divorce their wives but wives could not divorce their husbands. In rabbinic circles, only males were allowed to study the Torah. Jesus challenged these arrangements. Although he called only men to be his apostles, Jesus readily accepted women into his circle of friends and disciples. He also banned divorce, except in cases of adultery.

The early Christians heeded his example. In its initial stages, at least, the church strove to become an egalitarian society: in Christ, wrote Paul, "there is neither Jew nor Greek, slave nor free man, male or female." Although Paul's household code for Christians (Ephesians 5:22–23) called for wives to be subordinate to their husbands, both were equally subject to God.

Christianity's appeal for women was a major reason that it grew so rapidly in competition with other religions of the Roman Empire. Then, as now, most Christians were women. The new religion offered women not only greater status and influence within the church but also more protection as wives and mothers. For one thing, the church did away with the common practice of marrying girls of 11 or 12 to much older men. The result was a stronger, "more symmetrical marriage," says sociologist Stark. For another, Christianity carried over from Jewish tradition a profound respect for marriage. Eventually, the Catholic Church made marriage a sacrament, declaring the bond between Christian husband and wife insoluble.

In an even more radical challenge to the social mores of the ancient world, the church made room for virgins—both male and female—who consecrated their lives to Christ. In this way, says McGinn, consecrated Christian virgins "broke the bonds by which families controlled the fate of their members"—especially women. Thus, Christianity made it possible for celibate females or males to claim a complete life and identity apart from marriage and procreation.

The church also protected children from the whims of tyrannical fathers. Under Roman law, fathers could and often did commit infanticide. Female babies were especially vulnerable because they were nothing but an expense. From a study of gravestones at Delphi, Stark says, we know that of 600 upper-class families, "only half a dozen raised more than one daughter." From the beginning, Christians also opposed abortion, defending both mother and child from barbarous procedures that often left women either dead or sterile.

In a less direct way, Christianity also transformed the way that masculinity was defined throughout the ancient world. In place of the dominant image of the male as warrior, Jesus counseled men to be peacemakers—to "turn the other cheek" rather than strike back. "A woman preaching that people must be patient and meek and mild would have sounded just like a woman," argues Michael Novak, who covers religion and public policy at the American Enterprise Institute— and, he implies, would have been dismissed by men. But to believe, as Christians did, that this was the Son of God speaking meant that Christians could never make war with a clear conscience.

OPPOSITION TO WAR

NONVIOLENCE WAS EASY TO ESPOUSE AS long as Christians had no power. As Yale church historian Jaroslav Pelikan observes, "They never imagined that Caesar might become a Christian"—which he did when Constantine converted in 312—much less that theirs would become the official religion of the Roman Empire. With establishment came the power to wage war and to stamp out heretics. From his imperial throne in Constantinople, Constantine did both as protector of the church. But in the West, as "eternal" Rome fell to invaders from the North, Augustine laid down severe restrictions if the conduct of war between states is to be considered just. Among other principles outlined in his monumental "The City of God," Augustine said that only defensive wars could be justified. They should be brief, a last resort and never for spoils or gains. The means of war should never be excessive but always proportional to its goals. Noncombatants were to be immune from harm, and once the war was over, the aim of the winners was to be peace, not revenge.

While Augustine's just-war principles have never prevented wars from happening—including those waged in Jesus' name—they have, over the centuries, at least prompted some statesmen to try to make warfare less barbarous. We are still a long way from nonviolence. "But before Christ," notes Stark, "conquerors butchered people for the hell of it."

Ironically, once Christianity was identified with the state, many Christians found it more difficult to follow Christ than when they were a persecuted sect. To escape an increasingly worldly and compromised church, many Christian men and women fled to the desert (as some Jewish sects before them had done), where they could live in complete poverty, chastity and obedience. These became the basis of the Rule of Saint Benedict—"one of the most influential documents of Western civilization," according to Pelikan—which established monastic communities as places set apart for those called to fully "participate in the life of Christ."

The effects of monasticism on Western society can hardly be exaggerated. For more than a millennium, the monasteries produced saints who established the diverse forms of Christian mysticism and spirituality that are so much in revival today. The monks were also the church's reformers, calling popes to task for their worldliness and eventually becoming popes themselves. Through the example of the monks, celibacy became required of bishops in the East and, eventually, of all priests in the West.

MONKS AND MODERNITY

IT WAS THE MONKS WHO BECAME CHRIStianity's greatest missionaries, planting the church in England, Ireland and other outposts of no-longer eternal Rome. As the barbarians dismantled the empire, the monks copied and later disseminated the Latin classics, thus preserving much of the old civilization and laying the foundations of the new. They also cre-

ated music and chants, magnificent liturgies and marvelous illuminated manuscripts. In the so-called Dark Ages—a fiction created by anti-religious *philosophes* of the French Enlightenment—it was the monks who founded the first European universities in cities like Paris and Bologna. It was a Dominican friar, Thomas Aquinas, who crowned the Middle Ages with his towering synthesis of philosophy and theology, the "Summa Theologica." And it was another monk, Martin Luther, who fathered the Protestant Reformation.

One measure of Christian influence on Western culture is the extent to which innovations of the church have survived in secular form. The law is a prime example. "Much of medieval canon law has passed over—often unnoticed—into the laws of the state," says Harold Berman, professor of law emeritus at Harvard law school. "And many of the legal reforms the medieval papacy promoted command respect even seven and eight centuries later." Among them: rational trial procedures, which replaced trial by ordeal; the necessity of consent as the foundation of marriage; the need to show wrongful intent for conviction of crime, and legal protection of the poor against the rich.

The legacy of medieval "Christendom" had its darker side as well. From Christmas Day in 800, when Pope Leo III crowned Charlemagne as "Holy Roman Emperor," politics and religion were seldom separate. The results were mixed at best. Had the secular powers not defended Christianity, Europe might well be Muslim today. But the medieval Crusades to rescue the Holy Land from the Turks became excuses for plunder by conscripted thugs. Once church and state were yoked, almost any military action could be justified.

Although the New Testament contains no outline for a Christian society, medieval Christianity was one long effort to establish one. The doctrine the church preached became the doctrine the king enforced. Even Augustine had reluctantly concluded that the secular arm of society could be used to crush heresy. Acting on the premise that error has no rights, the church created the Inquisition, dispatching traveling squads

of Franciscans and Dominicans to ferret out heretics. In 1252 Pope Innocent IV allowed suspects to be tortured. The guilty were imprisoned and sometimes put to death. Two centuries later, the Spanish monarchs Ferdinand and Isabella created a separate Inquisition aimed at discovering and expelling converted Jews and Muslims who secretly

---

In the next millennium, which one of the following do you think should be organized Christianity's top priority?

PERCENT CHRISTIANS RESPONDING

38	Returning to traditional moral values
32	Spreading the faith
13	Increasing tolerance
7	Righting social ills

---

practiced their own religion. Even old women and children were tortured, and their descendants barred from universities and public office. In subsequent centuries Inquisitors expanded their list of heretics to include suspected Protestants and practitioners of witchcraft. Altogether, the Inquisition remains a monument to religious intolerance and a reminder of what can happen when church and state share total authority.

The Reformation shattered the old Christendom but also unleashed new energies. Protestants translated the Bible into vernacular languages and encouraged lay learning and initiative. From Europe, Christian missionaries dispersed to Asia, Africa and the Americas. In many cases, it was a matter of the cross following the flag—a shameless blessing of imperialism and colonialism. But there are other ways of measuring the missionaries' impact. From the 16th-century Jesuits to the 19th-century Protestants, missionaries developed written languages for many "indigenous" peoples who had none—not to mention grammars and dictionaries. In this way, Protestant and Catholic missionaries "preserved local cultures that otherwise would have been swept away by global forces," says Mark Noll, professor of history at Wheaton College. The missionaries also established countless schools and hospitals, bringing literacy and modern medicine to those that the indigenous elites ignored. "Nelson Mandela," notes Noll, " is a graduate of two missionary schools."

As the world moves toward the third millennium, Christianity seems far removed from the Jesus movement of its birth. And yet, the same gospel is being preached. Christians are still being persecuted: in the 20th century alone, there were many times more martyrs—especially under Hitler and Stalin—than all the victims of the Caesars combined. But the differences from times past are also striking. Post-Christian Europe seems spiritually exhausted. In the United States, secularism is the reigning ideology. However, there is more unity among Christians now than at any time since the Reformation. Despite the Holocaust—or perhaps because of it— "the people to whom Jesus belonged, and the people who belong to Jesus," as Pelikan puts it, are no longer spiritual enemies. Science and religion, once thought to be implacable adversaries, are beginning to talk to each other: the hubris of the Enlightenment has run its course.

Numerically, it is already clear, the future of Christianity lies with the youthful churches of Africa, the Hispanics of the Americas and—who knows?—the millions of stalwart Christians in China. Christianity already comprises the most diverse society known to humankind. But what new ideas and forms the gospel will inspire await the birth of the third millennium. Of the future, the Book of Revelation has only this to say: "Behold, I make all things new."

The Other Jesus

To Christians, he is the Son of God. But the world's other great religions have their own visions of a legendary figure.

By Kenneth L. Woodward

Christ is absolutely original and absolutely unique. If He were only a wise man like Socrates, if He were a prophet like Muhammad, if He were enlightened like the Buddha, without doubt He would not be what He is.
—*John Paul II*

EVER SINCE HIS ELECTION, JOHN Paul II has wanted one thing: to walk where Jesus walked, preach where Jesus taught and pray where Jesus was crucified, died and was buried. This week the pope finally gets his chance. Weary in body but ecstatic in spirit, John Paul makes his long-anticipated pilgrimage to the Holy Land. For him it is a personal "journey with God"; there will be no intruding television cameras when, lost in prayer, he communes alone at Christianity's holiest shrines. But the land of his heart's desire is holy to Jews and Muslims as well. And so the pope will visit the Western Wall, Judaism's most sacred site, and the Mosque of El Aqsa atop the Temple Mount. He will also meet with Muslim and Jewish religious leaders and—in one particularly resonant moment—pause to pray at Yad Vashem, Israel's memorial to victims of the Holocaust.

Like his powerful plea for forgiveness a fortnight ago, the pope's trip is also an exercise in religious reconciliation. More than 90 times since he took office, John Paul has acknowledged past faults of the church and begged pardon from others—Muslims and Jews, as well as Protestant and Orthodox Christians— for sins committed in the name of Catholicism. Like the sound of one hand clapping, however, his efforts have brought few echoing responses. Now, at

the high point of this jubilee year for the church, he comes to Jerusalem, the city of peace, hoping to erect bridges among the three monotheistic faiths.

There are, of course, important commonalities among these three religious traditions. All three believe in one God who has revealed his will through sacred Scriptures. They all look to an endtimes when God's justice and power will triumph. And they all recognize the figure of Abraham as a father in faith. What is often overlooked, however, is another figure common to the three traditions: Jesus of Nazareth.

The Christ of the Gospels is certainly the best-known Jesus in the world. For Christians, he is utterly unique—the only Son of God and, as the pope puts it, the one "mediator between God and humanity." But alongside this Jesus is another, the Jesus whom Muslims since Muhammad have regarded as a prophet and messenger of Allah. And after centuries of silence about Jesus, many Jews now find him a Jewish teacher and reformer they can accept on their own terms as "one of us."

Jesus has become a familiar, even beloved, figure to adherents of Asian religions as well. Among many contemporary Hindus, Jesus has come to be revered as a self-realized saint who reached the highest level of "God-consciousness." In recent years, Buddhists like the Dalai Lama have recognized in Jesus a figure of great compassion much like the Buddha. "I think as the world grows smaller, Jesus as a figure will grow larger," says Protestant theologian John Cobb, a veteran of interfaith dialogues.

Perhaps. Each of these traditions— Judaism, Islam, Buddhism and Hindu-

ism—is rich in its own right, and each has its own integrity. As the pope calls for better understanding among the world's great religions, it is important to recognize that non-Christian faiths have their own visions of the sacred and their own views of Jesus.

JUDAISM

THAT JESUS WAS A JEW WOULD SEEM to be self-evident from Gospels. But before the first Christian century was out, faith in Jesus as universal Lord and Savior eclipsed his early identity as a Jewish prophet and wonder worker. For long stretches of Western history, Jesus was pictured as a Greek, a Roman, a Dutchman—even, in the Germany of the 1930s, as a blond and burly Aryan made in the image of Nazi anti-Semitism. But for most of Jewish history as well, Jesus was also a deracinated figure: he was *the* apostate, whose name a pious Jew should never utter.

Indeed, the lack of extra-Biblical evidence for the existence of Jesus has led more than one critic to conclude that he is a Christian fiction created by the early church. There were in fact a half dozen brief passages, later excised from Talmudic texts, that some scholars consider indirect references to Jesus. One alludes to a heresy trial of someone named Yeshu (Jesus) but none of them has any independent value for historians of Jesus. The only significant early text of real historical value is a short passage from Falvius Josephus, the first-century Jewish historian. Josephus describes Jesus as a "wise man," a "doer of startling deeds" and a "teacher" who was cruci-

HIS ROOTS: Christian and Jewish scholars accept that much of what Jesus taught can be found in Jewish Scriptures, but Jews still see Christ as an 'admirable Jew,' not the Son of God

fied and attracted a posthumous following called Christians. In short, argues Biblical scholar John P. Meier of Notre Dame, the historical Jesus was "a marginal Jew in a marginal province of the Roman Empire"—and thus unworthy of serious notice by contemporary Roman chroniclers.

Christian persecution of the Jews made dialogue about Jesus impossible in the Middle Ages. Jews were not inclined to contemplate the cross on the Crusaders' shields, nor did they enjoy the forced theological disputations Christians staged for Jewish conversions. To them, the Christian statues and pictures of Jesus represented the idol worship forbidden by the Torah. Some Jews did compile their own versions of a "History of Jesus" ("Toledoth Yeshu") as a parody of the Gospel story. In it, Jesus is depicted as a seduced Mary's bastard child who later gains magical powers and works sorcery. Eventually, he is hanged, his body hidden for three days and then discovered. It was subversive literature culled from the excised Talmudic texts. "Jews were impotent in force of arms," observes Rabbi Michael Meyer, a professor at Hebrew Union Seminary in Cincinnati, "so they reacted with words."

When skeptical scholars began to search for the "historical Jesus" behind the Gospel accounts in the 18th century,

The Pilgrimage

On his historic trip to the Holy Land, Pope John Paul II will call for peace and reconciliation as he visits ancient sites holy to Jews, Christians and Muslims. Planned papal stops:

JORDAN

1 Mount Nebo: The pope will visit the site Christians believe is Moses' resting place

2 Wadi al-Kharrar: On the eastern bank of Jordan River. Jordanians believe this is where Jesus was baptized. (Israel has a rival site.)

'Memorial of Moses' on Mount Nebo: Sacred to both Christians and Jews. Where Moses first saw the Promised Land. Overlooking West Bank and Dead Sea.

WEST BANK

3 Qasr al-Yahud: In Israeli military zone; on the western bank of Jordan River. Israel claims this is Jesus' baptismal site. The pope was pressured to include this stopover.

4 Bethlehem: Birthplace of Jesus. Pope will hold mass at Manger Square and pray at Church of the Nativity.

5 Dheisheh refugee camp: Palestinians hope a visit here will signal papal support for statehood

Baptismal-site squabble: The pope's stop at Wadi al-Kharrar made Israel demand a detour to its side of the Jordan Valley at Qasr al-Yahud

An Exodus?

The Christian population has risen slightly after falling in recent years.

IN THOUSANDS

160
120
80
40
0

1949   1997

Mediterranean Sea

G A Z A

(Continued on next page)

few Jewish intellectuals felt secure enough to join the quest. One who did was Abraham Geiger, a German rabbi and early exponent of the Reform Jewish movement. He saw that liberal Protestant intellectuals were anxious to get beyond the supernatural Christ of Chris-

tian dogma and find the enlightened teacher of morality hidden behind the Gospel texts. From his own research, Geiger concluded that what Jesus believed and taught was actually the Judaism of liberal Pharisees, an important first-century Jewish sect. "Geiger argued

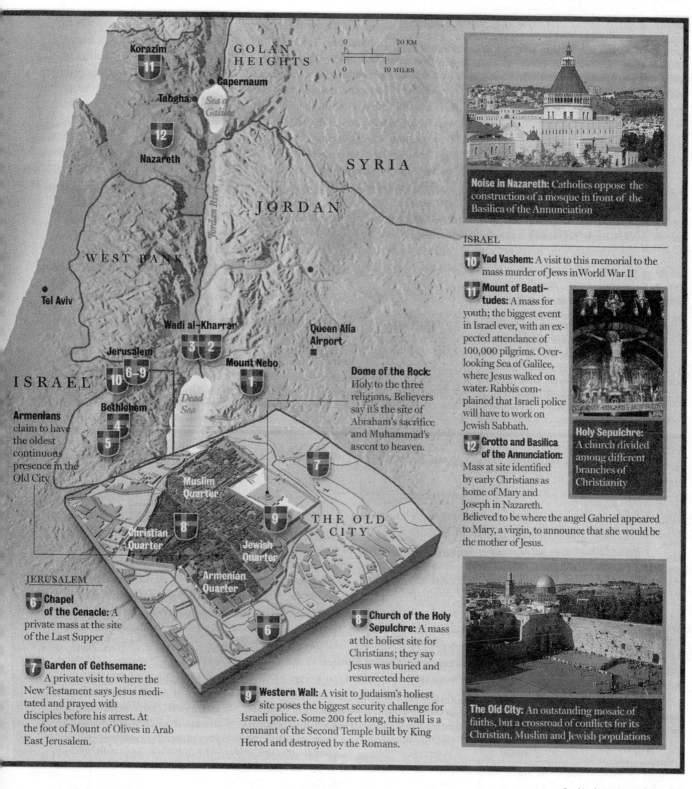

Noise in Nazareth: Catholics oppose the construction of a mosque in front of the Basilica of the Annunciation

ISRAEL

10 Yad Vashem: A visit to this memorial to the mass murder of Jews in World War II

11 Mount of Beatitudes: A mass for youth; the biggest event in Israel ever, with an expected attendance of 100,000 pilgrims. Overlooking Sea of Galilee, where Jesus walked on water. Rabbis complained that Israeli police will have to work on Jewish Sabbath.

12 Grotto and Basilica of the Annunciation: Mass at site identified by early Christians as home of Mary and Joseph in Nazareth. Believed to be where the angel Gabriel appeared to Mary, a virgin, to announce that she would be the mother of Jesus.

Holy Sepulchre: A church divided among different branches of Christianity

The Old City: An outstanding mosaic of faiths, but a crossroad of conflicts for its Christian, Muslim and Jewish populations

Dome of the Rock: Holy to the three religions. Believers say it's the site of Abraham's sacrifice and Muhammad's ascent to heaven.

Armenians claim to have the oldest continuous presence in the Old City

JERUSALEM

6 Chapel of the Cenacle: A private mass at the site of the Last Supper

7 Garden of Gethsemane: A private visit to where the New Testament says Jesus meditated and prayed with disciples before his arrest. At the foot of Mount of Olives in Arab East Jerusalem.

8 Church of the Holy Sepulchre: A mass at the holiest site for Christians; they say Jesus was buried and resurrected here

9 Western Wall: A visit to Judaism's holiest site poses the biggest security challenge for Israeli police. Some 200 feet long, this wall is a remnant of the Second Temple built by King Herod and destroyed by the Romans.

Graphics by Kevin Hand/Newsweek

Sources: Central Bureau of Statistics, Israel, News Reports. Research by Fe Con way.

that Jesus was a reformist Pharisee whose teachings had been corrupted by his followers and mixed with pagan elements to produce the dogmas of Christianity," says Susannah Heschel, professor of Jewish studies at Dartmouth. Thus, far from being a unique religious genius—as the liberal Protestants claimed—Geiger's Jesus was a democratizer of his own inherited tradition. It was, he argued, the Pharisees' opponents, the Saducees, who became the first Christians and produced the negative picture of the Pharisees as legalistic hypocrites found in the later Gospel texts. In sum, Geiger—and after him, other Jewish scholars—distinguished between the faith *of* Jesus, which they saw as liberal Judaism, and

The Karma of the Gospel

A spiritual leader finds connections between Christian teachings and his own traditions.

BY THE DALAI LAMA

AS A BUDDHIST, MY attitude toward Jesus Christ is that he was either a fully enlightened being, or a bodhisattva of a very high spiritual realization. I see common notes between Buddhism and Christianity. Here are a few:

Transfiguration. In Buddhism, when an individual practitioner reaches a high degree of realization in his or her spiritual evolution, the transformation can manifest itself at the physical level, as well. We find such stories about the Buddha in the sutras. They begin when Buddha's disciples notice a physical change in his appearance. A radiance shines from his body. Then one of the disciples asks the Buddha, "I see these changes in you. Why are these changes taking place?" These parables are similar to the Gospel passages on the Transfiguration when Jesus' face is suddenly glowing.

Karma. In another Gospel passage, Jesus says: "I have not come to judge the world but to save it.... The word I have spoken will be his judge on the last day." I feel this closely reflects the Buddhist idea of karma. There is not an autonomous being (God) "out there" who arbitrates what you should experience and what you should know; instead, there is the truth contained in the casual principle itself. If you act in an ethical way, desirable consequences will result; if you act in a negative way, then you must face the consequences of that action as well.

Faith. In the Buddhist tradition, we speak of three different types of faith. The first is faith in the form of admiration that you have toward a particular person or a particular state of being. The second is aspiring faith. There is a sense of emulation: you aspire to attain that state of being. The third type is the faith of conviction.

All three types of faith can be explained in the Christian context as well. A practicing Christian can have a very strong devotion to and admiration for Jesus by reading the Gospel. That is the first level of faith, the faith of admiration and devotion. After that, as you strengthen your admiration and faith, it is possible to progress to the second level, which is the faith of aspiration. In the Buddhist tradition, you would aspire to Buddhahood. In the Christian context you may not use the same language, but you can say that you aspire to attain the full perfection of the divine nature, or union with God. Then, once you have developed that sense of aspiration, you can develop the third level of faith, a deep conviction that it is possible to perfect such a state of being.

Empathy. One of the grounds on which the presence of Buddha-nature in all people is argued is the human capacity for empathy. Some people may have a stronger force, others less; but all of us share this natural capacity to empathize. This Buddha-nature, this seed of enlightenment, of perfection, is inherent in all of us. To attain perfection, however, it is not enough that a spiritual practitioner merely possess such a nature; this nature must be developed to its fullest potential. In Buddhist practice, you require the assistance of an enlightened guide, a guru or teacher. Christians believe that all of us share this divine nature but it is only through Jesus that one perfects it. Through Jesus it comes into full bloom and becomes unified, one, with the Father.

THE DALAI LAMA *is the author of "The Good Heart"* (Wisdom Publications, Boston), *from which this is excerpted.*

the faith *in* Jesus, which became Christianity.

The implications of this "Jewish Jesus" were obvious, and quickly put to polemical use. Jews who might be attracted by the figure of Jesus needn't convert to Christianity. Rather, they could find his real teachings faithfully recovered in the burgeoning Reform Jewish movement. Christians, on the other hand, could no longer claim that Jesus was a unique religious figure who inspired a new and universal religion. Indeed, if any religion could claim universality, it was monotheistic Judaism as the progenitor of both Christianity and Islam.

The Holocaust occasioned yet another way of imagining Jesus. If some Jews blamed Christians—or God himself—for allowing the ovens of Auschwitz, a few Jewish artists found a different way to deal with the horror of genocide: they applied the theme of the crucified Christ to the Nazis' Jewish victims. This is particularly evident in harrowing paintings of Marc Chagall, where the dying Jesus is marked by Jewish symbols. And in "Night," his haunting stories of the death camps, Elie Wiesel adopted the Crucifixion motif for his wrenching scene of three Jews hanged from a tree, like Jesus and the two thieves on Golgotha. The central figure is an innocent boy dangling in protracted agony because his body is too light to allow the noose its swift reprieve. When Wiesel hears a fellow inmate cry, "Where is God?" the author says to himself; "Here He is. He has been hanged here, on these gallows." "There's no lack of suffering in Judaism," says Alan Segal, professor of Jewish Studies at Barnard College and Columbia University, "and no reason why Jews shouldn't pick up an image central to Christianity."

Today, the Jewishness of Jesus is no longer a question among scholars. That much of what he taught can be found in the Jewish Scriptures is widely accepted by Christian as well as Jewish students of the Bible. At some seminaries, like Hebrew Union, a course in the New Testament is now required of rabbinical candidates. Outside scholarly circles, there is less focus on Jesus, and most Jews will never read the Christian Bible. And, of course, Jews do not accept the Christ of faith. "They see Jesus as an admirable Jew," says theologian John Cobb, "but they don't believe that any Jew could be God."

ISLAM

AT THE ONSET OF RAMADAN LAST year, Vatican officials sent greetings to the world's Muslims, inviting them to reflect on Jesus as "a model and permanent message for humanity." But for Muslims, the Prophet Muhammad is the perfect model for humankind and in the Qur'an (in Arabic only), they believe, the very Word of God dwells among us. Even so, Muslims recognize Jesus as a great prophet and revere him as Isa ibn Maryam—Jesus, the son of Mary, the only woman mentioned by name in the Qur'an. At a time when many Christians deny Jesus' birth to a virgin, Muslims find the story in the Qur'an and affirm that it is true. "It's a very strange situation, where Muslims are defending the miraculous birth of Jesus against western deniers," says Seyyed Hossein Nasr, professor of Islamic studies at George Washington University. "Many Westerners also do not believe that Jesus ascended into heaven. Muslims do." Indeed, many Muslims see themselves as Christ's true followers.

What Muslims believe about Jesus comes from the Qur'an—not the New Testament, which they consider tainted by human error. They also draw upon their own oral traditions, called *hadith*,

and on experts' commentaries. In these sources, Jesus is born of Mary under a palm tree by a direct act of God. From the cradle, the infant Jesus announces that he is God's prophet, though not God's son, since Allah is "above having a son" according to the Qur'an.

Nonetheless, the Muslim Jesus enjoys unique spiritual prerogatives that other prophets, including Muhammad, lack. Only Jesus and his mother were born untouched by Satan. Even Muhammad had to be purified by angels before receiving prophethood. Again, in the Qur'an Muhammad is not presented as a miracle worker, but Jesus miraculously heals the blind, cures lepers and "brings forth the dead by [Allah's] leave." In this way Jesus manifests himself as the Messiah, or "the anointed one." Muslims are not supposed to pray to anyone but Allah. But in popular devotions many ask Jesus or Mary or John the Baptist for favors. (According to one recent estimate, vi-

sions of Jesus or Mary have occurred some 70 times in Muslim countries since 1985.)

Although Muhammad supersedes Jesus as the last and greatest of the prophets, he still must die. But in the Qur'an, Jesus does not die, nor is he resurrected. Muslims believe that Jesus asked God to save him from crucifixion, as the Gospels record, and that God answered his prayer by taking him directly up to heaven. "God would not allow one of his prophets to be killed," says Martin Palmer, director of the International Consultancy on Religion, Education and Culture in Manchester, England. "If Jesus had been crucified, it would have meant that God had failed his prophet."

When the end of the world approaches, Muslims believe that Jesus will descend to defeat the antichrist—and, incidentally, to set the record straight. His presence will prove the Crucifixion was a myth and eventually

---

A Rabbi Argues With Jesus

A noted Talmudic scholar insists that Jews must remain faithful to the words of the Torah.
BY JACOB NEUSNER

IMAGINE WALKING ON A dusty road in Galilee nearly 2,000 years ago and meeting up with a small band of youngsters, led by a young man. The leader's presence catches your attention: he talks, the others listen, respond, argue, obey—care what he says, follow him. You don't know who the man is, but you know he makes a difference to the people with him and to nearly everyone he meets. People respond, some with anger, some with admiration, a few with genuine faith. But no one walks away uninterested in the man and the things he says and does.

I can see myself meeting this man, and, with courtesy, arguing with him. It is my form of respect, the only compliment I crave from others, the only serious tribute I pay to the people I take seriously. I can see myself not only meeting and arguing with Jesus, challenging him on the basis of our shared Torah, the Scriptures Christians would later adopt as the "Old Testament." I can also imagine myself saying, "Friend, you go your way, I'll go mine, I wish you well—without me. Yours is not the Torah of Moses, and all I have from God, and all I ever need from God, is that one Torah of Moses."

We would meet, we would argue, we would part friends—but we would part, He would have gone his way, to Jerusalem and the place he believed God had prepared for him; I would have gone my way, home to my wife and my children, my dog and my garden. He would have gone his way to glory, I my way to my duties and my responsibilities.

Why? Because the Torah teaches that the kingdom that matters is not in heaven, but the one we find ourselves in now: sustaining life, sanctifying life, in the here and the now of home and family, community and society. God's kingdom is in the

humble details of what I eat for breakfast and how I love my neighbor.

Can the Kingdom of God come soon, in our day, to where we are? The Torah not only says yes, it shows how. Do I have then to wait for God's Kingdom? Of course I have to wait. But while waiting, there are things I have to do. Jesus demanded that to enter this Kingdom of Heaven I repudiate family and turn my back on home: "Sell all you have and follow me." That is not what the Torah says.

On Sinai Moses told how to organize a kingdom of priests and a holy people, conduct workday affairs, love God—how to build God's kingdom, accepting the yoke of God's commandments. As a faithful Jew, what I do is simply reaffirm the Torah of Sinai over and against the teachings of Jesus. Moses would expect no less of us. So when I say, if I heard those words, I would have offered an argument, my dispute would have been with a mortal man walking among us and talking with us. Only the Torah is the word of God.

I think Christianity, beginning with Jesus, took a wrong turn in abandoning the Torah. By the truth of the Torah, much that Jesus said is wrong. By the criterion of the Torah, Israel's religion in the time of Jesus was authentic and faithful, not requiring reform or renewal, demanding only faith and loyalty to God and the sanctification of life through carrying out God's will. Jesus and his disciples took one path, and we another. I do not believe God would want it any other way.

NEUSNER *has just been named research professor of religion and theology at Bard College. He is the author of "A Rabbi Talks With Jesus."*

A TRUE SAVIOR: The Christ of the Gospel is the best-known Jesus in the world. For Christians, he is unique—the only Son of God.

he will die a natural death. "Jesus will return as a Muslim," says Nasr, "in the sense that he will unite all believers in total submission to the one God."

HINDUISM

THE GOSPELS ARE SILENT ABOUT the life of Jesus between his boyhood visit to the Jerusalem Temple with his parents, and the beginning of his public ministry at the age of 30. But in India there is a strong tradition that the teenage Jesus slipped away from his parents, journeyed across Southeast Asia learning yogic meditation and returned home to become a guru to the Jews. This legend reveals just how easily Hinduism absorbs any figure whom others worship as divine. To Hindus, India is the Holy Land, its sacred mountains and rivers enlivened by more than 300,000 local deities. It is only natural, then, that Jesus would come to India to learn the secrets of unlocking his own inherent divinity.

As Gandhi was, many Hindus are drawn to the figure of Jesus by his compassion and nonviolence—virtues taught in their own sacred Scriptures. But also like Gandhi, Hindus find the notion of a single god unnecessarily restrictive. In their perspective, all human beings are sons of God with the innate ability to become divine themselves. Those Hindus who read the Gospels are drawn to the passage in John in which Jesus proclaims that "the Father and I are one." This confirms the basic Hindu belief that everyone is capable through rigorous spiritual practice of realizing his or her own universal "god-consciousness." The great modern Hindu saint Ramakrishna recorded that he meditated on a picture of the Madonna with child and was transported into a state of *samadhi*,

a consciousness in which the divine is all that really exists. For that kind of spiritual experience, appeal to any god will do. "Christ-consciousness, God-consciousness, Krishna-consciousness, Buddha-consciousness—it's all the same thing," says Deepak Chopra, an Indian popularizer of Hindu philosophy for New Age Westerners. "Rather than 'love thy neighbor,' this consciousness says, 'You and I are the same beings.' "

BUDDHISM

THE LIFE STORIES OF JESUS AND THE Buddha are strikingly similar. Both are conceived without sexual intercourse and born to chaste women. Both leave home for the wilderness where each is tempted by a Satan figure. Both return enlightened, work miracles and challenge the religious establishment by their teachings. Both attract disciples and both are betrayed by one of them. Both preach compassion, unselfishness and altruism and each creates a movement that bears the founder's name. Thich Nhat Hanh, a Vietnamese Zen Buddhist monk with a large Western following, sees Jesus and Buddha as "brothers" who taught that the highest form of human understanding is "universal love." But there is at least one unbridgeable difference: a Christian can never become Christ, while the aim of every serious Buddhist is to achieve Buddhahood himself.

Thus when Buddhists encounter Christianity they depersonalize the Jesus who walked this earth and transform him into a figure more like Buddha. "Buddhists can think of Jesus Christ as an emanation or 'truth body' [*dharmakaya*] of the Buddha," says Buddhist scholar Robert Thurman of Columbia University. For Tibetan Buddhists, Jesus

strongly resembles a bodhisattva—a perfectly enlightened being who vows to help others attain enlightenment. But to reconfigure Jesus as a Buddhist is to turn him into something he was not. Jesus, after all, believed in God, the creator and sustainer of the universe, which Buddhists do not. He believed in sin, which is not a Buddhist concept. Jesus did not teach compassion as a way of removing bad karma, nor did he see life as a cycle of death and rebirth. In short, says the Dalai Lama, trying to meld Jesus into Buddha "is like putting a yak's head on a sheep's body." It doesn't work. Indeed, nothing shows the difference between the Jesus and the Buddha better than the way that each died. The Buddha's death was serene and controlled—a calm passing out of his final rebirth, like the extinction of a flame. Jesus, on the other hand, suffers an agonizing death on the cross, abandoned by God but obedient to his will.

Clearly, the cross is what separates the Christ of Christianity from every other Jesus. In Judaism there is no precedent for a Messiah who dies, much less as a criminal as Jesus did. In Islam, the story of Jesus' death is rejected as an affront to Allah himself. Hindus can accept only a Jesus who passes into peaceful samadhi, a yogi who escapes the degradation of death. The figure of the crucified Christ, says Buddhist Thich Nhat Hanh, "is a very painful image to me. It does not contain joy or peace, and this does not do justice to Jesus." There is, in short, no room in other religions for a Christ who experiences the full burden of mortal existence—and hence there is no reason to believe in him as the divine Son whom the Father resurrects from the dead.

Even so, there are lessons all believers can savor by observing Jesus in the mirrors of Jews and Muslims, Hindus and Buddhists. That the image of a benign Jesus has universal appeal should come as no surprise. That most of the world cannot accept the Jesus of the cross should not surprise, either. Thus the idea that Jesus can serve as a bridge uniting the world's religions is inviting but may be ultimately impossible. A mystery to Christians themselves, Jesus remains what he has always been, a sign of contradiction.

With ANNE UNDERWOOD *and*
HEATHER WON TESORIERO

CONFUCIUS

Confucianism, once thought to be a dead doctrine, has made an astonishing comeback during the past 20 years. Cited as a major force behind East Asia's economic "miracles," it is now finding a renewed following among mainland Chinese grown disillusioned with communism. Yet what exactly Confucianism means is hard to say. All the more reason, Jonathan Spence urges, to return to the man himself—and to the little we know about his life and words.

Jonathan D. Spence

Jonathan D. Spence is George B. Adams Professor of History at Yale University. His many books include The Death of Woman Wang *(1978),* The Gate of Heavenly Peace *(1981),* The Search for Modern China *(1990), and, most recently,* Chinese Roundabout *(1992).*

Across the centuries that have elapsed since he lived in northern China and lectured to a small group of followers on ethics and ritual, the ideas of Confucius have had a powerful resonance. Soon after his death in 476 B.C., a small number of these followers dedicated themselves to recording what they could remember of his teachings and to preserving the texts of history and poetry that he was alleged to have edited. In the fourth and third centuries B.C., several distinguished philosophers expanded and systematized ideas that they ascribed to him, thus deepening his reputation as a complex and serious thinker. During the centralizing and tyrannical Ch'in dynasty that ruled China between 221 and 209 B.C., the works of Confucius were slated for destruction, on the grounds that they contained material antithetical to the obedience of people to their rulers, and many of those who prized or taught his works were brutally killed on the emperor's orders.

Despite this apparently lethal setback, Confucius's reputation was only enhanced, and during the Han dynasty (206 B.C.–A.D. 220) his ideas were further edited and expanded, this time to be used as a focused source for ideas on good government and correct social organization. Despite the pedantry and internal bickering of these self-styled followers of Confucius, his ideas slowly came to be seen as the crystallization of an inherent Chinese wisdom. Surviving the importation of Buddhist metaphysics and meditative practices from India in the third to sixth centuries A.D., and a renewed interest in both esoteric Taoist theories of the cosmos and the hard-headed political realism of rival schools of legalistically oriented thinkers, a body of texts reorganized as "Confucian," with their accumulated commentaries, became the basic source for competitive examinations for entrance into the Chinese civil service and for the analysis of a wide spectrum of political and familial relationships: those between ruler and subject, between parents and children, and between husband and wife. In the 12th century A.D., a loose group of powerful philosophers, though differing over the details, reformulated various so-called Confucian principles to incorporate some of the more deeply held premises of Buddhism, giving in particular a dualistic structure to the Confucian belief system by separating idealist or universalist components—the inherent principles or premises, known as the *li*—from the grosser matter, or manifestations of life-in-action (the *ch'i*).

A final series of shifts took place in the last centuries of imperial China. During the 16th century elements of Confucian doctrine were deepened and altered once again by philosophers who emphasized the inherent morality of the individual and tried to overcome the dualism that they felt Confucians had erected between nature and the human emotions. In the 17th century Confucian scholars confronted the promise and challenge of newly imported scientific ideas from the West,

From *The Wilson Quarterly*, Autumn 1993, pp. 30–38. © 1993 by Jonathan D. Spence. Reprinted by permission of the author.

brought by Jesuits and other Catholic missionaries. During the following century Confucian scholars embarked on a newly formulated intellectual quest for the evidential basis of historical and moral phenomena, one that led them cumulatively to peaks of remarkable scholarship. In the 19th century these scholars began to cope with Western technology and constitutional ideas and with the development of new modes of education. But in the 20th century Confucian ideas were attacked from within and without China as contributing to China's economic backwardness, myopic approach to social change, denial of the idea of progress, resistance to science, and a generally stultified educational system.

These attacks were so devastating that as recently as 20 years ago, one would have thought that the chances of Confucius ever again becoming a major figure of study or emulation were slight indeed, in any part of the world. In Communist China, where he had been held up to ridicule or vilification since the Communist victory of 1949, his name was invoked only when mass campaigns needed a symbol of the old order to castigate, as in the "Anti-Confucius and anti-Lin Biao Campaign" of 1973–74. But in that case the real focus of the campaign was Chairman Mao's former "closest comrade-in-arms," General Lin Biao, not the discredited sage of Lu. In Taiwan, though constant lip service was paid to the enduring values of Confucianism, the doctrine that lived on under that name was slanted in content and attracted few of the brightest young minds. It was a version of Confucian belief that followed along lines first laid down by Nationalist Party ideologues during the 1930s in an attempt to boost their own prestige and give a deeper historical legitimacy to party leader Chiang Kai-Shek. Although in Taiwan as in other parts of Asia there were great scholars who continued to explore the sage's inner meaning, in many Asian schools Confucius was also invoked in support of authoritarian and hierarchical value systems. In Europe and the United States, though Confucian texts were studied in East Asian and

Oriental studies centers, they did not arouse much excitement, and the young—if they were interested in earlier Asian studies at all—were likely to be far more interested in Taoism or Buddhism.

Now, however, the revival is in full swing. Confucian study societies have sprung up inside the People's Republic of China, with government approval. In Taiwan, Confucianism is studied as a central aspect of philosophical inquiry, and so-called New Confucians are linking his ideas on conduct and the self to certain preoccupations in modern ethics. In the United States especially, many colleges now teach sophisticated and popular courses in "Confucian belief," and a distinguished stream of "Confucian" academics jet around the world as conference participants and even as consultants to foreign governments on the sage. Translations of Confucius's work, and that of his major followers, are in print with popular presses, often in variant editions. And "Confucian principles" are cited approvingly as being one of the underpinnings of the disciplined work habits and remarkable international economic success of a number of Asian states.

The renewed interest in Confucius is not the result of any rush of new information about him. There has been no newly discovered cache of intimate details about him or his family that could engage the public interest, no fresh sources that can be ascribed to him and thus deepen our sense of his achievement, or that could serve as the basis for new controversies. The scraps of information about Confucius are so slight that they barely give us an outline, let alone a profile, of the man. (The modern name Confucius is an early Western rendering of the sage's Chinese honorific name, "K'ung-fu'tsu.") We are almost certain that he was born in 551 B.C. We have a definite year of death, 479 B.C. He was born in the kingdom of Lu, one of the many small states into which China was then divided and which corresponds roughly to the area of modern Shandong province. His parents might have had aristocratic roots, but they were neither prominent nor wealthy, and though Confucius received a good education in historical and ritual matters,

his parents died when he was young, and the youth had to fend for himself. He acquired a number of skills: in clerical work, music, accounting, perhaps in charioteering and archery, and in certain "menial activities" on which we have no other details. Sometime between 507 and 497 B.C. he served in the state of Lu in an office that can be translated as "police commissioner" and that involved hearing cases and meting out punishments. Before and after that stint of service he traveled to various neighboring states, seeking posts as a diplomatic or bureaucratic adviser but meeting with little success. Because of some feud he was, for a time, in mortal danger, but he handled himself with calmness and courage. He married and had one son and two daughters. His son predeceased him, but not before producing an heir. One of his daughters married a student of Confucius who had served time in jail. Confucius approved the match because he believed that the young man had in fact done no wrong. During his later years Confucius was a teacher of what we might now call ethics, ritual, and philosophy; the names of 35 of his students have come down to us.

To compound the problems caused by this paucity of biographical information, we have nothing that we can be completely sure was written by Confucius himself. What we do have is a record of what some of his disciples and students—or their students—said that he said. Usually translated as *The Analects of Confucius,* this collection is brief, aphoristic, and enigmatic. But the *Analects,* despite the problem of indirect transmission, remain our crucial source on Confucius's beliefs, actions, and personality. Not surprisingly, scholars disagree on how to interpret many passages and how much to believe in the authenticity of the different parts of this text. The best and perhaps the only gauges of authenticity are internal consistency, tone, and coherence. One can also look at the construction of each book—there are 20 in all, each running about five pages in English translation—and search for obvious distortions and later additions. The last five of the books, for example, have lengthy sections that present Confucius either as a butt to the Taoists or as an uncritical transmitter of doctrines with which he can be shown in earlier chapters to have disagreed. It is a fairly safe assumption that these were added to the original text by persons with a special cause to plead. Other books give disproportionate space to Confucius's praise of a particular student whom we know from other passages that he rather disliked. Perhaps in such cases we are witnessing attempts to correct the record by later followers of the student concerned. There does not seem to be any political censorship; indeed, one of the mysteries of the later uses of Confucianism concerns the way that the original text as we now have it has been preserved for two millennia even though it seems quite obviously to contradict the ideological uses to which it was being put. Interpretation and commentary, that is to say, carried more weight with readers than did the original words.

Given the bewildering array of philosophical and political arguments that Confucianism has been called on to support, and given, in particular, the generally held belief that Confucius was a strict believer in hierarchy and the values of absolute obedience to superiors, and that he lacked flexibility and imagination, it is an intriguing task to read the *Analects* with open eyes and without any presuppositions drawn from later interpretative attempts. What was, in fact, the central message of the man Confucius himself?

Personally, almost two and a half millennia after his death, I find that Confucius is still especially valuable to us because of the strength of his humanity, his general decency, and the fervor of his belief in the importance of culture and the act of learning. He emphatically did not feel that he had any monopoly on truth. Rather, he was convinced that learning is a perpetual process that demands flexibility, imagination, and tenacity. He scolded students who would not get up in the morning, just as he scolded those who were unctuous or complacent. He said that he had no interest in trying to teach those who did not have the curiosity to follow up on a philosophical argument or a logical sequence of ideas after he had given them an initial prod in the right direction. He let his students argue among themselves—or with him—and praised those who were able to make moral decisions that might benefit humankind in general. But at the same time he adamantly refused to talk about the forces of heaven or to speculate on the nature of the afterlife, since there was so much that he did not know about life on this Earth that he was convinced such speculations would be idle.

It is clear that Confucius derived great pleasure from life. Once, one of his students could not think what to say to an influential official who had asked what sort of a person Confucius really was. Hearing of the incident, Confucius gently chided his student with these words: "Why did you not simply say something to this effect: He is the sort of man who forgets to eat when he tries to solve a problem that has been driving him to distraction, who is so full of joy that he forgets his worries and who does not notice the onset of old age?"

This brief exchange comes from *The Analects of Confucius*, book VII, section 19, and it is typical of words that Confucius left us, words through which we can in turn analyze his character.[*] Another example could be taken from Confucius's views concerning loyalty to the state and the value of capital punishment. In later periods of Chinese history, it was commonplace to assert that "Confucian" bureaucrats and scholars should always put their duty to the state and the dynasty they served ahead of personal and family loyalties. Chinese history is also replete with grim details of executions carried out in the name of "Confucian" ideology against those who violated the state's laws. But in the most clearly authenticated books of the *Analects* that we have, we find completely unambiguous views on these central matters of human practice and belief. What could be clearer than this?

The Governor of She said to Confucius, "In our village there is a man nicknamed 'Straight Body.' When his father stole a sheep, he gave evidence against him." Confucius answered, "In our village those who are straight are quite different. Fathers cover up for their sons, and sons cover up for their fathers. Straightness is to be found in such behavior." (XIII/18)

On executions, Confucius was equally unambiguous:

Chi K'ang Tzu asked Confucius about government, saying, "What would you think if, in order to move closer to those who possess the Way, I were to kill those who do not follow the Way?" Confucius answered, "In administering your government, what need is there for you to kill? Just desire the good yourself and the common people will be good. The virtue of the gentleman is like wind; the virtue of the small man is like grass. Let the wind blow over the grass and it is sure to bend." (XII/19)

If it were humanly possible, Confucius added, he would avoid the law altogether: "In hearing litigation, I am no different from any other man. But if you insist on a difference, it is, perhaps, that I try to get the parties not to resort to litigation in the first place." (XII/13) In the long run, the fully virtuous state would be forever free of violent death: "The Master said, 'How true is the saying that after a state has been ruled for a hundred years by good men it is possible to get the better of cruelty and to do away with killing.' " (XIII/11)

Since the words of Confucius have been preserved for us mainly in the form of aphorisms or snatches of dialogue—or the combination of the two—one way to find a coherent structure in his thought is to track the remarks he made to specific individuals, even if these are widely scattered throughout the *Analects*. Sometimes, of course, there is only one remark, especially in the case of those whose behavior Confucius considered beyond the pale. My favorite example here is his dismissal of Yuan Jang, allegedly once his friend: "Yuan Jang sat waiting with his legs spread wide. The Master said, 'To be neither modest nor deferential when young, to have passed on nothing worthwhile when grown up, and to refuse to die when old, that is what I call being a pest.' So saying, the Master tapped him on the shin with his stick." (XIV/43) That tapping on the shin, perhaps playful, perhaps in irritation, shows an unusual side of Confucius. Was he trying to add physical sting to his sharp words? More commonly with him, it was a laugh or a shrug that ended a potentially confrontational exchange.

With several of his students, Confucius clearly felt a deep rapport, even when they did not see eye to eye. One such student was Tzu-lu, who was more a man of action than a scholar. Confucius loved to tease Tzu-lu for his impetuosity. Thus, after telling his students that if he were on a raft that drifted out to sea, Tzu-lu would be the one to follow him, Confucius added wryly that that would be because Tzu-lu had at once more courage and less judgment than his teacher. On another occasion, when Tzu-lu asked if Confucius thought he, Tzu-lu, would make a good general, Confucius replied that he would rather not have as a general someone who would try to walk across a river or strangle a tiger with his bare hands. (V/7 and VII/11)

Different in character, but still very much his own man, was the merchant and diplomat Tzu-kung. Confucius acknowledged that Tzu-kung was shrewd and capable, and made a great profit from his business deals. He even agreed that Tzu-kung's type of intelligence was especially useful in the world of literature and thought: "Only with a man like you can one discuss the Odes. Tell such a man something and he can see its relevance to what he has not been told." (I/16) But Confucius did not like Tzu-kung's insistence on always trying to put people in a ranked order of priorities, as if they were so many objects—"For my part I have no time for such things," Confucius observed—and he was equally upset if he felt that Tzu-kung was skimping things that really mattered because of his private feelings: "Tzu-kung wanted to dispense with the practice of ritually killing a sacrificial sheep at the announcement of the new moon. The Master said, 'You love the sheep, but I love the Rites.' " (XIV/29 and III/17)

Most readers of the *Analects* feel that the student called Yen Yuan was clearly Confucius's favorite, and the one closest to the Master by behavior and inclination. Yen Yuan was poor but lived his life without complaining. He did not allow poverty to sour or interrupt his search for the Way, and his intelligence was truly piercing. As Tzu-kung, not a modest man, put it, "When he[Yen Yuan] is told one thing he understands 10. When I am told one thing I understand only two." To which Confucius sighed in agreement, "Neither of us is as good as he is." (V/9) In a similar vein, Confucius praised Yen Yuan's prudence, contrasting it with Tzu-lu's bravado. As Confucius phrased it, Yen Yuan was the kind of man who "when faced with a task, was fearful of failure," and who knew how "to stay out of sight when set aside;" furthermore, Yen Yuan was not above making mistakes, but more important, "he did not make the same mistake twice." (VII/11 and VI/3) When Yen Yuan died young, before being able to achieve his full promise, Confucius gave way to a conspicuous display of immoderate grief. When some of his students remonstrated with him for showing such "undue sorrow," Confucius's answer was brief but powerful: "If not for him for whom should I show undue sorrow?" (IX/10)

Confucius lived to a fine old age, and not even regret over the loss of his favorite student and his own son could blunt the pleasures he felt at his own mounting experience and the attainment of something that might be approaching wisdom. He did not boast about the knowledge he had acquired—indeed he thought he was lucky to have got as far as he had. As he put it once to Tzu-lu: "Shall I tell you what it is to know? To say you know when you know, and to say you do not know when you do not, that is knowledge." (II/17) His own greatest ambition, as he once told Yen Yuan and Tzu-lu jointly, was "to bring peace to the old, to have trust in my friends, and to cherish the young." (V/26) On another occasion he went even further, telling his followers, "It is fitting that we hold the young in awe. How do we know that the generations to come will not be the equal of the present?" (IX/23) In the passage that is perhaps the most famous of his sayings, Confucius gave his own version of the stages of life, and it is as different as anything could be from Shakespeare's "Seven Ages of Man," with its heart-rending account of man's descent into the weakness and imbecility of old age after a brief phase of youthful vigor. Whereas according to the *Analects*, the Master said, "At 15 I set my heart on learning; at 30 I took my stand; at 40 I came to be free from doubts; at 50 I understood the Decree of Heaven; at 60 my ear was attuned; at 70 I followed my heart's desire without overstepping the line." (II/4)

Certainly we should not read Confucius as though he were always right. And as we read through the *Analects* we can find Confucius revealing a fussy and sometimes impatient side. Some of his vaunted arguments seem like quibbles, and he could be punctilious to the point of prudishness. His political motivations are often obscure, and he seems to appreciate various struggling rulers' foibles less than his own. But cleared of the accumulation of unsubstantiated details and textual over-interpretations that have weighed him down across the centuries, we find to our surprise an alert, intelligent, and often very amusing man.

How then did he get the reputation that he did, one at once more austere, more pompous, harsh even, and as a reinforcer of the status quo? Strangely enough, part of the reappraisal resulted from the efforts of the man who is undeniably China's greatest historian, Ssu-ma Ch'ien, who lived from around 145 to 89 B.C., during the Han dynasty. In his life's work, a composite history of China entitled simply *Historical Records*, which was completed between 100 and 95 B.C., Ssu-ma Ch'ien aimed to integrate the histories of all China's earlier states and rulers with the steady and inexorable rise to power of the centralizing Ch'in dynasty (221–209 B.C.), and he determined to give Confucius an important role in this process. Thus Ssu-ma Ch'ien paid Confucius the ultimate accolade by placing his story in the section devoted to the ruling houses of early China, as opposed to placing him with other individual thinkers and statesmen in the 70 chapters of biographies that conclude the *Historical Rec-*

ords. In the summation of Confucius's worth with which he ended his account, Ssu-ma Ch'ien gave concise and poignant expression to his homage:

> In this world there have been many people—from kings to wise men—who had a glory while they lived that ended after their death. But Confucius, though a simple commoner, has had his name transmitted for more than 10 generations; all those who study his works consider him their master. From the Son of Heaven, the princes, and the lords on down, anyone in the Central Kingdom who is dedicated to a life of learning, follows the precepts and the rules of the Master. Thus it is that we call him a true Sage.

To give substance to this judgment, Ssu-ma Ch'ien took all known accounts written over the intervening three centuries that purported to describe Confucius, following the principle that if there was no clear reason for discarding an item of biographical information, then he should include it, leaving for later generations the task of winnowing the true from the false. Thus was Confucius given courageous ancestors, his birth described in semi-miraculous terms, his own physical distinction elaborated upon. In one curious addition, Confucius's father was described as being of far greater age than the sage's mother: By one interpretation of the phrase used by Ssu-ma Ch'ien, that the marriage was "lacking in proportion," Confucius's father would have been over 64, while his mother had only recently entered puberty. Confucius's precocious interest in ritual and propriety, his great height and imposing cranial structure, the fecundity of the flocks of cattle and sheep that he supervised in one of his first official posts, his preternatural shrewdness in debate, his instinctive brilliance at interpreting unusual auguries—all of these were given documentary precision in Ssu-ma Ch'ien's account. The result is that Confucius not only emerges as a key counselor to the rulers of his native state of Lu, but the meticulousness of his scholarship and his flair for editing early texts of poetry, history, and music are presented as having attracted an ever-widening circle of hundreds or even thousands of students from his own and neighboring states.

Having constructed this formidable image of a successful Confucius, Ssu-ma Ch'ien was confronted by the need to explain the reasons for Confucius's fall from grace in Lu and for his subsequent wanderings in search of rulers worthy of his service. Being one of China's most gifted storytellers, Ssu-ma Ch'ien was up to this task, presenting a convincing scenario of the way the sagacity of Confucius's advice to the ruler of Lu made him both respected and feared by rival rulers in northern China. One of them was finally able to dislodge Confucius by sending to the ruler of Lu a gift of 24 ravishing female dancers and musicians, along with 30 magnificent teams of chariot horses. This gift so effectively distracted the ruler of Lu from his official duties—most important, it led him to forget certain key ritual sacrifices—that Confucius had no choice but to leave his court.

In various ways, some subtle, some direct, the portrait of Confucius that Ssu-ma Ch'ien wove incorporated diverse levels of narrative dealing with the unpredictability of violence. This was surely not coincidental, for the central tragedy of Ssu-ma Ch'ien's own life had been his court-ordered castration, a savage punishment inflicted on him by the Han dynasty emperor Wu-ti (r. 141–87 B.C.). Ssu-ma Ch'ien's "crime" had been to write a friend a letter in which he incautiously spoke in defense of a man unjustly punished by the same emperor. Despite this agonizing humiliation, which placed the historian in the same physical category as the venal court eunuchs he so deeply despised, Ssu-ma Ch'ien refused to commit suicide; he maintained his dignity by making his history as grand and comprehensive as possible—his presentation of Confucius being a stunning example of his dedication to craft and content. Thus he describes Confucius as a man who had the bureaucratic power to make major judicial decisions but who did so only with care and consideration of all the evidence. When Confucius acted harshly, according to Ssu-ma Ch'ien, it was only when the long-term threat to his kingdom was so strong that leniency would have been folly. This explains one shattering moment in Ssu-ma Ch'ien's biography. One rival leader was planning to overthrow the ruler of Lu, but each of his ruses was seen through and foiled by Confucius. At last, in desperation, the rival ruler ordered his acrobats and dwarfs to perform wild and obscene dances at a ritual occasion that the ruler of Lu was attending. Confucius, according to Ssu-ma Ch'ien, ordered the dwarfs killed.

In another dissimilar but equally powerful comment on violence, Ssu-ma Ch'ien showed that even the descendants of a man of Confucius's integrity could not escape Emperor Wu-ti's willful power. Thus at the very end of his long biography, before the final summation, Ssu-ma Ch'ien lists all of Confucius's direct descendants in the male line. When he comes to the 11th in line, An-kuo, the historian mentions tersely that An-kuo had died "prematurely" under the "ruling emperor." Ssu-ma Ch'ien knew—and knew that his readers knew—that An-kuo had been executed on Wu-ti's orders for involvement in an alleged court coup. The line had not, however, been stamped out, because An-kuo's wife had borne a son before her husband was killed.

Ssu-ma Ch'ien's attempt to reconstruct a convincing psychological and contextual universe for Confucius was a brilliant one, and his version was elaborated upon and glossed by scores of subsequent scholars, even as suitable pieces of the Confucian legacy were seized upon by later rulers and bureaucrats to justify some current policy decision or to prove some philosophical premise. But after more than two millennia of such accretions, it seems time to go back to the earlier and simpler version of the record and try to see for ourselves what kind of a man Confucius was. The results, I feel, in our overly ideological age, are encouraging to those who value the central premises of humane intellectual inquiry.

Note

1. *All citations of the *Analects* are from D. C. Lau's Penguin Books translation, *Confucius, The Analects*. In some cases I have made minor modifications to his translations.

Unit 6

Key Points to Consider

❖ Compare life in 1000 with that of the Roman Empire (see Unit 4, "The Year One"). Was there any change?

❖ Compare common life around the world, including the Americas.

❖ Evaluate the evidence for warfare among the Indians of the Southwest. Is it convincing?

❖ What is the importance of Arab scholarship in world history?

❖ What was the contribution of the Vikings to world history?

❖ Would you agree that the clock is the single most important invention of Western civilization? Why, or why not?

 **Links**   **www.dushkin.com/online/**

These sites are annotated on pages 4 and 5.

World historians have some difficulty with this period of time. In the history of Europe, the Middle Ages, or the medieval period, is a time of retreat after the fall of Rome. The thousand-year span covers feudalism, the growth of nation-states, the bubonic plague (called the Black Death), reestablishment of long-distance trade, the domination of the Roman Catholic Church, and the emergence of Western civilization. For world historians, Western developments during this period of time are important for the future, but they pale in comparison to the achievements of China and Islam and to the changes that people elsewhere in the world were experiencing.

Lifespan and comfort for most people in the year 1000 was little improved from that of year one during the reign of the Roman Empire. "If You Had Lived Back Then" looks briefly at some successful careers around the world during the Middle Ages. In the Western Hemisphere, at that time, the North American Indian town of Cahokia flourished and then declined. It provided a less sophisticated example of town and temple building north of Mesoamerican civilization. Another echo of the civilization of the Aztecs and Mayas was the pueblo builders in the American Southwest. Although long thought to be peaceful farmers, recent evidence presented by Stephen Lekson in "Chaco Death Squads" indicates that warfare and perhaps cannibalism were much more common that anyone cared to believe.

Meanwhile, this period of time represents a golden age for Islamic power and culture. The Arabs rescued Greek writings, became interested in astronomy, impressed the world with its architecture, and advanced medicine. David W. Tschanz describes in "The Arab Roots of European Medicine" how people of the Middle East established the first hospitals and pharmacies. Fouad Ajami, in "An Iberian Chemistry," provides a glimpse of Islamic Cordova at the end of the tenth century when it was one of the great cities of the world. It was noted for its libraries, mosques, baths, tolerance, and trade. Islamic civilization spread its culture, religion, and language through North Africa, into Spain, through the Middle East, and eventually into Eastern Europe.

Europe, meanwhile, was ravaged by Viking raiders until the eleventh century. These Norsemen,

however, were more than marauders. They attempted colonization westward along the North Atlantic rim all the way to the New World, and eastward into Russia. In their part of the world, it was the age of the Vikings, as Arne Emil Christensen explains. At about the time that Viking raids ceased, Western civilization began to develop. Farming improved in the West, nations formed, in England the first halting step for civil liberties was taken with the signing of Magna Carta, and in the thirteenth century some unknown genius invented the mechanical clock. This key invention, as described by David Landes, changed attitudes about time and inspired further developments, such as miniaturization of parts and mass production. It pointed the way to the industrial revolution. By the fifteenth century the Europeans were ready to reach out into the world as no other civilization had done.

The World of the Middle Ages, 500–1500

If you had lived back then

Who would you have been? Most likely, a peasant

At the turn of the last millennium, most of Europe's population was dirt-poor, scratching out an existence at the whim of a lord. Elsewhere, things weren't much better, though a lucky few could control their destinies.

A SOLDIER'S FORTUNE

As the third son born to a chieftain of a small principality in Turkistan, Abu Mansur Subuktigin seemed destined for a life of shepherding and marauding. But by the time of his death in A.D. 997, he had become a renowned statesman and founded the powerful Islamic Ghaznavid dynasty.

Such was life for the ambitious Islamic slave soldier.

The import of slaves to be used as soldiers probably began on a large scale in A.D. 833. Al-Mu'tasim, an Abbasid caliph, was in search of a few good men to guard his palace in Baghdad—preferably bright, strapping young fellows who were good with bows and arrows. Local boys were out of the question—

ISLAMIC MAMELUKES were multi-talented fighters, "the atomic weapon of the Middle Ages."

Arabs were not inclined to be warriors. But young Turkic men were. Already a hot commodity on the slave market as house servants and male sex partners, Turks also had a reputation as excellent archers and horsemen.

Young Turks. The caliph snapped up an army of them. And what started as a small personal guard became a sophisticated regiment that helped Abbasid

ILLUSTRATION BY MATTHEW FREY—WOOD RONSAVILLE HARLIN INC. FOR *USN&WR*

successors conquer Pakistan, Afghanistan, Uzbekistan, and parts of Kazakhstan. Soon other caliphs and sultans were regularly dispatching agents to the steppes of Central Asia to buy boys as young as 10 from their families or warlords. Thus began 10 centuries of mamelukes—in Arabic, "owned ones,"—who, like Subuktigin, sometimes ended up quite the opposite.

Mamelukes were not slaves in the traditional sense. Although they were indeed owned by caliphs, sultans, and anyone else who could afford a private army, they were elite members of Islamic society—so admired that several

Muslims were caught trying to sell themselves into slavery (under Islamic law, Muslims cannot become slaves but slaves can become Muslims).

Their fierce loyalty was instilled in a vigorous training course that could span most of a boy's adolescence. Young, malleable boys emerged as disciplined, well-connected, state-of-the-art fighters. Georgetown University Prof. John Voll calls them "the atomic weapon of the Middle Ages," referring to their unique ability to shoot arrows from all directions (including backward) while at full gallop.

The mamelukes displayed skills off the battlefield, too. After the last Ayyubid sultan was killed by Louis IX's crusaders in 1249, mamelukes murdered his successors, and a mameluke named Baybars became the first ruler of the Mameluke dynasty, which lasted until Ottoman Turks invaded Cairo in 1517. At its height, this slave meritocracy controlled Egypt, Syria, Medina, and Mecca—the religious and commercial centers of the Middle East—making it the most prosperous and longest surviving Islamic dynasty in history. *—Margaret Loftus*

PEASANT DANGERS

The Anglo-Saxon elite are no great mystery to scholars. Scores of texts recounting their regal dress, lavish feasts, and political machinations have survived the centuries. The peasantry, by contrast, is virtually absent from the chronicles of the day. The paucity of information is so frustrating, says Henry Weisser, a Colorado State University professor and author of the forth

FOR THE PEASANT, the line between subsistence and hunger was fine, and a single misfortune could spell doom.

coming *England: An Illustrated History,* that he remembers a colleague once remarking that "he would give his right arm to know how a peasant felt."

Still, archaeological digs and a few documents like tax decrees or church handbooks provide a dim picture of hardscrabble peasant life. The typical hut was whitewashed sod with a thatched roof, no windows, and a dirt floor. A few stones at the center harbored hot coals for warmth and cooking. Straw-filled pallets served as bedding; families slept alongside their underfed animals.

The day began before dawn, with black bread and herb-spiced ale. Clad in simple, coarse cloaks, men headed out to plow their tiny plots, while women tended to the beasts or prepared gruel. The line between subsistence and hunger was fine, and a single misfortune—an early frost, sick oxen—could spell doom. Though plain, the peasant diet of peas, beans, and whole-grain breads was much healthier than the aristocratic fare of fatty game and honeyed treats. But good health was evasive; as many as a third of peasant children never celebrated their first birthday. Icy winters and dysentery were deadly. Fungus-ridden grain, eaten during famines, could lead to ergotism, or "St. Anthony's fire," a poisoning that causes hallucinations and limb loss. Settlements were routinely pillaged and burned by the merciless Norse.

Players. Yet woe was not the peasant's sole companion. There was ale-soaked celebration on Midsummer's Day, with wrestling bouts or other rough games. Though parish churches were rare, religious devotion was the centerpiece of life. "Peasants would sort of worship at the fringes," says Allen Frantzen, an English professor at Loyola University Chicago and general editor of the journal *Essays in Medieval Studies.* "There might well have been peasants who would only have worshiped with roaming preachers in the open air."

ILLUSTRATIONS BY KAREN BARNES—WOOD RONSAVILLE HARLIN INC.-FOR *USN&WR*

Survival was foremost in the peasant mind, a preoccupation scarcely changed by one of the new millennium's most seminal events—the Norman Conquest of 1066, which barely registered. "The [new] lord would look alien and foreign and speak a different language," says Weisser. "But as far as life goes for a peasant, it was still nasty, brutish, and short." —*B.I.K.*

BEST AND BRIGHTEST

When Al Gore set out to "reinvent" government, he probably didn't have the sweeping transformations of Song dynasty China in mind. Pity. Because at the turn of the last millennium, an elite corps of scholar-officials established one of the world's first meritocracies—a civil service based on brains, not bloodlines—and set the stage for a host of innovations that would endure for centuries, from school systems and foreign aid to the use of paper currency.

These so-called mandarins (the term was later coined by the British) were China's best and brightest—moral

authorities versed in Confucian classics and plucked to serve as imperial ministers or town magistrates by passing a series of rigorous local, provincial, and palace exams. Getting accepted to Harvard is a snap by comparison. "The magnitude of their accomplishments is impressive," says Stephen West, a professor of Chinese literature at the University of California–Berkeley. "It would be as if a Henry Kissinger was as gifted a poet as Robert Hass. Or if W. H. Auden was also a superb governmental policy specialist."

Scholars in training. The process began around age 5, when boys learned to bow respectfully and recite lines from classical texts. Families, many of them wealthy landowners or merchants, then might hire tutors to teach the writing of Chinese characters and the study of Confucius. Only the most promising teenagers would head to the capital city of Kaifeng to master the poetry, essay writing, and Confucian scholarship that formed the core of the palace-level

exam. Many failed. Only 50 students aced the highest, or *jin-shi,* test in 998, and Song literature is filled with tales of young scholars led astray by wine and women.

THE POOREST PUJARI from the humblest fishing village in
the Indian realm of Chola was superior to the king himself.

Such brilliance was required to manage the burgeoning commercial and cultural hub that China had become during the 10th century. Tea, originally imported from Southeast Asia more than 100 years earlier, now was the most popular drink on the planet, and the central government included an elaborate bureaucracy to regulate trade and collect taxes. Mandarins managed the money supply, maintained security in the provinces, and settled legal wrangles.

Serving the government was a noble and powerful profession, but it also was hard work. Court began at 5 a.m., and 10-day workweeks were the norm, with two days off in between. Still, life was hardly glum. Along with banquets every other day, many mandarins had household entertainers and concubines. Research by University of California–Davis Chinese historian Beverly Bossler suggests that some of these consorts—as well as many mothers and sisters—may have been almost as well educated as the men in their lives. —*Mary Lord*

BORN TO PRAY

For a Brahman around 1000, apocalypse would come in the blink of an eye, but the next one wasn't due for another 427,898 years. The blink would be that of the god Shiva, who'd open the third eye in the center of his forehead and incinerate the entire universe with his all-piercing sight. He'd done it an infinite number of times before, would do it an infinite number of times again, so there wasn't much cause for alarm. Indians in the year 1000 were living in the Kali Yuga, the last (and most miserable) phase of an endless cycle of birth, florescence, decay, and death.

Even to a small-town *pujari* (ritual priest), such knowledge would be commonplace. Pujaris were just one of the many types of Brahmans, each of whom had distinct responsibilities. The task of the pujari caste was to perform pujas,

religious ceremonies held on any occasion that might benefit from a bit of divine oversight. Any Brahman could recite the holy scriptures, but a Hindu paying for a puja for, say, a daughter's wedding would want to hire a trained professional.

Higher than king. A pujari might have assisted in the coronation of one of the Chola dynasty's greatest monarchs. People in the tropical parts of India knew A.D. 1000 as the 15th year in the reign of King Rajaraja (the name is modestly translatable as "King Kingking"). In a ritual sense, however, the poorest pujari from the humblest fishing village in the Chola realm was superior to King Kingking himself; the mightiest monarch was still a mere Kshatriya—one of a class of knights and nobles inferior to the Brahmans. While not necessarily rich or powerful, Brahmans were considered human manifestations of the divine spirit itself. Even a small-town pujari had to safeguard his purity with an elaborate set of taboos. He could eat neither meat nor (if he was

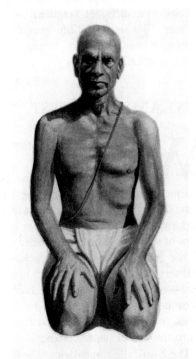

ILLUSTRATIONS BY WILL WILLIAMS (TOP) AND ROB WOOD (BOTTOM)—WOOD RONSAVILLE HARLING, INC. FOR *USN&WR*

particularly strict) animal products such as eggs, cheese, or milk. He had to avoid defilement by members of ritually polluting castes, such as latrine cleaners, leather tanners, and brewers of alcohol. Not only was he forbidden to have physical contact with people then seen as "untouchable"; a Brahman couldn't eat food prepared by them, drink water drawn from their wells, or even (in some parts of the South) let one of their shadows dart across his toe.

The son of a washerman became a washerman; the son of a pujari became a pujari. No change in this life—but there were an infinite number of lives left to live. An untouchable butcher who worked hard might be reincarnated as a respectable craftsman. An unjust king might return as the lowest hauler of trash in all the lands he once ruled. Dharma, the law of the cosmos, is also a Sanskrit word for justice. —*Jonah Blank*

Felonious monks

Religious reform is always tricky, but a millennium ago, the rival kings of Tibet managed to agree on a remarkably modern solution: They hired an outside consultant.

Coaxed north by a hefty sum of gold, legendary Indian guru Atisha trekked to the rugged Tibetan highlands in 1042. He and his followers were faced with a challenge: The Buddhism that had been introduced to Tibet centuries earlier was corrupt, rife with misinterpretations, and mixed with the popular, shamanistic Bon religion.

Later writings describe a land in chaos. An empire that had rivaled China's just two centuries earlier was now broken and divided. Worse, some people had taken sacred metaphors far too literally. "These 'robber-monks' kidnapped and killed men and women, ate them, drank alcohol, and indulged in sexual intercourse," according to historian Rolf Alfred Stein, in *Tibetan Civilization*.

Atisha to the rescue. The famed 60-year-old monk set down strict rules barring sex, possessions, travel, and intoxicants. Other Buddhist teachers followed in his wake, many fleeing Muslim persecution in India. The religious orders founded by Atisha and those who followed him were sponsored by noble families, who gained credibility through the association.

In exchange, the learned lamas served as teachers, adminstrators, and priests. Typically, the head of each Tibetan monastery was the son of a noble family, and the office was hereditary. Since monks were celibate, control would pass from uncle to nephew. Educated and worldly, the lamas helped run the monastic estates and counseled the kings.

Bureaucrats. "After the 13th century, the lamas gradually came to form

a bureaucracy, administering the country but ultimately accountable to the kings and noble families," says Robert Thurman, professor of Indo-Tibetan Buddhist studies at Columbia. Scholars believe life in the monasteries changed little over the centuries. Unlike Europeans at the time, Tibetan monks ate well. The staple of monastic and peasant life was barley grown in mountain fields that were irrigated by glacial melt. Monks supplemented their diet with a wide variety of yak products, including milk, cheese, butter, and meat.

The monasteries grew in power, thriving until the Chinese invasion of Tibet in 1950, when many of the largest monasteries and centuries-old religious libraries were destroyed. Led by the Dalai Lama, the monks who fled the country continue to follow the traditions set down by Atisha. —*Andrew Curry*

The Americas

By Lewis Lord

America was different then. Eagles soared over the oak and poplar forests of Manhattan, where the fragrance of wild roses filled the air and deer, turkeys, and great horned owls inhabited what would become Fifth Avenue. Boston teemed with beavers. Herds of buffalo trod Chicago. And in the heart of the Midwest in that year—A.D. 1000—the first city in what is now the United States was on the verge of becoming an Indian metropolis.

Archaeologists know it as Cahokia, the busiest spot north of the Rio Grande when the new millennium began. At a time when few settlements had even 400 or 500 residents, this 6-square-mile community on the Illinois side of the Mississippi River boasted several thousand. In its 12th-century heyday, Cahokia may have had 20,000 or 25,000 residents, roughly the number in contemporary London. Not until 1800, when Philadelphia counted 30,000, would any U.S. city have more.

Cahokia enjoyed the same advantages that strengthened urban centers of the 19th and 20th centuries: a specialized labor force, an organized government, public construction projects, and a trade network that extended the length of the Mississippi River and reached east to the Atlantic and west to Oklahoma and Nebraska. But it also was bedeviled by problems not unlike those that plague modern cities, especially the

havoc created by too much growth. Five or six centuries after its birth, America's first city, unable to cope with change, was a ghost town.

Yet, while the people vanished, their monuments remained, as can be seen in a visit to Cahokia Mounds State Historical Site, a 2,200-acre tract of open fields and Indian mounds 8 miles east of downtown St. Louis maintained by the state of Illinois. Among the scores of mounds still intact in the rich river bottomland is Monks Mound, towering as high as a 10-story building and covering more ground than the biggest of Egypt's pyramids. From atop this grassy structure—the largest prehistoric earthen mound in the western hemisphere—visitors see in the distance St. Louis's Gateway Arch. Much closer, they hear the whine below of 18-wheelers on an interstate highway built in the 1960s across the ancient city's site.

Corn boom. One millennium ago, Cahokia was emerging from centuries in which people in the region foraged for nuts and berries. Cahokia's rise very likely began with a breakthrough, the introduction around A.D. 800 of a variety of corn suited as much for the Midwest as for Mexico, the land where corn began. New technology also helped: Someone fastened a stone blade to a pole, and farmers in the heartland began cultivating soil with a hoe instead of scratching it with a digging stick. All

around Cahokia, corn-fed villages sprang up on the plain made fertile by floods of the Mississippi and Illinois rivers.

Indians for centuries had built mounds in many shapes—octagons, circles, even the zigzag of a snake. Around A.D. 900, Cahokia developed another form: the four-sided pyramid with a flat top. To this day, no one has shown that a single Mexican ever visited Cahokia. But someone, somehow, had Mexican ideas: Cahokia's earthen mounds were very similar to the stone pyramids built by Mexico's then fading Mayans. And atop Cahokia's mounds stood thatched-roof temples and houses for the privileged, like structures crowning the Mayan platforms.

To build Monks Mound (so named after a local 19th-century Trappist monastery), Cahokians hauled 55-pound basket loads of dirt on their backs from nearby borrow pits. After they did this 14.7 million times over three centuries, constructing one rectangular platform atop another, the 22-million-cubic-foot mound was complete.

Cahokia-style. The French explorers who ventured into the Mississippi Valley in the 1600s found nothing around Cahokia but vine-covered mounds, which they probably mistook for natural hills. But further south along the Mississippi, they came across Indian tribes with lifestyles that scholars believe were

Then: Artist's rendering shows Cahokia in its heyday, 1100-1200.

MICHAEL HAMPSHIRE—CAHOKIA MOUNDS STATE HISTORIC SITE

remarkably like Cahokia's. The Cahokians are considered perhaps the earliest of a people known to anthropologists as "Mississippians"—Indians of the Mississippi Valley and the Southeast who formed villages beside rivers, raised corn, built temple mounds, and worshiped the sun. In the early 1700s, in what is now Mississippi, French colonists settled among perhaps the last Mississippian tribe—the Natchez—and, before annihilating them 30 years later, kept detailed accounts of their habits.

Along with archaeological findings at Cahokia, the Natchez records give scholars plenty of clues about Cahokian life. Evidence suggests, for instance, that each morning at Cahokia a millennium ago likely found a cluster of old men in a house atop Monks Mound raising their arms and emitting frightful howls as a man covered in tattoos arose from his bed. Not once did the Great Sun, as Mississippian chiefs were known, bother to look at them. Instead,

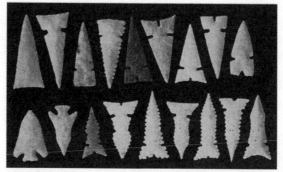

CAHOKIA MOUNDS STATE HISTORIC SITE

Arrowheads were found in one of Cahokia's mounds.

he stepped outside and howled a greeting to his perceived brother, the real sun, as it emerged over the wooded flatlands. Then he lifted a hand above his head and drew a line across the sky, from east to west. That showed the sun which way to go.

Cahokia's great suns apparently expected an eternity of female companionship. Excavation of a small mound a half mile south of Monks Mound revealed the skeleton of an early leader, a

man about 40 years old, resting on a bird-shaped platform of nearly 20,000 marine-shell beads. Nearby lay the remains of more than 100 women between 15 and 25 years old, plus four male skeletons—apparently the chief's attendants—with no heads or hands. When a Natchez sun died, many of his subjects volunteered to be strangled so they could join him in his afterlife. A mass sacrifice, scholars believe, was also precipitated by the death of Cahokia's great sun.

A re-creation of the Cahokia chief's burial, complete with the 20,000 beads, is part of a life-size diorama at the historical site's museum near Collinsville, Ill. Among other scenes: a young woman grinding corn, children playing with a doll made of cattails, a man with tattoos on his face and shoulders (indicating high status) trading salt for a knife, and a boy heating rocks for a sweat lodge, where townspeople expected steam to cleanse their bodies and spirits.

Cahokians could neither read nor write, but they had a knack for astronomy. West of Monks Mound stands a reconstructed circle of 48 wooden posts every day. You could probably smell Cahokia before you saw it."

Most of the trees from the nearby forests, Iseminger suspects, were cut for

---

Cahokia wrestled daily with challenges that would confront Americans a millennium later: military defense, runaway growth, smog.

---

that scholars dubbed "Woodhenge" because of its functional similarity to England's Stonehenge. Nearly 10 centuries ago, such a circle apparently served as the Cahokians' calendar: A pole at the center, when aligned with the circle's easternmost post and the front of Monks Mound, marked the equinoxes of spring and fall.

Wall of woe. The original Woodhenge went up when the city was on the rise, and its replica symbolizes Cahokian achievement. Just east of Monks Mound stands another re-creation—a portion of a 20-foot-high wall—that represents the community's decline. "More and more people were settling in Cahokia, and a lot of problems developed," explains archaeologist William Iseminger, the museum curator. "They likely had smog from all the fires that burned

construction and firewood. This damaged the habitat of animals that provided meat for diets not only in Cahokia but also in surrounding communities. Reduction of the forests also probably led to silt buildups in streams, resulting in floods that wrecked croplands. "Cahokia was competing with other people for resources," Iseminger says, "and warfare may have resulted."

What ensued was a defense program that apparently helped spell Cahokia's demise. Around A.D. 1100, the Cahokians enclosed their inner city within a 2-mile-long stockade built from the foot-thick trunks of 20,000 oak and hickory trees. Problems endured, but the wall didn't. Thrice in the next 200 years, the Cahokians rebuilt their wooden perimeter, each time at a cost of 20,000 trees and 130,000 work-hours. Ca-

hokia's forests were being exhausted and so, too, were its people.

By 1200, a gradual exodus from the inner city and its suburbs was underway. The wall still shielded Cahokia from rival chiefdoms, but inside the city, shortages of fuel and food grew steadily worse. No one is sure whether other problems emerged, such as inept leadership, the rise of a more charismatic chief somewhere else, a ruinous change in climate, or diseases brought on by diminished diets and faulty sanitation.

Nor does anyone know where the Cahokians were going. Conceivably they canoed down the Mississippi to Memphis or Natchez, or up the Ohio and the Tennessee to Alabama or Georgia. In all those places, Mississippian communities with platform mounds and a culture akin to Cahokia's would emerge and endure into the 16th century, only to vanish in the wake of Hernando De Soto's epidemic-spreading 1540 trek across the South. Whether Cahokia's refugees inhabited any of the towns is anyone's guess. But the archaeological findings that focus on Cahokia itself are clear: By 1400, it was abandoned.

After a half-millennium run, the country's first city had become its first victim of urban stress.

Chaco Death Squads

Two new books address prehistoric warfare in the Southwest; one suggests a reign of terror by a warrior cult from Mexico.

By Stephen H. Lekson

THESE ARE TROUBLED TIMES FOR the ancient southwest. The story of the great Pueblo period—the tenth through the fifteenth centuries A.D. at Chaco Canyon, Mesa Verde, and Casas Grandes—is being revised, and the new version is brutal, grim, and unpopular.

The public attitude towards Pueblo prehistory had been consistently, even relentlessly, positive. At the beginning of our century, social philosophers offered ancient Pueblo towns as a New World contrast to the Old World order: Southwestern pueblos were independent, democratic communities of yeoman farmers. They were quintessentially American. Mesa Verde, Chaco Canyon, and other sites were painted in those same warm colors. Later, in the wake of the Great War, pop-psychology books presented Pueblo Indians (and, by extension, their ancient ancestors) as paragons of peace. Pueblo ceremonies and philosophies appealed, eclectically, to flower children in the 1960s and to New Agers in the 1980s, thousands of whom flocked to Chaco for the Harmonic Convergence. Hundreds of articles, dozens of books, and an unbroken chorus of park rangers still present the last thousand years of native Southwestern society as happy, its peaceful people in harmony with their environment.

Peace no more. At the turn of our millennium, the ancient Southwest is beset by famine, flood, and war. Famine and flood we can handle. Drought-induced famines were always a hazard in the desert Southwest, and they have been blamed for the thirteenth-century abandonment of Chaco and Mesa Verde. Floods are implicated in the fourteenth-century fall of the remarkable Hohokam civilization of southern Arizona. These were natural processes; this was the environment with which ancient Southwestern people sought harmony. War, however, is unnatural, and not part of white America's romantic vision of the ancient Southwest. But recent archaeological studies now reveal that warfare—and worse—was common practice in the ancient Southwest.

THE NEED FOR WAR

The twentieth century has seen warfare on an almost incomprehensible scale. Fifty million people died in World War II. The Cold War brought visions of a conflict that could end civilization. Philosophers and policy makers, pondering war, often proceed from the hopeful premise that the world has not always been so violent. Ancient, preindustrial communities are routinely offered as examples of societies without the need for war. But Lawrence H. Keeley demonstrated, in his landmark study *War Before Civilization* (New York: Oxford University Press, 1996), that warfare has been ubiquitous among agricultural peoples everywhere, through-

out the course of history. He even reported that casualty rates were typically much higher in ancient than in modern warfare: prehistoric wars were small but lethal.

Steven A. LeBlanc cites Keeley's book as a "seminal work" for his *Prehistoric Warfare in the American Southwest* (Salt Lake City: University of Utah Press, 1999). An archaeologist at the University of Southern California, LeBlanc worked in New Mexico in the Mimbres area and the El Morro Valley near Zuni. He is not the first to study Southwestern warfare. From the earliest days of archaeology in the region, sites revealed unburied bodies, burned buildings, warrior images, and other evidence of violence. A long but thin thread of articles on Southwestern warfare appeared in scientific journals, but they were usually discounted in favor of more peaceful explanations. In 1989, David Wilcox of the Museum of Northern Arizona and Jonathan Haas of the Field Museum of Anthropology reopened the debate with an influential paper, fancifully titled "Scream of the Butterfly" (a tag from an old Doors' song). Haas and Winifred Creamer expanded the discussion in an important monograph, *Stress and Warfare Among the Kayenta Anasazi of the Thirteenth Century A.D.* (Chicago: Field Museum of Natural History, 1993). LeBlanc's new book, building on these earlier efforts, is by far the most comprehensive and ambitious review of warfare in the ancient Southwest.

LeBlanc reviews many kinds of evidence—weapons technology, defensive placement of sites, settlement patterns, fortified architecture, burning, unburied bodies, bones with indications of wounds, images of warfare on pottery and rock art. He concludes that there were three distinct periods of warfare, spanning the whole history of village life in the Pueblo Southwest. First, from A.D. 200 to 900, small-scale warfare (raiding, ambush) was commonplace, almost a condition of life. From A.D. 900 until 1250 (LeBlanc's middle period), endemic violence greatly diminished; indeed, the very nature of violence changed significantly—this was the remarkable Chacoan era, to which we will shortly return. Then, from A.D. 1250 until, at least, 1500, warfare exploded. Violence was large in scale and devastating in effect:

The most compelling evidence for this period of increased conflict comes in the form of settlement patterns and site configurations as seen in the Colorado Plateau and White Mountains. The site configuration change—from small to large to compact—is quite dramatic. Most of the large sites were quite big— many times larger than previous villages— with 500 or more rooms common.

Many of these new large villages were found to be burned, with unburied bodies scattered through their rooms and plazas. This, and other evidence, conclusively demonstrates a different Southwest: not the happy, peaceful Southwest conjured up by Americans seeking Eden, but history of a piece with Keeley's real world—economies, communities, religion, and art in constant tension with socially sanctioned violence. Ancient Southwesterners raided, fought battles, and waged wars. In short, they were much like other societies, including our own. If that conclusion is depressing, our discouragement says more about America's need to idealize the Southwest than it does about the actual culture of that ancient religion. Pueblo people did not live their lives for our approval.

LeBlanc may not be correct in every particular of his interpretation (nor would he claim to be), but this book ensures that new emphasis will be placed upon ancient warfare in any discussion of Southwestern archaeology. LeBlanc's argument may well become Southwestern orthodoxy, and war a major theme in Southwestern prehistory.

At Chaco LeBlanc sees violence, but not warfare. We will return to that anomaly after a brief digression into the region and its times. Chaco Canyon, it has been argued, was central to Pueblo prehistory from A.D. 900 to about 1125, and an influence for centuries to come. Monumental "Great Houses" formed the core of a small "ceremonial city." Chaco's population numbered perhaps 3,000, of which half were upper-class. Chaco was the political capital of a well-defined region that encompassed most of the Four Corners country, with more than 150 outlying Great Houses scattered over an area about the size of Ireland.

Conditions on the periphery hint at the grim nature of the Chacoan center. Debra Martin, in a paper titled "Violence Against Women in the La Plata River Valley, A.D. 1000–1300," argues that evidence of battered women indicates an underclass of, perhaps, slaves. (Martin's paper appeared in *Troubled Times: Violence and Warfare in the Past* [Amsterdam: Gordon and Breach, 1997]). The La Plata Valley, in my opinion, was a periphery of the Chacoan world; several Great Houses are known this small district, 60 miles north of Chaco. If domestic slavery existed out on the edges, how much more stratified was society at the center? Chaco Canyon, I think, was socially stratified and politically centralized. The few had power over the many and, although they may have had slaves, there was no war during the Chacoan era.

A few years ago, I speculated about the absence of warfare during Chaco's era, and called this the Pax Chaco. Le-Blanc examined the data more systematically, and corrected my conjecture; he calls Chaco's era the "Pax With a Twist." LeBlanc notes that the quantity of violence dramatically decreased during Chaco's reign, but from A.D. 900 to

about 1150 the quality of violence developed in disturbing new ways:

The [Chacoan] pattern does not look like one caused by warfare. Instead, the presence of bodies and body parts seems to be part of an overall pattern of badly treating some individuals at the time of death. Many seem to have been killed violently and their bodies not formally buried; and in some cases bodies were actually deliberately mangled.

PUBLIC VIOLENCE

At Yucca House, a Chaco Great House near Mesa Verde, apparently as many as 90 people were killed and their bodies tossed into a single kiva. At least 25 of them showed unmistakable signs of mutilation and butchering. LeBlanc cites this and numerous others as examples of what he guardedly calls "disrespectful treatment of human remains" or "processing"—but not warfare.

If not war, then what caused these ugly events? LeBlanc sees little evidence of organized conflict between polities or societies of comparable size. I think he is correct. Chaco stood alone; it was the biggest kid on the block and, perhaps, a thoroughgoing bully. In this view, Chacoan violence, concentrated and brutal, appears to represent government terror: the enforcement of Chaco's rule by institutionalized force. Violence was public, intended to appall and subdue the populace. Chacoan death squads (my term, not LeBlanc's) executed and mutilated those judged to be threats to Chacoan power, those who broke the rules. It's not a pretty picture.

And it gets worse: Arizona State University anthropologist Christy G. Turner II adds cannibalism. "Cannibals of the Canyon," a 1998 *New Yorker* article, previewed the most extreme of these new histories: Turner's sensational revision of the received Southwest in which Chaco Canyon was a cannibal kingdom where Toltec thugs ruled in a reign of terror—to gloss his argument, slightly. Turner's ideas, presented in *Man Corn* (Salt Lake City: University of Utah Press, 1999), are understandably upsetting and unwelcome both to New Agers who bury crystals at Chaco and to Pueblo Indians who claim Chaco as their ancestral city. Many, perhaps most, archaeologists also dislike the cannibal question. LeBlanc steps carefully around the possibility of cannibalism:

The evidence that large numbers of individuals were being killed and their bodies processed as if they were animals is overwhelming. However, the evidence for consumption of meat—especially if considered starvation-driven—is weak or not convincing.

Cannibalism is a big taboo, far worse than warfare. Nobody wants to hear about it in the Southwest. Turner's exposure in the *New Yorker* article was preceded by several newspaper accounts of his work and by Timothy White's *Prehistoric Cannibalism at Mancos 5MTUMR2346* (Princeton: Princeton University Press, 1992). Each mention of cannibalism brought outraged objections from anthropologists, archaeologists, and Indians. Turner was denied the podium at one of the Southwest's annual conferences, sparking arguments about research and censorship. He is well aware of the fire storm of criticism that *Man Corn* will ignite.

Turner specializes in osteology, the study of human bones. During his long career, he and his late wife and co-author, Jacqueline A. Turner, examined an impressive range of human remains from scores of excavations, old and new, in the Southwest and Mexico. The bulk of *Man Corn* consists of case-by-case descriptions of human remains from 76 sites where archaeologists have made claims for cannibalism or violence. The Turners examined bones for shattering, cut-marks, and other tell-tale signs of butchering, burning, and cooking. In at least four cases, they disagreed with others' claims of cannibalism, but in the majority of cases, they found what they consider to be evidence of it.

A particularly compelling example comes from Peñasco Blanco, a Great House in Chaco Canyon. A room excavated in 1898 contained a remarkable number of human bones. In the words of an archaeologist who was there,

Some of these, including portions of the skull, were charred, and the ma-

jority of the long bones had been cracked open and presented the same appearance as do the animal bones that have been treated in a similar way for the extraction of the marrow.

Later archaeologists dismissed the account. The Turners, too, were initially skeptical of this turn-of-the-century claim and therefore "spent an extraordinary amount of time and energy examining the remains, now at the American Museum of Natural History, to make certain the damage had been inflicted at or very near the time of death. They concluded that the humans at Peñasco Blanco had definitely been cannibalized.

Analysis of human bones convinced the Turners that violence was present throughout Southwestern prehistory, but cannibalism was peculiar to Chacoan times and the Chacoan region. Turner's Chacoan cannibalism represents the same events as LeBlanc's "deliberately mangled bodies." But why this brutal violence in a time of peace? Turner independently reached LeBlanc's conclusion—terror as Chacoan social control—but adds a new level of brutality: "cannibalism and human sacrifice as conspicuous elements of terrorism might quickly and easily dominate small farming communities." The death squad killed you, cut you up, and then ate you in front of your relatives and neighbors.

These, of course, are not popular conclusions, and Turner's case may not be helped by his contentious nature. The *New Yorker* articles described Turner as "legendarily difficult. He seems to relish being on the unpopular side of an academic fight." Not surprisingly, other archaeologists are quick to respond. Peter Bullock of the Museum of New Mexico, Kurt Dongoske of the Hopi Tribe, and Andrew Darling of the Smithsonian Institution, in separate articles, suggest that Turner is simply wrong in his observations, or that similar patterns of bone damage could be produced by other, less disturbing cultural practices: burial processing, ritual mutilation of enemies, or dismembering a witch—the penalty once invoked by several Southwestern tribes against those deemed guilty of witchcraft. Turner has little patience with these criticisms, finding, for

example "no parallels between prehistoric multiple-body charnel deposits and accounts or legends of Puebloan witch killings." LeBlanc, in *Prehistoric Warfare,* also dismissed these alternate explanations, castigating the more extreme of them as "based on little more than their proponent's opinion that they do not believe cannibalism could have taken place." This will be a hot debate.

PUEBLO PERSPECTIVE

Where are contemporary Pueblo Indian people in all this? Magazine articles and newspaper accounts of cannibalism must be painful and distressing, and a heated academic debate will only keep the topic in the public eye. Pueblo people know their histories not from the *New Yorker* or ARCHAEOLOGY or academic journals, but from meticulously memorized traditional narratives. Those traditional histories do include violence. *Hopi Ruins Legends* (Lincoln: University of Nebraska Press, 1993), collected by Ekkehart Malotki, tells Homeric tales of warfare and tragedy. Class conflict—revolution, in fact—is the principal theme of Pima histories in *Short Swift Time of Gods on Earth* (Berkeley: University of California Press, 1994), by Donald Bahr and others, a point first noted by Lynn Teague of the Arizona State Museum. Traditional histories recount occasional

Man Corn Seems . . . Egregiously Offensive

violence, but those incidents are remembered as examples of how *not* to make a good world. My Pueblo colleagues are puzzled by scientists' fixation not on the good, but on the bad and the ugly. They find it insulting; imagine a well-funded Asian research institute dedicated to needling white Americans about slavery.

The two dozen Pueblos of Arizona and New Mexico remember Chaco in their histories, and many consider it an important ancestral site. *Man Corn* comes at a time when tribal claims for autonomy and laws such as the Native American Graves Protection and Repatriation Act are encouraging the Pueblos to assert more control over sites like Chaco, and over the public interpretation of Pueblo history. In this context, *Man Corn* seems ill timed and egregiously offensive—another white scholar making obviously debatable academic claims, which Indians will find deeply insulting.

Several years ago, Turner's paper on one case of possible cannibalism near Hopi was angrily and publicly denounced by Ivan Sydney, then chair of the Hopi Tribe. Sydney's response made national news. While Turner denies any "intent to shame, ridicule, or belittle any prehistoric American Indian people . . . or their possible living descendants," this disclaimer in *Man Corn* suggests that he knows exactly how Pueblo people will view his book and its attendant publicity.

Those who read *Man Corn* will discover that Turner, in fact, avoids implicating Pueblo people in Chacoan cannibalism. Instead, in his denouement Turner introduces a surprise villain from outside the Southwest. It was not Pueblo people who ruled Chaco, but Mexicans—Native Americans from one of the civilizations of central Mexico, such as Tula. Turner does not name the Mexican city, but he is surprisingly specific in his descriptions: the death squads were a "sociopathic cannibal warrior cult from Mexico, with a Charles Manson-like leader" (Turner's words, compressed). He continues, suggesting that,

> They entered the San Juan Basin [Chaco's setting] around A.D. 900 and found a suspicious but pliant population, whom they terrorized into reproducing the theocratic life-style they had previously known in Mesoamerica.

Why Mexico? Is it safer to annoy our southern neighbor than our indigenous Natives? Well, no; Mexican death squads are not an intellectual bait-and-switch. Ritual cannibalism has great time-depth in Mexico. Turner summarizes its history in *Man Corn,* and Car-

men Pijoan and Josefina Mansilla give an excellent review in "Evidence for Human Sacrifice, Bone Modification, and Cannibalism in Ancient Mexico," a chapter in *Troubled Times.*

"Man corn" is a literal translation of the Nahuatl word *tlacatlaolli,* which Turner expands as meaning a "sacred meal of sacrificed human meat, cooked with corn." The Chaco killings, as he presents them, seem more brutal than sacred. UCLA's Patricia Anawalt notes that the Aztec *tlacatlaolli* was a profound ritual event. Man corn was neither a meal nor an act of state terror, but a devout, honorable, almost eucharistic ceremony. Turner acknowledges that it is a perilous stretch from Nahuatl man corn to Chacoan death squads. Blaming Chaco cannibalism on goons from Tula may get Turner off the hook with outraged Pueblo officials, indignant archaeologists, and annoyed park rangers, but don't bet on it.

MEXICO AND THE SOUTHWEST

Turner's cannibal warrior cult is the latest variation on a familiar Southwestern theme: Mexican intervention. Ever since Adolf Bandelier's pioneer fieldwork in the region for the Archaeological Institute of America in 1880, Southwestern scholars have wondered about the region's relationship to ancient Mexico. Opinions have varied from complete isolation to virtual dependency. Contemporary Southwestern archaeology rejects Mexican entanglements; we have the North American Free Trade Agreement today, but the ancient border between the U.S. and Mexico remains doggedly patrolled. Turner's story is a good example of a Mexican *deus ex machina* controlling Southwestern prehistory. I propose another version that splices Southwest and Mexico but sustains a unique Southwestern history.

In the pages of ARCHAEOLOGY (January/February 1997, pp. 52–55) and in a new book *Chaco Meridian: Centers of Political Power in the Ancient Southwest* (Walnut Creek, CA: Altamira Press, 1999), I outline a political history of the ancient Southwest. Chaco was the first of three ceremonial cities that dominated the Pueblo Southwest: Chaco from A.D. 900 to 1125, Aztec Ruins from A.D. 110 to

1275, and Paquime (also called Casas Grandes) from A.D. 1250 to 1500. Aztec and Paquime were as impressive as Chaco. Each of the three cities served as the largest and most important political, ceremonial, and economic center of its time. Each controlled, to varying degrees, large regions. These claims are based on widely accepted chronologies, regional surveys, and social reconstructions for each of these sites.

I suggest further that Chacoan political forms and structures—and, perhaps, lineages—were perpetuated and maintained at Aztec Ruins and Paquime. Much as emerging dynasties in ancient Mesoamerica claimed historical affinity with great cities and rulers of their past, the rulers of Aztec Ruins and Paquime appealed to Chaco to legitimate their regimes. They manipulated Chacoan symbols to demonstrate that connection and to show their own power. Some of the most spectacular symbols of Southwestern power, employed by Chaco Canyon, Aztec Ruins, and Paquime, were also Mesoamerican: colonnades, ballcourts, copper objects, tropical feathers. Control of interaction over great distances showed political strength.

Southwest political history begins at Chaco. Aztec Ruins and Paquime built on that foundation and developed new structures to meet changing economic and political situations. They apparently eschewed Chacoan social violence; the reigns of Aztec and Paquime were marked by warfare, but not by "deliberately mangled bodies." This political history corresponds, in many ways, to the prehistories presented by LeBlanc and Turner. I agree with LeBlanc that the Pax Chaco may have been generally peaceful, but specifically ugly. Both LeBlanc and Turner recognize shifts in the nature of violence from pre-Chaco, to Chaco, to post-Chaco; and Chacoan violence was, in many ways, the most disturbing. Chacoan rulers apparently used brutal, murderous, institutionalized violence to enforce order, no different from many societies, ancient and modern.

I also agree with LeBlanc that the jury is out on cannibalism as a routine tactic of Chacoan power. Turner's *Man Corn* will certainly provoke highly critical research. If *Man Corn* survives those tests, I could accept that Chacoan ruthlessness extended to Turner's lengths; Chaco was, in many ways, a grim place. But I think that Turner is wrong about the source of Chacoan power. Chacoan

The Jury Is Out on Cannibalism

politics, like all politics, was local. We don't need adventurers from Tula to establish a Mesoamerican theocracy, because Chaco *was,* inherently, a Mesoamerican polity.

Culturally, the ancient Southwest was part of Mexico. Mesoamerica's frontiers extended north far beyond present national borders. There was a lot of empty space within that territory. Discontinuous, hop-scotch distributions of ideologies, political forms, and architectural styles were as much the norm in the ancient New World as compact, contiguous empires. Try thinking of Chaco as a banana republic on the fringe of the grasping, materialistic Mesoamerican world. It was something like that.

The old Southwest just ain't what it used to be. Political capitals, dynasties, warfare, death squads, cannibalism—these are not things you will read in coffee-table books or hear from tour guides at Mesa Verde. The ancient Southwest produced wonderful art and powerful architecture. We can be sure that there was song and poetry, and the deep spiritual connection that marks Pueblo peoples' feelings toward the land. But there was also a darker side that places the Southwest, for better or worse, amid myriad human societies. Archaeology is all about learning, developing new ideas about the past that fit the facts better than old ideas. New ideas about the ancient Maya have altered our perception of their rulers from philosopher-poet-priests to bloody warrior kings; the ancient Southwest is also changing.

STEPHEN H. LEKSON *is a professor of anthropology at the University of Colorado in Boulder.*

The Arab Roots of European Medicine

Wel knew he the olde Esculapius and Deyscorides and eek Rufus Olde Ypocras, Haly and Galeyn, Serapion, Razi and Avycen, Averrois, Damascien and Constantyn, Bernard and Gatesden and Gilbertyn.

Written by David W. Tschanz

In the "General Prologue" of *The Canterbury Tales,* Geoffrey Chaucer identifies the authorities used by his "Doctour of Physic" in the . . . lines quoted above. The list includes four Arab physicians: Jesu Haly (Ibn'Isa), Razi (Al-Razi, or Rhazes), Avycen (Ibn Sina, or Avicenna) and Averrois (Ibn Rushd, or Averroes). These four did not make Chaucer's list only to add an exotic flavor to his late-14th-century poetry. Chaucer cited them because they were regarded as among the great medical authorities of the ancient world and the European Middle Ages, physicians whose textbooks were used in European medical schools, and would be for centuries to come. First collecting, then translating, then augmenting and finally codifying the classical Greco-Roman heritage that Europe has lost, Arab physicians of the eighth to eleventh century laid the foundations of the institutions and the science of modern medicine.

After the collapse of the western Roman empire in the fifth century, Europe lost touch with much of its intellectual heritage. Of Greek science, all that remained were Pliny's *Encyclopedia* and Boethius's treatises on logic and mathematics; the Latin library was so limited that European theologians found it nearly impossible to expand their knowledge of their own scriptures.

The center of Europe's new world view became the church, which exerted profound new influences in medicine. Because Christianity emphasized compassion and care for the sick, monastic orders ran fine hospitals—but they did not function as hospitals do today. They were simply places to take seriously ill people, where they were expected to either recover or die as God willed. There were no learned physicians to attend them, only kindly monks who dispensed comfort and the sacraments, but not medicines.

Because the Christian church viewed care of the soul as far more important than care of the body, medical treatment and even physical cleanliness were little valued, and mortification of the flesh was seen as a sign of saintliness. In time, nearly all Europeans came to look upon illness as a condition caused by supernatural forces, which might take the form of diabolical possession. Hence, cures could only be effected by religious means. Every malady had a patron saint to whom prayers were directed by the patient, family, friends and the community. Upper respiratory infections were warded off by a blessing of the throat with crossed candles on the feast of Saint Blaise. Saint Roch became the patron of plague victims. Saint Nicaise was the source of protection against smallpox. Kings, regarded as divinely appointed, were believed to be able to cure scrofula and skin diseases, among other maladies, with the "royal touch."

With the study of disease and of patients neglected, licensed medicine as an independent craft virtually vanished.

Those physicians who endured were mostly connected with monasteries and abbeys. But even for them, the generally accepted goal was less to discover causes, or even to heal, than to study the writings of other physicians and comment on their work. In the middle of the seventh century, the Catholic church banned surgery by monks, because it constituted a danger to their souls. Since nearly all of the surgeons of that era were clerics, the decree effectively ended the practice of surgery in Europe.

At roughly the same time, another civilization was rising in the east. The coming of Islam, also in the seventh century (See *Aramco World,* November/December 1991), led to a hundred years of continuous geographical expansion and an unprecedented era of ferment in all branches of learning. The Arabs rapidly melded the various cultures of the Islamic domain, and Arabic—the language of the Qur'an—became the universal language. By the 10th century a single language linked peoples from the Rann of Kutch to the south of France, and Arabic became to the East what Latin and Greek had been to the West—the language of literature, the arts and sciences, and the common tongue of the educated.

Medicine was the first of the Greek sciences to be studied in depth by Islamic scholars. After Plato's Academy was closed in 529, some of its scholars found refuge at the university at Jun-

Reprinted from *Aramco World,* May/June 1997, pp. 20-31. © 1997 by Aramco Services Company.

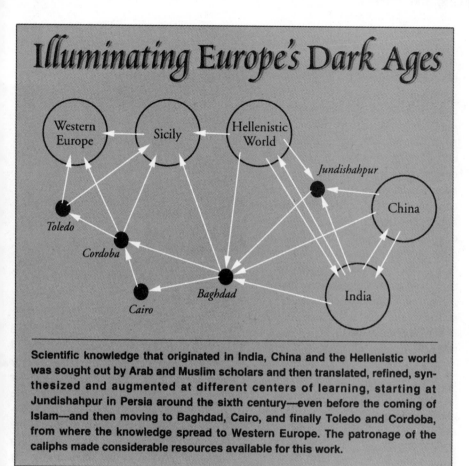

Illuminating Europe's Dark Ages

Scientific knowledge that originated in India, China and the Hellenistic world was sought out by Arab and Muslim scholars and then translated, refined, synthesized and augmented at different centers of learning, starting at Jundishahpur in Persia around the sixth century—even before the coming of Islam—and then moving to Baghdad, Cairo, and finally Toledo and Cordoba, from where the knowledge spread to Western Europe. The patronage of the caliphs made considerable resources available for this work.

DIAGRAM AND CAPTION ADAPTED FROM *THE CREST OF THE PEACOCK: NON-EUROPEAN ROOTS OF MATHEMATICS* BY GEORGE GHEVERGHESE JOSEPH (PENGUIN BOOKS/I.B. TAURIS) © 1991. USED BY PERMISSION OF PENGUIN BOOKS LTD.

dishahpur, the old Sassanid capital of Persia, which had also sheltered excommunicated Nestorian Christian scholars—among them physicians—in 431. Persia became part of the Islamic world in 636, and Arab rulers supported the medical school at Jundishahpur; for the next 200 years it was the greatest center of medical teaching in the Islamic world. There, Islamic physicians first familiarized themselves with the works of Hippocrates, Galen and other Greek physicians. At the same time, they were also exposed to the medical knowledge of Byzantium, Persia, India and China.

Recognizing the importance of translating Greek works into Arabic to make them more widely available, the Abbasid caliphs Harun al-Rashid (786–809) and his son, al-Ma'mun (813–833) established a translation bureau in Baghdad, the Bayt al-Hikmah, or House of Wisdom, and sent embassies to collect Greek scientific works in the Byzantine Empire. (See *Aramco World*, May/June

1982.) This ushered in the first era in Islamic medicine, whose effects we feel today: the period of translation and compilation.

The most important of the translators was Hunayn ibn Ishaq al-'Ibadi (809–73), who was reputed to have been paid for his manuscripts by an equal weight of gold. He and his team of translators rendered the entire body of Greek medical texts, including all the works of Galen, Oribasius, Paul of Aegin, Hippocrates and the *Materia Medica* of Dioscorides, into Arabic by the end of the ninth century. These translations established the foundations of a uniquely Arab medicine.

Muslim medical practice largely accepted Galen's premise of humors, which held that the human body was made up of the same four elements that comprise the world—earth, air, fire and water. These elements could be mixed in various proportions, and the differing mixtures gave rise to the different tem-

peraments and "humors." When the body's humors were correctly balanced, a person was healthy. Sickness was due not to supernatural forces but to humoral imbalance, and such imbalance could be corrected by the doctor's healing arts.

Muslim physicians therefore came to look upon medicine as the science by which the dispositions of the human body could be discerned, and to see its goal as the preservation of health and, if health should be lost, assistance in recovering it. They viewed themselves as practitioners of the dual art of healing and the maintenance of health.

Even before the period of translation closed, advances were made in other health-related fields. Harun al-Rashid established the first hospital, in the modern sense of the term, at Baghdad about 805. Within a decade or two, 34 more hospitals had sprung up throughout the Islamic world, and the number grew each year.

These hospitals, or *bimaristans,* bore little resemblance to their European counterparts. The sick saw the *bimaristan* as a place where they could be treated and perhaps cured by physicians, and the physicians saw the *bimaristan* as an institution devoted to the promotion of health, the cure of disease and the expansion and dissemination of medical knowledge. Medical schools and libraries were attached to the larger hospitals, and senior physicians taught students, who were in turn expected to apply in the men's and women's wards what they had learned in the lecture hall. Hospitals set examinations for their students, and issued diplomas. By the 11th century, there were even traveling clinics, staffed by the hospitals, that brought medical care to those too distant or too sick to come to the hospitals themselves. The *bimaristan* was, in short, the cradle of Arab medicine and the prototype upon which the modern hospital is based.

Like the hospital, the institution of the pharmacy, too, was an Islamic development. Islam teaches that "God has provided a remedy for every illness," and that Muslims should search for those remedies and use them with skill and compassion. One of the first pharmacological treatises was composed by

169

The Caliphs' Researches

Fourteenth-century historian and political scientist Ibn Khaldun wrote about the intellectual curiosity that helped to preserve Greek learning.

When the Byantine emperors conquered Syria, the scientific works of the Greeks were still in existence. Then God brought Islam, and the Muslims won their remarkable victories, conquering the Byzantines as well as all other nations. At first, the Muslims were simple, and did not cultivate learning, but as time went on and the Muslim dynasty flourished, the Muslims developed an urban culture which surpassed that of any other nation.

They began to wish to study the various branches of philosophy, of whose existence they knew from their contact with bishops and priests among their Christian subjects. In any case, man has always had a penchant for intellectual speculation. The caliph al-Mansur therefore sent an embassy to the Byzantine emperor, asking him to send him translations of books on mathematics. The emperor sent him Euclid's *Elements* and some works on physics.

Muslim scholars studied these books, and their desire to obtain others was whetted. When al-Ma'mun, who had some scientific knowledge, assumed the caliphate, he wished to do something to further the progress of science. For that purpose, he sent ambassadors and translators to the Byzantine empire, in order to search out works on the Greek sciences and have them translated into Arabic. As a result of these efforts, a great deal of material was gathered and preserved.

Jabir ibn Hayyan (ca. 776), who is considered the father of Arab alchemy. The Arab pharmacopoeia of the time was extensive, and gave descriptions of the geographical origin, physical properties and methods of application of everything found useful in the cure of disease. Arab pharmacists, or *saydalani,* introduced a large number of new drugs to clinical practice, including senna, camphor, sandalwood, musk, myrrh, cassia, tamarind, nutmeg, cloves, aconite, ambergris and mercury. The *saydalani* also developed syrups and juleps—the words came from Arabic and Persian, respectively—and pleasant solvents such as rose water and orange-blossom water as means of administering drugs. They were familiar with the anesthetic effects of Indian hemp and henbane, both when taken in liquids and inhaled.

By the time of al-Ma'mun's caliphate, pharmacy was a profession practiced by highly skilled specialists. Pharmacists were required to pass examinations and be licensed, and were then monitored by the state. At the start of the ninth century, the first private apothecary shops opened in Baghdad. Pharmaceutical preparations were manufactured and distributed commercially, then dispensed by physicians and pharmacists in a variety of forms—ointments, pills, elixirs, confections, tinctures, suppositories and inhalants.

The blossoming of original thought in Arab medicine began as the ninth century drew to a close. The first major work appeared when Abu Bakr Muhammad ibn Zakariya Al-Razi (ca. 841–926) turned his attention to medicine.

Al-Razi, known to the West as Rhazes, was born in Persia in the town of Rayy, near Tehran. After a youth spent as a musician, mathematician and alchemist, Al-Razi went to Baghdad to take up the study of medicine at the age of 40. Completing his studies, he returned to Rayy and assumed the directorship of its hospital. His reputation

grew rapidly and within a few years he was selected to be the director of a new hospital to be built in Baghdad. He approached the question of where to put the new facility by hanging pieces of meat in various sections of the city and checking the rate at which they spoiled. He then ordered the hospital built at the site where the meat showed the least putrefaction.

Al-Razi is regarded as Islamic medicine's greatest clinician and its most original thinker. A prolific writer, he turned out some 237 books, about half of which dealt with medicine. His treatise *The Diseases of Children* has led some historians to regard him as the father of pediatrics. He was the first to identify hay fever and its cause. His work on kidney stones is still considered a classic. In addition, he was instrumental in the introduction of mercurial ointments to treat scabies. Al-Razi advocated reliance on observation rather than on received authority; he was a strong proponent of experimental medicine and the beneficial use of previously tested medicinal plants and other drugs. A leader in the fight against quacks and charlatans—and author of a book exposing their methods—he called for high professional standards for practitioners. He also insisted on continuing education

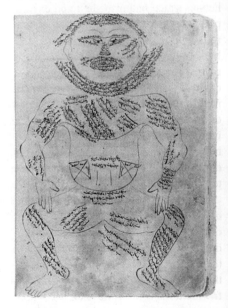

Seeds of *Silene gallica* (top left), called *hashishat al-thubban,* or *flyweed,* in Arabic, were effective in a snakebite antiodote, according to Dioscorides. Above, Persian notations detail the human muscle system in Mansur ibn Ilyas' late-14th-century Tashrih-i Badan-i Insan (The Anatomy of the Human Body).

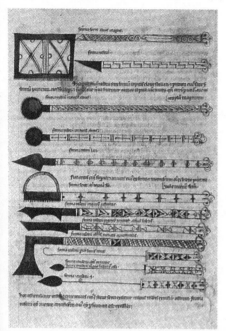

Surgical instruments are shown in detail in a 13th-century Latin translation of The Method *(above), a 30-part medical text written by Islam's greatest medieval surgeon, Abu al-Qasim, who practiced in 10th-century Córdoba.*

for already licensed physicians. Al-Razi was the first to emphasize the value of mutual trust and consultation among skilled physicians in the treatment of patients, a rare practice at that time.

Following his term as hospital director in Baghdad, he returned to Rayy where he taught the healing arts in the local hospital, and he continued to write. His first major work was a 10 part treatise entitled *Al-Kitab al-Mansuri,* so called after the ruler of Rayy, Mansur ibn Ishaq. In it, he discussed such varied subjects as general medical theories and definitions; diet and drugs and their effect on the human body; mother and child care, skin disease, oral hygiene, climatology and the effect of the environment on health; epidemiology and toxicology.

Al-Razi also prepared *Al-Judari wa al Hasbah,* the first treatise ever written on smallpox and measles. In a masterful demonstration of clinical observation (see column at right), Al-Razi became the first to distinguish the two diseases from each other. At the same time, he provided still-valid guidelines for the sound treatment of both.

His most esteemed work was a medical encyclopedia in 25 books, *Al-Kitab al-Hawi,* or *The Comprehensive Work,*

the *Liber Continens* of Al-Razi's later Latin translators. Al-Razi spent a lifetime collecting data for the book, which he intended as a summary of all the medical knowledge of his time, augmented by his own experience and observations. *In Al-Hawi,* Al-Razi emphasized the need for physicians to pay careful attention to what the patients' histories told them, rather than merely consulting the authorities of the past. In a series of diagnosed case histories entitled "Illustrative Accounts of Patients," Al-Razi demonstrated this important tenet. One patient, who lived in a malarial district, suffered from intermittent chills and fever that had been diagnosed as malaria, but nonetheless seemed incurable. Al-Razi was asked to examine him. Upon noting pus in the urine, he diagnosed an infected kidney, and he treated the patient successfully with diuretics.

Al-Razi's clinical skill was matched by his understanding of human nature, particularly as demonstrated in the attitudes of patients. In a series of short monographs on the doctor-patient relationship, he described principles that are still taught a millennium later: Doctors and patients need to establish a mutual bond of trust, he wrote; positive comments from doctors encourage patients, make them feel better and speed their recovery; and, he warned, changing from one doctor to another wastes patients' health, wealth and time.

Not long after Al-Razi's death, Abu'Al al-Husayn ibn 'Abd Allah ibn 'Sina (980–1037) was born in Bukhara, in what today is Uzbekistan. Later translators Latinized his name to Avicenna. It is hard to describe Ibn Sina in anything other than superlatives. He was to the Arab world what Aristotle was to Greece, Leonardo da Vinci to the Renaissance and Goethe to Germany. His preeminence embraced not only medicine, but also the fields of philosophy, science, music, poetry and statecraft. His contemporaries called him "the prince of physicians."

Ibn Sina's life was in fact the stuff of legend. The son of a tax collector, he was so precocious that he had completely memorized the Qur'an by age 10. Then he studied law, mathematics,

physics, and philosophy. Confronted by a difficult problem in Aristotle's *Metaphysics,* Ibn Sina re-read the book 40 times in his successful search for a solution. At 16 he turned to the study of

A Physician

Observes

In Al-Judari wa al-Hasbah, *Al-Razi distinguished smallpox from measles for the first time in medical history. This passage shows his skill as a medical observer, a competence on which he placed great importance.*

The eruption of the smallpox is preceded by a continued fever, pain in the back, itching in the nose and terrors in the sleep. These are the more peculiar symptoms of its approach, especially a pain in the back with fever; then also a pricking which the patient feels all over his body; a fullness of the face, which at times comes and goes; an inflamed color, and vehement redness in both cheeks; a redness of both the eyes, heaviness of the whole body; great uneasiness, the symptoms of which are stretching and yawning; a pain in the throat and chest, with slight difficulty in breathing and cough; a dryness of the breath, thick spittle and hoarseness of the voice; pain and heaviness of the head; inquietude, nausea and anxiety; (with this difference that the inquietude, nausea and anxiety are more frequent in the measles than in the smallpox; while on the other hand, the pain in the back is more peculiar to the smallpox than to the measles;) heat of the whole body; an inflamed colon, and shining redness, and especially an intense redness of the gums.

Above: Mandrake (Mandragora officinalis; al-luffah in Arabic) was described in the 10th century by Al-Biruni as a useful soporific.

medicine, which he said he found "not difficult." By 18, his fame as a physician was so great that he was summoned to treat the Samanid prince Nuh ibn Mansur. His success with that patient won him access to the Samanid royal library, one of the greatest of Bukhara's many storehouses of learning.

Testing New Medicines

In his voluminous writings, Ibn Sina laid out the following rules for testing the effectiveness of a new drug or medication. These principles still form the basis of modern clinical drug trials.

1 The drug must be free from any extraneous accidental quality.

2 It must be used on a simple not a composite, disease.

3 The drug must be tested with two contrary types of diseases, because sometimes a drug cures one disease by its essential qualities and another by its accidental ones.

4 The quality of the drug must correspond to the strength of the disease. For example, there are some drugs whose heat is less than the coldness of certain diseases, so that they would have no effect on them.

5 The time of action must be observed, so that essence and accident are not confused.

6 The effect of the drug must be seen to occur constantly or in many cases, for if this did not happen, it was an accidental effect.

7 The experimentation must be done with the human body, for testing a drug on a lion or a horse might not prove anything about its effect on man.

BODLEIAN LIBRARY

At 20, Ibn Sina was appointed court physician, and twice served as vizier, to Shams al-Dawlah, the Buyid prince of Hamadan, in western Persia. His remaining years were crowded with adventure and hard work, yet he somehow found time to write 20 books on theology, metaphysics, astronomy, philology and poetry and 20 more on medicine—including *Kitab al-Shifa'*, or *The Book of Healing*, a medical and philosophical encyclopedia.

His supreme work, however, is the monumental *Al-Qanun fi al-Tibb, The Canon of Medicine*. Over one million words long, it was nothing less than a codification of all existing medical knowledge. Summarizing the Hippocratic and Galenic traditions, describing Syro-Arab and Indo-Persian practice and including notes on his own observations, Ibn Sina strove to fit each bit of anatomy, physiology, diagnosis and treatment into its proper niche.

The Canon stressed the importance of diet and the influence of climate and environment on health. It included discussions of rabies, hydrocele, breast cancer, tumors, labor and poisons and their treatment. Ibn Sina differentiated meningitis from the meningismus of other acute diseases; and described chronic nephritis,

facial paralysis, ulcer of the stomach and the various types of hepatitis and their causes. He also expounded the dilation and contraction of the pupils and their diagnostic value, described the six motor muscles of the eye and discussed the functions of the tear ducts, and he noted the contagious nature of some diseases, which he attributed to "traces" left in the air by a sick person.

The Canon also included a description of some 760 medicinal plants and the drugs that could be derived from them. At the same time Ibn Sina laid out the basic rules of clinical drug trials, principles that are still followed today. (*See box, "Testing New Medicines".*)

Not surprisingly, *The Canon* rapidly became the standard medical reference work of the Islamic world. Nizami-i Arudi of Samarkand spoke for generations of physicians when he wrote, in the early 12th century, "From him who manages the first volume [*of The Canon*], nothing will be hidden concerning the general theory and principles of medicine." *The Canon* was used as a reference, a teaching guide and a medical textbook until well into the 19th century, longer than any other medical work.

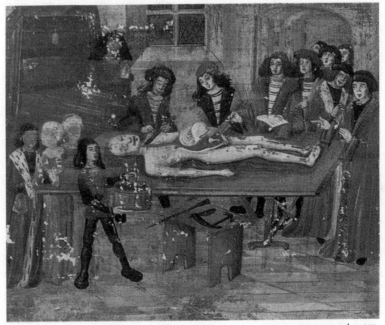

ART RESOURCE/MUSEÉ ALGER

This depiction of mandrake before flowering (left) appeared in an Arabic version of De Materia Medica *titled* Khawass al-Ashjar (The Properties of Plants), *translated in Baghdad in 1240. Above, an anatomy lesson at the medical school at Montpellier—one of Europe's earliest—from de Chauliac's 1363* Grande Chirurgie.

During the 10th century, when Arab astronomical texts were first translated in Catalonia, Europe began to reap the intellectual riches of the Arabs and, in so doing, to seek out its own classical heritage. The medical works of Galen and Hip-

Ibn Sina's *Canon* made its first appearance in Europe by the end of the 12th century, and its impact was dramatic. Copied and recopied, it quickly became the standard European medical reference work. In the last 30 years of the 15th century, just before the Euro-

University of Paris. In *The Inferno*, Dante placed Ibn Sina side by side with antiquity's two greatest physicians, Hippocrates and Galen. Roger Bacon consulted Ibn Sina to further his own inquiries into vision.

But it was not only Al-Razi and Ibn Sina who influenced Europe. Translations of more than 400 Arab authors, writing on such varied topics as ophthalmology, surgery, pharmaceuticals, child care and public health, deeply influenced the rebirth of European science.

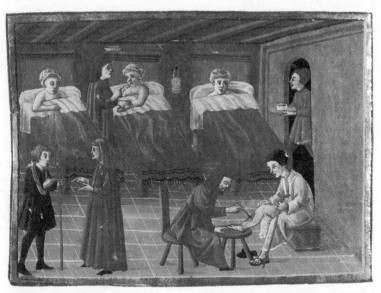

ART RESOURCE/BIBLIOTECA LAURENZIANA

At the Benedictine monastery at Monte Cassino in the 10th century, the Middle Eastern traveler Leo Africanus translated Arab medical texts and supervised a hospital run on Arab principles. Between that time and the Renaissance, European hospitals, like the one above, from an undated Italian manuscript, were increasingly modeled on the Arab bimaristan.

pocrates returned to the West by way of the Middle East and North Africa, recovered through Latin translations of what had become the Arab medical classics. Through the intellectual ferment of the Islamic present, Europe recovered some of its past.

The two main translators of classical material from Arabic into Latin were Constantinus (also known as Leo) Africanus (1020–1087), who worked at Salerno and in the cloister of Monte Cassino, and Gerard of Cremona (1140–1187), who worked in Toledo. It was no accident that both translators lived in the Arab-Christian transition zone, where the two cultures fructified each other. And it was no coincidence that Salerno, Europe's first great medical faculty of the Middle Ages, was close to Arab Sicily, nor that the second, Montpellier, was founded in 1221 in southern France, near the Andalusian border.

pean invention of printing, it was issued in 16 editions; in the century that followed more than 20 further editions were printed. From the 12th to the 17th century, its *materia medica* was the pharmacopoeia of Europe, and as late as 1537 *The Canon* was still a required textbook at the University of Vienna.

Translations of Al-Razi's *Al-Kitab al-Hawi* and other works followed rapidly. Printed while printing was still in its infancy, all of Al-Razi's works gained widespread acceptance. The ninth book of *Al-Kitab al-Mansuri* ("Concerning Diseases from the Head to the Foot") remained part of the medical curriculum at the University of Tübingen until the end of the 15th century.

Contemporary Europeans regarded Ibn Sina and Al-Razi as the greatest authorities on medical matters, and portraits of both men still adorn the great hall of the School of Medicine at the

Despite their belief in now superseded theories such as humors and miasmas, the medicine of Ibn Sina, Al-Razi and their contemporaries is the basis of much of what we take for granted today.

It was those Arab physicians who made accurate diagnoses of plague, diphtheria, leprosy, rabies, diabetes, gout, cancer and epilepsy. Ibn Sina's theory of infection by "traces" led to the introduction of quarantine as a means of limiting the spread of infectious diseases. Arab doctors laid down the principles of clinical investigation and drug trials, and they uncovered the secret of sight. They mastered operations for hernia and cataract, filled teeth with gold leaf and prescribed spectacles for defective eyesight. And they passed on rules of health, diet and hygiene that are still largely valid today.

Thus the Islamic world not only provided a slender but ultimately successful line of transmission for the medical knowledge of ancient Greece and the Hellenic world, it also corrected and enormously expanded that knowledge before passing it on to a Europe that had abandoned observation, experimentation and the very concept of earthly progress centuries before. Physicians of different languages and religions had cooperated in building a sturdy structure whose outlines are still visible in the medical practices of our own time.

David W. Tschanz lives and works in Saudi Arabia as an epidemiologist with Saudi Aramco. He holds master's degrees in both history and epidemiology, and writes about the history of medicine.

An Iberian chemistry

It was a time and place to blend Muslim and Jewish cultures

By Fouad Ajami

Long before the rise of Spain and Spanish culture, before that special run of historical events that took the Iberian Peninsula from the Catholic sovereigns Ferdinand and Isabella to the golden age of Cervantes and El Greco and Velázquez, there was another golden age in the peninsula's southern domains. In Andalusia's splendid and cultured courts and gardens, in its bustling markets, in academies of unusual secular daring, Muslims and Jews came together—if only fitfully and always under stress—to build a world of relative tolerance and enlightenment. In time, decay and political chaos would overwhelm Muslim Spain, but as the first millennium drew to a close, there had arisen in the city of Cordova a Muslim empire to rival its nemesis in the east, the imperial world around Baghdad.

We don't know with confidence the precise population of Cordova in the closing years of the 10th century. The chroniclers and travelers spoke of a large, vibrant city, which could have had a population of some 250,000 people. One 10th-century traveler wrote with awe of a city that had no equal in Syria, Egypt, or Mesopotamia for the "size of its population, its extent, the space occupied by its markets, the cleanliness of its streets, the architecture of its mosques, the number of its baths and caravansaries." Cordova had no urban rival in Western Europe at the time. Its equivalents were the great imperial centers of Baghdad and Constantinople, and cities in remote worlds: Angkor in Indochina, Tchangngan in China, Tollán in Mexico.

City life. A Pax Islamica held sway in the Mediterranean region, and Cordova's merchants and scholars took part in the cultural and mercantile traffic of that world. In fact, the city made a bid of its own for a place in the sun in the early years of the 10th century. One of its great rulers, Abd al-Rahman III, had taken for himself the title of caliph—or successor to the prophet Mohammed—and staked out Cordova's claim to greatness.

In the seven or eight decades that followed, the city would become a metropolis of great diversity. Blessed with a fertile countryside, the city had some 700 mosques, 3,000 public baths, illuminated streets, luxurious villas on the banks of the Guadalquivir River, and countless libraries. Legend has it that the caliph's library stocked some 400,000 volumes.

Andalusia was a polyglot world, inhabited by Arabs, Jews, Berbers from North Africa, blacks, native Christians, and Arabized Christians called Mozarabs, as well as soldiers of fortune drawn from the Christian states of Europe. The Jews did particularly well in this urban world of commerce, philosophy, and secularism. The Jewish

An age of artistic richness

LOUVRE, PARIS—GIRAUDON/ART RESOURCE

documents of that age depict a truly cosmopolitan world in which Jewish merchants traveled between Spain and Sicily, to Aden and the Indian Ocean, from Seville to Alexandria. Jewish academies were launched in Cordova, Granada, Toledo, and Barcelona. By the end of the 10th century, Iberian Jews had declared their independence from the Talmudists of the Babylonian academies in Baghdad. A rich body of Judeo-

From the *U.S. News & World Report*, August 16-23, 1999, pp. 44, 48, 50. © 1999 by U.S. News & World Report. Reprinted by permission.

Arabic literature became the distinctive gift of this age.

Terror and plunder. Even given these great cultural accomplishments, the success—and the hazards—of the Andalusian world are best seen through the deeds and valor of the Muslim soldier and strongman of Cordova, Almanzor. Cordova's de facto ruler, the first minister of the court in the final years of the 10th century, Almanzor was an able and ambitious ruler descended from the early Arab conquerors of Spain. He had risen to power in 976 and made the caliphate an instrument of his own ambitions. By some estimates, Almanzor led more than 50 expeditions against neighboring Christian states. In 997 he undertook his most daring symbolic campaign, sacking Santiago de Compostela, the Christian shrine and pilgrimage center in Galicia. He laid waste to the church and took the church bells for the Great Mosque of Cordova. Three years later, in the year 1000, he cut a swath of terror through much of Castile and plundered Burgos. He died on horseback in 1002, on his way back to Cordova from a military campaign in La Rioja.

Almanzor had given Cordova's political center a military vocation but undone its prosperity at the same time. He had brought into this Andalusian setting wholesale contingents of Berber tribesmen from North Africa, and the enmity between Berbers and Arabs would push the Cordovan world into its grave. What unity the Andalusian political structure had once possessed was irretrievably lost. The opening years of the 11th cen-

A mingling of cultures in Andalusia's golden age

GRANGER COLLECTION

JEWS AND MUSLIMS, though always wary of one another, built a unique world of relative tolerance and enlightenment.

tury would be terrible years for Cordova. The city was sacked by Catalan mercenaries in 1010; the Guadalquivir overflowed its banks in the year that followed; and a terrible mass slaughter took place in 1013 when merciless Berber soldiers besieged the city, put a large number of its scholars to the sword, and torched its elegant villas. Many of the city's notables, Muslims and Jews alike, took to the road.

One of these exiles was a talented Jewish child of Cordova, one Samuel Ibn Neghrela. He was given the gift of Cordova's greatness: He was a poet, learned in Arabic and Hebrew and Latin, the Berber and Romance tongues. But he also inherited the legacy of Cordova's collapse. He fled Cordova's upheaval to the coastal city of Málaga, then made his way to the court of Granada, where he prospered as courtier and chief min-

---

VILLAS & MOSQUES

Constructing Andalusia

Andalusia's architects thrived on Cordova's cultural stew, and their work fused myriad regional and cultural styles. The city's villas, built around patios and lined by terraces, are imitated to this day. The Jewish quarter was home to synagogues inspired by the sun-baked edifices of North Africa. But the most spectacular triumphs were the mosques, and chief among them was La Mezquita, or Great Mosque, a 6-acre giant built to hold 35,000.

When the Moors arrived in 711, the existing temples were plain affairs. The newcomers remade mosque interiors with marble columns taken from Roman and Visigothic ruins, creating dense thickets of pillars to support wooden roofs; it is said that one caliph asked his architects to simulate palm tree groves, as a reminder of his native Syria. A vital innovation, adapted from the Visigoths, was the horseshoe arch, a semicircular support that became the Moorish trademark. In the Great Mosque, these arches were made from alternating bands of red brick and white stone, a pattern that tricks the eye into perceiving the interior as limitless in size.

—*Brendan I. Koerner*

ister. He saw through the splendor and the hazards of that world. In a poignant poem, entitled "A Curse," he wrote of his wandering and exile: "Heart like a pennant / On a ship's mast, in a storm; / An exile is ink / In God's book. Across my soul, and every shore; / And all on whom wandering is written / Are driven like Jonah, and scavenge like Cain."

Distant memory. It twisted and turned, that world that had risen in the West. Ten years after Neghrela's death, his son and heir, Joseph, was killed by a mob in Granada, in an anti-Jewish riot in which some 1,500 Jewish families perished. By then the unity of the Andalusian world had become a distant memory. The age that followed was dubbed the *mulak al-tawa'if,* a time when warlords and pretenders carved up Muslim Spain into petty, warring turfs. No fewer than 30 ministates claimed what had once been a coherent dominion. The robust mercantile economy eroded.

Calamity soon struck this world. In 1085, Toledo, the ancient capital of the Visigothic kingdom, was conquered by Alfonso VI, King of León. For Christians this was a sign of divine favor, and the conqueror claimed no less than that. "By the hidden judgment of God," a charter of Alfonso read, "this city was for 376 years in the hands of the Moors, blasphemers of the Christian faith. . . . Inspired by God's grace I moved an army against this city, where my ancestors once reigned in power and wealth." Cordova itself fell in 1236. Its conqueror, Ferdinand III of Castile, claimed the Great Mosque of Cordova in a "purification" ceremony, and his bishops consecrated it for Christian worship as the Catedral de Santa María. The foundations of the Great Mosque had been laid down in the closing years of the eighth century, and successive rulers had adorned and enlarged it. It was the symbol of Andalusian authority, a sublime architectural wonder into which rulers and patrons poured their reverence and ambition, their desire for a new Muslim frontier as grand as the best Baghdad or Damascus could boast. In the peninsula, one people's golden age was always another's decline. What had once been a

LIFE ON THE MARGIN
A Zionist in Andalusia's golden age

The Spanish rabbi-poet Judah Halevi lived in a society in which he and other Jews were socially powerless and influenced heavily by the dominant Islamic culture. Still, he used his poetry to explore both conflict and harmony among Arabs and Jews. An outgoing physician and court poet with many friends, he wrote a collection of secular poetry and a huge body of religious verses, some of which have made their way into modern Jewish prayer books. (His famed *Ode to Zion* has been read for centuries in religious services.) The poetry brought forth a deeper sense of intellectual words. Jews watched their Arab counterparts closely and learned to be astronomers, philosophers, scientists, and poets.

Signs of status. But this was a time of only partial autonomy. Jews were free to live in the Islamic world as long as they paid a special tax to Muslim rulers and submitted to an order forbidding them to own Muslim slaves. Jews had their own legal system and social services, were forbidden to build new synagogues, and were supposed to wear identifying clothing.

These restrictions led to a profound sense of alienation for some Jews. It was, says Raymond Scheindlin, professor of medieval Hebrew literature at New York's Jewish Theological Seminary, a demoralizing daily reminder "that you are part of a losing team." Halevi reacted to that message. To him, life in Spain—though comfortable in between harrowing bouts of perseuction—was like slavery compared with the life intended for Jews in Palestine.

Allied neither with the crescent nor the cross, Halevi instead focused on a different destiny. To him, the Jews were a calamitous and wounded people, unsure of their place in human history. He wanted Jews to believe what he was confident of: that Hebrew was superior to Arabic, Palestine to Spain, and they were the chosen people.

Some Spanish Jews felt at home in Islamic society.
GRANGER COLLECTION

Jewish spirituality that had been unheard of in previous generations.

With Islam and Christianity locked in a battle of religious giants, the Jewish minority in medieval Spain was left with few privileges. Although some Jews felt at home in an Islamic society, many, like Halevi, longed for a world in which their own people could rise to the top.

In fact, the years between 900 and 1200 in Spain and North Africa are known as the Hebrew "golden age," a sort of Jewish Renaissance that arose from the fusion of the Arab and Jewish

When he was 50, Halevi underwent an emotional upheaval and decided to devote himself to God by going on a pilgrimage to the Holy Land. Legend has it that he met his death upon finally arriving in Israel, where he was run over by an Arab horseman. With the vision of Jerusalem set before him, he recited the last verse of his *Ode to Zion.*
—*Lindsay Faber*

land of three faiths would in time be cleansed of its Muslims and Jews. A militant new doctrine—called *limpieza* *de sangre,* or "purity of blood"—would dispense with all that tangled past and its richness.

The Age of
The Vikings

Norse Seafarers Plundered, Traded, and Settled From Canada to Russia

A.D. 793 was a particularly nasty year along the northeastern coast of England. First came the "fierce, foreboding omens," and the "wretchedly terrified" populace watched fiery dragons dance across the sky. A great famine struck. And then "the ravaging of heathen men destroyed God's church at Lindisfarne through brutal robbery and slaughter." And so began the Age of the Vikings.

By Arne Emil Christensen

This *Anglo-Saxon Chronicle* description of the first major Viking raid is typical of contemporary accounts of the Norsemen. In a remarkably violent time, the Vikings were feared above all others in Europe. Yet they were much more than brutal warriors. The Norse proved themselves to be colonizers, city-builders, law-givers, architects, explorers, and merchants.

For 250 years, from about A.D. 800 until 1050, people of Denmark, Sweden, and Norway played a potent role in European history far out of proportion to the size and population of their mother countries. They plundered, traded, and settled from deep into Russia all the way to Newfoundland on the edge of the New World. They terrorized powerful, established kingdoms like France and England.

The Norse sailed up the rivers of France and Spain, laid siege to Paris, and attacked coastal towns in Italy. In

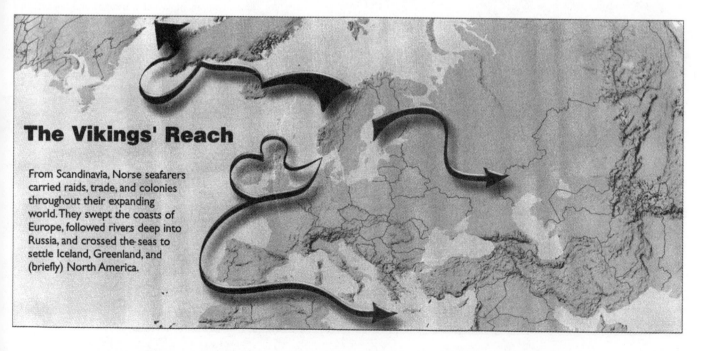

The Vikings' Reach

From Scandinavia, Norse seafarers carried raids, trade, and colonies throughout their expanding world. They swept the coasts of Europe, followed rivers deep into Russia, and crossed the seas to settle Iceland, Greenland, and (briefly) North America.

From *Scientific American Discovering Archaeology*, September/October 2000, pp. 40-47. © 2000 by Scientific American Discovering Archaeology.

NORSE GRAVES REVEAL THE PARADOX OF WAR AND PEACE

BURYING VIKINGS

An Arab traveling through Russia nearly 1,200 years ago happened upon an extraordinary sight: the fiery burial of a Viking chieftain.

The leader's great ship was hauled ashore and his valuables loaded aboard it. The body was dressed in fine clothes and placed on the ship. A slave woman who had chosen to follow her master into the afterlife was killed and her body was placed aboard. Then the chieftain's horse and dog were sacrificed for the grave. Finally, the ship was set ablaze and a mound built over the ashes of the funeral pyre.

Ibn Fadlans described the ninth-century A.D. scene in his journal—the only eyewitness account of a Viking burial. Fortunately for archaeologists, not all Norse funerals involved burning the remains; sometimes whole ships were buried with their owners and property, offering a remarkable glimpse into the life and times of the Norsemen.

The graves give mute testimony to the violence of the Viking age. Nearly all males were buried with weapons. A warrior fully equipped for the next world was interred with his sword, ax, and spear, and often with a bow and arrows. A wooden shield with a central iron boss was the usual protection. The helmets and armor seen on modern representations are extremely rare, and the horned helmet of cartoon Vikings has never been seen in a real Norse grave.

The graves also reveal the paradox of the Vikings: Alongside the fearsome set of arms, the accouterments of peace are also found. Craftsmen were buried with their tools, blacksmiths with their hammer, tongs, and files. Farmers had their hoe, scythe, and sickle; and along the coasts, the dead were often buried with their boats and fishing equipment. Women took with them their personal jewelry, as well as textiles and kitchen tools.

Only metal objects survive the centuries in most graves, but conditions at a few, especially beneath the blue clay on the Oslo Fjord, preserved even wood, leather, and textiles. The clay and tightly stacked turf used in some of the burials produced graves as well sealed as hermetic jars. Everything sacrificed in such graves has been preserved in the moist, oxygen-free conditions.

The preserved contents of three extremely rich ship graves—from *Oseberg, Gokstad,* and *Tune*—are among Norway's national treasures. At the time of the burial, the ships were pulled ashore on rollers and placed in a pit dug into the ground. A burial chamber was built on board to hold the body and provisions needed for a life after death. Then a huge mound was built over the grave.

The remains of a man were found in the *Gokstad* grave, and the *Tune* ship probably also held a male. But the *Oseberg* grave was the resting place for two women, one 50 to 60 years old and the other in her 20s. The *Oseberg* and *Gokstad* graves had been robbed, so the fine weapons and jewelry that must have been among the original grave goods were not found. Articles of wood, leather, and textiles, however, did not interest the robbers and have survived.

It is unclear which of the *Oseberg* women was the recipient of the grave, and which was the after-death companion. Women often held high status in Norse society, and the *Oseberg* grave belonged to a high-ranking women.

Her grave held the evidence of her role as the main administrator of a manor. Even after death, she was equipped to spin and weave and supervise milking, cheese-making, and work in the fields. For land travel, she had three sleds and a wagon complete with sacrificed horses and two tents. Cooking equipment, wooden troughs and buckets, a cauldron, a frying pan, and a carving knife were at hand, as were two oxen, grain, apples, and blueberries.

Objects such as the wagon and several finely carved wooden animal heads probably were religious icons, suggesting the woman may have been both a political and religious leader. The many decorated wooden objects seem to be the work of several different woodcarvers. Except for this grave, our knowledge of Viking art is based mainly on preserved metalwork that generally is smaller than the wooden objects. But whether metal or wood, the artistic goal was the same: to create a carpet of intertwined, fantastic animals.

The number of different artisans represented suggests the "*Oseberg* queen" was a patron of the arts who assembled the best woodcarvers and weavers at her court. The woodcarvings prove that some Vikings were as handy with chisel and knife as with sword and spear. AEC

UDO ARCHIVES/COURTESY OF SMITHSONIAN INSTITUTION

The most famous of Viking ships came from the Oseberg Burial Mound, shown here during excavations in 1904. The impermeable blue clay of the mound in the Oslo Fjord protected the ship and its contents for more than 1,000 years.

THE PERFECT WAR MACHINE

Viking warships were fearsome works of art. The sight of that curved prow suddenly cresting the horizon could send whole cities into panic a millennium ago.

The Scandinavian shipbuilders who created these unique and pioneering craft were quite possibly the most important factor in establishing Norse military supremacy and creating a far-flung web of trade and colonization. A leading Swedish archaeologist, Bertil Almgren, called Viking ships the only ocean-going landing craft ever devised—which would explain how small bands of warriors could terrorize settled societies.

Early accounts of Norse attacks demonstrate the military value of these unique craft and the shattering amphibious tactics they permitted. The ships—light, flexible, and free to maneuver in shallow water—had no need of harbors. They could be easily beached by their crews, who then transformed themselves from oarsmen to fierce, shock troops who swarmed over their terrified targets.

A surprise amphibious attack could hit almost anywhere along Europe's coasts and rivers. Then after a quick and bloody battle, the Norsemen were gone—far out to sea again before a counterattack could be mounted. The Vikings learned early how to tack their ships against the wind, allowing immediate escape even with the wind at their faces. At a time

when civilized armies were supposed to march overland, the amphibious tactics of the Norsemen were devastating.

The Viking ship, that near-perfect war machine of its day, was the culmination of a long Scandinavian shipbuilding tradition that dates back to at least 350 B.C. Many of the techniques developed by Norse shipbuilders are still used for small boats today, so 1,000-year-old problems can be answered by living boatbuilders.

The sail came rather late to Viking ships, probably not until early in the eighth century. But the new sailing ships were perfected through four generations to serve raiders and traders alike.

Even with a full crew, the *Gokstad* could float in one meter (just over three feet) of water. She could be beached by the crew and was well suited for surprise attacks on foreign shores.

The Viking ships were clinker built: Long planks were overlapped and fastened together with iron rivets to form the hull. This planking shell was built first, then the ribs inserted afterwards for strength and stability. This method produces much lighter, more flexible ships than those that began with the stout interior frame to which outer planking was added.

Norse shipbuilders gained even more flexibility by lashing the ship's ribs and planking together. The backbone of keel

and stems fore and aft increased strength. Most ships were built of oak; pine was also used.

As society changed during the Viking Age, different kinds of ships were developed. Warships were long and slender, built for speed with large crews who could man the oars. Cargo ships were much wider and slower and relied more on sails than did the warships. Busy trade routes from Western Norway to Iceland and Greenland required seaworthy ships.

Much of what we know about Viking shipbuilding comes from the Norse practice of burying important personages in their ships. Three especially notable excavated ship burials come from Oseberg, Gokstad and Tune in Norway. All three are exhibited in the Viking Ship Museum at Bygdoy in Oslo.

Norway's National Museum recently used tree-ring analysis to date these three pristine ships. The *Oseberg* was built between A.D. 815 and 820, the other two in the A.D. 890s. The *Oseberg* is 22 meters (72 feet) long and could be rowed by 30 men. The *Gokstad* stretches 24 meters (78 feet) with room for 32 oarsmen, while the *Tune* was probably about 20 meters (65 feet) long.

All three had a mast amidships, with the sail of *Gokstad* estimated at about 120 square meters (1,300 square feet). Sails were made of wool, and the task of collecting wool, and sorting, spinning, weaving, and sewing such a sail must have been a greater task than building the ship.

The *Oseberg* was less seaworthy than the later *Gokstad* and *Tune* ships, but still well-suited for trips across the North Sea in summer. It is probably typical of the warship used for the early raids. The seaworthiness of the *Gokstad* has been proved by the three replicas which have crossed the North Atlantic in modern times, yet the ship could float freely in as little as one meter (just over three feet) of water.

Most of the routes taken by Viking Age seafarers were in coastal waters or across fairly short stretches of open sea. Navigation was based on landmarks; and in coastal waters, it was usual to find a good harbor for the night and camp on the shore. Only on the long stretches of open water from Western Norway to Iceland and Greenland would sailors be out of sight of land for several days.   AEC

BETTMANN/CORBIS; PAINTED BY EDWARD MORAN

This golden box brooch with silver inlays, recovered from Gotland Island, demonstrates the high level of Norse craftsmanship.

the east, they traded with Arab merchants at Bulgar on the Volga and raided as far east as the Caspian Sea. From Kiev, they traveled downriver to the Black Sea and attempted an attack on the Byzantine capital of Constantinople.

MEN FROM THE SEA   Scandinavia was hardly unknown to the rest of Europe when the surprise raids began. Archaeological evidence shows cultural contacts dating back several millennia, but the distant Nordic area was of little import to the rest of Europe.

That changed suddenly in A.D. 793, when "men from the sea" plundered Lindisfarne monastery on Northumberland Island. Within a few years, every summer brought a wave of attacks on Ireland, England, France, and the North Sea's Frisian Islands.

Some of the Viking raiders stayed behind to build well-planned cities like Dublin and Kiev or take over existing ones like York. Others came with family and livestock to settle as farmers in Eng-

land, Scotland, Normandy, and Russia. For 200 years, their ships sailed all the known waters of Europe and ventured where ships had never been.

Great ventures under famous chiefs often involved men from throughout Scandinavia, but the three countries divided their world into distinct spheres of interest.

The Swedes sailed mainly to the east, trading and settling along the Russian rivers and settling in towns as far south as Kiev. They must have played a role in creating the Russian state, although the importance of the role is debated. The Norsemen's eastern expansion was less warlike than the move against Western Europe. Trade was key in the east, and the enormous quantities of ancient Arab coins found in Sweden demonstrate how far the trade networks reached.

SWEEPING ACROSS EUROPE   The Danes sailed south to Friesland (in northern Europe), France, and southern England, occasionally reaching even

Spain and Italy. Much of England became known as the "danelaw." In France, the embattled king invited Rollo, a Norse chieftain, to settle in Normandy as a French duke—in exchange for keeping other Vikings at bay.

Norway held sway in the west and northwest. Norwegian settlements on Orkney and Shetland may predate the Viking Age, when Norway drilled deep roots into northern England, Scotland, and Ireland. Scandinavian jewelry recovered from English graves tell of whole families emigrating, while Celtic names in Iceland suggest some settlers came from Ireland with Irish wives.

Farther west, the settlers came upon virgin land: the Faroe Islands, Iceland, and Greenland. The settlement of Iceland intensified around A.D. 900, when Norwegian kings strengthened their central government, according to a unique source, *Landnamabok*, which tells the story of the settlement and names many of the settlers.

Chiefs often preferred to emigrate rather than submit to higher authority; family and friends usually followed. Some settlers had no choice after being outlawed at home. The man who led the colonization of Greenland, Eirik the Red, was expelled from Iceland for killing and other mayhem.

NEW WORLD COLONY   Sailing still farther westward, the Norse reached North America and launched a settlement around A.D. 1000. Conflicts with the original inhabitants of the New World doomed the colony, however, and the settlers returned to Greenland.

The location—and even the existence—of the Norsemen's North American settlement has been hotly debated for more than a century, with suggestions ranging from Labrador to Manhattan. Unassailable proof was discovered in the 1960s by Helge and Anne Stine Ingstad with their excavations at L'Anse aux Meadows on northern Newfoundland. Houses like those excavated on Iceland and Greenland, Viking artifacts, and radiocarbon dates of about A.D. 1000 proved this to be a site built and used by Norse people.

What accounts for this rapid, violent expansion? Well-organized states such

ROLAND HEJDSTRÖM

This oval brooch from Sweden's Gotland Island was made in Karelia, Russia.

as France and the Anglo-Saxon kingdoms of England were taken by complete surprise and were rarely able to resist the amphibious attacks.

Written accounts from the time, which were hardly objective, paint the Vikings as merciless pirates, robbers, and brigands. And, indeed, they no doubt were. But these were violent times. Accounts from Ireland state that the Irish themselves plundered about as many monasteries and churches as the Vikings. The Frankish Empire grew via long and bloody wars, and the Anglo-Saxon kingdoms fought one another repeatedly. The Vikings may well have been just the most efficient raiders of their day.

But they were more than warriors. Some of their leaders not only won great battles, but founded kingdoms in conquered lands, planned cities, and gave laws that are still in force. The remains of fortresses that could house an army have been found in Denmark. Dating to the end of the Viking Age, the circular forts are laid out with a precision that impresses modern surveyors. The forts testify to an advanced knowledge of geometry and surveying.

FARMERS AND BLACKSMITHS   In their homelands, the Norse mostly were farmers and stockbreeders who supplemented their larder by fishing and hunting. Barley, oats, and some wheat were cultivated; and cattle, horses, sheep, goats, and pigs were raised. Iron-making was an important resource in Sweden and in Norway, with bog ore to supply the iron and ample wood to fuel the furnace pits. Some

areas quarried steatite for cooking vessels and slate for whetstones.

The farmers were generally self-reliant, although luxury goods and such necessities as salt formed the basis of thriving trade. Steatite items survive the centuries well and turn up in excavations outside Scandinavia; but such perishable goods as furs, ropes of seal and walrus skins, and dried fish must also have been important trade items. Many Arab coins have been found in Scandinavia, and although we do not know what was purchased with the coins, iron and slaves are possibilities.

Warfare was rarely allowed to interfere with trade. As Alfred of Wessex fought desperately to block a Viking invasion, he was visited by Ottar, a Norwegian merchant. Ottar's story was written down and survives as the only contemporary report on Viking society by a Viking. Ottar lived in the far north of Norway and collected his trade goods as taxes paid by nearby indigenous people, the Saami. He mentions furs, eiderdown, and skin ropes, as well as walrus teeth—the "ivory of the Arctic."

A SOURCE OF WARRIORS   One force driving Norse expansion may have been the *odel,* which seems to extend back to Viking times. The *odel* dictated that a farm should not be divided but inherited intact by the oldest son. Younger sons and daughters received far less and likely had to clear new land or go abroad to acquire a farm. Landless younger sons may have given chieftains the manpower they needed to raid Europe.

Although West European sources tell a grim story of the Vikings, archaeological excavations paint a much more varied picture. Excavated farms and graves reveal artifacts from a peaceful life centered on the rhythm of a year that revolved around agriculture. Piles of stones tell of careful clearing of the land, and we have found the furrows left by a plowing 1,100 years ago.

As the years progressed, Norse society changed. Fewer chieftains controlled

more and more resources, forming the basis of kingdoms until each of the three countries united into a central kingdom along roughly the same borders as today. Marketplaces grew into towns with well-planned streets and plots for homes.

From Staraya Ladoga and Kiev in Russia to Dublin in Ireland, we find evidence of townspeople basing their life on trade and handicraft. Garbage disposal was not a high priority, and the thick layers of ancient refuse are now gold mines for archaeologists. Excavations illuminate everything from changing fashions to the kinds of lice that bedeviled the townspeople.

CHRISTIAN VIKINGS   The Viking Age ended in the eleventh century, as Scandinavian kingdoms adopted Christianity. The raids gradually ended, and the pantheon of warrior gods faded. Viking gods lived on as our days of the week: Tuesday, Wednesday, Thursday and Friday. Ty and Thor were war gods; Wotan (or Odin) was the chief god with power over life, death, and poetry; Frey and his sister Freya were the gods of fertility. We know little of Viking religion, as written sources are late and colored by Christian belief. The gods demanded sacrifice, and temples and holy forests were probably dedicated to these deities. Like their Greek and Roman counterparts, the Viking gods had human traits.

The northern countries, once the scourge of a continent, became a regular part of Christian Europe and great changes ensued. But for the people of the Norselands, life went on. They continued to sow and reap, and herd and hunt as they had for generations beyond counting.

ARNE EMIL CHRISTENSEN, of the University Museum of National Antiquities in Oslo, specializes in shipbuilding history and craftsmanship in the Iron Age and Viking period.

CLOCKS
REVOLUTION
IN TIME

Ancient Clepsydra

The question to ask is: Why clocks? Who needs them? After all, nature is the great time-giver, and all of us without exception, live by nature's clock. Night follows day; day, night; and each year brings its succession of seasons. These cycles are imprinted on just about every living being in what are called circadian ('about a day') and circannual biological rhythms. They are stamped in our flesh and blood; they persist even when we are cut off from time cues; they mark us as earthlings.

These biological rhythms are matched by societal work patterns: day is for labour, night for repose, and the round of seasons is a sequence of warmth and cold, planting and harvest, life and death.

Into this natural cycle, which all people have experienced as a divine providence, the artificial clock enters as an intruder.

David Landes

WHEN IN THE LATE SIXTEENTH century Portuguese traders and Christian missionaries sought entry into China, they were thwarted by a kind of permanent quarantine. Chinese officials correctly perceived these foreigners as potential subversives, bringing with them the threat of political interference, material seduction, and spiritual corruption. The ban was not lifted for decades, and then only because Matteo Ricci and his Jesuit mission brought with them knowledge

and instruments that the Celestial Court coveted. In particular, they brought chiming clocks, which the Chinese received as a wondrous device. By the time Ricci, after numerous advances and retreats, finally secured permission from the court eunuchs and other officials to proceed to Peking and present himself to the throne, the emperor could hardly wait. 'Where', he called, 'are the self-ringing bells?' And later, when the dowager empress showed an interest in her son's favourite clock, the emperor

had the bell disconnected so that she would be disappointed. He could not have refused to give it to her, had she asked for it; but neither would he give it up, so he found this devious way to reconcile filial piety with personal gratification.

The use of these clocks as a ticket of entry is evidence of the great advance European timekeeping had made over Chinese horology. It had not always been thus. The Chinese had always been much concerned to track the stars for astrological and horoscopic purposes. For the emperor, the conjunctions of the heavenly bodies were an indispensable guide to action, public and private—to making war and peace, to sowing and reaping, to conceiving an heir with the empress or coupling with a concubine. To facilitate the calculations required, court mechanicians of the Sung dynasty (tenth and eleventh centuries) built a series of remarkable clock-driven astraria, designed to track and display the apparent movements of the stars. The clock mechanism that drove the display was hydraulic—a water clock (clepsydra) linked to a bucket wheel. As each bucket filled, it activated a release mechanism that allowed the big drive wheel to turn and bring the next bucket into position. The water clock in itself was no more accurate than such devices can be; but in combination with the wheel, it could be adjusted to keep time within a minute or two a day. By way of comparison, the ordinary drip or flow water clocks then in use in Europe probably varied by a half-hour or more.

These astronomical clocks marked a culmination. The greatest of them, that built by Su Sung at the end of the eleventh century, was also the last of the series. When invasion and war forced the court to flee, the clock was lost and its secret as well. From this high point of achievement, Chinese timekeeping retrogressed to simpler, less accurate instruments, so that when the Jesuits arrived some five hundred years later with their mechanical clocks, they found only objects that confirmed their comfortable sense of technological, and by implication moral, superiority.

Meanwhile European timekeeping made a quantum leap by moving from hydraulic to mechanical devices. The new clocks, which took the form of weight-driven automated bells, made their appearance around 1280. We don't know where—England possibly, or Italy—and we don't know who invented them. What we do know is that the gain was immense and that the new clocks very rapidly swept the older clepsydras aside. Since these first mechanical clocks were notoriously inaccurate, varying an hour or more a day, and unreliable, breaking down frequently and

needing major overhauls every few years, one can only infer that water clocks left even more to be desired. The great advantage of the mechanical clock lay in its relative immunity to temperature change, whereas the drip or flow of the water clock varied with the seasons while frost would halt it altogether (the temperature did not have to go down to freezing to increase viscosity and slow the rate). In the poorly heated buildings of northern Europe, especially at night, this was a near-fatal impairment. Dirt was another enemy. No water is pure, and deposits would gradually choke the narrow opening. The instructions for use of a thirteenth-century water clock installed in the Abbey of Villers (near Brussels) make it clear that no one expected much of these devices: the sacristan was to adjust it daily by the sun, as it fell on the abbey windows; and if the day was cloudy, why then it was automatically ten o'clock at the end of the morning mass.

Why Europe should have succeeded in effecting this transition to a superior technology and China not is an important historical question. Anyone who looked at the horological world of the eleventh or twelfth century would have surely predicted the opposite result. (He would have also expected Islam to surpass Europe in this domain.) The Chinese failure—if failure is the right word—cannot be sought in material circumstances. The Chinese were as troubled and inconvenienced by the limitations of the water clock as were the Europeans; it can get very cold in Peking. (The Chinese tried substituting mercury or sand for water, but mercury kills and neither behaves very well over time.) Instead the explanation must be sought in the character and purposes of Chinese timekeeping. It was, in its higher forms, a monopoly of the imperial court, as much an attribute of sovereignty as the right to coin money. In this instance, dominion over time and

Illustrations courtesy of Bodleian Library Film Strip Service, Oxford.

A monastic water-driven wheel clock of thirteenth-century Europe. The mechanism is hard to make out, but the picture suggests that water-driven wheel clocks of the Chinese type were used (or at least known) in Europe before the advent of the weight-driven wheel-clock.

Manuscript illustrations from the fifteenth century show the metaphorical importance clocks had in a medieval application of the concept of time. The goddess Attemprance, half-figure in a cloud, grasps a clock with hanging bells in both hands; large bell above. A French manuscript illustration of the late fifteenth century.

Manuscript illustration of 1450 showing a huge, intricate clock, standing on earth, but with its open and visible wheel-work and dial and bell in heaven. The four traditional symbols of the evangelists are shown on the four corners of the dial. The goddess Attemprance, resting on the clouds, is winding the clock.

taken as special projects, the work of a team assembled for the occasion. Each of these machines was a *tour de force*, and each built on earlier models, researched in the archives by way of preparation. There was, then, no continuous process of construction and emendation; no multiplicity of private initiatives; no dynamic of continuing improvement. Instead we have these occasional peak moments of achievement, highly fragile, vulnerable to political hostility and adventitious violence, easily buried and forgotten once the team of builders had dissolved or died.

Outside these rarefied circles, the Chinese people had little interest in time measurement for its own sake. Most of them were peasants, and peasants have no need of clocks. They wake with the animals in the morning, watch the shadows shorten and lengthen as the sun crosses the sky, and go to bed once night falls—because they are tired, illumination is costly and they must get up very early. They are not unaware of the passage of time, but they do not have to measure it. Time measurement is an urban concern, and in medieval China the authorities provided time signals (drums, trumpets) in the cities to mark the passage of the hours and warn the residents of such things as the closing of the gates to the separate quarters or neighbourhoods. But such noises could not easily be used to order the daily round of activities, for the Chinese did

calendar was a major aspect of power, for it laid the cognitive foundation for imperial decisions in every area of political and economic life. So much was this the case that each emperor began by proclaiming his own calendar, often different from that of his predecessor;

by so doing, he affirmed his legitimacy and identity.

Timekeeping instruments were therefore reserved to the court and certain of its officials; there was no civilian clock trade. Such great astronomical clocks as were built for the throne were under-

not number the hours sequentially; rather they named them, so that auditory signals transmitted limited information. Such as they were, they sufficed, for the organisation of work created no need for closer or continuous timing. The typical work unit was the household shop, comprising master, assistants, and apprentices. The day started at dawn, when the youngest or newest apprentice woke to make the fire and wake the rest; and work continued until night imposed its interruption. This mode of production set no artificial *clocktime* limited to labour; nature fixed the bounds.

In contrast, medieval Europe did have a constituency concerned to track and use time. This was the Christian church, especially those monastic orders that followed the rule of Benedict. This rule, which was defined in the sixth century, became over time the standard of monachal discipline in western Europe. The aim of the rule was to ensure that the entire day be ordered and devoted to the service of God—to pray above all, but also to work, which was defined as

another kind of prayer. The daily prayer offices numbered seven (later eight), six (later seven) in the daytime and one at night. The institution of a nocturnal office was peculiar to Christianity and sharply differentiated it from the other monotheistic religions. It went back to the prayer vigils conducted by the earliest Christians in imminent expectation of the *parousia*, or second coming. It was these vigils that were later merged with the morning prayer to constitute the canonical hour known as matins.

The obligation to rise to prayer in the dark imposed a special condition on Christian worship. Whereas Jews (and later Muslims) set their times of prayer by natural events (morning, afternoon, and evening) that do not require the use of an artificial timekeeper, Christians needed some kind of alarm to wake to matins. In the cities of the Roman empire, the night watch could give the signal. In medieval Europe such municipal services had long disappeared, and most abbeys were located in rural areas. Each house, then, had to find its own way to

satisfy the requirement, usually by means of an alarm device linked to a water clock. This would rouse the waker, usually the sacristan, who would then ring the bells that called the others to prayer. Most house rules—for although the principal was general, there was little uniformity in the details of practice—enjoined the sacristan to be scrupulous in his performance of this duty, for his neglect imperilled the salvation of his brethren (and the larger church) as well as his own. 'Nothing, therefore, shall be put before the Divine Office', says the Rule.

To the ordinary monk, getting up in the dark of the night was perhaps the hardest aspect of monastic discipline. Indeed the practical meaning of 'reforming' a house meant first and foremost the imposition (reimposition) of this duty. The sleepy-heads were prodded out of bed and urged to the offices; they were also prodded during service lest they fail in their obligations. Where the flesh was weak, temptation lurked. Raoul Glaber (early eleventh century) tells the tale of a demon who successfully seduced a monk by holding the lure of sweet sleep:

> As for you, I wonder why you so scrupulously jump out of bed as soon as you hear the bell, when you could stay resting even unto the third bell. . . but know that every year Christ empties hell of sinners and brings them to heaven, so without worry you can give yourself to all the voluptuousness of the flesh. . . .

The same Glaber confesses to two occasions when he himself woke late and saw a demon, 'come to do business with the laggards'. And Peter the Venerable, Abbot of Cluny in the twelfth century, tells the story of Brother Alger, who woke thinking he had heard the bell ring for nocturns. Looking around, he thought he saw the other beds empty, so he drew on his sandals, threw on his cloak, and hastened to the chapel. There he was puzzled not to hear the sound of voices lifted in prayer. Now he hurried back to the dormitory, where he found all the other monks fast asleep. And then he understood: this was all a temptation of the devil, who had awakened him at the wrong time, so that when the bell

A sketch of a clock tower by Villard de Honnecourt, circa 1225–1250. An early example of a chiming clock tower which kept equal hours and provided regular signals—a constraint for worker and employer alike.

for nocturns really rang, he would sleep through it.

These, I suggest, are what we now know as anxiety dreams. They clearly reflect the degree to which time-consciousness and discipline had become internalised. Missing matins was a serious matter, so serious that it has been immortalised for us by perhaps the best known of children's songs:

Frère Jacques, Frère Jacques,
Dormez-vous? dormez-vous?
Sonnez les matines, sonnez les matines,
Ding, dang, dong; ding, dang, dong.

We know far less than we should like about monastic horology in the Middle Ages, and such information as we have is confused by the use of the general term *(h)orologium* for any and all kinds of timekeeper. It seems clear, however, that the century or two preceding the appearance of the mechanical clock saw important improvements in technique and a growing emphasis on the details of the monastic time service. The enhanced temporal consciousness may be related to the revival of monastic life after the millennium and in particular to the needs of the Cistercian order—that economic empire with its agricultural, mining, and industrial enterprises, its ever-turning water wheels, its large labour force of lay brethren, its place in the forefront of European technology.

One of the innovations of this period seems to have been the combination clepsydra/mechanical alarm. This worked as follows: when the water in the recipient vessel reached an appropriate height, it tripped a weight-driven escape wheel, so called because it meshed with pallets that alternately blocked and released it (allowed it to escape). This stop-go motion in turn imparted a to-and-fro oscillation to the rod or *verge* holding the pallets; hence the name *verge escapement*. Attach a small hammer to the end of the verge, and it could ring a bell. Put an oscillating cross bar on the end, and you had a controller for a clock.

The first clocks were probably alarms converted in this manner. The very name *clock* meant bell, and these were essentially machines to sound the passing

hours. Their use entailed a drastic change in the character of European timekeeping. Because the mechanical clock beat at a more or less uniform rate, it sounded equal-length hours—what later came to be known as mean (average) time. But the standard of medieval Europe was the sun, and the hours were natural, equal fractions of the day and night. Thus as days got longer, daylight hours lengthened and night hours shrank; and vice versa. These seasonally variable hours (often called temporal hours) were easily measured by the water clock; all one had to do was change the scale with the seasons. But an automated bell was another story: changing the times of ringing to take account of changing hours would have been a difficult and time-consuming task. So Europeans learned a new time standard in which the sun rose and set at different hours as the days passed. This seems natural enough to us, but it must have come as a shock at first. (Some places chose to start their day at sunrise, which took care of one end of the problem, though not the other).

In effect the new clock offered a rival time standard in competition with the older church time. It was not only the hours that differed; it was the signals also. The old water clocks did not sound public, tower bells. They told the time for the bell ringer, who usually rang, not the unequal, temporal hours, but the hours of prayer, the so-called canonical hours. These were not equally spaced and did not lend themselves to the kind of calculation we take for granted: how long since? how long until? It was equal hours that made this possible and thereby contributed significantly to the growing numeracy of the urban population. Insofar as the medieval church resisted the new time standard, it gave over an important symbol of authority to the secular power. Where once people punctuated their day by such marks as sext, none, and vespers, now they thought in terms of hours and, very soon, minutes.

The transition from church time to lay time was at once sign and consequence of the rise of a new, urban social order. The new machines appealed from the start to the rich and powerful, who

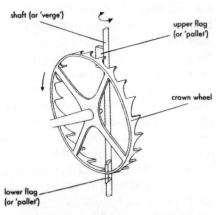

Diagram illustrating the 'verge' escapement. An escapement is the mechanism which could control and slow down the speed at which the weights of a clock dropped. The 'verge' escapement is the earliest surviving form.

made them the preferred object of conspicuous consumption. No court, no prince would be without one. But far more important in the long run was the rapid acceptance of the new instrument in cities and towns, which had long learned to regulate many aspects of civil life by bells—bells to signal the opening and closing of markets, waking bells and work bells, drinking and curfew bells, bells for opening and closing of gates, assembly and alarms. In this regard, the medieval city was a secular version of the cloister, prepared by habit and need to use the clock as a superior instrument of time discipline and management.

The pressure for time signals was especially strong in those cities that were engaged in textile manufacture—the first and greatest of medieval industries. There the definition of working time was crucial to the profitability of enterprise and the prosperity of the commune. The textile industry was the first to go over to large-scale production for export, hence the first to overflow the traditional workshop and engage a dispersed work force. Some of these workers—the *ciompi* in Florence, the 'blue nails' (stained by dye) in Flanders—were true proletarians, owning none of the instruments of production, selling only their labour power. They streamed early every morning into the dye shops and fulling mills, where the high consumption of energy for heating the vats and driving the hammers encouraged concentration in large units. Other branches of the manufacture could be conducted in the rooms and cottages of the workers: employers liked this so-called putting out because it shifted much of the burden of overhead costs to the employee, who was paid by the piece rather than by time; and the workers preferred it to the time discipline and supervision of the large shops. They could in principle start and stop at will, for who was to tell them what to do in their own home?

The bells would tell them. Where there was textile manufacture, there were work bells, which inevitably gave rise to conflict. Part of the problem was implicit in the effort to impose time discipline on home workers. In principle, payment by the piece should have taken care of the matter, with workers responding to wage incentives. In fact, the home workers were content to earn what they felt they needed, and in time of keen demand, employers found it impossible to get them to do more, for higher pay only reduced the amount of work required to satisfy these needs. The effort to bring the constraints of the manufactory into the rooms and cottages of spinners and weavers made the very use of bells a focus of resentment.

Meanwhile in the fulling mills and dyeshops the bells posed a different kind of problem, especially when they were controlled by the employer. Consider the nature of the wage contract: the worker was paid by the day, and the day was bounded by these time signals. The employer had an interest in getting a full day's work for the wages he paid; and the worker in giving no more time than he was paid for. The question inevitably arose how the worker could know whether bell time was honest time. How could he trust even the municipal bells when the town council was dominated by representatives of the employers?

Under the circumstances, workers in some places sought to silence the *werk-clocke*: at Therouanne in 1367 the dean and chapter promised 'workers, fullers, and other mechanics' to silence 'forever the workers' bell in order that no scandal or conflict be born in city and church as a result of the ringing of a bell of this type'. Such efforts to eliminate time

The clockmaker at work, from a sixteenth-century wood engraving.

signals never achieved success: as soon suppress the system of wage labour. Besides, once the work day was defined in temporal rather than natural terms, workers as well as employers had an interest in defining and somehow signalling the boundaries. Time measurement here was a two-edged sword: it gave the employer bounds to fill, and to the worker bounds to work. The alternative was the open-ended working day, as Chrétien de Troyes observed of the silk weavers of Lyons in the twelfth century:

... nous sommes en grand'misère,
Mais s'enrichit de nos salaires
Celui pour qui nous travaillons.

Des nuits grand partie nous veillons
Et tout le jour pour y gagner
... we are in great misery,
The man who gets rich on our wages
Is the man we worked for.
We're up a good part of the night
And work all day to make our way. ...

It was not the work bells as such, then, that were resented and mistrusted, but the people who controlled them; and

it is here that the chiming tower clock made its greatest contribution. It kept equal hours and provided regular signals, at first on the hour, later on at the halves or quarters, and these necessarily limited the opportunities for abuse. With the appearance of the dial (from the word for day), of course, it was possible for all interested parties to verify the time on a continuous basis.

The early turret clocks were very expensive, even when simple. Wrought iron and brass needed repeated hammering, hence much labour and much fuel. The casting of the bells was a precarious operation. The placement of the mechanism usually entailed major structural alterations. The construction and installation of a tower clock might take months if not years. Teams of craftsmen and labourers had to be assembled on the site and there lodged and boarded. Subsequent maintenance required the attendance of a resident technician, repeated visits by specialised artists, and an endless flow of replacement parts.

These costs increased substantially as soon as one went beyond simple time-keepers to astronomical clocks and/or automata. The medieval accounts show this process clearly: the sums paid to painters and woodcarvers bear witness to the growing importance of the clock as spectacle as well as time signal. The hourly parade of saints and patriarchs; the ponderous strokes of the hammer-wielding *jaquemarts*; the angel turning with the sun; the rooster crowing at sunrise; the lunar disc waxing and waning with the moon—and all these movements and sounds offered lessons in theology and astronomy to the upgrazing multitude that gathered to watch and wonder at what man had wrought. They hourly pageant was an imitation of divine creation; the mechanism, a miniaturisation of heaven and earth. As a result, the show clock was to the new secular, urbanising world of the later Middle Ages what the cathedrals had been to the still worshipful world of the high Middle Ages: a combination of a sacrifice and affirmation, the embodiment of the highest skills and artistry, a symbol of prowess and source of pride. It was also a source of income—the lay analogue to the religious relics that were so potent an attraction to medieval travellers. When Philip the Bold of Burgundy defeated the Flemish burghers at Rosebecke in 1382 and wanted to punish those proud and troublesome clothiers, he could do no worse (or better) than seize the belfry clock at Courtrai and take it off to his capital at Dijon.

These public clocks, moreover, were only the top of the market. They are the ones that history knows best, but we know only a fraction of what was made. In this regard, the records are misleading: they have preserved the memory of a spotty, biased selection and largely omitted the smaller domestic clocks made to private order. As a result, it was long thought that the first mechanical clocks were turret clocks, and that the smaller domestic models were the much later product of advances in miniaturisation. Yet there was no technical impediment to making chamber clocks once the verge escapement had been invented. Indeed, since the mechanical clock is a development of the timer

alarm, itself made to chamber size, small may well have preceded big.

Whichever came first, the one logically implied the other, so that we may fairly assume that both types of clock were known and made from the start. In the event, the first literary allusion to a mechanical clock refers to domestic timepieces. This goes back to the late thirteenth century, in Jean de Meung's additional verse to *Le roman de la rose*. Jean, a romantic poet of curiously worldly interest, attributes to his Pygmalion a fair array of chamber clocks:

Et puis faire sonner ses orloges
Par ses salles et par ses loges
A roues trop subtillement
De pardurable mouvement.

And then through halls and chambers,
Made his clock chime
By wheels of such cunning
Ever turning through time.

By the end of the fourteenth century, hundreds of clocks were turning in western Europe. A new profession of horologers had emerged, competing for custom and seeking severally to improve their product. There could be no surer guarantee of cumulative technical advance. Few inventions in history have ever made their way with such ease. Everyone seems to have welcomed the clock, even those workers who toiled to its rules, for they much preferred it to arbitrary bells. *Summe necessarium pro omni statu hominum* was the way Galvano Fiamma, chronicler of Milan, put it when he proudly marked the erection in 1333 (?) of a clock that not only struck the hours but signalled each one by the number of peals. And this in turn recalls an earlier inscription on a clock installed in 1314 on the bridge at Caen:

Je ferai les heures ouir
Pour le commun peuple rejouir.

I shall give the hours voice
To make the common folk rejoice.

Even the poets liked the new clocks. That is the most astonishing aspect of these early years of mechanical horology, for no group is by instinct and sensibility so suspicious of technical innovation. Here, moreover, was an in-

vention that carried with it the seeds of control, order, self-restraint—all virtues (or vices) inimical to the free, spontaneous imagination and contemplation so prized by creative artists. Yet it would be anachronistic to impute these ideals to the thirteenth and fourteenth centuries; they came much later. The medieval ideal was one of sobriety and control, along with due respect for worthy models. Besides, it was surely too soon to understand the potential of the new device for forming the persona as well as dictating the terms of life and work. Instead, the availability of this new knowledge gave all a sense of power, of enhanced efficiency and potential, of ownership of a new a valuable asset, whereas we, living by the clock, see ignorance of or indifference to time as a release from constraint and a gain in freedom. Everything depends, I suppose, on where one is coming from. In any event, the early celebrators of the clock were no mere poetasters: thus Dante Alighieri, who sang in his *Paradise* (Canto X) the praises of the 'glorious wheel' moving and returning 'voice to voice in timbre and sweetness'—*tin tin sonando con si dolce nota* (almost surely a reference to a chamber clock, unless Dante had a tin ear), therein echoing the pleasure that Jean de Meung's Pygmalion took in his chiming clocks a generation earlier. And a half-century later we have Jean Froissart, poet but more famous as historian, composer of 'love ditties', among them *L'horloge amoureuse* (1369):

... The clock is, when you think about it,
A very beautiful and remarkable instrument,
And it's also pleasant and useful,
Because night and day it tells us the hours
By the subtlety of its mechanism
Even when there is no sun.
Hence all the more reason to prize one's machine,
Because other instruments can't do this
However artfully and precisely they may be made
Hence do we hold him for valiant and wise
Who first invented this device
And with his knowledge undertook and made
A thing so noble and of such great pride.

The invention and diffusion of the mechanical clock had momentous consequences for European technology, culture, and society—comparable in their significance to the effects of the later invention of movable type and printing. For one thing, the clock could be miniaturised and, once small enough, moved about. For this, a new power source was needed, which took the form of a coiled spring, releasing energy as it unwound. This came in during the fifteenth century and gave rise to a new generation of small domestic clocks and, by the early sixteenth, to the watch, that is, a clock small enough to be worn on the person. Domestic clocks and, even more, the watch were the basis of the private, internalised time discipline that characterises modern personality and civilisation—for better or worse. Without this discipline, we could not operate the numerous and complex activities required to make our society go. (We could, no doubt, have recourse to public signals, as in the army. But that would mean a very different kind of collectivity).

For another thing, the mechanical clock was susceptible of great improvement in accuracy, even in its smaller form. This potential lay in its revolutionary principle of time measurement. Whereas earlier instruments had relied on some continuous movement—of shadow (the sundial) or fluid (the clepsydra)—to track the passage of time, the mechanical clock marked time by means of an oscillating controller. This took the form of a bar or wheel swinging to and fro. The swings (pulses or beats) could then be counted and converted to time units—hours, minutes, and eventually sub-minutes. To the ancients who invented the sundial and water clock, a continuous controller on what we would not call the analogue principle seemed only logical, for it was an imitation of time itself, always passing. But in the long run, its possibilities for improvement were limited not only by the inherent flaws of sunlight (no use at night or in cloudy weather) and flowing liquids, but by the difficulty of sustaining and even, continuously moving display. Time measurement by beats or pulses, on the other hand—the digital principle—had no bounds of accuracy. All that was needed was an even, countable frequency. The oscillating controller of the first medieval clocks usually beat double-seconds. Frequency was decidedly uneven, hence the large variation in rate. It took almost four hundred years to invent a vastly superior controller in the form of the pendulum, which in its seconds-beating form could keep time within less than a minute a day. Today, of course, new controllers have been invented in the form of vibrating quartz crystals (hundreds of thousands or even millions of beats per second), which vary less than a minute a year; and atomic resonators (billions of vibrations per second), which take thousands of years to gain or lose a second. These gains in precision have been an important impetus to scientific inquiry; indeed, almost all of them came about because scientists needed better time-keeping instruments. How else to study process and rates of changes?

Finally, the clock with its regularity came to stand as the model for all other machines—the machine of machines, the essence of man's best work in the image of God; and clock-making became the school for all other mechanical arts. No one has said it better than Lewis Mumford in *Technics and Civilization*:

> The clock, not the steam engine, is the key-machine of the modern industrial age . . . In its relationship to determinable quantities of energy, to standardization, to automatic action, and finally to its own special product, accurate timing, the clock has been the foremost machine in modern technics; and at each period it has remained in the lead: it marks a perfection toward which other machines aspire.

All of this was there in germ in the oscillating controllers of the first mechanical clocks. The builders of those clocks did not know what they had wrought. That the clock was invented in Europe and remained a European monopoly for some five hundred years, and that Europe then built a civilisation organised around the measurement of time;—these were critical factors in the differentiation of West from Rest and the definition of modernity.

FOR FURTHER READING

David S. Landes, *Revolution in Time: Clocks and the Making of the Modern World* is published by Harvard University Press; on January, 16th at £17. Ernest von Bassermann-Jordan, *The Book of Old Clocks and Watches* (4th ed., revised by Hans von Bertele; New York: Crown, 1964); Eric Bruton, *The History of Clocks and Watches* (New York: Rizzoli, 1979); Carlo Cipolla, *Clocks and Culture, 1300–1700* (New York: Walker, 1967); Jacques Le Goff, *Time, Work, and Culture in the Middle Ages* (University of Chicago Press, 1980); Lewis Mumford, *Technics and Civilization* (New York: Harcourt, Brace, 1934); Joseph Needham, Wang Ling, and Derek J. de Solla Price, *Heavenly Clockwork: The Great Astronomical Clocks of Medieval China* (Cambridge University Press, 1960); also articles in *Antiquarian Horology*, the journal of the Antiquarian Horological Society of Great Britain.

Unit 7

Key Points to Consider

❖ Why did the Chinese fail in their efforts to explore the world?

❖ Was Columbus unique? If he had not sailed to the west, would someone else have done it? Explain.

❖ How should historians treat Columbus? Does every generation rewrite history?

❖ Did the massive death of Native Americans mean genocide, as some critics say about the coming of Europeans to the Western Hemisphere?

❖ Why were spices so important as a trade item?

❖ What is the significance of Magellan's voyage? What does it mean in respect to Western civilization and the world?

 **Links** **www.dushkin.com/online/**

These sites are annotated on pages 4 and 5.

It might be argued that the most important event in the formation of the modern world is the industrial revolution. In that case, textbooks should divide at that point. A date of 1800 could roughly mark the start not only of the industrial revolution, but also the liberal political revolts in France, the United States, and Latin America. Yet, 1500 is the time of the Reformation, the Renaissance, and the great global explorations. This is the start of the Western domination of the world that continues into the present. Therefore, most world historians accept 1500 as a suitable breaking point for teaching purposes. So it is with the two volumes of *Annual Editions: World History*.

In global exploration, the Scandinavians might have led the way with their colonies in Iceland, Greenland, and Nova Scotia. But, their attempt failed for ecological reasons. The Chinese also might have led the way if it had not been for indifference, internal economic problems, politics, and, perhaps, arrogance. Zheng He, a court eunuch and Muslim, directed a powerful fleet westward on successful explorations that carried him to India and the eastern coast of Africa. But, the Chinese government stopped the voyages and destroyed the ships. Like those of the Vikings, the Chinese discoveries were left unexploited.

The discoveries were left to the Europeans, who had the ambition as well as the technology. The Portuguese sailed southward around Africa, while Christopher Columbus headed westward. His encounter with a new world changed the course of history, and other Europeans followed quickly in the wake of his ships to exploit the new lands and peoples. The quincentenary of his 1492 voyage brought criticism from native activist groups as never before. Columbus appeared as a symbol of oppression. John Noble Wilford assesses this development in "Columbus and the Labyrinth of History."

There is no doubt that the spread of European diseases had a catastrophic effect on native populations, although no one knows the exact numbers. Still, driven by greed and religion, the Europeans explored the world. *The Economist* investigates the desire to pursue the spice trade in the article, "A Taste of Adventure," that drove the Portuguese on to India. Simon Winchester describes Magellan's first circumnavigation of the world, a feat accomplished by no other civilization, in "After Dire Straights, an Agonizing Haul Across the Pacific." Through these explorations Europeans were able to bypass the Middle East to open up trade lanes, and that marked the beginning of a global shift of commerce. Time and technology was on the side of the West.

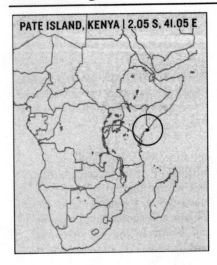

PATE ISLAND, KENYA | 2.05 S, 41.05 E

1492:
The Prequel

Decades before Columbus, Zheng He sailed from China with 300 ships and 28,000 men. His fleet got as far as Africa and could have easily reached America, but the Chinese turned back. What happened?

By Nicholas D. Kristof

From the sea, the tiny East African island of Pate, just off the Kenyan coast, looks much as it must have in the 15th century: an impenetrable shore of endless mangrove trees. As my little boat bounced along the waves in the gray dawn, I could see no antennae or buildings or even gaps where trees had been cut down, no sign of human habitation, nothing but a dense and mysterious jungle.

The boatman drew as close as he could to a narrow black-sand beach, and I splashed ashore. My local Swahili interpreter led the way through the forest, along a winding trail scattered with mangoes, coconuts and occasional seashells deposited by high tides. The tropical sun was firmly overhead when we finally came upon a village of stone houses with thatched roofs, its dirt paths sheltered by palm trees. The village's inhabitants, much lighter-skinned than people on the Kenyan mainland,

emerged barefoot to stare at me with the same curiosity with which I was studying them. These were people I had come halfway around the world to see, in the hope of solving an ancient historical puzzle.

"Tell me," I asked the first group I encountered, "where did the people here come from? Long ago, did foreign sailors ever settle here?"

The answer was a series of shrugs. "I've never heard about that," one said. "You'll have to ask the elders."

I tried several old men and women without success. Finally the villagers led me to the patriarch of the village, Bwana Mkuu Al-Bauri, the keeper of oral traditions. He was a frail old man with gray stubble on his cheeks, head and chest. He wore a yellow sarong around his waist; his ribs pressed through the taut skin on his bare torso. Al-Bauri hobbled out of his bed, resting on a cane and the arm of a grandson. He claimed

to be 121 years old; a pineapple-size tumor jutted from the left side of his chest.

"I know this from my grandfather, who himself was the keeper of history here," the patriarch told me in an unexpectedly clear voice. "Many, many years ago, there was a ship from China that wrecked on the rocks off the coast near here. The sailors swam ashore near the village of Shanga—my ancestors were there and saw it themselves. The Chinese were visitors, so we helped those Chinese men and gave them food and shelter, and then they married our women. Although they do not live in this village, I believe their descendants still can be found somewhere else on this island."

I almost felt like hugging Bwana Al-Bauri. For months I had been poking around obscure documents and research reports, trying to track down a legend of an ancient Chinese shipwreck that had led to a settlement on the African coast. My interest arose from a fascination with what to me is a central enigma of the millennium: why did the West triumph over the East?

For most of the last several thousand years, it would have seemed far likelier that Chinese or Indians, not Europeans, would dominate the world by the year 2000, and that America and Australia would be settled by Chinese rather than by the inhabitants of a backward island called Britain. The reversal of fortunes of East and West strikes me as the biggest news story of the millennium, and one of its most unexpected as well.

As a resident of Asia for most of the past 13 years, I've been searching for an explanation. It has always seemed to me that the turning point came in the early 1400's, when Admiral Zheng He sailed from China to conquer the world. Zheng He (pronounced JUNG HUH) was an improbable commander of a great Chinese fleet, in that he was a Muslim from a rebel family and had been seized by the Chinese Army when he was still a boy. Like many other prisoners of the time, he was castrated—his sexual organs completely hacked off, a process that killed many of those who suffered it. But he was a brilliant and tenacious boy who grew up to be physically imposing. A natural leader, he had the good fortune to be assigned, as a houseboy, to the household of a great prince, Zhu Di.

In time, the prince and Zheng He grew close, and they conspired to overthrow the prince's nephew, the Emperor of China. With Zheng He as one of the prince's military commanders, the revolt succeeded and the prince became China's Yongle Emperor. One of the emperor's first acts (after torturing to death those who had opposed him) was to reward Zheng He with the command of a great fleet that was to sail off and assert China's pre-eminence in the world.

Between 1405 and 1433, Zheng He led seven major expeditions, commanding the largest armada the world would see for the next five centuries. Not until World War I did the West mount anything comparable. Zheng He's fleet included 28,000 sailors on 300 ships, the longest of which were 400 feet. By comparison, Columbus in 1492 had 90 sailors on three ships, the biggest of

which was 85 feet long. Zheng He's ships also had advanced design elements that would not be introduced in Europe for another 350 years, including balanced rudders and watertight bulwark compartments.

The sophistication of Zheng He's fleet underscores just how far ahead of the West the East once was. Indeed, except for the period of the Roman Empire, China had been wealthier, more advanced and more cosmopolitan than any place in Europe for several thousand years. Hangzhou, for example, had a population in excess of a million during the time it was China's capital (in the 12th century), and records suggest that as early as the 7th century, the city of Guangzhou had 200,000 foreign residents: Arabs, Persians, Malays, Indians, Africans and Turks. By contrast, the largest city in Europe in 1400 was probably Paris, with a total population of slightly more than 100,000.

A half-century before Columbus, Zheng He had reached East Africa and learned about Europe from Arab traders. The Chinese could easily have continued around the Cape of Good Hope and established direct trade with Europe. But as they saw it, Europe was a backward region, and China had little interest in the wool, beads and wine Europe had to trade. Africa had what China wanted—ivory, medicines, spices, exotic woods, even specimens of native wildlife.

In Zheng He's time, China and India together accounted for more than half of the world's gross national product, as they have for most of human history. Even as recently as 1820, China accounted for 29 percent of the global economy and India another 16 percent, according to the calculations of Angus Maddison, a leading British economic historian.

Asia's retreat into relative isolation after the expeditions of Zheng He amounted to a catastrophic missed opportunity, one that laid the groundwork for the rise of Europe and, eventually, America. Westerners often attribute their economic advantage today to the intelligence, democratic habits or hard work of their forebears, but a more important reason may well have been the folly of 15th-century Chinese rulers. That is why

I came to be fascinated with Zheng He and set out earlier this year to retrace his journeys. I wanted to see what legacy, if any, remained of his achievement, and to figure out why his travels did not remake the world in the way that Columbus's did.

ZHENG HE LIVED IN NANJING, THE OLD capital, where I arrived one day in February. Nanjing is a grimy metropolis on the Yangtze River in the heart of China. It has been five centuries since Zheng He's death, and his marks on the city have grown faint. The shipyards that built his fleet are still busy, and the courtyard of what had been his splendid 72-room mansion is now the Zheng He Memorial Park, where children roller-skate and old couples totter around for exercise. But though the park has a small Zheng He museum, it was closed—for renovation, a caretaker told me, though he knew of no plans to re-open it.

I'd heard that Zheng He's tomb is on a hillside outside the city, and I set out to find it. It wasn't long before the road petered out, from asphalt to gravel to dirt to nothing. No tomb was in sight, so I approached an old man weeding a vegetable garden behind his house. Tang Yiming, 72, was still lithe and strong. His hair was gray and ragged where he had cut it himself, disastrously, in front of a mirror. Evidently lonely, he was delighted to talk, and offered to show me the path to the tomb. As we walked, I mentioned that I had read that there used to be an old Ming Dynasty tablet on Zheng He's grave.

"Oh, yeah, the old tablet," he said nonchalantly. "When I was a boy, there was a Ming Dynasty tablet here. When it disappeared, the Government offered a huge reward to anyone who would return it—a reward big enough to build a new house. Seemed like a lot of money. But the problem was that we couldn't give it back. People around here are poor. We'd smashed it up to use as building materials."

A second mystery concerned what, if anything, is actually buried in Zheng He's tomb, since he is believed to have died on his last voyage and been buried at sea. So I said in passing that I'd heard tell the tomb is empty, and let my voice trail off.

"Oh, there's nothing in there," Tang said, a bit sadly. "No bones, nothing. That's for sure."

"How do you know?"

"In 1962, people dug up the grave, looking for anything to sell. We dug up the ground to one and a half times the height of a man. But there was absolutely nothing in there. It's empty."

The absence of impressive monuments to Zheng He in China today should probably come as no surprise, since his achievement was ultimately renounced. Curiously, it is not in China but in Indonesia where his memory has been most actively kept alive. Zheng He's expeditions led directly to the wave of Chinese immigration to Southeast Asia, and in some countries he is regarded today as a deity. In the Indonesia city of Semarang, for example, there is a large temple honoring Zheng He, located near a cave where he once nursed a sick friend. Indonesians still pray to Zheng He for a cure or good luck.

Not so in his native land. Zheng He was viewed with deep suspicion by China's traditional elite, the Confucian scholars, who made sure to destroy the archives of his journey. Even so, it is possible to learn something about his story from Chinese sources—from imperial archives and even the memoirs of crewmen. The historical record makes clear, for example, that it was not some sudden impulse of extroversion that led to Zheng He's achievement. It grew, rather, out of a long sailing tradition. Chinese accounts suggest that in the fifth century, a Chinese monk sailed to a mysterious "far east country" that sounds very much like Mayan Mexico, and Mayan art at that time suddenly began to include Buddhist symbols. By the 13th century, Chinese ships regularly traveled to India and occasionally to East Africa.

Zheng He's armada was far grander, of course, than anything that came before. His grandest vessels were the "treasure ships," 400 feet long and 160 feet wide, with nine masts raising red silk sails to the wind, as well as multiple decks and luxury cabins with balconies. His armada included supply ships to carry horses, troop transports, warships, patrol boats and as many as 20 tankers to carry fresh water. The full contingent of 28,000 crew members included interpreters for Arabic and other languages, astrologers to forecast the weather, astronomers to study the stars, pharmacologists to collect medicinal plants, ship-repair specialists, doctors and even two protocol officers to help organize official receptions.

In the aftermath of such an incredible undertaking, you somehow expect to find a deeper mark on Chinese history, a greater legacy. But perhaps the faintness of Zheng He's trace in contemporary China is itself a lesson. In the end, an explorer makes history but does not necessarily change it, for his impact depends less on the trail he blazes than on the willingness of others to follow. The daring of a great expedition ultimately is hostage to the national will of those who remain behind.

IN FEBRUARY I TRAVELED TO CALICUT, A port town in southwestern India that was (and still is) the pepper capital of the world. The evening I arrived, I went down to the beach in the center of town to look at the coastline where Zheng He once had berthed his ships. In the 14th and 15th centuries, Calicut was one of the world's great ports, known to the Chinese as "the great country of the Western ocean." In the early 15th century, the sight of Zheng He's fleet riding anchor in Calicut harbor symbolized the strength of the world's two greatest powers, China and India.

On this sultry evening, the beach, framed by long piers jutting out to sea, was crowded with young lovers and ice-cream vendors. Those piers are all that remain of the port of Calicut, and you can see at a glance that they are no longer usable. The following day I visited the port offices, musty with handwritten ledgers of ship visits dating back nearly a century. The administrator of the port, Captain E. G. Mohanan, explained matter-of-factly what had happened. "The piers got old and no proper maintenance was ever carried out," he said, as a ceiling fan whirred tiredly overhead. "By the time we thought of it, it was not economical to fix it up."

So in 1989, trade was halted, and one of the great ports of the world became no port at all.

The disappearance of a great Chinese fleet from a great Indian port symbolized one of history's biggest lost opportunities—Asia's failure to dominate the second half of this millennium. So how did this happen?

While Zheng He was crossing the Indian Ocean, the Confucian scholar-officials who dominated the upper echelons of the Chinese Government were at political war with the eunuchs, a group they regarded as corrupt and immoral. The eunuchs' role at court involved looking after the concubines, but they also served as palace administrators, often doling out contracts in exchange for kickbacks. Partly as a result of their legendary greed, they promoted com-

The village's inhabitants, much lighter-skinned than people on the Kenyan mainland, emerged barefoot to stare at me with the same curiosity with which I was studying them. These were people I had come halfway around the world to see, in the hope of solving an ancient historical puzzle.

merce. Unlike the scholars—who owed their position to their mastery of 2,000-year-old texts—the eunuchs, lacking any such roots in a classical past, were sometimes outward-looking and progressive. Indeed, one can argue that it was the virtuous, incorruptible scholars who in the mid-15th century set China on its disastrous course.

After the Yongle Emperor died in 1424, China endured a series of brutal power struggles; a successor emperor died under suspicious circumstances and ultimately the scholars emerged trium-

ILLUSTRATION BY DUGALD STERMER

25 feet — ZHENG HE'S TREASURE SHIP 400 FEET LONG — Santa Maria: 85 feet

Zheng He's armada was the largest the world would know for 500 years. The grandest vessels had nine masts and were 400 feet long. By comparison, Columbus's largest ship measured 85 feet.

phant. They ended the voyages of Zheng He's successors, halted construction of new ships and imposed curbs on private shipping. To prevent any backsliding, they destroyed Zheng He's sailing records and, with the backing of the new emperor, set about dismantling China's navy.

By 1500 the Government had made it a capital offense to build a boat with more than two masts, and in 1525 the Government ordered the destruction of all oceangoing ships. The greatest navy in history, which a century earlier had 3,500 ships (by comparison, the United States Navy today has 324), had been extinguished, and China set a course for itself that would lead to poverty, defeat and decline.

Still, it was not the outcome of a single power struggle in the 1440's that cost China its worldly influence. Historians offer a host of reasons for why Asia eventually lost its way economically and was late to industrialize; two and a half reasons seem most convincing.

The first is that Asia was simply not greedy enough. The dominant social ethos in ancient China was Confucianism and in India it was caste, with the result that the elites in both nations looked down their noses at business. Ancient China cared about many things—prestige, honor, culture, arts, education, ancestors, religion, filial piety—but making money came far down the list. Confucius had specifically declared that it was wrong for a man to make a distant voyage while his parents were alive, and he had condemned profit as the concern of "a little man." As it was, Zheng He's ships were built on such a grand scale and carried such lavish gifts to foreign leaders that the voyages were not the huge money spinners they could have been.

In contrast to Asia, Europe was consumed with greed. Portugal led the age of discovery in the 15th century largely because it wanted spices, a precious commodity; it was the hope of profits that drove its ships steadily farther down the African coast and eventually around

the Horn to Asia. The profits of this trade could be vast: Magellan's crew once sold a cargo of 26 tons of cloves for 10,000 times the cost.

A second reason for Asia's economic stagnation is more difficult to articulate but has to do with what might be called a culture of complacency. China and India shared a tendency to look inward, a devotion to past ideals and methods, a respect for authority and a suspicion of new ideas. David S. Landes, a Harvard economist, has written of ancient China's "intellectual xenophobia"; the former Indian Prime Minister Jawaharlal Nehru referred to the "petrification of classes" and the "static nature" of Indian society. These are all different ways of describing the same economic and intellectual complacency.

Chinese elites regarded their country as the "Middle Kingdom" and believed they had nothing to learn from barbarians abroad. India exhibited much of the same self-satisfaction. "Indians didn't go to Portugal not because they couldn't but because they didn't want to," mused M. P. Sridharan, a historian, as we sat talking on the porch of his home in Calicut.

The 15th-century Portuguese were the opposite. Because of its coastline and fishing industry, Portugal always looked to the sea, yet rivalries with Spain and other countries shut it out of the Mediterranean trade. So the only way for Portugal to get at the wealth of the East was by conquering the oceans.

The half reason is simply that China was a single nation while Europe was many. When the Confucian scholars re-asserted control in Beijing and banned shipping, their policy mistake con-demned all of China. In contrast, Euro-pean countries committed economic suicide selectively. So when Portugal slipped into a quasi-Chinese mind-set in the 16th century, slaughtering Jews and burning heretics and driving astrono-mers and scientists abroad, Holland and England were free to take up the slack.

WHEN I FIRST BEGAN RESEARCHING ZHENG He, I never thought I'd be traveling all the way to Africa to look for traces of his voyages. Then I came across a few intriguing references to the possibility of an ancient Chinese shipwreck that might have left some Chinese stranded on the island of Pate (pronounced PAH-tay). One was a skeptical reference in a schol-arly journal, another was a casual con-versation with a Kenyan I met a few years ago and the third was the epilogue of Louise Levathes's wonderful 1994 book about China's maritime adven-tures, "When China Ruled the Seas." Levathes had traveled to Kenya and found people who believed they were descended from survivors of a Chinese shipwreck. So, on a whim and an ex-pense account, I flew to Lamu, an island off northern Kenya, and hired a boat and an interpreter to go to Pate and see for myself.

Pate is off in its own world, without electricity or roads or vehicles. Mostly jungle, it has been shielded from the 20th century largely because it is acces-sible from the Kenyan mainland only by taking a boat through a narrow tidal channel that is passable only at high tide. Initially I was disappointed by what I found there. In the first villages

PHOTOGRAPH BY GUEORGUI PINKHASSOV/MAGNUM, FOR THE NEW YORK TIMES

The keeper of oral traditions, Bwana Mkuu Al-Bauri.

I visited, I saw people who were light-skinned and had hair that was not tightly curled, but they could have been part Arab or European rather than part Chi-nese. The remote villages of Chundwa and Faza were more promising, for there I found people whose eyes, hair and complexion hinted at Asian ancestry, though their background was ambiguous.

And then on a still and sweltering af-ternoon I strolled through the coconut palms into the village of Siyu, where I met a fisherman in his 40's named Ab-dullah Mohammed Badui. I stopped and stared at the man in astonishment, for he had light skin and narrow eyes. For-tunately, he was as rude as I was, and we stared at each other in mutual sur-prise before venturing a word. Eventu-ally I asked him about his background and appearance.

"I am in the Famao clan," he said. "There are 50 or 100 of us Famao left here. Legend has it that we are descend-ed from Chinese and others.

"A Chinese ship was coming along and it hit rocks and wrecked," Badui continued. "The sailors swam ashore to the village that we now call Shanga, and they married the local women, and that is why we Famao look so different."

Another Famao, with the same light complexion and vaguely Asian features,

approached to listen. His name was Ath-man Mohammed Mzee, and he, too, told of hearing of the Chinese shipwreck from the elders. He volunteered an in-triguing detail: the Africans had given giraffes to the Chinese.

Salim Bonaheri, a 55-year-old Famao man I met the next day, proudly de-clared, "My ancestors were Chinese or Vietnamese or something like that." I asked how they had got to Pate.

"I don't know," Bonaheri said with a shrug. Most of my conversations were like that, intriguing but frustrating dead ends. I was surrounded by people whose appearance seemed tantalizingly Asian, but who had only the vaguest notions of why that might be. I kept at it, though, and eventually found people like Khalifa Mohammed Omar, a 55-year-old Famao fisherman who looked somewhat Chi-nese and who also clearly remembered the stories passed down by his grand-father. From him and others, a tale emerged.

Countless generations ago, they said, Chinese sailors traded with local African kings. The local kings gave them gi-raffes to take back to China. One of the Chinese ships struck rocks off the east-ern coast of Pate, and the sailors swam ashore, carrying with them porcelain and other goods from the ship. In time they married local women, converted to Islam and named the village Shanga, af-ter Shanghai. Later, fighting erupted among Pate's clans, Shanga was de-stroyed and the Famao fled, some to the mainland, others to the village of Siyu.

Every time I heard the story about the giraffes my pulse began to race. Chi-nese records indicate that Zheng He had brought the first giraffes to China, a fact that is not widely known. The giraffe caused an enormous stir in China be-cause it was believed to be the mythical *qilin*, or Chinese unicorn. It is difficult to imagine how African villagers on an island as remote as Pate would know about the giraffes unless the tale had been handed down to them by the Chi-nese sailors.

Chinese ceramics are found in many places along the east African coast, and their presence on Pate could be the re-sult of purchases from Arab traders. But the porcelain on Pate was overwhelm-

Westerners often attribute their economic advantage today to the intelligence or hard work of their forebears, but a more important reason may well have been the folly of the 15th-century Chinese rulers who dismantled Zheng He's fleet.

---

ingly concentrated among the Famao clan, which could mean that it had been inherited rather than purchased. I also visited some ancient Famao graves that looked less like traditional Kenyan graves than what the Chinese call "turtle-shell graves," with rounded tops.

Researchers have turned up other equally tantalizing clues. Craftsmen on Pate and the other islands of Lamu practice a kind of basket-weaving that is common in southern China but unknown on the Kenyan mainland. On Pate, drums are more often played in the Chinese than the African style, and the local dialect has a few words that may be Chinese in origin. More startling, in 1569 a Portuguese priest named Monclaro wrote that Pate had a flourishing silk-making industry—Pate, and no other place in the region. Elders in several villages on Pate confirmed to me that their island had produced silk until about half a century ago.

When I asked my boatman, Bakari Muhaji Ali, if he thought it was possible that a ship could have wrecked off the coast near Shanga, he laughed. "There are undersea rocks all over there," he said. "If you don't know exactly where you're going, you'll wreck your ship for sure."

If indeed there was a Chinese shipwreck off Pate, there is reason to think it happened in Zheng He's time. For if the shipwreck had predated him, surviving sailors would not have passed down stories of the giraffes. And if the wreck didn't occur until after Zheng He, its survivors could not have settled in Shanga, since British archeological digs indicate that the village was sacked, burned and abandoned in about 1440—very soon after Zheng He's last voyage.

Still, there is no hard proof for the shipwreck theory, and there are plenty of holes in it. No ancient Chinese characters have been found on tombs in Pate, no nautical instruments have ever turned up on the island and there are no Chinese accounts of an African shipwreck. This last lacuna might be explained by the destruction of the fleet's records. Yet if one of Zheng He's ships did founder on the rocks off Pate, then why didn't some other ships in the fleet come to the sailors' rescue?

AS I MADE MY WAY BACK THROUGH THE jungle for the return trip, I pondered the significance of what I'd seen on Pate. In the faces of the Famao, in those bits of pottery and tantalizing hints of Chinese culture, I felt as though I'd glimpsed the shadowy outlines of one of the greatest might-have-beens of the millennium now ending. I thought about the Columbian Exchange, the swap of animals,

plants, genes, germs, weapons and peoples that utterly remade both the New World and the Old, and I couldn't help wondering about another exchange—Zheng He's—that never took place, yet could have.

If ancient China had been greedier and more outward-looking, if other traders had followed in Zheng He's wake and then continued on, Asia might well have dominated Africa and even Europe. Chinese might have settled in not only Malaysia and Singapore, but also in East Africa, the Pacific Islands, even in America. Perhaps the Famao show us what the mestizos of such a world might have looked liked, the children of a hybrid culture that was never born. What I'd glimpsed in Pate was the high-water mark of an Asian push that simply stopped—not for want of ships or know-how, but strictly for want of national will.

All this might seem fanciful, and yet in Zheng He's time the prospect of a New World settled by the Spanish or English would have seemed infinitely more remote than a New World made by the Chinese. How different would history have been had Zheng He continued on to America? The mind rebels; the ramifications are almost too overwhelming to contemplate. So consider just one: this magazine would have been published in Chinese.

Nicholas D. Kristof is the Tokyo bureau chief of The New York Times. He is the author, with Sheryl WuDunn, of "China Wakes."

Columbus and the Labyrinth of History

Every generation creates the Columbus it needs. As the Quincentenary of his 1492 voyage approaches, observers are torn between celebrating a brave visionary and condemning the first representative of an age of imperial exploitation. Here Pulitzer Prize-winning journalist John Noble Wilford explores the various Columbus legends and discovers, beneath them, a very human figure and an adventure unprecedented in boldness.

John Noble Wilford

John Noble Wilford has been a science correspondent for the New York Times *since 1965. Twice winner of the Pulitzer Prize, Wilford is the author of* The Mapmakers *(1981),* The Riddle of the Dinosaur *(1985),* Mars Beckons *(1990), and* Mysterious History of Columbus *(1991).*

History has not been the same since Christopher Columbus. Neither has he been the same throughout history.

During the five centuries since his epochal voyage of 1492, Columbus has been many things to many people: the protean symbol of the adventuring human spirit, the lone hero defying both the odds and entrenched thinking to change the world; the first modern man or a lucky adventurer blinded by medieval mysticism; an icon of Western faith in progress or an object of scorn for his failings of leadership and intellect; a man virtually deified at one time and roundly vilified today for his part in the initiation of an international slave trade and European imperialism. We hardly know the real Columbus. Such, it seems, is the fate of historical figures whose deeds reverberate through time.

The Columbus story surely confirms the axiom that all works of history are interim reports. What people did in the past is not preserved in amber, a moment captured and immutable through the ages. Each generation looks back and, drawing from its own experiences, presumes to find patterns that illuminate both past and present. This is natural and proper. A succeeding generation can ask questions of the past that those in the past never asked themselves. Columbus could not know that he had ushered in what we call the Age of Discovery, with all its implications, any more than we can know what two world wars, nuclear weapons, the collapse of colonial empires, the end of the Cold War, and the beginning of space travel will mean for people centuries from now. Perceptions change, and so does our understanding of the past.

Accordingly, the image of Columbus has changed through the years, sometimes as a result of new information, more often because of changes in the lenses through which we view him. Once a beneficiary of this phenomenon, Columbus in times of reigning optimism has been exalted as a mythic hero. Now, with the approach of the Quincentennial, he has fallen victim to a more self-critical society, one prone to hero-bashing and historical pessimism.

As recently as 1974, Samuel Eliot Morison, the biographer of Columbus, concluded one of his books with a paean to European influence on America: "To the people of the New World, pagans expecting short and brutish lives, void of hope for any future, had come the Christian vision of a merciful God and a glorious heaven." It is hard to conceive of those words being written today. In a forward to the 1983 edition of Morison's *Admiral of the Ocean Sea: A Life of Christopher Columbus,* British historian David Beers Quinn criticizes Morison for ignoring or dismissing Columbus's failings. Columbus, Quinn writes, "cannot be detached from the imperialist exploitation of his discoveries and must be made to take some share of responsibility for the brutal exploitation of the islands and mainlands he found."

By and large, this new perspective has produced a more realistic, demythologized version of the Columbus story. The temptation, though, is to swing too far in the other direction, rewriting history as we wish it would have been or judging people wholly by anachronistic political standards. This has happened all too often regarding Columbus, producing myth and propaganda in the guise of history.

All the more reason for us to sift through the romantic inventions and enduring misconceptions that have clouded the real Columbus and to recognize that so much of the man we celebrate or condemn is our own creation. He is the embodiment of our running dialogue about the human potential for good and evil.

Some of the facts about Columbus—who he was and what he did—are beyond serious dispute. This mariner of humble and obscure origins was possessed of an idea that became an obsession. He proposed to sail west across the uncharted ocean to the fabled shores of the Indies, the lands of gold and spices celebrated in the tales of Marco Polo and the goal of an increasingly expansionist Europe in the 15th century. The Portuguese had sought a route around the tip of Africa. Some Florentine cosmographers had pondered the prospect of a westward sea route. But Columbus was apparently the first with the stubborn courage to stake his life on the execution of such a daring scheme.

After years pleading his case before the courts of Portugal and Spain, dismissed as a hopeless visionary or a tiresomely boastful nuisance, Columbus finally won the reluctant support of Ferdinand and Isabella. At the little Andalusian port of Palos de la Frontera, he raised a fleet of three ships and enlisted some 90 seamen. Whatever the sailors' trepidations or their opinion of Columbus when he arrived at Palos, their destiny was to share with him a voyage "by which route," Columbus wrote in the prologue to his journal, "we do not know for certain anyone previously has passed."

Columbus was never more in command of himself and his destiny than on

that day, August 3, 1492, when he weighed anchor at Palos. He was a consummate mariner, as all his contemporaries agreed and historians have not contradicted, and here he was doing what he did best and so sure of his success. Of course, he never made it to the Indies, as head-shaking savants had predicted, then or on any of his three subsequent voyages. His landfall came half a world short of them, on an unprepossessing island inhabited by naked people with no knowledge whatsoever of Marco Polo's Great Khan.

On the morning of October 12, Columbus and his captains, together with their most trusted functionaries, clambered into armed launches and headed for the sandy beach and green trees. They carried the flags of the Christian monarchs of Spain. A solemn Columbus, without so much as a thought that it was anything but his to take, proclaimed possession of the island for the king and for the queen. Columbus and his officers then dropped to their knees in prayer.

It did not escape Columbus that these islanders "go around as naked as their mothers bore them; and the women also." This was not prurience but culture shock. Columbus was generally admiring in his initial descriptions of the people. They were "guileless and generous." Bringing cotton, parrots, and javelins to trade, they paddled out to Columbus's ships in their dugouts, each made from a single tree and so long that they held 40 men; the West Indian term for these dugouts was *canoa*—and thus a New-World word entered European speech. Columbus was pleased to note that they had no firearms. When he had shown them some swords, "they took them by the edge and through ignorance cut themselves." "They should be good and intelligent servants," he concluded, "for I see that they say very quickly everything that is said to them; and I believed they would become Christians very easily, for it seemed to me that they had no religion." Columbus the anthropologist had his priorities.

Unfortunately, we have no record of the first impressions that the people Columbus called Indians had of the Europeans. What did they think of these

white men with beards? Their sailing ships and their weapons that belched smoke? Their Christian God and their inordinate interest in gold and a place beyond the horizon called the Indies? We will never know. They could not put their feelings into writing; they had no writing. And the encounter itself doomed them. Within a generation or two, they became extinct, mainly through exposure to European diseases, and so could not pass on by word of mouth stories about the moment white men entered their lives.

Columbus made certain by his words and actions that his discovery would not be lost to history. On the homeward voyage, after visiting a string of other islands and more people, he composed a letter to the court of Ferdinand and Isabella in which he announced his discovery. He had made good his boast to one and all. He may have harbored some disappointment in not reaching the Asian mainland, but he had sailed across the Ocean Sea and found lands and peoples unknown to Europeans. And he wanted the court to read about it in his own words, especially since this justified his own claim to the titles and wealth due him pursuant to the deal he had struck with the court.

The letter Columbus wrote was also his bid for a place in history. He understood that the achievement would go for naught unless the news got back to others. To explore (the word, in one version of its etymology, comes from the Latin "to cry out") is to search out and exclaim discovery. Simply reaching a new land does not in itself constitute a discovery. It must be announced and then recorded in history so that the discovery can be acted upon.

Others besides the indigenous people preceded Columbus in finding parts of America. This is no longer an issue of consuming dispute in Columbian studies. Almost certainly the Norse under Leif Ericson landed at some northern islands and established a short-lived settlement at Newfoundland. Ericson and others may have reached America, but they failed to discover it. For nothing came of their deeds. Columbus, in writing the letter, was making sure his deeds

'Gardens the Most Beautiful I Ever Saw'

The following account of October 10–13, 1492, is taken from Columbus's **Diario,** *as abstracted by Bartolomé de las Casas and adapted by William Carlos Williams.*

Wednesday, 59 leagues, W. S. W., but counted no more than 44. Here the people could endure no longer. All now complained about the length of the voyage. But I cheered them as best I could, giving them good hopes of the advantages they might gain by it. Roused to madness by their fear, the captains declared they were going back but I told them then, that however much they might complain, I had to go to the Indies and they along with me, and that I would go until I found them, with the help of our Lord. And so for a time it passed but now all was in great danger from the men.

Thursday, 11th of October. The course was W. S. W. More sea [spilling over the deck] than there had been during the whole of the voyage. Sandpipers and a green reed near the ship. And for this I gave thanks to God as it was a sure sign of land. Those of the Pinta saw a cane and a pole, and they took up another small pole which appeared to be worked with iron; also another bit of cane, a land plant, and a small board. The crew of the caravel Niña also saw signs of land, and a small plant covered with berries.

. . . I admonished the men to keep a good lookout on the fore-castle and to watch well for land and to him who should first cry out that he had seen land I would give a silk doublet besides the other rewards promised by the Sovereigns which were 10,000 *maravedis* to him who should first see it. Two hours past midnight, the moon having risen at eleven o'clock and then shining brightly in the sky, being in its third quarter, a sailor named Rodrigo de Triana sighted the land at a distance of about two leagues. At once I ordered them to shorten sail and we lay under the mainsail without the bonnets, hove to waiting for daylight.

On Friday, the 12th of October, we anchored before the land and made ready to go on shore. Presently we saw naked people on the beach. I went ashore in the armed boat and took the royal standard, and Martin Alonzo and Vincent Yañez, his brother, who was captain of the *Niña*. And we saw the trees very green, and much water and fruits of diverse kinds. Presently many of the inhabitants assembled. I gave to some red caps and glass beads to put round their necks, and many other things of little value. They came to the ship's boats afterward, where we were, swimming and bringing us parrots, cotton threads in skeins, darts—what they had, with good will. As naked as their mothers bore them, and so the women, though I did not see more than one young girl. All I saw were youths, well made with very handsome bodies and very good countenances. Their hair short and coarse, almost like the hairs of a horse's tail. They paint themselves some black, some white, others red and others of what color they can find. Some paint the faces and others paint the whole body, some only round the eyes and others only on the nose. They are themselves neither black nor white.

On Saturday, as dawn broke, many of these people came to the beach, all youths. Their legs are very straight, all in one line, and no belly. They came to the ship in canoes, made out of the trunk of a tree, all in one piece, and wonderfully worked, propelled with a paddle like a baker's shovel, and go at marvelous speed.

Illustration from the Granger Collection, New York

Bright green trees, the whole land so green that it is a pleasure to look on it. Gardens of the most beautiful trees I ever saw. Later I came upon one man in a canoe going from one island to another. He had a little of their bread, about the size of a fist, a calabash of water, a piece of brown earth, powdered then kneaded, and some dried leaves which must be a thing highly valued by them for they bartered with it at San Salvador. He also had with him a native basket. The women wore in front of their bodies a small piece of cotton cloth. I saw many trees very unlike those of our country. Branches growing in different ways and all from one trunk; one twig is one form and another is a different shape and so unlike that it is the greatest wonder of the world to see the diversity; thus one branch has leaves like those of a cane, and others like those of a mastic tree; and on a single tree there are five different kinds. The fish so unlike ours that it is wonderful. Some are the shape of dories and of the finest colors, so bright that there is not a man who would not be astounded, and would not take great delight in seeing them. There are also whales. I saw no beasts on land save parrots and lizards.

On shore I sent the people for water, some with arms, and others with casks; and as it was some little distance I waited two hours for them.

During that time I walked among the trees, which was the most beautiful thing which I had ever seen. . . .

would have consequences and his achievement would enter history.

The letter eventually reached the court in Barcelona and had the desired effect. The king and queen received Columbus with pomp and listened to his story with genuine interest and pleasure. They instructed him to return to the new-found lands with a larger fleet including soldiers and settlers. America had entered world history, though Columbus insisted to his dying day that he had reached the Indies.

This familiar story of Columbus has been embellished to create an enduring popular legend. Some of the tales (though not all of them) have been laid to rest through historical research.

Columbus did not, for example, have to prove that the world was round: All educated people in Europe at the time accepted this as a given. Isabella did not have to pawn her jewels to raise money for the expedition; though the Crown, following its wars against the Moors, was strapped for cash, the financial adviser Luis de Santangel arranged a loan from the ample coffers of the state police and from some Italian merchant bankers. And Columbus did not set sail with a crew of hardened criminals. Only four men, accused of murdering a town crier, took advantage of a promised amnesty, and even they were seasoned mariners and acquitted themselves well on the voyage.

More troublesome for historians have been certain other mysteries and controversies.

Where, for example, did the first landfall occur? We know it was a small island the inhabitants called Guanahani and Columbus christened San Salvador. It was in the Bahamas or thereabouts, far from the Asian mainland he was seeking, but which island? No fewer than nine different possible islands have been identified from the few ambiguous clues in Columbus's journal. The site favored by most experts is the Bahamian island once called Watling's but renamed San Salvador in 1924 to help solidify its claim.

Did Columbus really come from Genoa? Nearly every European nation has at one time or another laid some claim to him. Was he Jewish? Such conjecture originated in the 19th century and was promoted in 1940 in Salvadore de Madriaga's vivid biography, *Christopher Columbus*. But the evidence is circumstantial. Records in Genoa indicate that, whatever his more remote ancestry, Columbus's family had been Christian for several generations.

When and how in the mists of his rootless life did Columbus conceive of his audacious plan? Was it sheer inspiration bolstered by rational research? Or did he come into some secret knowledge? Was he really seeking the Indies? How was he finally able to win royal backing? What were his ships like?—no caravel wreck from that period has ever been recovered. Scholars and amateur sleuths have spent lifetimes trying to resolve these questions, usually without notable success.

Part of the problem lies with the passage of time. Although the record of Columbus by contemporaries is more substantial than that of any other 15th-century explorer, surviving accounts are often difficult to assess from this distance. Whose version is to be trusted: The letters of Peter Martyr, the courtier in Spain who never ventured to the New World? The biography by Hernando Columbus, the devoted son protective of his father's fame? The history of the New World by Bartolomé de las Casas (1474–1566), the Dominican friar and champion of the Indians who never missed a chance to condemn the brutality of the early explorers and colonists? Even the few extant writings of Columbus himself, who could be vague, contradictory and self-serving?

Hero worship has further distorted history. We want—or used to want—our heroes to be larger than life. The result can be a caricature, a plaster saint inviting iconoclasts to step forward with their own images, which can also ignore the complexity of human reality.

We are left, therefore, with enough material to mold the Columbus we choose to extol or excoriate, but not enough ever to feel sure we truly know the man.

Nothing better illustrates history's changing images of Columbus than the succession of portraits of him that have appeared over the centuries. They show a man of many faces—handsome and stalwart, heavy and stolid, shadowed and vaguely sinister. Artistic interpretation, like history, changes with the times.

Yet, there should be little confusion over the man's physical appearance. His son Hernando, who should have known, said he was "a well-built man of more than average stature, the face long, the cheeks somewhat high, his body neither fat nor lean. He had an aquiline nose and light colored eyes; his complexion too was light and tending to be red. In youth his hair was blond, but when he reached the age of 30 it all turned white."

The son went on to describe his father's character: "In eating and drinking, and in the adornment of his person, he was very moderate and modest," Hernando wrote. "He was affable in conversation with strangers and very pleasant to the members of his household, though with a certain gravity. He was so strict in matters of religion that for fasting and saying prayers he might have been taken for a member of a religious order."

Hernando may be guilty of some exaggeration. Columbus could not be too gentle and modest if he were to promote his vision before skeptical courts and if he could control a crew of rough seamen who suspected they might be headed to their deaths. He could be harsh in meting out punishment to seamen and in ordering punitive raids against Indian villages. Like others of that time, and to this day, he presumably saw no contradiction between his behavior and his religious beliefs. By all accounts Columbus was a demonstrably pious man. Late in life, his writings portrayed a mind filled with mysticism and a belief in his divine mission to carry Christianity to all people and prepare them for the impending end of the world.

Of this mysticism, Hernando has nothing to say. He is also frustratingly reticent or misleading about the genesis of his father's consuming dream and even about his origins. Columbus himself chose to reveal very little about his early life.

Every verifiable historical document, however, indicates that Columbus was born in Genoa, which was an independent city-state (the lesser rival to Venice) whose ships traded throughout the entire Mediterranean world. He was probably born in 1451, and both his father Domenico and his father's father were wool weavers; his mother, Susanna Fontanarossa, was a weaver's daughter. Christopher was probably their eldest child. Bartholomew, the chart-maker who would share many of Columbus's adventures, was a year or two younger. The other children who grew to adulthood were a sister named Bianchetta and a brother Giacomo, better known by the Spanish equivalent, Diego, who joined Christopher on the second voyage. All in all, the Columbuses of Genoa were fruitful and humble tradespeople—and nothing for a young man to be ashamed of.

At a "tender age," as Columbus once wrote, he cast his lot with those who go to sea. At first, he probably made short voyages as a crewman, and then longer ones on trading ships to the Genoese colony of Chios in the Aegean Sea. But even more crucial to Columbus's development than his ancestry or his birthplace was the timing of his birth. He was born two years before the fall of Constantinople, Christendom's eastern capital, to the Ottoman Turks in 1453. Young Columbus was to grow up hearing about the scourge of Islam, the blockage of regular trade routes to the spices of the East, and the parlous times for Christianity. Priests and popes were calling for a new crusade to recapture Constantinople and Jerusalem. All of this could have nourished the dreams of a great adventure in an ambitious young man with nautical experience.

The most significant mystery about Columbus concerns how he came up with his idea for sailing west to the Indies. As in everything else, Columbus's own words on the subject obfuscate more than elucidate. It was his practice, writes the Italian historian Paolo Emilio Taviani, "never to tell everything to everyone, to say one thing to one man, something else to another, to reveal only portions of his arguments, clues, and evidence accumulated over the years in his mind." Perhaps Columbus told so many partial stories in so many different versions that, as Morison suspects, he himself could no longer remember the origins of his idea.

In all probability he formulated the idea in Portugal sometime between 1476 and 1481. Columbus had come to Portugal quite literally by accident. When the Genoese fleet he had shipped with was attacked and destroyed in the summer of 1476, Columbus was washed ashore at the Portuguese town of Lagos. He made his way to Lisbon, where the talk of seagoing exploration was everywhere. He heard stories of westering seamen who found islands far out in the ocean and saw maps sprinkled with mythical islands. On voyages north perhaps so far as Iceland and south along the coast of Africa, he gained a taste for Atlantic sailing. There may even be something to the story of the unknown pilot from whom Columbus supposedly obtained secret knowledge of lands across the ocean. But as far as anyone can be sure—and volumes have been written on the subject—there was no sudden revelation, no blinding flash of inspiration.

Nor did Columbus derive his plan from a careful reading of scholars. He was not then, and never became, a man who read to learn; he read to gather support for what he already thought to be true. His familiarity with the travel accounts of Marco Polo and the *Travels of Sir John Mandeville,* a 14th-century collection of travelers' tales from around the world, did not so much inform his concept as inflame a mind already stoked with the dry tinder of desire. From other sources—from a recent Latin translation of Claudius Ptolemy's second-century *Geography,* which described many Southeast Asian spice islands, to Pierre d'Ailly's *Imago Mundi,* a compendium of contemporary knowledge about the world which argued that the Western Sea was not very wide—Columbus made some calculations of global distances. Like d'Ailly, he conveniently managed to constrict the unknown he proposed to challenge, grossly underestimating the distance from Europe to Japan. Had he unwittingly deceived himself? Or had he deliberately contrived calculations to deceive those he looked to for support? All that can be said with assurance is that Columbus was by then a man consumed by an enthusiasm that willed away obstacles and brooked no doubt.

His marriage in Portugal may have indirectly contributed to his growing conviction. In 1479, he wed Felipa Perestrello de Moniz, a daughter of lesser nobility. Her widowed mother showed Columbus the journals and maps left by her husband, who had sailed for Prince Henry the Navigator. From the papers of Bartolomeo Perestrello and other Portuguese seamen, Columbus concluded, his son Hernando wrote, "for certain that there were many lands West of the Canary Islands and Cape Verde, and that it was possible to sail to, and discover them." The social position of his wife's family also smoothed the way for Columbus's introduction to the court of Portugal's King John II.

When Columbus finally laid out his plan before John II, probably in 1483 or 1484, the court cosmographers, a Portuguese historian wrote, "considered the words of Christovae Colom as vain, simply founded on imagination, or things like that Isle Cypango of Marco Polo."

Columbus refused to accept rejection. By this time, his wife had died, and in 1485 he took their son, Diego, and left Portugal for Palos, across the border in Spain. Tradition has it that Columbus and little Diego, penniless and hungry, got off the ship and trudged along a dusty road to the Franciscan monastery of La Rabida. He knocked at the portal to beg for water and bread. If the legend is true, the father may have been taking the son there to be a boarding student, freeing himself to pursue his dream.

Though a secretive man and often portrayed as a loner, Columbus must not have been without charm, even charisma. He had insinuated himself into the influential society of Lisbon and would do so again in Spain. "Columbus's ability to thrust himself into the circles of the great was one of the most remarkable things about him," writes Harvard historian John H. Parry. It was also in his character that he seldom acknowledged the help of others.

At La Rabida, Columbus won the friendship and confidence of a Franciscan official knowledgeable in cosmography and through him gained introductions to wealthy patrons and eventually his first audience with Ferdinand and Isabella. They referred his proposal to a commission of learned men at the University of Salamanca. Washington Irving, in his fanciful biography, has the commissioners saying that the "rotundity of the earth was as yet a matter of mere speculation." Many of them no doubt deserved Irving's condemnation as a "mass of inert bigotry," but they were right (and Columbus wrong) in their judgment that Asia could not be reached by ships sailing west. They recommended that the monarchs reject the venture.

Columbus was nothing if not persistent. With a modest retainer from the court, he continued to solicit support from influential courtiers. While in Cordoba, waiting for some sign of royal encouragement, he met Beatriz Enriquez de Arana, a peasant woman, and they became lovers. In August 1488 she gave birth to an illegitimate son, Hernando. (They never married, and sometime after his first voyage, they drifted apart. He likely felt a peasant woman was beneath his station.)

Through another friar at La Rabida, Columbus gained other audiences with the monarchs in 1491 and again in early 1492, just after the Moorish capital of Granada fell to the Christian forces. He had been led to believe that, after the burden of the prolonged war was lifted, the queen especially might be disposed to give her approval. Some writers have let themselves imagine that Isabella saw more in Columbus than an insistent supplicant. Such speculation of a sexual relationship between the two, Taviani says, is "a sheer fairy-tale, rejected by all historians."

Nothing seemed to change with the fall of Granada. Columbus was turned away, this time with an air of finality. Behind the scenes, however, Luis de Santangel, the chief financial adviser, interceded with assurances to the queen that financing the expedition need not be an insurmountable obstacle. No one

knows why the king and queen finally relented. They might have been persuaded by the argument that they had little to lose and much to gain if this importunate foreigner just happened to be on to something.

After his first voyage, when he was the toast of Barcelona, Columbus supposedly faced down his first critics. At a banquet, some noblemen insisted that if Columbus had not undertaken the enterprise, someone else, a Spaniard and not a foreigner, would have made the same discovery. At this, Columbus called for an egg and had it placed on the table. "Gentlemen," he was reported to have said, pointing to the egg, "you make it stand here, not with crumbs, salt, etc. (for anyone knows how to do it with meal or sand), but naked and without anything at all, as I will, who was the first to discover the Indies." When it was Columbus's turn, he crushed one end of the egg and had no trouble making it stand up on the table.

The anecdote has proved irresistible to historians and storytellers to illustrate the singular role of Columbus in history. But it never happened—one more Columbian myth. The story was not only apocryphal, Morison points out, but it "had already done duty in several Italian biographies of other characters."

In reality, Columbus would not so easily put down the critics who dogged him the rest of his life—and through history. If only he had stopped with the first voyage, the echo of those fanfares in Barcelona might not have faded so fast.

A fleet of 17 ships, carrying some 1,200 people, left Cadiz in the autumn of 1493 with instructions to establish a permanent settlement on the island of Hispaniola. There, near the present city of Puerto Plata in the Dominican Republic, Columbus built a fort, church, and house for what would be his colonial capital, La Isabela. The experiment was disastrous. The site had no real harbor, insufficient rainfall, and little vegetation. Sickness and dissension brought work to a standstill and the colony to the point of starvation. Expeditions into the mountains failed to find any rich

lodes of gold. As Las Casas wrote, they "spread terror among the Indians in order to show them how strong and powerful the Christians were." Bloody warfare ensued.

With little gold to show for his efforts, Columbus ordered a shipment of Taino Indians to be sold as slaves in Spain. The best that can be said in defense of Columbus is that he was now a desperate man. His power to rule La Isabela was waning. His visions of wealth were fading. He feared that his influence back in Spain would be irreparably diminished by critical reports from recalcitrant officers who had returned to Spain. And he had failed again to find a mainland. His desperation was such that he forced all his crew to sign a declaration that, at Cuba, they had indeed reached the mainland of Cathay. Sick and discouraged, he sailed home in 1496.

The third voyage did nothing to restore his reputation. Departing from Seville in May 1498, he steered a southerly course and reached an island off the northeastern coast of South America, which he named Trinidad, for the Holy Trinity. A few days later, he saw a coastline to the south. Columbus recognized that the tremendous volume of fresh water flowing from the Orinoco River was evidence of a large land, but he failed to appreciate that this might be a continent or to pursue his investigations. Instead, his mind drifted into speculation that the river must originate in the Earthly Paradise. Bound to medieval thinking, the man who showed the way across the ocean lost his chance to have the New World bear his name. The honor would soon go to a man with a more open-minded perspective, Amerigo Vespucci, who on his second voyage of exploration (1501–2) concluded that the South American landmass was not Asia but a new continent.

Columbus turned his back on South America and sailed to Santo Domingo to attend to the colony there. He found that his brothers, Bartholomew and Diego, had lost control. Some of the colonists had mutinied, and the crown had dispatched a new governor empowered to do anything necessary to restore order. It was then that Columbus was ar-

Illustration from the Granger
Collection, New York

Columbus disgraced, 1500. Charged with malfeasance as governor of Hispaniola, Columbus returned to Spain a prisoner in chains.

rested, stripped of his titles, and sent back in irons to Spain in October 1500.

It was an ignominious end to Columbus's authority and to his fame in his lifetime. The crown eventually restored his titles, but never again was he allowed to serve as viceroy. The monarchs now were under no illusions about Columbus. He had failed as a colonial administrator, and they had strong doubts about the validity of his claims to have reached the Indies.

Columbus was given permission for one final voyage, which lasted from 1502 to 1504. He was specifically barred from returning to Santo Domingo. Instead, he explored the coast of Central America and attempted without success to establish a settlement in Panama.

Historians cite the last voyage as one of his many "missed opportunities." With luck and more persistence, Columbus might have stumbled upon the Maya civilization or the Pacific Ocean. As it was, he barely made it back to Spain. He was marooned a year on Jamaica, where he wrote a pathetic letter to the monarchs. "I implore Your Highnesses' pardon," he wrote. "I am ruined as I have said. Hitherto I have wept for others; now have pity upon me, Heaven, and weep for me, earth! I came to Your Highnesses with honest purpose and sin-

cere zeal, and I do not lie. I humbly beg Your Highnesses that, if it please God to remove me hence, you will aid me to go to Rome and on other pilgrimages."

Columbus in his last years was a dispirited man who felt himself to be misunderstood and unappreciated. He sought to define himself in a remarkable manuscript now known as *Libro de las profecías,* or *The Book of Prophecies.* Between the third and fourth voyages, Columbus collected passages of biblical scriptures and the words of a wide range of classical and medieval authors. According to his own description, this was a notebook "of sources, statements, opinions and prophecies on the subject of the recovery of God's Holy City and Mount Zion, and on the discovery and evangelization of the islands of the Indies and of all other peoples and nations."

The document reveals the depth and passion of Columbus's belief that he had a special relationship with God and was acting as the agent of God's scheme for history. He marshaled evidence from the prophecies of the Bible to show that his recent discoveries were only the prelude to the realization of a greater destiny. It was as if he saw his role as being not unlike John the Baptist's in relation to

Christ. The wealth from his voyages and discoveries had given the king and queen of Spain the means to recover the Holy Land for Christendom, and thereby he had set the stage for the grandiose climax of Christian history, the salvation of all the world's peoples and their gathering at Zion on the eve of the end of time.

Most historians who studied the document have tended to dismiss it as the product of his troubled and possibly senile mind. His other writings at the time sometimes betrayed a mind verging on paranoia. Delno C. West, a historian who has recently translated the *Book of Prophecies,* suspects that historians were "reluctant to admit that the first American hero was influenced by prophetic ideas." If the book indeed reflects Columbus's thinking even before 1492, it undermines the popular image of Columbus as a man of the modern age who applied reason in conceiving his venture. It exposes him as a person thoroughly mired in the medieval world, obsessed with eschatology, and driven by a supposed call from God to carry out a mission of apocalyptic dimensions.

West contends that this spirituality, which fed Columbus's apocalyptic view of history, lay at the heart of the man and shaped his actions. Rather than some map or unknown pilot's tale, this may have been the "secret knowledge" that inspired Columbus. Certainly, without his unwavering belief in himself and his destiny, Columbus might not have sustained the single-minded persistence it took to win support for the enterprise and to see it through. "The Lord purposed that there should be something clearly miraculous in this matter of the voyage to the Indies," Columbus wrote in the *Prophecies,* "so as to encourage me and others in the . . . Household of God." Beginning in 1493, he began signing nearly all of his letters and documents *Christoferens,* a Latinization of his given name that means "Christbearer."

New attention to the spiritual side of Columbus does not, however, necessarily bring this complex man into focus. Images of a superstitious spiritualist and the modern explorer must be superimposed to produce a stereoscopic picture of Columbus, revealing the depth and

Columbus's Mysterious Signature

In 1498, Columbus instructed all of his heirs to continue to "sign with my signature which I now employ which is an X with an S over it and an M with a Roman A over it and over them an S and then a Greek Y with an S over it, preserving the relation of the lines and the points." At the top, thus, is the letter S between two dots. On the palindromic second row are the letter S A S, also preceded, separated, and ended with dots. The third row has the letters X M and a Greek Y, without dots. Below that is the final signature, Xpo Ferens, a Greco-Latin form of his given name.

To this day no one can decipher the meaning Columbus had in mind, but it almost certainly bears on his religious outlook. The simplest explanations hold that the letters stand for seven words. It has been suggested that the four letters stand for "Servus Sum Altissimi Salvatoris," for "Servant I Am of the Most High Savior." The three letters of the third line could be an invocation to Christ Jesus and Mary, or to Christ, Mary, and Joseph. Another proposed solution is that the seven letters are the initials for "Spiritus Sanctus Altissimi Salvator Xristus Maria Yesus."

John Fleming, a medievalist at Princeton University, believes he has cracked the code, finding it to be an "acrostic of considerable complexity committed to a more or less learned and hermetic mystical theology." Columbus, he concludes, was borrowing from two medieval traditions in formal signatures, that of the church worthies, like St. Francis, who devised intricate crucigrams, and that of the church mariners who often included in their craft marks anchors, masts, fishhooks, and so forth. For his signature, Fleming says, Columbus seems to have combined religious

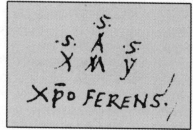

Reproduction from the collection of the Library of Congress

and nautical symbolism. The unifying idea is the medieval association of the Virgin Mary with Stella Maris, the indispensable navigational star also known as Polaris, or the North Star. The first cross bar stands for StellA MariS. The vertical "mast" stands for "Stella Ave Maris," after the vesper hymn *Ave, stella maris.* By design, the structure represents both a Christian cross and a ship's mast. The line X M Y may have one meaning, *"Jesus cum Maris sit nobis in via"* (an invocation with

which Columbus opened much of his writing), with the Y representing the fork in the road and the symbolism for his having chosen the hard way to destiny's fulfillment. Fleming suggests a double meaning. The X and Y at either end of the bottom line could also stand for "Christophorus," his name and destiny, and "Jacobus," for "St. James," whose feast day and Christopher's are the same and who is, not incidentally, the patron saint of Spain, Santiago—Sant Yago.

Fleming's cryptographic skills have uncovered other clues in the signature to Columbus's "religious imagination." But, for understanding Columbus the mystical discoverer, Fleming draws insight from his associations with Mary, Christopher, and Santiago. He writes: "In Columbus's heavenly city, the Virgin Mary stands ever firm between her two Christ-bearing guards, Christophorus on the one hand, San Yago the Moorslayer on the other. And in the larger meaning of these two saints, both celebrated by the Roman church on a single day, which was of course Columbus's nameday, we may see adumbrated much of the glory, and much of the tragedy, of the European encounter with the New World."

heights of the mental terrain through which he traveled as he found America and then lost his way in failure, self-pity, and a fog of mysticism.

Columbus was probably no more than 55 years old when he died on May 20, 1506, in Valladolid, Spain. But he was much older in body and in tormented mind. His last voyages had left him crippled with arthritis and weak from fever. He was reduced to a sad figure, spending his last years in disgrace while stubbornly pressing his claims for the restoration of titles and the wealth due him.

Contrary to legend, he was neither destitute nor alone at the end. His two sons were with him, in a comfortable home. We cannot be sure of the traditional story, that he died believing he had reached the Indies. He never gave explicit expression to any recognition that he had found something other than Asia. All the evidence, though, suggests that he died unsatisfied.

His death went unheralded. There was no public ceremony of mourning and no recorded expressions of grief at the royal court. The man who rose from obscurity died in obscurity. His remains have been moved so many times over the centuries, from Spain to the New World and presumably back again, that no one is sure of his final resting place.

In the first century after his voyages, Columbus languished in the backwaters of history. His reputation suffered from his many failures as a colonial governor. The 1519–1522 Magellan circumnavigation left no doubt about the magnitude of Columbus's error in thinking he had reached the Indies. Conquering explorers such as Cortes and Pizarro won greater immediate fame by their dazzling exploits against the Aztecs and Incas. Cartographers saw fit to name the New World after Vespucci, not Columbus. Books of general history scarcely mentioned Columbus or ignored him altogether.

Within 50 years of Columbus's death, Bartolomé de las Casas, the Dominican bishop who extolled and defended the Indians, produced the first revisionist history. In his *History of the Indies,* Las Casas wrote eloquently of the atrocities committed against the Indians. To sail to the islands Columbus had discovered, Las Casas wrote, one needed only to follow the floating corpses of Indians that marked the way. His accounts of torture and killings documented the so-called

Black Legend of Spanish cruelty that was seized upon by the English, Dutch, and French to fan the fires of national rivalries and religious hatreds.

As the Age of Discovery flourished during the late 16th century, Columbus began to be rescued from oblivion. He was celebrated in poetry and plays, especially in Italy and later in Spain. A glimmer of history's future hero could be seen in a popular play by Lope de Vega in 1614. In *The New World Discovered by Christopher Columbus,* he portrayed Columbus as a dreamer up against the establishment, a man of singular purpose who triumphed, the embodiment of that spirit driving humans to explore and discover.

It was in the New World, though, that Columbus would be transformed almost beyond human recognition into an icon.

By the late 17th century, people in the British colonies of North America were beginning to think of themselves as Americans and sought to define themselves in their own terms and symbols. Samuel Sewell, a Boston judge, suggested that the new lands should rightfully be named for Columbus, "the magnanimous hero . . . who was manifestly appointed by God to be the Finder out of these lands." The idea took root. In time, writers and orators used the name "Columbia" as a poetic name for America. Joel Barlow's poem *The Vision of Columbus,* appearing in 1787, has an aged Columbus lamenting his fate until he is visited by an angel who transports him to the New World to see what his discovery had brought to pass. There he could glimpse the "fruits of his cares and children of his toil."

Indeed, the young republic was busy planning the 300th anniversary of the landfall, in October 1792, when it named its new national capital the District of Columbia—perhaps to appease those who demanded that the entire country be designated Columbia. Next to George Washington, Columbus was the nation's most exalted hero. In him the new nation without its own history and mythology found a hero from the distant past, one seemingly free of association with the European colonial powers and Old-World tyranny. Americans invoked Columbus, the solitary individual who had challenged the unknown, as they contemplated the dangers and promise of their own wilderness frontier. "Instead of ravaging the newly found countries," Washington Irving wrote in his 1828 biography, Columbus "sought to colonize and cultivate them, to civilize the natives."

This would be the Columbus Americans knew and honored throughout the 19th and into the present century. With the influx of millions of immigrants after the Civil War, he was even made to assume the role of ethnic hero. In response to adverse Protestant attitudes and to affirm their own Americanism, Irish Catholic immigrants organized the Knights of Columbus in 1882. The fraternity's literature described Columbus as "a prophet and a seer" and an inspiration to each knight to become "a better Catholic and a better citizen." Catholics in both America and Europe launched a campaign to canonize Columbus on the grounds that he had brought the "Christian faith to half the world." The movement failed not because of Columbus's brutal treatment of Indians but mainly because of the son he had sired out of wedlock.

Columbus's reputation was never higher than on the 400th anniversary of his first voyage. There were parades and fireworks, the naming of streets and dedicating of monuments. The World's Columbian Exposition in Chicago, with its lavish displays of modern technology, was less a commemoration of the past than the self-confident celebration of a future that Americans were eager to shape and enjoy. Americans ascribed to Columbus all the human virtues that were most prized in that time of geographic and industrial expansion, heady optimism, and unquestioning belief in progress. A century before, Columbus had been the symbol of American promise; now he was the symbol of American success.

The 20th century has dispelled much of that. We have a new Columbus for a new age. He is the creation of generations that have known devastating world wars, the struggle against imperialism, and economic expansion that ravages nature without necessarily satisfying basic human needs. In this view, the Age of Discovery initiated by Columbus was not the bright dawning of a glorious epoch but an invasion, a conquest and Columbus himself less a symbol of progress than of oppression.

Columbus scholarship has changed. More historians are writing books from the standpoint of the Indians. They are examining the consequences—the exchange of plants and animals between continents, the spread of deadly diseases, the swift decline of the indigenous Americans in the face of European inroads. The Quincentennial happens to come at a time of bitter debate among Americans over racism, sexism, imperialism, Eurocentrism, and other "isms." Kirkpatrick Sale's 1990 book about Columbus said it all in its title, *The Conquest of Paradise.*

Was Columbus a great man, or merely an agent of a great accomplishment, or perhaps not a very admirable man at all? His standing in history has varied whenever posterity reevaluated the consequences of Europe's discovery of America. Ultimately, Columbus's reputation in history is judged in relation to the place that is accorded America in history.

Europeans took a long time appreciating their discovery. Columbus and succeeding explorers looked upon the islands and mainland as an inconvenience, the barrier standing in their way to Asia that must be breached or circumnavigated.

As early as Peter Martyr, Europeans tried to assimilate the new lands into what they already knew or thought, rejecting the utter newness of the discovery. This was, after all, during the Renaissance, a period of rediscovering the past while reaching out to new horizons. And so the peoples of the New World were described in terms of the Renaissance-ancient image of the "noble savage," living in what classical writers had described as the innocent "Golden Age." The inhabitants of the New World, Martyr wrote, "seem to live in that golden world of which old writers speak so much, wherein men lived simply and innocently without enforcement of laws, without quarreling, judges and libels, content only to satisfy nature, without further vexation for knowledge of things to come."

1991: Cerebration, Not Celebration

It was in 1982 that I first became aware that the 500th anniversary of Columbus's 1492 Voyage of Discovery was a minefield, where the prudent celebrant stepped lightly and guardedly.

To my long-time friend Ramon, in an institute attached to the foreign ministry in Madrid, I said on the telephone one day that year, "Ramon, here at Florida we're beginning to get interested in the Columbus Discovery Quincentenary."

"Why do you say Columbus?" he responded. "He was an Italian mercenary. It was Spain that discovered America, not Columbus."

"But, Ramon," I protested, "we can't celebrate 1492 in the United States without mentioning Columbus."

"In your country," he lectured me, "Columbus Day is an Italian holiday. But the ships, the crews, the money were all Spanish. Columbus was a hired hand."

"But—"

"So when Cape Canaveral space center holds its 100th anniversary, are you going to call it the Werner von Braun celebration?"

I was grateful to Ramon for alerting me, in his way, to the sensitive character of this anniversary. Soon afterwards I learned that "Discovery," too, is a term freighted with ethnic and cultural contentions, as many descendants of the native peoples in the Americas argue against its Eurocentric and paternalistic coloring. "We were already here," they reminded me. And they were here so long ago, 10 to 25,000 years the anthropologists say. I was left to wonder, which was the Old World and which was the New?

As the past ten years have shown, the Spanish-Italian tension has softened, but the European-Native American disjunction has hardened, as historians, epidemiologists, moralists, romanticists, and native spokespersons have clashed over the benefits, if any, that European entrance onto the American stage brought the societies of both worlds, particularly this one.

Certainly huge numbers of indigenous people died as a result of the collision: some, it is true, from the sword, but by far the majority from the Europeans' unwitting introduction of pathogens—smallpox, measles, tuberculosis, the plague—to which the native peoples had no immunities. Recognizing the dimensions of that calamity, many Westerners acknowledge that there is little to celebrate. In Spain, where a 500th Year Worlds' Fair will open in Seville, many of that country's intellectuals are decrying what they call a 15th- and 16th-century *genocidio*.

In the margins of the debate, native descendants and their advocates are publicizing a long list of grievances against the Caucasians who abused their liberties, expropriated their lands, and despoiled an environmental paradise. On July 17–21, 1990, some 400 Indian people, including a delegation from the United States, met in Quito, Ecuador, to plan public protests against 500 years of European "invasion" and "oppression." Even before that, the first sign of reaction in the United States had already come when, in December 1989, representatives of the American Indian Movement, supported by a group of university students, began picketing the "First Encounters" archaeology exhibition mounted by the Florida Museum of Natural History as it traveled from Gainesville to Tampa, Atlanta, and Dallas. (In Tampa, their presence was welcomed because it boosted paid attendance.) In 1992, a loose confederation of North American Indian groups will picket in all U.S. cities where the Columbus replica ships will dock. They seek, one of their leaders told me, "not confrontation but media attention to present-day Native American problems."

African Americans also remind their fellow citizens that the events of 1492 and afterwards gave rise to the slave trade. And Jews appropriately notice that 1492 was the year when they were forcibly expelled from their Spanish homeland. In a counter-counteraction in all this Quincentenary skirmishing, however, the National Endowment for the Humanities decided not to fund a proposed television documentary about the early contact period because, reportedly, it was too biased against the Europeans. (Spain, by contrast, is acting uncommonly large-minded: It has agreed to fund the Smithsonian-Carlos Fuentes television production, "The Buried Mirror," a show that is highly critical of Spain's colonial practices.)

It is this "politically correct" dynamic that, most likely, will keep 1992 from being quite the exuberant and careless celebration that the Bicentennial was in 1976. Anglo-Saxon and Celtic Americans felt comfortable with the Bicentennial because it reinforced their ethnic and cultural givens (Plymouth Rock, Virginia, Washington, Jefferson, the English language, Northern European immigration, etc.). Today, nervous about what is happening to "their" country and learning that citizens of Hispanic origins are projected soon to be the largest U.S. minority, the old line white majority may not be enthusiastic about celebrating the 500th coming of the Hispanics—especially since they sense no continuing need for Columbus as a unifying principle or symbol.

What is likely to happen in 1992? Occasional public celebrations and observances will be produced by civic, ethnic, and cultural bodies. Reproductions of Columbus's ships will arrive in various ports from Spain. Tall ships may parade in New York harbor. Fireworks will explode here and there. People will view two television mini-series and read countless ambivalent newspaper stories.

The Federal Quincentenary Jubilee Commission that was appointed to superintend our exultations is in disarray, its chairman forced out on a charge of mishandling funds, its coffers empty of federal dollars, its principal private donor, Texaco, pulling the plug. Some states, and numerous individual cities (especially those named after Columbus, 63 at last count), have plans for observances, large or small. Florida which has the best reasons, geographically and temporally, to do something, has no state-wide plans, two commissions having collapsed and a third now being stripped of its funds.

But now the good news: In anticipation of the 500th anniversary an enormous amount of intellectual activity has occurred, in the form of archival discoveries, archaeological excavations, museum and library exhibitions, conferences, and publications. Some 30 new and upcoming adult titles have been enumerated by *Publishers Weekly*. Over 100 exhibitions and conferences have been counted by the National Endowment for the Humanities. This remarkable efflorescence of original research and scholarship will leave a lasting legacy of understanding and good. On the twin principles that cerebration is more valuable than celebration and that correcting one paragraph in our children's schoolbooks is worth more than a half-million dollars worth of fireworks exploded over Biscayne Bay, 1992 should be the best 1492 anniversary ever.

—Michael Gannon

Michael Gannon *is Director of the Institute for Early Contact Period Studies at the University of Florida.*

The innocence of the indigenous Americans was more imagined than real. To one degree or another, they knew warfare, brutality, slavery, human sacrifice, and cannibalism. Columbus did not, as charged, "introduce" slavery to the New World; the practice existed there before his arrival, though his shipments of Tainos to Spain presaged a transoceanic traffic in slaves unprecedented in history.

This idealized image of people living in nature persisted until it was too late to learn who the Americans really were and, accepting them for what they were, to find a way to live and let live. Disease and conquest wiped out the people and their cultures. In their place Europeans had begun to "invent" America, as the Mexican historian Edmundo O'Gorman contends, in their own image and for their own purposes. They had set upon a course, writes historian Alfred W. Crosby, of creating "Neo-Europes." This was the America that took its place in world history.

In the 18th century, however, European intellectuals did engage in a searching reappraisal. A scientific movement, encouraged by the French naturalist Georges-Louis Leclerc de Buffon (1707–1788), spread the idea that America was somehow inferior to the Old World. As evidence, Buffon offered denigrating comparisons between the "ridiculous" tapir and the elephant, the llama and the camel, and the "cowardly" puma and the noble lion. Moreover, Old-World animals introduced there fared poorly, declining in health and size, with the sole exception of the pig. It was Buffon's thesis that America suffered an arrested development because of a humid climate, which he attributed to its relatively late emergence from the waters of the Biblical flood.

Buffon's ideas enjoyed a vogue throughout the 18th century and inspired more extreme arguments about "America's weakness." Not only were the animals inferior, so were the Americans, and even Europeans who settled there soon degenerated.

Unlike the proud patriots in colonial and post-Revolutionary North America, European intellectuals began expressing strong reservations about the benefits of the American discovery. There was no gainsaying its importance. Few disputed the opinion of Adam Smith: "The discovery of America, and that of a passage to the East Indies by the Cape of Good Hope, are the two greatest and most important events recorded in the history of mankind."

But there were negative assessments, not unlike today's. The anti-imperialist Samuel Johnson (1709–1784) wrote: "The Europeans have scarcely visited any coast but to gratify avarice, and extend corruption; to arrogate dominion without rights, and practice cruelty without incentive." He was also one of the first to make an unflattering connection between the conquest of America and its original conqueror. Columbus, Johnson said, had to travel "from court to court, scorned and repulsed as a wild projector, an idle promiser of kingdoms in the clouds: nor has any part of the world had reason to rejoice that he found at last reception and employment."

The French philosopher Abbé Guillaume-Thomas Raynal (1713–1796) challenged others to consider the following questions: Has the discovery of America been useful or harmful to mankind? If useful, how can its usefulness be magnified? If harmful, how can the harm be ameliorated? He offered a prize for the essay that would best answer those questions.

The respondents whose essays have survived were evenly divided between optimists and pessimists. Although "Europe is indebted to the New World for a few conveniences, and a few luxuries," Raynal himself observed, these were "so cruelly obtained, so unequally distributed, and so obstinately disputed" that they may not justify the costs. In conclusion, the abbé asked, if we had it to do over again, would we still want to discover the way to America and India? "Is it to be imagined," Raynal speculated, "that there exists a being infernal enough to answer this question in the affirmative?"

Pangs of guilt and expressions of moral outrage were futile, however; nothing stayed the momentum of European expansion in America. Most of the immigrants had never heard of the "American weakness" or read the intellectuals who idealized or despised the Indians or deplored Europe's blood-stained seizure of the lands. By the millions—particularly after the introduction of the steamship and on through World War I—immigrants flocked to a promised land where people could make something of themselves and prepare a better life for their children. There had been nothing quite like this in history. This was reflected in the image of Columbia. Little wonder that Columbus's standing in history was never higher than it was when the achievements and promise of America seemed so bright and were extravagantly proclaimed at home and abroad.

The "primary factor behind our [current] reassessment of the encounter," Crosby writes, "is a general reassessment of the role of rapid change, even catastrophe, in human history, and even the history of the earth and of the universe." The earlier faith in progress was founded on a Western belief that change came gradually and almost invariably for the better. In 19th-century science, the uniformitarian geology of Charles Lyell and the evolutionary theory of Charles Darwin were widely accepted because they seemed to confirm the idea of progress: The present world and its inhabitants were the products not of global disasters and multiple creations but of slow and steady change.

By contrast, Crosby observes, the 20th century has experienced the two worst wars in history, genocide, the invention of more ominous means of destruction, revolutions and the collapse of empires, rampant population growth, and the threat of ecological disaster. Catastrophism, not steady progress, is the modern paradigm. Even the universe was born, many scientists now believe, in one explosive moment—the Big Bang.

"The rapidity and magnitude of change in our century," Crosby concludes, "has prepared us to ask different questions about the encounter than the older schools of scientists and scholars asked."

If Abbé Raynal held his essay contest today, the pessimists might outnumber the optimists. Indeed, almost everything about Columbus and the discovery of America has become controversial.

And perhaps the greatest controversy of all is whether or not to celebrate the Quincentennial. The critics who advocate not celebrating it are correct, if to celebrate perpetuates a view of the encounter that ignores the terrible toll. This must be acknowledged and memorialized in the hope that nothing like it is ever repeated. Even so, it would be unhistorical to ignore the more salutary consequences. The New World, for example, changed Europe through new ideas, new resources, and new models of political and social life that would spread through the world. William H. McNeill is one of many historians who believe this led to the Enlightenment of the 18th century and thus to the philosophical, political, and scientific foundations of modern Western civilization. It should not be overlooked that this is the kind of society that encourages and tolerates the revisionists who condemn its many unforgivable transgressions in the New World.

Of course, attributing so much to any one historical development makes some historians uneasy. In cautioning against the "presentism" in much historical interpretations, Herbert Butterfield recalled "the schoolboy who, writing on the results of Columbus's discovery of America, enumerated amongst other things the execution of Charles I, the war of the Spanish Succession and the French Revolution." No one will ever know what the world and subsequent events would have been like if the discovery had not been made, or if it had not occurred until much later. But the impact of that discovery can hardly be underestimated. And it did start with Christopher Columbus.

That brings up another issue central to the Quincentenary debates: Columbus's responsibility for all that followed. It must be remembered who he was—not who we wish he had been. He was a European Christian of the 15th century sailing for the crown of Spain. There can be no expiation, only understanding. His single-mindedness and boldness, as well as the magnitude of his achievement, give him heroic standing. Others did not have Columbus's bold idea to sail across the unknown ocean, or if they did, they never acted upon it. Columbus did. In so many other respects, he failed to rise above his milieu and set a more worthy example, and so ended up a tragic figure. But he does not deserve to bear alone the blame for the consequences of his audacious act.

We must resist the temptation to shift blame for our behavior to someone dead and gone. Mario Vargas Llosa, the Peruvian novelist, finds little to admire in the early Spanish conquerors but recognizes the dangers inherent in transferring to them an inordinate share of the blame for modern America.

"Why have the post-colonial republics of the Americas—republics that might have been expected to have deeper and broader notions of liberty, equality, and fraternity—failed so miserably to improve the lives of their Indian citizens?" Vargas Llosa asks. "Immense opportunities brought by the civilization that discovered and conquered America have been beneficial only to a minority, sometimes a very small one; whereas the great majority managed to have only a negative share of the conquest.... One of our worst defects, our best fictions, is to believe that our miseries have been imposed on us from abroad, that others, for example, the conquistadores, have always been responsible for our problems.... Did they really do it? We did it; we are the conquistadores."

People have choices, but they do not always choose well. One wishes Columbus had acquitted himself more nobly, in the full knowledge that, even if he had, others who came after would have almost surely squandered the opportunity presented to them to make a truly fresh start in human history—a new world in more than the geographic sense. But wishes, yesterday's self-congratulation or today's self-flagellation, are not history.

Columbus's failings, as well as his ambitions and courage, are beyond historical doubt—and are all too human. The mythic Columbus of our creation is something else. His destiny, it seems, is to serve as a barometer of our self-confidence, our hopes and aspirations, our faith in progress, and the capacity of humans to create a more just society.

How Many People Were Here Before Columbus?

One of the few certainties: The Indian populations of North and South America suffered a catastrophic collapse after 1492

By Lewis Lord

George Catlin, the 19th-century artist, revered the American Indians—"a numerous and noble race of HUMAN BEINGS," he called them, "fast passing to extinction." In the 1830s, he traveled among four dozen tribes to paint nearly 600 portraits and scenes of Indian life; most now hang in the Smithsonian. During his visits, his hosts extolled the blissful age before the settlers came, a time when tribes were much larger. "The Indians of North America," Catlin would speculate in his diary, "were 16 millions in numbers, and sent that number of daily prayers to the Almighty."

Few contemporaries agreed with Catlin's lofty estimate of the Indian population before contact with the white man. "Twaddle about imaginary millions," scoffed one Smithsonian expert, reflecting the prevailing view that Indians were too incompetent to have ever reached large numbers. Alexis de Tocqueville's cheery assertion that America before Columbus was an "empty continent . . . awaiting its inhabitants" was endorsed by no less than the U.S. Census Bureau, which in 1894 warned against accepting Indian "legends" as facts. "Investigation shows," the bureau said, "that the aboriginal population within the present United States at the beginning of the Columbian period could not have exceeded much over 500,000."

A century later the question remains far from settled. But modern scholarship tends to side with the painter. Some experts believe that perhaps 10 million people lived above the Rio Grande in 1492—twice as many as may have inhabited the British Isles at that time. The population of the Western Hemisphere may have exceeded 15th-century Europe's 70 million.

Driving the higher estimates is the relatively new view that most of America's Indians were wiped out by smallpox, measles, and other Old World diseases that swept across the hemisphere far faster than the Europeans that brought them. "Population decay was catastrophic," concluded historian William McNeill in his 1976 book, *Plagues and Peoples.*

But that still leaves unsolved the question of how many Indians inhabited the continent when the first Europeans arrived. No one, in fact, knows how many people lived *anywhere* in those days, except for perhaps a city or two in Europe. The first national censuses occurred centuries later: 1749 in Sweden, 1790 in the fledgling United States, 1801 in France and Britain; it was 1953 when China took a complete count.

George Catlin's means of counting Indians—the guesstimate—was the only method in his day. It was the same method the Census Bureau used in 1894 when it haughtily dismissed his idea that millions of Indians once inhabited the country.

The expert whose figures would dominate scholarly thought for the first

PHOTOGRAPHS BY EDWARD S. CURTIS FROM *THE NORTH AMERICAN INDIAN* COURTESY OF CHRISTOPHER CARDOZO INC.

LOST PEOPLES a gallery of portraits ca. 1900 by photographer Edward Curtis

half of this century, Smithsonian ethnologist James Mooney, did his share of guessing, too. Mooney pored through historical documents for accounts of tribal populations made by soldiers, missionaries, and others. But he suspected that his sources routinely exaggerated—soldiers to paint their conquests as more heroic, missionaries to pad their tallies of souls saved. So he often took the lowest count he could find and, to be safe, reduced it. His ultimate tribe-by-tribe estimate, published in 1928, showed an Indian population of 1,150,000 north of the Rio Grande.

Mooney was estimating the population not in 1492 but in periods that followed initial contacts with white men—including encounters in the American West as late as the 19th century. The common assumption in his day was that the Indians the whites came upon were probably as numerous as the Indians of 1492. That's what anthropologist Alfred Kroeber believed in 1934 when he produced an estimate of the entire hemisphere's pre-Columbian population that dominated academic thought into the 1960s. Kroeber took Mooney's tally, shrank it a bit, and extrapolated the figures to the rest of North and South America. With a map and a device called a planimeter, he measured off various cultural areas and assigned each a population density. For the eastern United States, he averaged fewer than 1 person per square mile. For the many regions below the Rio Grande—the lands of the Incas and Aztecs and others that obviously had been much more populous—he assigned much higher densities. He multiplied the densities by the square miles in each region and concluded that 8.4 million people inhabited the Americas in 1492. They were neatly divided: 4.2 million in North America and 4.2 million in South America and the Caribbean.

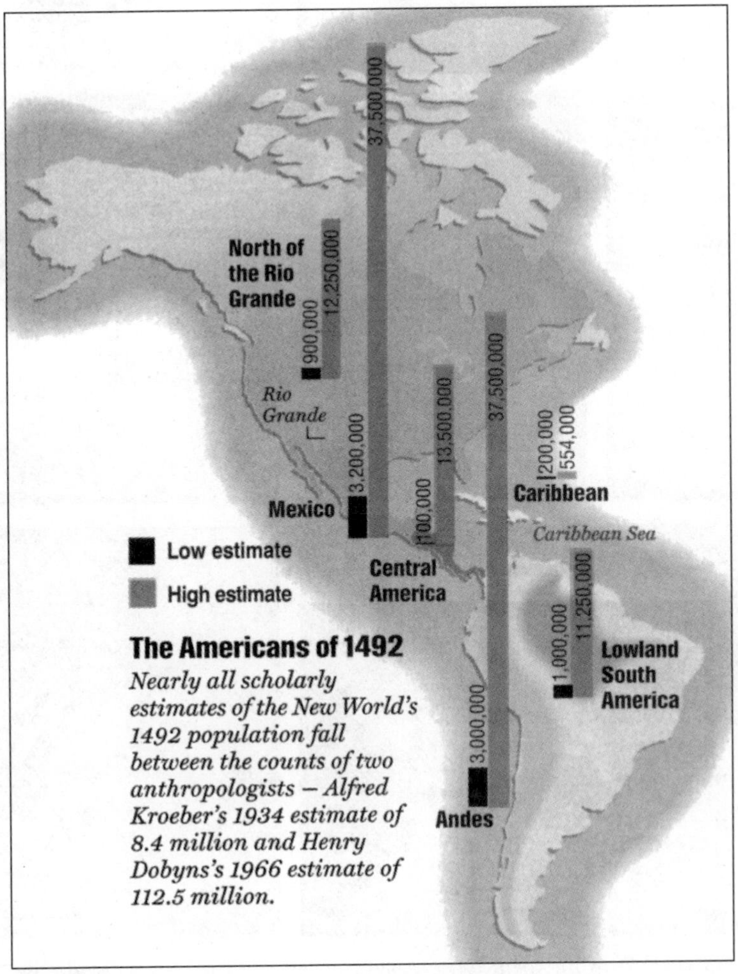

Canoe count. No one since Kroeber has made an estimate so low. In the past 40 years, scholars have sifted through thousands of volumes—from 16th-century Spanish reports of baptisms, marriages, and tax collections in Mexico to 17th-century accounts of epidemics in New England. Where the data failed to provide direct answers, the experts devised ingenious ways to draw inferences from them. Explorers, for instance, rarely estimated total populations; they tended to report only the number of warriors. Scholars now multiply the warrior counts by a correction factor such as 5 to come up with a total that includes women, children, and old men. Multiples likewise are applied to baptisms, Indian buildings, even canoes and acres of beans and corn. Archaeological sites containing heaps of oyster shells have been used to estimate how many oysters were eaten—and thus how many Indians ate them.

By the 1960s, scholars were concluding that just one spot—central Mexico—once had three times as many Indians as Kroeber had estimated in the whole hemisphere.

The highest estimate ever, made in 1966, was supported by a provocative theory. Anthropologist Henry Dobyns argued that disease reduced the Indian population by 95 percent or more throughout the hemisphere—a "depopulation ratio" that, he said, has commonly occurred even in modern times when epidemics strike peoples with no immunity. Dobyns took Indian populations at their nadirs—their lowest levels—and multiplied the numbers by 20 or 25. In America above the Rio Grande, for instance, the Indian population hit bottom early in this century when census figures reported 490,000; by Dobyns's calculation that means between 9.8 million and 12.2 million Indians once inhabited what's now the United States and Canada. For the hemisphere, he estimated a 1492 population of 90 million to 112.5 million.

Critics suspect Dobyns assumed too much. Epidemics, they say, were probably not as frequent or lethal as he claimed. Dobyns, who retired without revising his count, agrees that his method is simplistic; he proposed it "for

North of the Rio Grande

37,500,000
12,250,000
900,000

Rio Grande

3,200,000
13,500,000
100,000

1,200,000
554,000

Mexico

Caribbean

Caribbean Sea

Central America

1,250,000
1,000,000

Lowland South America

3,000,000

Andes

■ Low estimate
■ High estimate

The Americans of 1492

Nearly all scholarly estimates of the New World's 1492 population fall between the counts of two anthropologists – Alfred Kroeber's 1934 estimate of 8.4 million and Henry Dobyns's 1966 estimate of 112.5 million.

Sources: American Anthropologist, Current Anthropology
GRAPHIC BY STEPHEN ROUNTREE—USN&WR

lack of something better," he says, and localized studies, if thorough, can be more accurate. A colleague's on-the-scene research in Peru, for instance, convinced Dobyns that his Inca empire estimate of 30 million to 37 million Indians was perhaps 20 million too high. But in the 31 years since his *Current Anthropology* article, Dobyns has measured other regional populations with tools that other scholars use—warrior counts, food availability, and the like—and "fairly consistently" found that his 1966 assumptions were too low. He now believes that Florida in 1492 had perhaps 700,000 Indians—several times what he concluded in 1966. His article estimated the Caribbean's 1492 population at a half million; he now agrees with other scholars that it was 5 million or more.

How close will scholars ever come to the real numbers? A recent effort by geographer William Denevan to reconcile the many conflicting estimates, by using the best findings of various scholars, concludes that 54 million people inhabited the Americas in 1492, including 3.8 million above the Rio Grande. But how meaningful such numbers are is the question. With decades of careful research, historian Woodrow Borah once predicted, scholars eventually may produce an estimate with a margin of error of 30 to 50 percent. "If I had to pick the most unanswerable question in the world to get into heaven, that would be a good choice," says David Henige, a historian at the University of Wisconsin–Madison and author of the forthcoming book *Numbers From Nowhere.* "It is absolutely impossible to answer. Yet people have written tens of thousands of pages on it."

Even if the absolute total is forever unknowable, there are other numbers that tell a haunting tale. In the 1960s, a Berkeley geographer, Carl Sauer, cited evidence of a 1496 census that Columbus's brother Bartholomew ordered for tax purposes on Hispaniola (now Haiti and the Dominican Republic). The Spanish counted 1.1 million Indians. Since that sum covered only Hispaniola's Spanish-controlled half and excluded children, Sauer concluded that 3 million Indians once inhabited the island. But a generation after 1492, a Spanish resident reported Hispaniola's Indian population had shrunk below 11,000.

The island's collapse was only a preview. By 1650, records suggest that only 6 million Indians remained in all of North America, South America, and the Caribbean. Subtract 6 million from even a conservative estimate of the 1492 population—like Denevan's consensus count of 54 million—and one dreadful conclusion is inescapable: The 150 years after Columbus's arrival brought a toll on human life in this hemisphere comparable to all of the world's losses in World War II.

A Taste of Adventure

Kerala, India, and the Molucca Islands, Indonesia

The history of spices is the history of trade

SOON after dawn on May 21st 1498, Vasco da Gama and his crew arrived at Calicut after the first direct sea voyage from Europe to Asia. If history's modern age has a beginning, this is it. Europe's ignorance of, and isolation from, the cosmopolitan intellectual and commercial life of Asia were ended forever. With ships, weaponry and a willingness to use them both, the countries of Europe were about to colonise the rest of the world. To support this expansion, its merchant classes would invent new forms of commercial credit and the first great corporations, vital parts of capitalism's operating system, and spread their trading networks across the seven seas. And what did the men shout as they came ashore? "For Christ and spices!"

The proselytising part turned out to be disappointingly unnecessary: there were already plenty of Christians living on the Malabar coast, following the arrival of a Syrian contingent many centuries earlier. But as far as spice went, Da Gama and his crew were right on the money. Then, as now, Calicut was a gateway to the world's greatest pepper-growing region—indeed this was why the Syrians had moved there in the first place. As such it was at the heart of the spice trade, a network of sea routes and entrepots in the making for millennia: the world economy's oldest, deepest, most aromatic roots.

For thousands of years before Da Gama and hundreds of years afterwards, the secret of the spice trade was simple: great demand and highly controlled supply. Some of that control was enforced through political power or contrived through mercantile guile. Some was simply a gift from the gods of climate and botany. Legend has it that, before leaving, Da Gama dared to ask the zamorin of Calicut whether he could take a pepper stalk with him for replanting. His courtiers were outraged, but the potentate stayed calm. "You can take our pepper, but you will never be able to take our rains." He knew how important the region's unusual twin monsoon, both phases of which bring heavy rain, was to its fickle crop. To this day, though regions elsewhere grow pepper, Kerala reigns supreme in its quality, dominating the high end of the market.

If those vital downpours have not washed away what passes for the road, a few days travel into Kerala's rolling Western Ghats, where waterfalls roar and herds of wild elephants loom from soft mist, brings you to the ancestral home of *Piper nigrum*. High up in the middle of nowhere, Iddicki produces the finest pepper in the world, its peppercorns always dark and heavy, bursting with flavour. Its vines wind their way around almost every tree in sight, climbing ten metres or more into the sky.

After such a journey you might expect Iddicki to be a sleepy backwater. In its own idyllic way, though, it is a boomtown worthy of the Wild West. Fancy jeeps clog the narrow streets; shops overflow with the latest necessities of rural life, like washing machines and stereos. Giant satellite dishes shove their expensive snouts at the heavens from every other house. One of the world's largest stashes of gold is in rural India, and to judge by its glittering jewellery shops this town has considerably more than its fair share. "Black gold," explains one pepper farmer with a broad grin, is fetching top prices on the world market.

And what did the men shout as they came ashore? "For Christ and spices!"

Until you talk to them about that world market, Iddicki's residents seem much like farmers anywhere else in the developing world—scraping a living at the margins of the market economy. Thomas Thomas, one of the several hundred thousand smallholders who grow Kerala's pepper, is a good example. A humble man of the earth, he speaks softly and still wears his *dhothi,* a traditional loincloth, when he tills his soil. But with a little prompting he will give you an analysis of the pepper market sophisticated enough to make a Chicago commodities trader blush: current prices, the direction of the futures market, the costs versus benefits of holding stocks. A local spice dealer explains over a feast of fiery snapper and spiced tapioca at his spacious bungalow that "there is full price-discovery in this market." The farmers who sell their crops to him (for resale at the big market in Jewtown, which has replaced Calicut as the hub of Kerala's pepper trade) do so with the latest New York and Rotterdam prices in hand. One particularly sharp farmer, he moans, is cutting out the middlemen altogether and shipping his stocks directly to Europe.

The global aspect of the dealer's trade is nothing new. As far back as 2600 BC, there are records of the Egyptians feeding spices obtained from Asia to labourers building the great pyramid of Cheops, to give them strength. Archeological evidence suggests that cloves were quite popular in Syria not long after, despite the fact that, like nutmeg and mace, they came only from the spice islands of what is now Indonesia. Long before the 6th century BC, when Confucius advocated the use of ginger, the Chinese were obtaining spices from the tropics. Europe imported them before Rome was founded.

Today spices are chiefly flavourings for food, but a hundred other uses have contributed to the demand through history. In ancient Egypt cassia and cinnamon fetched a high price because they were essential for embalming; so too were anise, marjoram and cumin, used to rinse out the innards of the worthy dead. Hammurabi's legal code, which called for severe punishment of sloppy or unsuccessful surgeons, did much to encourage the use of medicinal spices in Sumeria.

Particularly in Europe, though, food came to matter most. Spices preserve, and they also make the poorly preserved palatable, masking the appetite-killing stench of decay. After bad harvests and in cold winters the only thing that kept starvation at bay was heavily salted meat—with pepper. And there was never enough of it. Thus pepper began the association with gold it still has in the streets of Iddicki, often at a one-to-one exchange rate. In order to call off their siege of Rome in 408 AD, the Visigoths demanded a bounty in gold, silver and pepper. In the Middle Ages plague added to the demand for medicinal spices; a German price table from the 14th century sets the value of a pound of nutmeg at seven fat oxen. At the same

time "peppercorn rents" were a serious way of doing business. When the *Mary Rose,* an English ship that sank in 1545, was raised from the ocean floor in the 1980s, nearly every sailor was found with a bunch of peppercorns on his person—the most portable store of value available.

The great beneficiaries of Europe's need were the Arabs. Spices could change hands a dozen times between their source and Europe, soaring in value with each transaction, and the Arabs were the greatest of the middlemen. Keen to keep it that way, they did everything possible to confuse consumers about the spices' origins. As early as the 5th century BC an Arab cover story fooled Herodotus into believing that cinnamon was found only on a mountain range somewhere in Arabia. The spices were jealously guarded by vicious birds of prey, he wrote, which made their nests of the stuff on steep mountain slopes. Arabs would leave out large chunks of fresh donkey meat for the birds to take back to their nests, which would crash to the ground under the weight. The brave Arabs then grabbed the nests, from under the talons of their previous owners.

Not everyone was fooled. In the 1st century AD the Roman historian Pliny grew concerned at the way the empire's gold flowed ever to the east, and set out to expose the truth and undercut the Arab monopolists who he reckoned to be selling pepper at prices a hundred times what they paid for it in India. It did not help that the gluttonous Romans were, in the words of Frederic Rosengarten, a spice historian, "the most extravagant users of aromatics in history". They used spices in every imaginable combination for their foods, wines and fragrances. Legionaries headed off to battle wearing perfume. The rich slept on pillows of saffron in the belief that it would cure hangovers.

Resentment against the Arab stranglehold had led Rome to launch an invasion of Arabia in 24 BC, an ill-fated expedition that ended in humiliation. But where military means failed, market intelligence prevailed. In 40 AD, Hip-

palus, a Greek merchant, discovered something the Arabs had long tried to obscure: that the monsoons which nourish India's pepper vines reverse direction mid-year, and that trips from Egypt's Red Sea coast to India and back could thus be shorter and safer than the empire had imagined. Roman trade with India boomed: the Arab monopoly broke.

Early in the 7th century, an obscure spice merchant named Muhammad re-established Arab dominance of the spice trade by introducing an aggressive, expansionary Islam to the world. When the muslims took Alexandria in 641 AD, they killed the trade which had long flourished between Rome and India. As they tightened their grip on the business over the next few centuries, prices in Europe rose dramatically. During the Middle Ages, spices became a luxury that only a few in Europe could afford. This was bad news for the poor and good news for Venice. Its shrewd merchants struck a deal with the Arabs that made them the trade's preferred—indeed almost exclusive—European distributors. Even during the crusades, the relationship bought wealth to all concerned.

The rest of Europe did not care at all for the Muslim Curtain, as the Islamic empire separating west from east came to be called, or for the Venetians. The final blow came in 1453 when the Ottoman Turks took Constantinople, shutting down the small overland trade that had previously evaded the Arab-Venetian monopoly. The Egyptians, gatekeepers of the trade with Venice, felt confident enough to impose a tariff amounting to a third of the value of spices passing through their fingers.

Salvation for the palates and exchequers of Europe's kings lay in finding a sea route to the Indies. In particular, the hunt was on for Malacca, the most important entrepôt in the spice trade and the fabled gateway to the Spice Islands. Spain and Portugal financed dozens of exploration parties in its general direction; half would never make it back home. The rationale for this expense and danger was simple: "He who is lord of Malacca has his hand on the throat of Venice."

It was as part of Portugal's *Drang nach Osten* that Vasco da Gama rounded Africa's Cape of Good Hope to reach India in 1498. As waves of Portuguese explorers returned to Lisbon with their loads of spices, the Venetians and the Egyptians were stunned: the price of pepper in Lisbon fell to one-fifth that in Venice.

"He who is lord of Malacca has his hand on the throat of Venice"

The Spaniards, too, were less than happy. They had sent Christopher Columbus to find a route to the Indies via the west, but he had failed, hitting upon the previously unknown Americas instead. In his zeal to convince his paymasters and himself that he had succeeded, he named the new world's natives as Indians and their sacred *chiles* "red" pepper—two unpardonable obfuscations that have confused people to this day.

Pope Alexander IV was drafted in to keep the two expansionist powers apart; the result was the treaty of Tordesillas, which granted all discoveries west of a mid-Atlantic meridian to Spain, and those east of it to Portugal. But the Spanish clung to the possibility of a western end-run to the Spice Islands, and financed Ferdinand Magellan on what would become the first circumnavigation of the earth. Magellan himself was killed in the Philippines, but his sidekick, Sebastian del Cano, completed the momentous journey—with a landfall at the Spice Islands en route. In 1522 his *Victoria* returned to Europe with a tonne of spices on board. The king awarded him a coat of arms embellished with two cinnamon sticks, three nutmegs and twelve cloves.

But the Portuguese had pipped Spain to the post. They had captured the vibrant free-trading port of Malacca, in what is now Malaysia, in 1511. Using the intelligence they gathered there, they made it to the promised land: the tiny Banda Islands, the world's only source of nutmeg and mace, which they

reached the following year. Nutmeg is the pit of the nutmeg tree's fruit, and mace, which commanded and still commands a higher price, is the delicate red aril which comes between the pit and the fruit's husky exterior. Chaucer extolled "nutemuge put in ale . . ." and it remains an essential part of Coca-Cola's secret formula.

After filling their holds, the Portuguese began their return. One ship ran aground, stranding its crew on a remote island. Hearing of a strange race of white men in his parts, the sultan of Ternate, the most powerful of the clove isles, sent for them—and so the Europeans found the last secret source of spice.

Look out from the expansive verandah of the sultan's palace in Ternate and one of history's great microcosms lies before you. Dominating one side is Gamalama, the island's temperamental volcano. Opposite it stands its equally fickle twin on the island of Tidore. The two spits of land, not a mile apart, are now almost unknown beyond their immediate vicinity. But five centuries ago their names were uttered with breathless excitement across Europe as their rulers, ancient rivals, played the new great powers off against each other with promises of limitless wealth.

Dark, husky aromas swirl through the palace as incense made specially of local spices finds its way into the thick tropical air. The place is overflowing with gifts from distant customers: priceless Chinese vases, exquisitely carved Indian daggers, fine Venetian glassware, all of them evidence of the influence these rulers once wielded. Ask politely, and you might be allowed to gaze—from a respectful distance, and only after much ceremony—at the sultan's magical crown, its hundred sparkling gemstones hanging heavy like ripe peaches. You are not the first impressionable tourist here. Francis Drake gushed about the palace, especially its 400-strong harem. And it seems that it's still good to be the king: one of the gifts on display is an enormous modern settee, helpfully labelled "Lazy chair: for the sultan to take naps."

For much of the 16th century, Spain and Portugal tried to win control of the

trade in cloves that made such a lifestyle possible. This meant entangling themselves in the long-running rivalry between the rulers of the two islands, who were in-laws. The European powers would build alliances and forts in one place and then the other, only to find themselves kicked out or caught up in endless intrigues and feuds. After decades of this Machiavellian palaver the Portuguese emerged as the top European player in the clove market, but they never really made it a monopoly. Indeed, they allowed the Dutch, who were growing increasingly anxious for a piece of the action, to be their chief distributors in the north and west of Europe. After Spain gobbled up Portugal in 1580, though, the trade changed again. The Spanish tightened control of the market to which they now had exclusive access, cutting the Dutch out of the picture and raising prices across the continent.

Convinced that they had to find a way to control the source of the spices, the Dutch got their act together. In 1602 they formed the Dutch East India Company (the *Vereenigde Oost-Indische Compagnie*, VOC), an association of merchants meant to reduce competition, share risk and realise economies of scale. Other European countries also formed East India companies—everyone from Portugal to Sweden to Austria had a go—but none was ever as successful in the spice trade as the VOC. By 1670 it was the richest corporation in the world, paying its shareholders an annual dividend of 40% on their investment despite financing 50,000 employees, 30,000 fighting men and 200 ships, many of them armed. The secret of this success was simple. They had no scruples whatsoever.

The VOC's first conquest was the Banda archipelago. Unlike the sultans of the clove islands, who relished the attention lavished upon them by their European suitors and the opportunities for mischief that came with it, the fiercely independent Islamic merchants of the Bandas had never allowed Spain or Portugal to build forts on their islands: they insisted on their freedom to trade with all nations. This independence proved their undoing, since it

Hot Chile

"Oh Blessed Incomparable Chile, ruler of all things . . . I give thee thanks for my digestive health, I give thee thanks for my very life!" Thus the Transcendental Capsaicinophilic Society, one of the worrying number of cults devoted to *capsicum*: chiles or "red" pepper.

If it sounds as if they are on drugs then so, in a way, they are. Paul Bosland of the Chile Pepper Institute in New Mexico reckons they and all chileheads are high on endorphins, painkillers released by the body to block the sting of the capsaicin which gives chiles their bite.

The addicts are spread all over the world. Travelling on the back of the European spice trade, America's chiles have since colonised every corner of the earth so thoroughly that everyone thinks they have always been around.

Even the top man at the Indian Spices Board refuses to accept that chiles are an import, pulling dubious sanskrit references from the Vedas to bolster his point. His clinching argument? "Indians can go months without touching black pepper, but not a day goes by that we don't eat chile peppers."

This is fast becoming true everywhere else, too. Americans' consumption of chile has doubled over the past two decades; they now use the spice in almost everything. Salsa now outsells ketchup as America's top condiment. But black pepper still gets all the glory as the world's most important traded spice. Unlike its fickle namesake, red pepper grows like mad all over the place. So though there may be a great demand for it, no one makes much money out of trading it.

Climb through the dense, aromatic forests that cover the steep slopes of Ternate's volcano, and you will find this living testament to the ultimate futility of monopoly. Nearly 40 metres tall and over 4 metres round, Afo is the world's oldest clove tree, planted in defiance of the Dutch ban nearly four centuries ago. Despite the VOC's extreme precautions, Afo's sister seedlings, stolen in 1770 by an intrepid Frenchman (curiously, named Poivre), ended up flourishing on the Seychelles, Réunion and especially Zanzibar, which later became the world's largest producer of cloves. By the end of the 18th century the emergence of these rivals had broken the Dutch monopoly for good.

By that time the VOC was already a hollow mockery of its original ghastly self. As early as the end of the 17th century, careful analysis of the books shows that its volume of trade was reducing every year. Even a monopoly so ruthlessly enforced could not help but leak, and the VOC's overheads were huge—tens of thousands of employees, garrisons, warships. Decades of easy rents had created a corrupt and inefficient beast. By 1735, dwindling spice income had been overtaken by textiles in the company's profit column. In 1799, the most vicious robber baron of them all met its final end. The VOC went bankrupt.

The demise of the VOC was not just a pleasing comeuppance. It was evidence that, in just two centuries, Europeans had changed the spice trade forever. The spices that were once limited to tiny islands in hidden archipelagoes were being grown around the world and in large quantities. Trade routes that spanned oceans were becoming commonplace and, as such, competitive. The Dutch did their best to buck the trend, destroying their stocks so blatantly that, according to one observer, the streets of Amsterdam were "flooded with nutmeg butter". But it was all in vain. Spices were no longer that hard to come by. Monopolies gave way to markets.

Those markets remained rich in romance; the allure of the trade, its role as a cultural crossroads, its many rival players, its uncertainties and its opportunities for smuggling (even relatively

---

encouraged the VOC to put the nutmeg trade first on its order of business.

For a taste of Banda's romance nothing beats a trip to Run, an explosion of nutmeg trees in the middle of a turquoise sea. Reaching it after a night aboard ship is a magical experience; scores of dolphins dart about your bow-wave as the first glints of sunrise streak across the sky. It feels much as it must have done when English adventurers first claimed the place, making it the country's first colony anywhere. Not much of a colony, it must be said: the island is so small that even a modest fishing vessel can come ashore only at

---

The secret of this success was simple. The Dutch had no scruples whatsoever

---

high tide. Yet this seemingly insignificant toe-hold in nutmeg-land so exercised the Dutch that they traded away a promising young colony on the other side of the world to secure it. That island was New Amsterdam, now better known as Manhattan.

The purchase of Run demonstrates the VOC's persistence; it does not do jus-

tice to the company's cruelty (normally, but not exclusively, meted out to non-Europeans). Its most successful head, Jan Pieterszoon Coen, had earlier convinced the reluctant Bandanese of his firm's God-given right to monopolise the nutmeg trade in a more typical style: he had had every single male over the age of fifteen that he could get his hands on butchered. Coen brought in Japanese mercenaries to torture, quarter and decapitate village leaders, displaying their heads on long poles. The population of the isles was 15,000 before the VOC arrived; 15 years later it was 600.

When they turned to the clove trade the Dutch had no time for the squabbling politics of Ternate and Tidore. The VOC uprooted all the Sultans' clove trees and concentrated production on Ambon, an island where its grip was tight. By 1681, it had destroyed three-quarters of all nutmeg trees in unwanted areas and reorganised farming into plantations. It imposed the death penalty on anyone caught growing, stealing or possessing nutmeg or clove plants without authorisation. It drenched every nutmeg with lime before export, to ensure that not one fertile seed escaped its clutches. Yet high on its hillside Afo lives to tell its tale.

cheap spices carry a lot of value for a given weight) kept the spice bazaars of Kerala, Ambon and Rotterdam fascinating. And lucrative, too; though no one could control the overall flow of spice any more, information could still be rushed ahead fast enough—or sequestered behind long enough—for people in the know to make a killing. Now, though, the information itself has started to flow freely. "There just aren't so many secrets any more," reflects a spice trader in Rotterdam. "The farmers in Vietnam are walking around with mobile phones. They know the market price as soon as I do."

Such traders are now caught in a trap. Their space for bargaining and trade, opened up with the end of monopoly production, is being hemmed in by ever more powerful purchasers—the food giants and spice multinationals. In an age of free-flowing information these buyers can bypass the markets and go directly to the source. From Jewtown, still the key pepper entrepot, to Rotterdam, London and New York, the main international markets, spice traders are a dying breed. One industry veteran reckons that only a fifth of the trading concerns that flourished 30 years ago are still in business.

Their problems stem from men like Al Goetze. Meet him in his office near Baltimore, at the staid headquarters of McCormick, the world's largest spice firm, and his conservative suit and dry manner might lead you to mistake him for a stuffy corporate type. But to his admiring colleagues he is "a modern day Marco Polo."

Procurement managers at food-processing firms were once content to purchase spices through brokers, never leaving the comfort of their air-conditioned offices. Mr Goetze hits the road. He and his men have travelled to nearly every country on earth that grows spices, again and again. McCormick has set up joint-ventures or wholly owned subsidiaries in over a dozen key spice-producing countries in recent years.

Once the reason for going to the source was price. Now, Mr Goetze says, quality is what matters. Both American and European regulators, prompted by increasing consumer awareness of food safety, have been cracking down hard on impurities. Mr Goetze points to an unlikely assortment of objects in a display case: stones, rusty nails, giant cockroaches, plastic beach sandals. All were crammed into bursting burlap bags and sold to McCormick with its spice. Big processing firms and marketers, frightened that such stuff—or, worse, microscopic impurities that come with it—might make it to the dinner plates of litigious customers, are going straight to the source to clean things up.

Alfons van Gulick, the head of Rotterdam's Man Producten, the world's biggest and most influential spice-trading firm, is understandably unimpressed: "McCormick should stick to polishing its brand and selling, rather

---

Stones, rusty nails, giant cockroaches, plastic beach sandals, all crammed into bursting burlap bags and sold with the spice

---

than telling countries how to produce spice." But the people for whose products McCormick and Man Producten compete have an interest in Mr Goetze's strategy. The Indian Spices Board is already helping members improve standards and obtain seals of approval such as ISO certification. The hope is that, over time, producers can go downstream and capture more of the fat margins that come with the "value-added" processing now done in rich countries.

Industry analysts are sceptical about vertical integration. In other commodities it has not been much of a success. Cutting out the middleman may pose unexpected problems for conservative multinationals, unfamiliar with the culture and risks involved in going upstream. And then there is volatility, on which middlemen thrive and which farmers and multinationals dislike. Asked whether the trade has lost its mystery, one animated trader replies "Mystery? I experience it every day when I try to figure out what is going on with prices in this market!"

Producers hate this, and have made various attempts to iron out the market's ups and downs. The International Pepper Community—which includes India, Indonesia and Brazil among its members—has tried for decades to form a producers' cartel to boost prices, without any success. Price fixing by vanilla growers in Madagascar succeeded for a while, but then Uganda flooded the market with cheaper beans. Indonesia and Grenada, the top producers of nutmeg, managed to boost prices for a few years by limiting supply, but cheating quickly scuppered the arrangement. Quiet talks are underway between top cardamom producers in India and Guatemala, who produce nearly all the world's output, to restrict supply; it may work for a while, but not for long.

Every decade or so, an ambitious individual trader tries to do with money what the producers cannot do by agreement. To corner the pepper market would offer huge riches, and so people regularly have a go. Half a century ago, it was an Armenian; a decade ago, an American. Now it appears that a shadowy Indonesian tycoon may be making a play for at least the white pepper market. But history teaches that such grandiose efforts at monopoly face an uphill struggle. And though it may be possible to milk them for a while, the modern day economics of the trade ensure that they cannot last. The spice trade, once the stuff of legends, has become a market much like any other. And a taste of luxury beyond the dreams of almost every human in history is available to almost everyone, almost everywhere.

After Dire Straits, An Agonizing Haul Across the Pacific

It was only a generation after Columbus that Magellan's tiny fleet sailed west, via his strait, then on around the world

Simon Winchester

Simon Winchester is the author of eight books that combine history and travel, including The Pacific *(Hutchinson), from which this article was adapted.*

Balboa found the ocean. Then, in their droves, explorers emerged to circle and probe and colonize it, but first, in that most daring of all endeavors, to cross it.

No one could be sure how wide it was. No one could be sure where lay the Terra Australis Incognita, which Ptolemy had postulated and which Mercator would argue was a necessary balance for a spherical world—without it the whole planet might simply topple over, to be lost among the stars. No one knew the weather or the currents or the winds. But one small certainty spurred the would-be circumnavigators onward. It was that the Spice Islands, the Moluccas, lay at the farthest side of whatever might lie beyond the waters, pacific or unpacific, that Balboa had discovered.

Traders buying nutmegs and cloves from Arabian merchants had known about the Spice Islands for centuries; in the 1200s Marco Polo knew roughly where they were, for he saw junk traffic in the ports of North China loaded with spices and manned by crews who had come from the south. In 1511 a Portuguese expedition led by Antonio d'Abreu actually discovered them by moving eastward, after passing the tip of Africa, to Malacca, thence down the strait and past the immense island of Borneo to the confused archipelago where nearly all known spices grew in wild profusion. To reach their goal, d'Abreu's men had gone halfway round the world from Europe to the Orient.

The geographical fact they established was of great political and imperial importance. Since 1494, when the Treaty of Tordesillas was signed, all of the unknown world to the east of an imaginary line that had been drawn 370 leagues west of the Cape Verde Islands would belong to Portugal. Everything to the west of that line would belong to Spain. So far as the Atlantic and the Indian oceans were concerned, there was no problem; but what about the other side of the world? Conquest, squatter's rights, annexation, force majeure—these cruder tools of geopolitics might well dictate its eventual position. Thus the Moluccas, if discovered by going eastward around the globe, would belong to Portugal—at least by the logic of some explorers. But the Moluccas claimed by a party going westward might belong to Spain. So while d'Abreu and his colleagues went off eastward, even braver or more foolhardy men, carrying the banner of Castile, were determined to discover—heroically and, as it turned out for many of them, fatally—the way to reach this same Orient by traveling westward across the vast unknown.

There is thus a nice irony in the fact that the man who undertook the seminal voyage, and did so in the name of Spain, was in fact Portuguese. He was born Fernao de Magalhaes, and the Portuguese—"He is ours," they insist—rarely care to acknowledge that he renounced his citizenship after a row, pledged his allegiance to King Charles I (later to be-

From *Smithsonian magazine*, April 1991, pp. 84-90, 92, 94-95. Originally "The Strait—and Dire Straits—of Magellan" from *Pacific Rising* by Simon Winchester. © 1991 by Simon Winchester. Reprinted by permission of the Sterling Lord Literistic, Inc.

come Emperor Charles V) and was given a new name: Hernando de Magallanes. The English-speaking world, which reveres him quite as much as does Iberia, knows him as Ferdinand Magellan.

He set off on September 20, 1519, with a royal mandate to search for a passage to El Mar del Sur, and thus to determine for certain that the Spice Islands were within the Spanish domains. He had not the foggiest notion of how far he might have to travel. For all Magellan's 237 men in their five little ships knew, Balboa's Panama and the northern coast of South America, which Columbus had sighted in 1498 on his third voyage, might be the equatorial portions of a continent extending without a break to the Antarctic pole, making the southern sea they sought quite unreachable from the west. Johann Schöner's globe of the world, then the best known, placed Japan a few hundred miles off Mexico. The historian Lópex de Gómara asserts that Magellan always insisted that the Moluccas were "no great distance from Panama and the Gulf of San Miguel, which Vasco Núñez de Balboa discovered." Magellan would rapidly discover precisely what "no great distance" was to mean.

The five vessels that would soon make history—the *Victoria*, the *Trinidada* (the *Trinidad*), the *San Antonio*, the *Concepción* and the *Santiago*—were small, the largest being 120 tons, and hopelessly unseaworthy. ("I would not care to sail to the Canaries in such crates," wrote the Portuguese consul in Seville, with obvious pleasure. "Their ribs are soft as butter.")

They set sail from the Guadalquivir River under the proud corporate title of the Armada de Molucca, amply armed but hopelessly provisioned, with crews composed of men of nine different nationalities including a lone Englishman. There was one Moluccan slave, Enrique, who would act as an interpreter if the crossing was accomplished. There was a journalist, too, Antonio Francesca Pigafetta, who may also have been a Venetian spy. In any case, Pigafetta's diaries remained the source for all future accounts of the voyage; he had joined the ships, he said, because he was "desirous of sailing with the expedition so

that I might see the wonders of the world."

The sorry tales of sodomy and mutiny, of yardarm justice and abrupt changes of command, and of all the other trials that attended the armada on its path south and west across the Atlantic do not belong here. The truly important phase of the journey starts on February 3, 1520, when the vessels left their anchorage near today's Montevideo and headed south. No charts or sailing directions existed then. The sailors were passing unknown coasts, and confronting increasingly terrifying seas and temperatures that dropped steadily, day by day.

They began to see penguins—"ducks without wings," they called them, *patos sin alas*—and "sea-wolves," or seals. Seeking a way to the Pacific, they explored every indentation in the coast off which they sailed, and with depressing regularity each indentation—even though some were extremely capacious and tempted the navigators to believe that they might be the longed-for straits—proved to be a cul-de-sac. They spent much of the winter, from Palm Sunday until late August, in the center of a chilly and miserable bay at what is now Puerto San Julian. The winter was made doubly wretched by an appalling mutiny and the consequent executions and maroonings that Captain-General Magellan ordered; by the wrecking of the *Santiago*, which he had sent on a depth-sounding expedition; and by the realization of the dreadful damage done to the remaining ships by the chomping of those plank-gourmets of the seas, teredo worms.

But one important discovery was made at Puerto San Julian: these southern plains were inhabited by enormous nomadic shepherds who herded not sheep, but little wild llamas known as guanacos, and who dressed in their skins. Magellan captured a number of these immense people—one pair by the cruel trick of showing them leg-irons and insisting that the proper way to carry the shackles was to allow them to be locked around their ankles. Magellan's men also liked the giants' tricks: one, who stayed aboard only a week but allowed himself to be called Juan and

learned some biblical phrases, caught and ate all the rats and mice on board, to the pleasure of the cook and the entertainment of the men. Magellan called these men "*patagones*"—"big feet"; the land in which he found them has been known ever since as Patagonia.

By late August the fleet set sail again. Two men had been left behind, marooned for mutiny by Magellan's orders. They had a supply of wine and hardtack, guns and shot, but when other, later expeditions entered the bay, no trace of them was found. They may have been killed by the giants; they may have starved to death. All that the men of the armada remembered were their pitiful wails echoing over the still waters as the ships sailed out of the bay into the open sea, and then south.

By the time the flotilla had reached 50 degrees south latitude (not far from the Falkland Islands), the men were restive. Their artless plea now was: If the expedition wanted to reach the Spice Islands, why not turn east toward them and pass below the Cape of Good Hope, as others had? Magellan, sensible enough to know this would make a nonsense of the whole plan to render the Spice Islands Spanish, refused. But he promised that if no strait was found by the time they had eaten up another 25 degrees of latitude, he would turn east as they wished. The murmurs stilled. The Captain-General clearly had no idea of the utter impossibility of navigating at 75 degrees south latitude, for on that longitudinal track his ships would get stuck fast in the thick ice of what is now the Weddell Sea, hemmed in by the yet unimagined continent and the unendurable cold of the Antarctic.

THE CAPTAIN-GENERAL SIGHTS A VIRGIN CAPE

On October 21, 1520, Magellan sighted a headland to starboard. Cabo Virjenes, which today is equipped with a lighthouse that flashes a powerful beam and a radio direction beacon, is an important navigation point on the South American coast. It marks, as Magellan was soon to discover, the eastern end of the strait that bears his name—the tortuous entrance, at long last, to the Pacific.

Ranges of immense, snow-covered mountains crowded into view; there could be, Magellan must have thought, no possible exit. Still, he ordered the *San Antonio* and the *Concepción* into the headwaters of the bay—only to be horrified when he saw them being swept into a huge maelstrom of surf and spindrift by unsuspected currents and winds. But he had no time to dwell on such miseries, for an immense storm broke over his own ship, the *Trinidad*, as well as the *Victoria*, alongside. Men were hurled overboard. One vessel was dismasted; the other nearly turned turtle several times. The storm went on and on and on. When relief finally came to the exhausted crews, the only recourse, it seemed, was to turn tail and head for home. The expedition was over, an abject failure.

Yet just at that moment (one occasionally suspects that the mythmakers have been at work on the story) the lookout sighted sails on the western horizon. They were indeed what they could only have been: the two scouting vessels had returned. Not shattered and aground, they were safe and sound. The joy Magellan must have felt at realizing his men were still alive was, however, as nothing when, as the *San Antonio* and the *Concepción* drew closer, he saw their yardarms hung with bunting, music being played, and the crews dancing and singing.

As an account of the long voyage puts it, "Suddenly, they saw a narrow passage, like the mouth of a river, ahead of them in the surf, and they managed to steer into it. Driven on by wind and tide they raced through this passage and into a wide lake. Still driven by the storm they were carried west for some hours into another narrow passage, though now the current had reversed, so what appeared to be a great ebb tide came rushing towards them. They debouched from this second straight into a broad body of water which stretched as far as the eye could see toward the setting sun. . . ."

By tasting the water and finding it salty, and then making sure that both the ebb tides and flood tides were of equal strength (tests that argued against this body of water being a river), the captains of the scout ships realized they had, indeed, discovered the way through. Magellan, believing that his ultimate goal was within his grasp, brushed aside the persistent doubter's view that he should, despite the discovery, turn back *eastward* for the Moluccas. "Though we have nothing to eat but the leather wrapping from our masts," he declared, "we shall go on!"

The Strait of Magellan is as darkly beautiful as it is useful. Before I first visited the strait I supposed, wrongly, that since its latitude to the south is more or less the same distance from the Equator as Maine's latitude is to the north, the coastline would also be vaguely similar. But it is much starker, more hostile, more grand. Heading west, as Magellan did, the land begins flat, and wind reduces such trees as there are to stunted survivors. Even today the strait is not an easy place for sailing vessels: " . . . both difficult and dangerous, because of incomplete surveys, the lack of aids to navigation, the great distance between anchorages, the strong current, and the narrow limits for the maneuvering of vessels," says the pilot manual.

"A CARGO OF FALSEHOOD AGAINST MAGELLAN"

For Magellan and his men it was a nightmare. The currents were treacherous. Unexpected winds, now known as williwaws, flashed down steep cliffs, threatening to drive the little fleet onto the rocks. He lost another ship; though he did not know it at the time, the *San Antonio* had turned tail and was heading back to Spain, "bearing a cargo of falsehood against Magellan." She also took away supplies vital for all of the fleet— one-third of the armada's biscuits, one-third of its meat and two-thirds of its currants, chickpeas and figs. The men began begging to turn back.

Days passed. Finally, on November 28, 1520, *Trinidad*, *Victoria* and *Concepción* passed beyond the horrors of the strait, and sailed westward into an evening that became, suddenly, magically serene. We are told that "the iron-willed Admiral" broke down and cried. Then he assembled his men on deck. Pedro de Valderrama, the *Trinidad*'s priest, stood on the poop deck and called down on the crew of all three remaining vessels the blessing of Our Lady of Victory. The men sang hymns. The gunners fired broadsides. And Magellan proudly unfurled the flag of Castile.

"We are about to stand into an ocean where no ship has ever sailed before," Magellan is said to have cried (though it has to be emphasized that there is no hard evidence that he did so). "May the ocean be always as calm and benevolent as it is today. In this hope I name it the Mar Pacifico." And just in case it was not Magellan who first uttered the name, then perhaps it was Pigafetta: "We debouched from that strait," he later wrote, "engulfing ourselves in the Pacific Sea."

THE EUROPEAN DAWN BREAKS ON THE PACIFIC

The concept of the Pacific Ocean, the greatest physical unit on Earth, had been born. Balboa had seen it. D'Abreu had ventured onto its western edges. Magellan had reached its eastern periphery. Now it was up to the explorers to try to comprehend the enormity of their discovery. But before they could do that, Magellan had to sail across it. This was his determined aim, and the aim of those who sponsored his venture.

So the Captain-General ordered the sails set to carry the shrunken, but now at long last triumphant, armada northward. He thought it might take three or four days to reach the Spice Islands. It was a savage underestimate—a tragically optimistic forecast, based quite probably on the terrible inability of long-distance navigators to calculate longitude (an inability that insured that not a single estimate then available to Magellan was even 80 percent of the true size of the ocean).

Not that anyone suspected tragedy as they breezed to the north of Cape Desado. Far from it. Once the armada had reached the lower southern latitudes, the winds began to blow balmily and unceasingly from the southeast. They were trade winds, just like those well known in the southern Atlantic and Indian oceans, and they were pleasantly warm. Their effect produced nothing but splendid sailing: no undue swells, no angry squalls, no cyclonic outbursts. Just endless days and nights of leisured running before a steady, powerful breeze. "Well was it named Pacific," wrote Pigafetta later, confirming his master's choice of name, "for during this period we met with no storms."

And for weeks and weeks, simply by wafting before the winds with sails unchanged, the fleet managed to miss every single one of the islands with which the Pacific Ocean is littered. Magellan's course, sedulously recorded by his pilot, Francisco Albo, shows him—almost uncannily—leading his vessels past the Juan Fernández Islands, past Sala y Gómez and Easter islands, past Pitcairn, Ducie, Oeno and Henderson and, indeed, past everything else. His astrolabe, his crude speed recorder, his hourglass (a watchkeeper would be flogged for holding it against his chest, since to warm it made the sand flow faster, the hour pass more quickly, the watch be more rapidly over) served Magellan admirably: he plotted the likely course to the Spice Islands, and his ships took him there, more or less.

Any deviation could have caused disaster. Had he strayed just 3 degrees north of Albo's recorded track, he would have hit the Marquesas; 3 degrees south, he would have come to Tahiti. He was a hundred miles off Bikini Atoll. He passed within half a day's sailing of razor-sharp coral reefs—thundering surfs, huge spikes and lances that would have ruined his ships forever. At this distance in time, it seems as if some guardian angel had Magellan's tiny fleet under benevolent invigilation for days and nights too numerous to count. Yet this providence had a less kindly face. Six weeks out of the strait, Magellan's men began to die. In the monotony of a long, landless passage, what proved unbearable was the lack of food aboard the sea-locked ships.

Much of the stores had already gone, carried off on the treacherous *San Antonio*. Such food as the three ships carried began to rot under the soggy tropical airs. The penguins and seals they had killed and salted in Patagonia started to turn putrid; maggots raged through the ships, eating clothes and supplies and rigging; water supplies turned scummy and rank. Men began to develop the classic symptoms of scurvy—their teeth loosened in their gums, their breath began to smell horribly sour, huge boils erupted from their shrunken frames, they sank into inconsolable melancholia.

In January men began to die. One of the Patagonian behemoths whom Magellan had persuaded aboard was, despite his immense physique and power, the first to go; he begged to be made a Christian, was baptized "Paul" and then died. By mid-January a third of the sailors were too sick to stagger along the decks. Their food was limited to scoops of flour stained yellow by the urine of rats, and biscuits riddled with weevils.

The depression and deep anxiety afflicted Magellan too. At one point he flung his charts overboard in a fit of rage. "With the pardon of the cartographers, the Moluccas are not to be found in their appointed place!" he cried. The fleet did, in fact, strike land in late January—a tiny island they called St. Paul's, and which seems to be the minute atoll now known as Pukapuka, in the French Tuamotu group. (Four centuries later, Pukapuka was the first island to be spotted by Thor Heyerdahl aboard the balsa raft *Kon-Tiki* after his long drift westward from Callao in Peru.) They stayed a week, replenishing their water butts and feasting on turtle eggs. They left in an optimistic mood; surely, they surmised, this island must be the first of a vast skein of atolls and lagoons stretching to the now close Moluccas. But it was not to be; the ships had barely traversed a third of their ocean. Soon the hunger pains, the racking thirst and the sense of unshakable misery began anew, and the dying began once more.

AFTER MEALS OF LEATHER—LAND!

More and more terrible the voyage steadily became. By March 4 the flagship had run out of food completely. Men were eating the oxhides and llama skins used to prevent the rigging from chafing (not too bad a diet—so long as the crew's scurvy-ridden teeth hung in). The smell of death, the knowledge that it was both inevitable and impending, gripped Magellan's sailors. And then dawned March 6, when a seaman called Navarro, the only man still fit enough to clamber up the ratlines, spied what everyone was waiting for—land.

A great cheer went up. Cannon were fired. Men fell to their knees in prayer. A squadron of tiny dugouts sped from shore to meet the Spaniards. Magellan had reached the islands he first called Las Islas de las Velas Latinas and later, after much of his cargo had been filched, Las Islas de Ladrones, the Islands of Thieves. He had made his landfall at what we now call Guam. It was March 6, 1521. Magellan had crossed the Pacific. A voyage the Captain-General had supposed might take three or four days had, in fact, occupied three and a half months.

The fleet stayed in Guam for only three days—to rest, make minor repairs and take on food (such as the "figs, more than a palm long," which must have been bananas) and fresh water. Then Magellan set off, still toward the Moluccas, standing down for the southwest and to the Philippines, islands of which all travelers to these parts had often heard, but which no European had ever seen. Though the Spice Islands, it must be recalled, were the armada's prescribed goal, the official mandate and ambition of Magellan was to discover, name and seize in the name of Spain the immense archipelago that lay north of them.

The only Briton on the expedition, Master Andrew of Bristol, died on this last, short passage. He was never to see the islands that, a novelist was later to write, were "as fair as Eden, with gold beaches, graceful palms, exotic fruits and soil so rich that if one snapped off a twig and stuck it into the ground it would start straightway to grow."

Magellan made his landfall on March 16 on an island at the southern end of the large Philippine island of Samar. Two days later, the first contact was made with Filipinos, though the name "Philippines" was not to be given to the place until 1543, when explorer Ruy

López de Villalobos named one after the Infante, later to become King Philip II, the Spanish monarch whose reign made the words "Spanish Armada" infamous. (The name "Philippines" caught on later to mean the entire island group.) The significant moment came two days later still, when the ships sailed down the Gulf of Leyte and the Surigao Strait, where, more than four centuries later in World War II, one of the world's last great naval battles was fought, and Adm. William F. Halsey reduced the Japanese Imperial Navy to vestigial strength.

Once through the strait, Magellan landed at the island that guarded its entrance, Limasawa. Eight inhabitants sailed out to the *Trinidad* in a small boat. On orders from the Captain-General, his Moluccan slave, Enrique, hailed them. In a moment that must have seemed frozen in time, it became clear that the men in the approaching boat understood the words of the Moluccan perfectly.

Their language was being spoken to them by a man on a huge ship that had come to them from the east. The linguistic globe—even if not necessarily the physical globe—had been circumnavigated. A man who had originated in these parts had traveled across Asia and around Africa to Europe as a slave, and had now returned home by the Americas and the Pacific. Enrique de Molucca may well have been, strictly speaking, the first of humankind to circumnavigate the world; he was never to be honored for so doing.

Nor, by the unhappy coincidence of ill-temper and wretched misfortune, was Ferdinand Magellan ever to be able to savor his own triumph. Just six weeks after landing he was dead, cut down on a Philippine island in a skirmish that is as unremembered as the place in which it happened is unsung—a flat and muddy little island called Mactan, where an airport has now been built to serve the city of Cebu.

The circumstances of the Captain-General's end, however, are riven into every Iberian schoolchild's learning, even today. Despite his crew's objections, Magellan insisted on exploring. He was pleased at the relative ease with which the people took to Christianity. (It

is perhaps worth remembering that the Catholic faith, which Magellan and his priests brought to Samar and Cebu and northern Mindanao, flourishes there still today. The Philippines, in fact, is the only predominantly Christian country in Asia, and the influence of the church contributed significantly to the recent overthrow of President Ferdinand Marcos.)

But the successful sowing of the seeds of Christianity were to be Magellan's undoing. His horribly inglorious end came in late April. The precise circumstances were chronicled. Magellan had demonstrated what he felt was his superior status to the local raja of Cebu, and had made Christians of him and all his followers. But significantly, the rest of the Philippine nobility did not go along. Many local junior rajas objected, especially the minor raja of Mactan, a man named Cilapulapu and now known to all Filipinos simply as Lapu Lapu. He declared that he was not going to pay fealty to this Christian interloper, come what may. He cared little enough for the raja of Cebu, let along the Cebuano's newfound foreign friends.

The Spaniards soon got wind of this rebellious mood, and on April 27 Magellan and 60 of his men paddled across the narrow strait to Mactan, in an attempt to bring Lapu Lapu to heel. "You will feel the iron of our lances," Lapu Lapu was told by Magellan's interlocutor. "But we have fire-hardened spears and stakes of bamboo," replied a defiant chieftain. "Come across whenever you like."

THE LAST STAND ON MACTAN ISLAND

The waters at the northern end of Mactan are very shallow and degenerate into warm swamps. A selected 48 of the Spaniards, dressed in full armor, had to wade the last few hundred yards to do battle with the Mactan warriors. They fought for an hour, thigh-deep in the water. Then Magellan plunged his lance into the body of an attacker and was unable to withdraw it quickly enough. It was a fatal delay. Another islander slashed Magellan's leg with a scimitar.

He staggered. Scores of others crowded around him as he fell, and as Pigafetta was to write, "thus they killed our mirror, our light, our comfort and our true guide."

It is worth remembering that Fernao de Magalhaes was a native Portuguese—of whom it used to be said, because they were such energetic explorers, "they have a small country to live in, but all the world to die in." There is a monument near the spot where he fell, a tall white obelisk, guarded solicitously for the past 15 years by a man with the splendid name of Jesus Baring. There are two accounts of the event, one engraved on either side of the cross. Señor Baring derives much amusement from showing his occasional visitors—and there are very few, considering how globally important this spot should be—how markedly they differ.

The one on the monument's eastern side—the side that pedant geographers will recognize as marginally nearer to the Spanish Main—records the event as a European tragedy. "Here on 27th April 1521 the great Portuguese navigator Hernando de Magallanes, in the service of the King of Spain, was slain by native Filipinos...." On the other side, by contrast, it is seen as an Oriental triumph—a heroic blow struck for Philippine nationalism. "Here on this spot the great chieftain Lapu Lapu repelled an attack by Ferdinand Magellan, killing him and sending his forces away...." Baring points to the latter and roars with laughter. "This is the real story. This is the one we Filipinos like to hear!"

Lapu Lapu is thus the first, and to many Filipinos the greatest, of Filipino heroes. These days his memory is being revived, his exploits retold, his adventures made the stuff of comic strips, films and popular songs. Each April there is a full-scale reenactment of the Battle of Mactan on the beach, with an improbably handsome Cebuano film star playing the part of the seminaked hero and, when I was last there, the Philippine Air Force officer Mercurion Fernadez playing the role of the armor-clad Magellan. The two sides struggle gamely in the rising surf until that epic moment when Officer Fernandez contrives to collapse into the shallow sea and grunts his last. The assembled thousands then cheer. Such is Filipino pride in the raja of Mactan that there are firebrands—in Manila as well as in Cebu—who believe their country should shed its present name, a reminder that it is a colonial conquest, and be reborn as LapuLapu-Land.

Little more needs to be said of the tiny armada now, save to note what most popular historians choose to forget. The *Concepción* was scuttled; the flagship *Trinidad*, which tried to make for home via the Pacific once more, was blown north as far as Hakodate in Japan, captured by a Portuguese battle group and became a total loss in the Spice Islands, which had been its original goal. But

one of the ships, the doughty little *Victoria*—at 85 tons she was the second smallest of the original five—did make it back to Spain.

The *Victoria* scudded home under the charge of Juan Sebastian d'Elcano, previously the executive officer of the *Concepción*. She made Java. She made it round the top of Africa, through the waters where freak waves sometimes cause modern oil tankers to founder. She made the Cape Verde Islands, where the crew realized that despite meticulous log-keeping, they had lost an entire day from their calendar: the concept of crossing the international date line was unknown—and profoundly unimaginable—to them.

On September 6, 1523, the *Victoria* made the harbor of Sanlucar de Barrameda, from where she had set off almost exactly three years before. Juan Sebastian d'Elcano had brought just 17 men back with him: 237 had started out. Circumnavigation, it happened, was a most costly business.

But well rewarded. D'Elcano was given an annual pension and a coat of arms as handsome as it was aromatic: a castle, three nutmegs, 12 cloves, two crossed cinnamon sticks, a pair of Malay kings bearing spice sticks, and above all, a globe circled by a ribbon emblazoned with the motto *Primus Circumdedisti me*. "Thou first circumnavigated me."

Test Your Knowledge Form

We encourage you to photocopy and use this page as a tool to assess how the articles in **Annual Editions** expand on the information in your textbook. By reflecting on the articles you will gain enhanced text information. You can also access this useful form on a product's book support Web site at **http://www.dushkin.com/ online/.**

NAME: DATE:

TITLE AND NUMBER OF ARTICLE:

BRIEFLY STATE THE MAIN IDEA OF THIS ARTICLE:

LIST THREE IMPORTANT FACTS THAT THE AUTHOR USES TO SUPPORT THE MAIN IDEA:

WHAT INFORMATION OR IDEAS DISCUSSED IN THIS ARTICLE ARE ALSO DISCUSSED IN YOUR TEXTBOOK OR OTHER READINGS THAT YOU HAVE DONE? LIST THE TEXTBOOK CHAPTERS AND PAGE NUMBERS:

LIST ANY EXAMPLES OF BIAS OR FAULTY REASONING THAT YOU FOUND IN THE ARTICLE:

LIST ANY NEW TERMS/CONCEPTS THAT WERE DISCUSSED IN THE ARTICLE, AND WRITE A SHORT DEFINITION:

ANNUAL EDITIONS revisions depend on two major opinion sources: one is our Advisory Board, listed in the front of this volume, which works with us in scanning the thousands of articles published in the public press each year; the other is you—the person actually using the book. Please help us and the users of the next edition by completing the prepaid article rating form on this page and returning it to us. Thank you for your help!

ANNUAL EDITIONS: World History Volume 1, Seventh Edition

ARTICLE RATING FORM

Here is an opportunity for you to have direct input into the next revision of this volume. We would like you to rate each of the 40 articles listed below, using the following scale:

1. Excellent: should definitely be retained
2. Above average: should probably be retained
3. Below average: should probably be deleted
4. Poor: should definitely be deleted

Your ratings will play a vital part in the next revision.
So please mail this prepaid form to us just as soon as you complete it.
Thanks for your help!

We Want Your Advice

RATING

ARTICLE

1. Once We Were Not Alone
2. The Scavenging of "Peking Man"
3. Mapping the Past
4. Japanese Roots
5. The Diffusionists Have Landed
6. New Clues Show Where People Made the Great Leap to Agriculture
7. In Dawn of Society, Dance Was Center Stage
8. When No One Read, Who Started to Write?
9. A Tale of Two Cultures
10. The Cradle of Cash
11. Indus Valley, Inc.
12. In China, Ancient History Kindles Modern Doubts
13. Five Ways to Conquer a City
14. Nabada: The Buried City
15. Out of Africa: The Superb Artwork of Ancient Nubia
16. Scythian Gold
17. Tiny Sacrifices at 22,000 Feet
18. In Classical Athens, a Market Trading in the Currency of Ideas
19. Old Sports
20. Cleopatra: What Kind of a Woman Was She, Anyway?

RATING

ARTICLE

21. The Year One
22. Secrets of a Desert Metropolis: The Hidden Wonders of Petra's Ancient Engineers
23. Ancient Jewel
24. What Is the Koran?
25. The Dome of the Rock: Jerusalem's Epicenter
26. 2000 Years of Jesus
27. The Other Jesus
28. Confucius
29. If You Had Lived Back Then
30. The Americas
31. Chaco Death Squads
32. The Arab Roots of European Medicine
33. An Iberian Chemistry
34. The Age of the Vikings
35. Clocks: Revolution in Time
36. 1492: The Prequel
37. Columbus and the Labyrinth of History
38. How Many People Were Here Before Columbus?
39. A Taste of Adventure
40. After Dire Straits, an Agonizing Haul Across the Pacific

(Continued on next page)

BUSINESS REPLY MAIL
FIRST-CLASS MAIL PERMIT NO. 84 GUILFORD CT

POSTAGE WILL BE PAID BY ADDRESSEE

McGraw-Hill/Dushkin
530 Old Whitfield Street
Guilford, CT 06437-9989

IIIₙₙₗₗₙₗₗₗₗₗₗₗₗₗₗ (barcode)

ABOUT YOU

Name _____   Date _____

Are you a teacher? ☐   A student? ☐
Your school's name

Department _____

Address _____ City _____ State ____ Zip _____

School telephone # _____

YOUR COMMENTS ARE IMPORTANT TO US !

Please fill in the following information:
For which course did you use this book?
_____

Did you use a text with this *ANNUAL EDITION*? ☐ yes ☐ no
What was the title of the text?
_____

What are your general reactions to the *Annual Editions* concept?
_____

Have you read any particular articles recently that you think should be included in the next edition?
_____

Are there any articles you feel should be replaced in the next edition? Why?
_____

Are there any World Wide Web sites you feel should be included in the next edition? Please annotate.
_____

May we contact you for editorial input? ☐ yes ☐ no
May we quote your comments? ☐ yes ☐ no